ALLEN-LEWIS and DAVISON-RIDGEWAY FAMILIES

Migrations to Missouri

Wesley E. Pippenger

HERITAGE BOOKS

2019

HERITAGE BOOKS
AN IMPRINT OF HERITAGE BOOKS, INC.

Books, CDs, and more—Worldwide

For our listing of thousands of titles see our website
at
www.HeritageBooks.com

Published 2019 by
HERITAGE BOOKS, INC.
Publishing Division
5810 Ruatan Street
Berwyn Heights, Md. 20740

Cover illustration: Sisters Janice Louise and Zora Eileene Davison

International Standard Book Number
Paperbound: 978-0-7884-5881-1

Dedicated to my Grandmother

Velma Pearl Allen Davison (1902-1990)

CONTENTS

LIST OF FIGURES

PREFACE

Even though it has been very difficult to try and sort out all of the many individual families with common surnames in this part of my heritage, i.e. Allen, Hicks, Johnson, Lewis, Ridgeway and Smith, I have been able to make some progress in documentation. I now take a moment to record what information has been obtained up to this point about the ancestors of my mother Zora "Eileene" Davison Pippenger, through her mother Velma Pearl Allen and her father Chester Leland Davison.

The whole idea of researching this family history started when one day my grandmother flashed an old picture in front of me. This was some time around 1970. It was a photograph showing where all of Samuel Gillion Allen's family were lined up on the front porch of their "not-so-fancy" farm house near Rhea's Mill, Washington County, Arkansas. Maybe they took advantage of an unusual happening, the passing of a photographer. I guess it is not often that poor farming families had their pictures taken. Anyway, Grandmother started pointing people out, and my fascination began.

I have delayed many years in preparing the information I have collected because I know of so few alive to share it with. Mother is from a small family. Now as the years add I present a sampling of what data has been collected on these families.

We are rather fortunate to have many photographs of several lines of ancestors. Selecting just which ones to use in this book was a difficult process, but what is presented here is just a sample of the photographs or illustrations that I believe are best viewed in this format.

Wesley E. Pippenger
Tappahannock, Virginia

ABBREVIATIONS USED

b.	born		ed.	Editor
bapt.	baptized		fol.	folio
Bk.	Book		ibid.	same as preceding source
bur.	buried		inv.	inventory of estate
c.	circa or about		m.	married
Cem.	Cemetery		op. cit.	source cited above
cert.	certificate		p. or pp.	page or pages
Co.	County		prov.	proved
comp(s).	compiler(s)		q.v.	see elsewhere
d.	died		rem.	removed
d.inf.	died in infancy		res.	resident of or resided
d.y.	died young		twp.	township
div.	divorced		wit.	witness or witnessed
dau.	daughter			

* * *

A plus sign "+" before the numbering system means this person's history is carried forward in his or her own sketch elsewhere in the work.

The letter "a" following a generation indicates an adopted child.

Ancestor Chart for Z.E. Davison

James Davison
b. c.1773, PA; d. c.1852, OH
Catherine (perhaps Long)

George W. Davison
b. 7 MAR 1816, OH
m. 12 OCT 1848, OH
d. 8 FEB 1893, OH
(2) Caroline Smith
b. c.1828, OH
d. 24 NOV 1899, MO
p.d. Kansas City MO
bur. Union Cem.

Ausburn Ridgeway
b. c.1770, VA; d. 8 AUG 1841, IL
Jane Phelps

Samuel Ridgeway
b. 7 SEP 1804, KY
m. 5 NOV 1855
d. 4 SEP 1879, MO
(2) Jennettie A. Fowler
b. 11 JAN 1820, TN
d. 4 OCT 1883, MO
bur. Randolph Co. MO

Thomas Allen
b. c.1800, NC; d. c.1893, AR
Lucy [perhaps Bell]

Samuel Gillion Allen
b. 15 AUG 1829, TN
m. 25 FEB 1876, AR
d. 3 JAN 1913, AR
Mary Ann Hicks
b. 5 OCT 1854, TX
d. 11 MAR 1931, AR
bur. Rhea's Mill AR

Samuel Robinson Hicks
b. 3 SEP 1820, TN; d. 1867
Grizell Ann Brison

Joab Lewis
b. 14 JUN 1825, d. 3 NOV 1865

William F. Lewis
b. 26 DEC 1833, TN; d. 1886, AR
Martha Ann Kelley
b. c.1834, d. bef. 1866

Watson M. Adair
b. c.1824, TN; d. bef. 1858
Mary Elizabeth "Polly" Sweazea
b. c.1828, d. JAN 1868

Charles Condus Davison
b. 4 JUL 1853
p.b. Clermont Co. OH
m. 25 DEC 1884, MO
d. 14 NOV 1917
p.d. K.C. MO
bur. Elmwood Cem.

Florence Evelyn Ridgeway
b. 11 DEC 1864
b.p. Corder MO
d. 21 AUG 1936
p.d. Aurora CO

Robert Edward Allen
b. 17 JAN 1879
p.b. Rhea's Mill AR
m. 30 AUG 1900
d. 7 MAY 1958
p.b. Kansas City MO
bur. Memorial Park Cem.

Mary Ellen Lewis
b. 18 OCT 1880
p.b. Randolph Co. AR
d. 30 AUG 1960
p.d. Kansas City MO

William F. Lewis

Sarah Elizabeth Adair
b. 12 JUN 1853, AR
d. 19 DEC 1935, MO

Chester
Leland Davison
b. 16 SEP 1901
p.b. K.C. MO
m. 11 OCT 1922
p.m. Olathe KS
d. 31 MAR 1991
p.d. K.C. MO
bur. Memorial Park

Velma Pearl Allen
b. 3 MAY 1902
p.b. Springtown AR
d. 14 JUL 1990
p.d. K.C. MO

Zora
Eileene Davison
b. 5 MAR 1932
p.b. K.C. MO
m. 7 JUN 1953
p.m. K.C. MO
to
Charles
Wesley Pippenger

ALLEN FAMILY

B y using the United States census records, I pieced together a pattern of movement for our Allen Family, starting perhaps in Virginia (pre-Revolutionary War) or North Carolina (1801); then Carroll County, Tennessee (1821); then DeSoto County, Mississippi (1850); then Hunt County, Texas (1860); and ending in Washington County, Arkansas about 1870.

Because I was told that my great-great-grandparents, Samuel Gillion Allen and his wife Mary Ann Hicks, lived for a large period of time in Washington County, Arkansas, it is here where I started to assemble clues to the ancestry of the family. The 1880 Federal census reveals that a Thomas Allen, born about 1801 in North Carolina, a widower, is living with the Samuel G. Allen family in Marr's Hill Township, Rhea's Mill, postoffice, Washington County, Arkansas. At this point it looks probable that Thomas is the father of Samuel. Indeed, the 1850 Federal census for DeSoto

Figure 2 - Sketch of Rhea's Mill

County, Mississippi shows Samuel as a child of Thomas Allen and his wife Lucy, along with eight other children.

ALLEN FAMILY PORTRAIT (c. 1910) Taken at farm of S.G. Allen near Rhea's Mill, Arkansas. (L-R): Robert Edward Allen, LeRoy Benton Allen, Samuel Wayne Allen, Mary Ellen (Lewis) Allen, Clara Allen, Maude Allen, Velma Pearl Allen, Samuel Gillion Allen, Mary Ann (Hicks) Allen, Homer Johnson Allen, Delmas Allen, Samuel Frank Allen, Margaret Vera Allen, and Mary Luana (Edmiston) Allen

Figure 3 - Samuel Gillion Allen Family at their home near Rhea's Mill, Arkansas, c.1910

From this I can construct the following:

1850 U.S. Census—DeSoto County, Mississippi, p. 319, 7 SEP 1850.

Family	Head	Age	Occupation	Birthplace
90	ALLEN, E.W.[1]	24	Farming	Tennessee
	, Palestine	18		Alabama
	, Sitha J.	4		Mississippi
93	ALLEN, Thomas	49	Farming	North Carolina
	, Lucy	47		North Carolina
	, John	21	Farming	Tennessee
	, Samuel	20	Farming	Tennessee
	, Sarah	17		Tennessee
	, Joseph	12		Tennessee
	, Susannah	10		Tennessee
	, Andrew J.	8		Tennessee
	, Winsey J.	6 F		Tennessee
	, Thomas	3		Tennessee
	, James	3/12		Mississippi

Thus, it shows the Allen Family moved from Tennessee to Mississippi sometime between the birth of Thomas and James, making it circa 1847-1849. Again, I had trouble tracking what happened to the family, and because of later land transactions for which we have found receipts in Sam's family belongings, our Allen Family is then found in Hunt County, Texas. From the following Federal census record, a few more interesting coincidences, or facts rather, come to light:

1860 U.S. Census - Hunt County, Texas, Precinct No. 9, Post Office Greenville, Texas, p. 18, 8 SEP 1860.

Family	Head	Age	Occupation	Birthplace
129	ALLEN, Isaac	66	Farmer	North Carolina
	, Martha	64		North Carolina
	, Lewis G.	30		Tennessee
	, Minta P.	22		Mississippi
	, George W.	20		Mississippi

Family	Head	Age	Occupation	Birthplace
130	ALLEN, Thomas	60	Farmer	North Carolina
	, Ruth	54		North Carolina
	, Samuel G.	29	Farm Labor	Tennessee

---

[1] No relationship has been established between Mr. E.W. Allen and Thomas Allen. E.W. Allen (1823-1889) and his first wife Palestine Stephenson (1832-1876) ended up in Paris, Lamar Co., Tex. where they were bur. in Friendship Cem. They were married in 1847 in Marshall Co., Miss. It appears entirely possible that E.W. Allen is the eldest child of Thomas and Lucy Allen.

, Sarah A.	23		Tennessee
, Susan M.	20		Tennessee
, Andrew J.	18	Farm Labor	Tennessee
, Wincy J.	14		Tennessee
, Thomas J.	12		Tennessee
, James W.	9		Mississippi
, Mary E.	6		Texas

We see several new events: Thomas Allen may have a different wife (the handwriting is almost impossible to read), it appears that Thomas Allen has a brother Isaac Allen, and a new child Mary E. Allen has been born in Texas to Thomas Allen.

Based on the information we have learned thus far, that (1) Samuel G. Allen was born in Carroll County, Tennessee, and (2) that his father Thomas was living next to a Isaac Allen in Texas [his brother], and (3) we will soon see it seems sure that Samuel Allen/Allin of Carroll County, Tennessee is their father.

In August 1870, Thomas Allen heads a family near Rhea's Mill,[1] Marr's Hill Township, Washington Co., Arkansas, with wife Lucy, and three daughters.

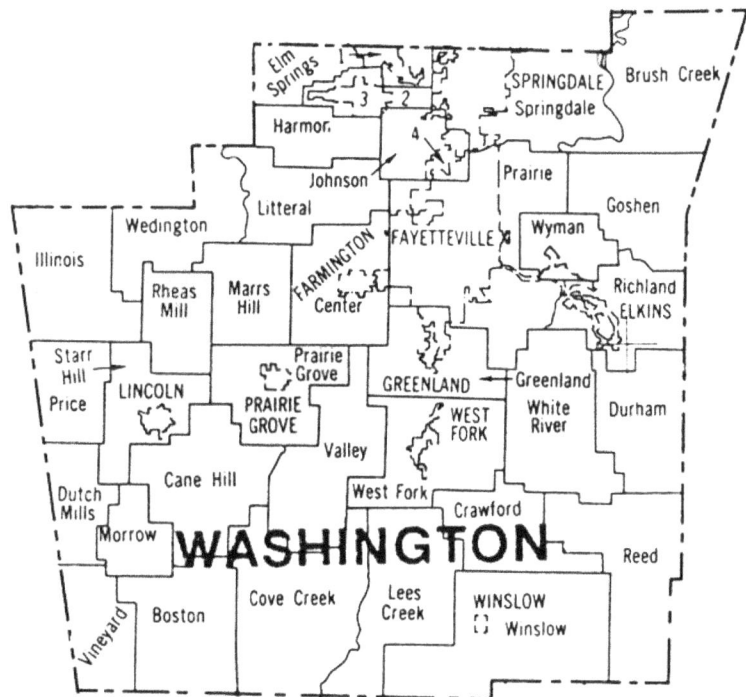

Figure 4 - Township map of Washington Co., Ark., showing Rheas Mill, Prairie Grove, and a bit up northeast is found Springdale

---

[1] A battle monument for Rhea's Mill reads as follows: This tower was the chimney of Rhea's Mill, which stood 6 miles northeast of this spot. The mill was operated by the Federal army before and after the Battle of Prairie Grove. General Blunt's supply train was at Rhea's during the battle, and under guard of General Frederick Salomon's troops. The tower is 55 feet high and weighs 200,000 pounds. It is 8 feet square at the base and tapers to 4 by 4 feet at the top. It contains 700 stones. The chimney was taken down at Rhea's and re-erected here as a memorial to the men who fought on this field December 7, 1862. The tower was given to Battlefield Park in 1957 by Mr. and Mrs. G.C. Mennecke.

Figure 5 - Marriage record extracted from the Robert E. Allen Family Bible (destroyed)

Samuel Allen
(c.1774-1827)

Samuel Allen was born c.1774,[1] either in Virginia or North Carolina.[2] He may have been a son of George Allen, born c.1730, who died 1806 in Orange County, North Carolina. Some researchers claim this George Allen was born 24 MAY 1730 in Coles Hill, Berkshire, England. Thus, the origin of our line of the Allen Family is yet uncertain.

This Samuel Allen is likely to have had brothers Andrew Allen and George Allen, as all three of them were listed on the 1799 tax list for Montgomery County, North Carolina, on the west fork of the Red River—Sam Allen had 100 acres while Andrew and George each had 200 acres there. Montgomery County was formed in 1779 from Anson County.

The first Federal census for Tennessee was not taken until 1810 and it covered the eastern portion of the state. It appears that the first child of Samuel Allen was born about 1794 in North Carolina, so the 1800 Federal census of North Carolina is the first to target for finding the correct household. The 1800 Federal census enumerates groups of data: the number of males in age groups 0-10, 10-16, 16-26, 26-45 and over 45; number of females in the same groupings; number of older free persons except Indians; and the number of slaves.

The most likely family for us is one of two Samuel Allen's residing in Montgomery County, North Carolina, for in 1800 is Samuel Allin with three sons under age 10 and 1 daughter under age 10. Perhaps the same person is enumerated as Sam Allen on the 1810 Federal census for Montgomery County (Green Township, page 567) with two sons under age 10 and five daughters (three under age 10, two between the age of 10 and 16 years). Other Allen Family heads of household nearby on the 1800 census for Montgomery County are Rubin, George and John Allin.

Earlier, we find a Samuel Allen grouped with George, Peggy, and Alexander Allen who all obtained land grants in Davidson County, Tennessee in the 1787 based on someone's military service in the Revolutionary War. Davidson County was formed in 1783 from Washington County, and the latter was created in 1777 by North Carolina. For a number of years, Davidson County was the only county in the western part of the state and was surrounded by Indian lands. The similar land grants are as follows:[3]

a. Samuel Allen, assignee of the heirs of John Jones, was granted 640 acres in Davidson County at the head of Gilkeson's Creek of Sulfur Fork of Red River. Warrant #508, 15 SEP 1787. Entry #2162. Book 63, p. 183.

b. George Allen, assignee of the heirs of Jeremiah Brantley, a private in the Continental Line, was granted 640 acres in Davidson County, at the west side of Wardraw Creek of Sulfur Fork of Red River. Warrant #508, 15 SEP 1787. Entry #2047. Book 63, p. 182.

---

[1] If the correct Samuel Allen is identified in Montgomery Co., N.C. in 1800 and 1810, this would make him between the age of 26 and 45 years for both census records, thus born sometime between 1755-1774.

[2] The 1880 Federal Census gives the birthplace of the parents of our Thomas Allen as: father (Virginia) and mother (North Carolina).

[3] North Carolina Land Grants in Tennessee are online through *Ancestry.com*, from the Tennessee State Archives.

c. <u>Peggy Allen</u>, assignee of the heirs of Matthew Lawless, a private in the Continental Line, was granted 640 acres in Davidson County on the north side of Sulphur Fork of Red River, adjacent to the boundary line of Col. Ezekiel Polk. Warrant #485, 15 SEP 1787. Entry #2059. Book 63, p. 176.

d. <u>Alexander Allen</u>, assignee of Jacob Moore, heir of Nicholas Moore, a private in the Continental Line, was granted 640 acres in Davidson County, on the east side of Sulfur Fork of Red River, adjoining the east boundary of Ezekiel Polk's survey, and adjacent to Messrs. Cantrell, Turner, and Renfroe. Warrant #136, 15 SEP 1787. Entry #2136. Book 63, p. 221.

Our Samuel Allen was married 19 MAR 1793, perhaps in Montgomery County, North Carolina, to Mary Rogers.

On 15 MAY 1827, Samuel Allin [sic] wrote his will in Carroll County, Tennessee, and it mentions his wife Mary,[1] who was born in North Carolina. Based on a land transaction of 1842 in Carroll County, Tennessee, the wife Mary Rogers is confirmed.[2] Carroll County was formed 7 NOV 1821 from Chickasaw Indian Lands or "The Western District."[3] Samuel Allen died 19 DEC 1827 in Carroll County, Tennessee.

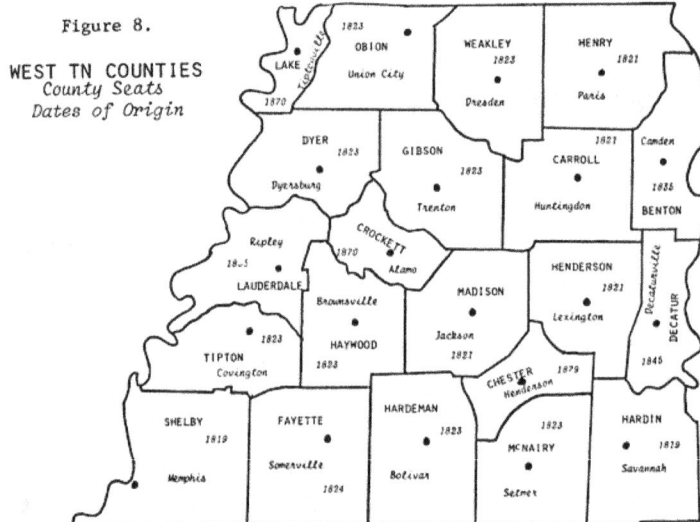

Figure 8.

WEST TN COUNTIES
County Seats
Dates of Origin

Figure 6 - Diagram showing position of Carroll County in western Tennessee

After Sam's death his sons Isaac, Levi, and John acquired individual land parcels in Carroll County, Tennessee. It is unclear whether Samuel Allen owned his own land or he was residing on land he inherited; however, it appears that he had applied for a land grant, but before the lengthy process ended he died, as on 30 JUN 1828, Samuel Allen was granted 150 acres of land in Carroll County, Tennessee, as assignee of John C. McLemore—the same day for grants to his three eldest sons.[4] Samuel Allen's grant was an "occupant" grant, meaning that it was a grant issued to someone who has already established themselves on the land prior to the date of issue.

---

[1] Carroll Co., Tenn. Wills, Bk. A, p. 10.
[2] Carroll Co., Tenn. Deeds, Bk. E, p. 399, dated 8 JAN 1842, between Basil Rogers and Mary Allen (dec.), of the one part and William Stoker; that Basil Rogers is administrator for land of Mary Allen (dec.) left to her by her husband Samuel Allen and sold to William Stoker and heirs.
[3] There was a fire at the courthouse in Huntingdon in 1931 and many records were damaged.
[4] Tennessee Land Grants, Bk. DD, p. 164, dated 30 JUN 1828, grant #25682, by survey of 2 JUN 1824, as assignee of John C. McLemore, a parcel of 150 acres in the 12th District of Carroll Co., in Range 5, Section 4, and beginning at a small hickory standing 10 poles west and 78 poles north from the 3-mile post south of the northeast corner of Section 4 in Range 5, running north 226½ poles to a white oak and two white oaks pointing, thence west 106¼ poles to a black oak hickory and post oak pointers, thence south 226½ poles to a hickory on the bank of a branch, thence east 106¼ poles to the beginning.

Probable children of Samuel Allen and Mary Rogers:

+ 1. ISAAC ALLEN, farmer, b. 19 DEC 1794 in Montgomery Co., N.C., d. OCT 1867 in Decatur, Wise Co., Tex., m. c.1818 to Martha "Patty" Green.

2. LEVI ALLEN,[1] b. c.1795 in Montgomery Co., N.C., d. between 1827 and 1848, probably in Carroll Co., Tenn. In 1827, he obtained a warrant for 20 acres on the waters of Hollow Rock Creek in Carroll Co., Tenn.[2] In 1848, his brother-in-law Joshua Maberry and other heirs, acquired 124 acres in Carroll Co. as part of Levi's former property.[3]

3. GRACE "Sally" ALLEN, b. c.1795 in Montgomery Co., N.C., d. December 1880 in Lenoir, Caldwell Co., N.C., m. 27 DEC 1814 in Wilkes Co., N.C. to Thomas Watson, d. 1880. Perhaps 16 children.

4. JOHN R. ALLIN, farmer, b. c.1796[4] in perhaps Montgomery Co., N.C., d. after 1860 in Carroll Co., Tenn., m. Catherine (unknown), b. c.1797 in N.C. In 1847, he acquired a land warrant for 133 acres on Allen's Creek in Carroll Co. that was adjacent to the 80-acre parcel of his brother Isaac Allen.[5] Enumerated in 1850 in District 17 of Carroll Co., Tenn. [family 2012; page 151, next door to Joshua Mabry], and on Federal census on 18 OCT 1860 for District 17, post office Marlsborough. Children:
   41. SAMUEL R. ALLIN, farmer, b. 1820 in Montgomery Co., N.C., m. 10 APR 1843 in Carroll Co., Tenn. to Margaret Auvenshine [Obenshine], b. 1827 in Tenn. Enumerated in 1850 in District 17 of Carroll Co. Children:
       411. CATHERINE ALLIN, b. 1843 in Tenn.
       412. JOHN WILLIS ALLIN, b. 1844 in Tenn.
       413. NANCY P. ALLIN, b. 1846 in Tenn.
       414. SUSAN ALLIN, b. 1851 in Tenn.
       415. WILLIAM ALLIN, b. 1853 in Tenn.
       416. ROSEANN ALLIN, b. 1854 in Tenn.
   42. WILEY ALLEN, farmer, b. c.1821 in Tenn., m. Elizabeth (unknown), b. c.1824 in Tenn. Children:
       421. ADELINE ALLEN, b. 1841 in Tenn.
       422. JOHN ALLEN, b. 1843 in Tenn.
       423. LUCINDA ALLEN, b. 1845 in Tenn.
       424. JAMES ALLEN, b. 1849 in Tenn.

---

[1] One researcher claims this Levi Allen, born c.1794 in N.C. was married to Tabitha Mills (1802-1870) and died in Smith Co., Miss. However, upon examination of the 1860 and 1870 Federal census for Smith Co., Miss., I find that the Levi there, with wife Tabitha, was born in 1788 in S.C.; thus a different person.

[2] Tennessee Land Grants, Warrant #511, dated 9 APR 1827, for 20 acres located in District 12, Range 6, Section 4.

[3] Tennessee Land Grants, Warrant #5323, dated 12 JAN 1848, based on survey dated 3 AUG 1847, Joshua Maberry assignee of three of the heirs of Levi Allen, dec., and Nancy C. Allen, the other heir, for 124 acres by survey dated 3 AUG 1847, in Range 6, Section 4, on Allen's Creek at the waters of Sandy River, bounded by lands of Levi Allen (his entry #2525), Mr. Hodges, the corner of John Allen's 268 acres (his entry #17), and entry #1,845 for 20 acres.

[4] The census taker for 1860 was a bit wild with age numbers as he records age 80.

[5] Tennessee Land Grants, Warrant #4161, dated 1 OCT 1847, beginning at the northwest corner of entry #1405 for 80 acres in the name of Isaac Allen, bounded on the south by entry #1404 for 80 acres by Isaac Allen, crossing Allen's Creek, adjacent to land of the heirs of John Hamit [Hammett], of entry #465 or 79 acres of Henry Dolon, and entry #17 by John Hodge (excluding 4 acres of the Pisgah Meeting House). As a point of interest, a John M. Hammett was a witness to the Last Will and Testament of Samuel Allin, written in 1827 in Carroll Co.

425.   MOSES ALLEN, b. 1851 in Tenn.
426.   JULIA ALLEN, b. January 1860 in Tenn.
43.   JOHN HENRY ALLIN, farmer, b. 1828 in Tenn, m. Mary "Polly" (unknown), b. 1815. Child:
431.   SARAH M. ALLIN, b. 1849 in Tenn.
44.   DAVID [or Davison] ALLEN, b. 1833 in Tenn., m. Milly (unknown), b. 1838 in Tenn. He's living in the household of Henry Dolan in District 17 of Carroll Co., Tenn. on the 1850 Federal census. Children:
441.   CAROLINE ALLEN, b. 1854 in Tenn.
442.   ELIZABETH ALLEN, b. 1856 in Tenn.
443.   JEFFERSON ALLEN, b. 1858 in Tenn.
44.   ISAAC ALLIN, b. 1834 in Tenn.
45.   FRANCES E. ALLIN, b. 1836 in Tenn.
46.   MOSES R. ALLEN, b. 1838 in Tenn.

5.   FANNY ALLEN, b. c.1799 in perhaps Montgomery Co., N.C.

+ 6.   THOMAS ALLEN (my ancestor), farmer, b. late 1800 in perhaps Montgomery Co., N.C., and d. c.1893 in Washington Co., Ark., m. (1) Ruth (unknown) and m. (2) Lucy (perhaps Bell).

7.   ELIZABETH ALLEN, b. 1803 in perhaps Montgomery Co., N.C., d. 1886 in Cross Co., Ark., bur. Tyer Cem., Hydrick, Poinsett Co., Ark., m. by 1830[1] (probably in Carroll Co., Tenn.) to William Ellis, farmer b. c.1797 in Rowan Co., N.C., d. 1866 in Marshall, Tenn. Enumerated in Carroll Co., Tenn. in 1830 [page 160]. Moved to Ark. in the 1850s and had land at Cherry Valley as late as the 1920s. Enumerated in 1850 in Poinsett Co., Ark. Issue:
71.   JOHN ALEXANDER ELLIS, b. c.1832 in Carroll Co., Tenn., d. 1865.
72.   ROBERT JAMES ELLIS, b. 6 JAN 1833 in Carroll Co., Tenn., d. 28 OCT 1905, bur. Tyer Cem., enlisted in Co. K, 13th Ark. Inf., C.S.A., m. (1) DEC 1855 to Sophia Burks, d. 1873. They returned for a short time to Shelby Co., Tenn., and in 1871 moved to Cherry Valley where he received 103 acres under the Homestead Act. Robert m. (2) in 1875 to Mollia Aires who died 4 years later, and he m. (3) in MAR 1879 to Martha Ann Mitchell (1837-1933). Issue:
721.   WILLIAM ALEXANDER ELLIS, b. 1840, d. 1880, bur. Tyer Cem.
722.   ELIZABETH ELLIS.
73.   THOMAS ELLIS, b. 1836.
74.   LUCINDA MARY ELLIS, b. 1837, d. 1910, m. (1) Mr. Smith, m. (2) Mr. Faulkner.
75.   NANCY ELLIS, b. 1838, d. 1859.
76.   WILLIAM F. ELLIS, b. 1840, d. 1880, bur. Tyer Cem., enlisted in Co. K, 13th Ark. Inf., C.S.A.
77.   GEORGE W. ELLIS, b. 1843 in Tenn., enlisted in Co. K, 13th Ark. Inf., C.S.A.
78.   JAMES ELLIS, b. 1844.

---

[1] Marriage records for Carroll Co., Tenn. start in 1838.

79. YANCY P. "Doc" ELLIS, b. 1845 in Ark., d. 1900, bur. Tyer Cem., Hydrick, Poinsett Co., Ark., m. Laura A. Shannon, b. 1861, d. 1910.

8. POLLY ALLEN, b. c.1804 in perhaps Montgomery Co., N.C.

9. NANCY C. ALLEN, b. c.1804-7 in perhaps Montgomery Co., N.C., d. in 1880 in Hunt Co., Tex., m. c.1823, probably in Carroll Co., Tenn. to Joshua Mabry/Mayberry, farmer, b. 14 FEB 1806 in Montgomery Co., N.C., d. 16 DEC 1896 in Hunt Co., Tex., son of Solomon Mabry. Enumerated in Carroll Co., Tenn. in 1830 [page 179, as Joshua Maberry]. Enumerated in 1850 in District 17 of Carroll Co., Tenn. [family 2014; page 151]. Enumerated in 1860 in Precinct #9 of Hunt Co., Tex. [family 88, page 301; post office Hookers], also in 1870 in Hunt Co. (Nancy cannot write), and 7 JUN 1880 in Hunt Co. where both her parents are shown as being born in *South Carolina*. Children:
91. ELIZA MABRY, b. 1824 in Carroll Co., Tenn.
92. MARY MELISSA MABRY, b. 29 OCT 1830 in Carroll Co., Tenn., d. 14 JAN 1865.
93. LUCINDA FRANCES MABRY, b. 30 MAR 1832 in Carroll Co., Tenn., d. 11 JAN 1853 in Henry Co., Tenn.
93. CAROLINE MABRY, b. 1833 in Carroll Co., Tenn., d. 14 JAN 1865 in Hunt Co., Tex.
94. NANCY B. MABRY, b. 1836 in Carroll Co., Tenn.
95. JOSHUA H. MABRY, b. 1841 in Tenn.
96. SOLOMON WESLEY MABRY, b. 1843 in Tenn.
97. ROSELLA PARLIE MABRY, b. 1 JAN 1846 in Carroll Co., Tenn., d. 18 JAN 1885 in Hunt Co., Tex., m. 25 MAR 1866 in Hunt Co. to Elbert Kelly Patrick (1833-1907).
98. WILLIAM M. MABRY, b. 1849 in Tenn.

10. HANNAH ALLEN, b. c.1810 in perhaps Montgomery Co., N.C. No further information.

11. PURITY ALLEN, b. c.1813 in perhaps Montgomery Co., N.C., d. after 10 DEC 1850, perhaps in Carroll Co., Tenn. The 1850 Federal census for District 15 of Carroll Co., Tenn. [family #1803], shows Purity Allen, age 37, is residing with her sister Sarah Allen Finch.

12. SARAH ALLEN, b. c.1815 in perhaps Montgomery Co., N.C., d. by 1858 in Ala., m. 1838 in Carroll Co., Tenn. to Edmund Finch (1815-1880), farmer, who m. (2) 12 AUG 1858 in Carroll Co. to Mary "Polly" Rowland and m. (3) 1869 in Carroll Co. to Melissa Jane Pinkston. Enumerated in 1850 in District 15 of Carroll Co. [family #1803]. Children:
121. MARY M. FINCH, b. 1839 in Tenn., m. 8 JAN 1857 in Carroll Co. to John W. White.
121. GEORGE W. FINCH, b. 1841 in Tenn.
122. WILLIAM NEWTON FINCH, b. 1843 in Tenn.
123. MARGARET A. FINCH, b. 1845 in Tenn.
124. EDMUND J. FINCH, b. 1849 in Tenn., m. Susan (unknown).

13.   DOLLY HARRIS ALLEN, b. c.1817 in perhaps Montgomery Co., N.C.

Will and Last Testament of Samuel Allin[1]
Carroll County, Tennessee, 1827

In the name of God Amen, I, Samuel Allin of the County of Carroll and State of Tennessee do this fifteenth day of May One thousand eight hundred & twenty seven being of sound mind and memory thanks be to God for the same but calling to mind the mortality of my body and knowing that it is appointed for all men to die. I make and ordain this my last will and Testament in manner and form following viz. first I will and bequeath unto my Daughter Fanny Allin One cow and calf one feather bed & furniture. 2nd I will and bequeath unto my Daughter Elizabeth Allin One cow and calf one feather bed and furniture. 3rd I will and bequeath unto my Daughter Hannah Allin One cow and calf one feather bed & furniture. 4th I will and bequeath unto my Daughter Purity Allin one cow and calf and feather bed & furniture. 5th I will and bequeath unto my Daughter Sally Allin One cow and calf and bed and furniture. 6th I will and bequeath unto my Daughter Dolly H. Allin One cow and calf and feather bed and furniture. I will and bequeath unto my beloved wife Mary Allin the <u>ballance</u> of my estate during her natural life time or widdowhood to dispose of in any way that she thinks proper at the end of her life or widdowhood. All to be sold and equally divided amongst my children, namely Isaac Allin, Levi Allin, John Allin, Fanny Allin, Thomas Allin, Elizabeth Allin, Polly Allin, Nancy Allin, Hannah Allin, Purity Allin, Sarah Allin, Dolly Harris Allin. I make or design my trusty & beloved son Levy Allin to Executor this my last will and Testament. In witness whereof I have hereunto set my hand and seal to this my last will and testament the day and above written. Signed Sealed in presence of us who were present at the time of signing and Sealing thereof.

	his
R. Green	Samuel "x" Allin (seal)
John M. Hammett	mark

Figure 7 - Transcript of Last Will and Testament of Samuel Allin, 1827

---

[1] Carroll Co., Tenn. Wills, Bk. A, p. 10.

Complexity of Researching Early Tennessee Lands

Early Tennessee land acquisition is probably more complex than any other state because of the different governments and the time involved in processing grants. Information from the Tennessee States Archives perhaps describes the situation best:

North Carolina, the United States Territory South of the Ohio River, and Tennessee, successively governed this land. Since the Indians assisted the British in the Revolutionary War, North Carolina believed they had relinquished their title to the land. The United States government honored Indian ownership and required title by treaty before granting land. In an 1806 compact, North Carolina, the United States, and Tennessee, agreed that Tennessee could issue grants, provided they honored all land warrants already issued by North Carolina, as well as any warrants they were required to issue. This took time.

When North Carolina took control of her lands from the Crown in 1777, she established land entry offices in each of her counties. At that time, all of the occupied land in what is now Tennessee was Washington County, North Carolina. Settlement was primarily confined to northeast Tennessee. For forty shillings per hundred acres, each head of a family could buy 640 acres for himself and 100 acres for his wife and each child. Any amount of land above that cost five pounds per 100 acres. By 1779, the population had increased and an entry takers office was opened in Sullivan County, North Carolina (now Tennessee). These offices closed in 1781.

Richard Henderson, by treaty with the Indians, purchased a large area in middle Tennessee and Kentucky; his land company, including the James Robertson and John Donelson groups, were the first people in Middle Tennessee. When North Carolina selected that area for their military district, they granted Richard Henderson 200,000 acres in Powell's Valley.

North Carolina's promise of land to her soldiers for their service in the Continental Line (the amount determined by rank) delayed the transfer of the right to issue land grants to Tennessee. It was many years before North Carolina could verify that all her soldiers had received a warrant for their service, and that grants had been issued for those warrants. It appears the only grant made by the United States Territory South of the Ohio River was for the town of Pulaski in Giles County.

There were six different types of land grants issued. **Purchase grants** were obtained by purchasing warrants from county offices and the Hillsboro, North Carolina office for land in particular areas. **Military grants** were issued to North Carolina soldiers of the Continental Line, based on their rank and length of service. **Pre-emption grants** were issued to those settlers in Middle Tennessee who settled upon the land when the North Carolina Commissioners surveyed the military district for North Carolina. Pre-emption grants were also issued in other areas to the first legal settler. **Surveyor grants**, also called service grants, were issued to surveyors and their assistants in compensation for their services in surveying the land. **Commissioner grants** were issued to those commissioners appointed by the North Carolina legislature to survey or "lay off" the military reservation, later known as District 1. **Legislative grants** were issued for special service to special individuals, including General Nathanael Greene and David Wilson for their special service, and to Richard Henderson in exchange for his company that settled in Middle Tennessee before it was selected as the military district.

Before the Revolutionary War, the person desiring the land paid the fees and obtained a warrant and grant from the governor's office. After the Revolution, the fees were paid to the entry taker's office. The enterer, or someone for him, such as a real estate agent, sometimes called a locator, actually went upon the land desired, marked the trees and wrote a rough description of the land desired, specifying its bounds and describing its monuments. This entry was taken to the entry taker at the local land office. The location of the appropriate land office depended upon the type of grant to be received, i. e., military, purchase, or pre-emption.

The entry taker searched his records, and if he determined no one had previously entered that particular land, he copied the entry into his well-bound book and gave it the next number in sequence, called an entry or location number. The entry taker used his own shorthand. In most entry books, "L" described the location or entry number; the "W" described the warrant number; the "D" described the date; the "A" described the acreage. Sometimes the locator was identified and other information pertaining to that particular entry may be given. Often, the date was specified only by day and it is necessary to search previous pages for the month and year. After three months, if no one else claimed that he had previously entered that land, the entry taker issued a warrant which authorized the surveyor to make the survey. The process, from application to grant took some time.

The surveyor used a thirty-three foot chain carried by two people in measuring the boundaries. Another person, called a marker, marked the land as it was measured. All were sworn "the truth to tell." The surveyor drew, to scale, the boundaries of the tract, giving an accurate description of the land, noting the streams, corner trees, etc. The drawing was called the plat and the boundary description was called the certificate of survey. The certificate of survey included the names of the sworn chain carriers indicated as "SCC."

The warrant and survey were sent to the North Carolina Secretary of State, who prepared the grant and attested the governor's signature to it. The grant was returned to the entry taker, who notified the recipient via the newspaper that he could pick up his grant from the land office. The process usually took 18 months to 2 years to complete during which time the recipient sat tax-free on his land.

The final step was for the recipient to have his grant recorded in the county where the land lay. There were a few occasions, because of Indian opposition, when the recipient was allowed to record his grant in the North Carolina county where he lived. At another time, recipients who lived out of the state were directed to record their grants in Hawkins County. These were temporary arrangements and only allowed when some cause prevented access to the register of the county where the land lay. The necessity of having the grants recorded in "the county where the land lay" is understandable, for it would be here that persons interested in knowing the ownership of the land would search. Also, the local county has always held jurisdiction over the collection of property taxes, as well as land transfer and the recording fees, and they were insistent upon this technicality.

In 1806, when Tennessee received the right to issue land grants, they discovered they had no records. A large North Carolina land fraud had caused the original records to be subpoenaed to North Carolina. Tennessee agents had to go to North Carolina and copy Tennessee records from the North Carolina books, which included both North Carolina and Tennessee grants. They also had to copy the entry and survey books. These records are in the Tennessee State Library and Archives, called Record Group 50, and are microfilmed.

West Tennessee (the area west of the Tennessee River) was known as the Congressional Reservation District. North Carolina had sold many large land grants in that area, but since an Indian treaty was not signed for it until 1818, the Federal Government closed the area until that time. In 1806, Middle Tennessee was known as West Tennessee. Tennessee set up two Boards of Commissioners—one for West (Middle) Tennessee and one for East Tennessee. Before Tennessee could issue a grant, it had to be approved by one of these boards. At the same time, Tennessee surveyed the land into districts and appointed land officers for each district. They tried to follow the Federal Government's edict that the land be surveyed in township and range, and in a few areas usage of both township and range, as well as metes and bounds were attempted. It did not work very well and eventually became metes and bounds. The record books of these two Boards are included in the microfilmed Record Group 50. The loose papers are not processed or microfilmed at this time.

The North Carolina Military District became District 1; Districts 2 through 8 were East Tennessee and Southern Middle Tennessee. The real West Tennessee, in 1818, was surveyed into Districts 9 through 13.

The record books and loose papers of these boards and districts are in the Tennessee State Library and Archives, but they have not been completely arranged and microfilmed and are not available for use. There are so many documents, in no order, that it has required the life-time work of several archivists. Each new archivist first has to learn the history of the land and the order the records are in before determining how to proceed.

Until these records are processed and made public, other records can be used. Each grant was registered in the county where the land lay and that record can be obtained from the deed books of that county. The records copied from the North Carolina record books have been microfilmed, and these films, known as Record Group 50, are available at the Tennessee State Library and Archives, although there are inconsistencies in RG 50 that require careful searching to locate the materials in question. In addition, the Tennessee State Library and Archives has purchased from North Carolina microfilmed copies of the warrants and surveys North Carolina used to issue grants for land in Tennessee.

1. Isaac Allen
(1794-1867)

Isaac Allen, son of Samuel Allen and Mary Rogers, was born 19 DEC 1794, perhaps in Montgomery County, North Carolina. He was married c.1818 to Martha "Patty" Green, born 19 DEC 1794 in North Carolina, who died in August 1866 and was buried in Lafayette Cemetery, Lafayette, Upshur County, Texas. Martha appears to be a daughter of Aaron Green (1765-1827) and Elizabeth Rowland of Carroll County, Tennessee.

In 1828, Isaac Allen, as assignee of John Christmas McLemore,[1] obtained two land grants in Carroll County, Tennessee.[2] The second was for 150 acres in Carroll County, Tennessee.[3] On 27 MAR 1830, Isaac Allen sold to Robert Stokes a 10-acre land tract that was lying in the 6th range and 4th section in Carroll County, Tennessee, being the northwest corner of his upper 80-acre tract.[4]

The family is enumerated in 1830 for Carroll County, Tennessee [page 156]. In 1841, a state census was taken in Mississippi and shows Isaac Allen in Marshall County—the household including six males and four females.

On 1 DEC 1849, Isaac Allen purchased from James Ozier, a 179-acre parcel in District 15 (part of grant No. 358) in Carroll County, Tennessee.[5]

During the time of the Federal census that was taken on 9 OCT 1850, Isaac Allen's family was living in the southern district of Marshall County, Mississippi [family #394; page 236], with the youngest children: Thomas, Martha, Araminta and George Allen.

---

[1] West Tennessee land speculator John C. McLemore was b. 1 JAN 1790 in Orange Co., N.C. In 1809 he moved to Nashville, where he became a surveyor's clerk. Five years later, he succeeded his uncle William Christmas as surveyor general of the Tennessee Military Tract. His name appeared in most county land books as a grant or land locator or as an official. Because of his character, generosity, and business acumen, contemporaries considered McLemore a potential gubernatorial or senatorial candidate, but he never ran for either office. Both Nashville and Memphis named an early street in his honor, an indication of his community status. In addition to his popularity and impressive good looks, McLemore's rise to prominence benefited from his marriage to Elizabeth Donelson, daughter of John Donelson, a longtime friend of Andrew Jackson. Before 1820 Jackson and McLemore cooperated in land development in northern Alabama with fellow brother-in-law and Jackson favorite General John Coffee. McLemore invested heavily in West Tennessee's development. Evidently he lent his name to McLemoresville and Christmasville in Carroll County. More importantly, the Jackson-McLemore tie resulted in the latter's early interest in Memphis and made him the fourth founding father of the city, along with Jackson, John Overton, and James Winchester. In competition with Overton and Winchester, McLemore speculated in risky ventures, namely Fort Pickering and the LaGrange and Memphis Railroad. Nearly bankrupt, he tried to recoup his losses in California's gold boom of 1850. Within a decade, McLemore returned to Memphis, where he d. 20 MAY 1864.

[2] Tennessee Land Grants, Bk. DD, p. 167, grant #25680, dated 30 JUN 1828, from a survey of 2 JUN 1824, lying in the 12th District of Carroll Co., in Range 6 Section 4, beginning at a post oak in the east boundary lines of entry No. 1404 made in the name of the said Allen, 40 poles north from the east corner of said entry, running east 88 poles to a post oak & post pointing thence south 100 poles to a small dogwood poplar and post oak pointing thence west 154½ poles to a stake thence north 60 poles to a stake in the south boundary of said Allen's 80-acre entry, thence east with the same to the southeast corner, thence north 40 poles to the beginning.

[3] Tennessee Land Grants, Bk. DD, p. 166, grant #25681, dated 30 JUN 1828, from a survey dated 2 JUN 1824, lying in the 12th District of Carroll Co., in Range 6 Section 4, beginning 92 poles east and 78 poles north from the 3-mile post south from the NW corner of Section 4 on a post oak running north 50 poles to a red oak, thence west 160 poles to a stake in a field, thence south 80 poles to a stake, thence east 160 poles to a stake, thence north 40 poles to the beginning. A Samuel Allen also obtained 150 acres that year; Bk. DD, p. 164, grant #25682.

[4] Carroll Co., Tenn. Deeds, Bk. C, p. 50, located near the range line, recorded December session 1832, registered 27 FEB 1833. I see no evidence of a wife releasing her right to the property, and the deed is signed only by Isaac Allen. The next deed recorded is that for Isaac's brother Thomas Allen to Robert Stokes.

[5] Carroll Co., Tenn. Deeds, Bk. H, p. 43, dated 1 DEC 1849, witnessed by James Allen and John K. Brown.

On 3 FEB 1854, Isaac Allen sold to Robert Hawthorn a 75-acre parcel in District 15, adjacent to land of James Ozier and the old Smyrna Meeting House in Carroll County.[1]

Isaac headed a household in 1860 Hunt County, Texas. [family 130; page 345; post office Greenville] with wife Martha. The 1860 Federal agriculture census shows Isaac Allen possessed 370 acres in Hunt County, and in 1861 he sold property there.

Isaac Allen died in October 1867 in Decatur, Wise County, Texas. Presumably, Martha died before 1870 as she is not found on a Texas census that year.

Children of Isaac Allen and Martha Green:

11.   ELIZABETH or POLLY ALLEN, b. between 1816-1820.[2]
12.   [ELI] WESLEY ALLEN, b. between 1821-1825 in Carroll Co., Tenn.
13.   JOHN ALLEN, b. between 1821-1825 in Carroll Co., Tenn.
14.   MOSES McQUELL ALLEN, b. 25 NOV 1825 in Carroll Co., Tenn., d. 11 MAY 1908 in China Grove, Scurry Co., Tex., bur. Dunn Cem., Scurry Co., Tex., m. 1847 to Susan Emma Ellis, b. 12 MAR 1833, d. 5 MAR 1905.   He served in the C.S.A. under Throckmorton's command. Issue:
   141.   ERASTUS HAYWOOD ALLEN, b. 20 OCT 1853 in Tex., d. 18 NOV 1929 in Mitchell Co., Tex., m. 6 MAR 1876 in Ellis Co., Tex. to Lucy Eulalie Pyles, b. 10 MAY 1859, d. 29 AUG 1939; both Dunn Cem. Issue.
   142.   SUSAN EMMA ALLEN, b. 26 FEB 1858 in Ellis Co., Tex., d. 26 SEP 1921 in Dunn, Tex., bur. Dunn Cem., m. 16 APR 1876 in Ellis Co., Tex. to Middleton Roberts House, b. 7 APR 1855, d. 31 JUL 1912, son of William House and Ediline Zumwald.
   143.   THOMAS ELLIS ALLEN, b. 31 JUL 1860, d. 3 NOV 1937 in Scurry Co., Tex., bur. Dunn Cem., m. 21 JUN 1885 in Jack Co., Tex. to Mollie Drusella Blackburn, b. 12 SEP 1870, d. 4 MAY 1943.
   144.   GEORGE MATTHEW ALLEN, b. 5 JAN 1863 in Ellis Co., Tex., d. 15 OCT 1948 in Roscoe, Nolan Co., Tex., bur. Dunn Cem., m. (1) 13 NOV 1892 in Sterling Co., Tex. to Lucinda Elizabeth Collier (1874-1926), dau. of Francis Collier and Louisa Taylor, m. (2) 1928 to Nannie Ballew (1875-1932), m. (3) 1935 to Cordelia Ann Kimberlin (1882-1967). Issue.
   145.   MISSOURI CATHERINE ALLEN, b. 10 MAR 1869 in Ellis Co., Tex., d. 30 AUG 1937 in Sydner, Scurry Co., Tex., bur. Lamesa Memorial Park, Lamesa, Dawson Co., Tex., m. 3 AUG 1888 in Tom Green Co. (later Sterling Co.) to Henry Reeves, b. 28 JUN 1861, d. 23 APR 1935, son of Pleasant Reeves and Martha Phifer.
15.   LEVI GREEN ALLEN, b. 20 DEC 1827 in Carroll Co., Tenn., d. 9 JUN 1886, m. Carolyn "Callie" Jane Foster, dau. of William Foster and Ararat Dunn, b. 19 DEC 1853, d. 31 JUL 1888, bur. Foster Cem. of Sterling, Tex. Issue:
   151.   WILLIAM EWING ALLEN, assessor, b. 1 SEP 1876 in Ennis, Tex., d. 15 MAR 1928 in Temple, Bell Co., Tex., m. Ruth Evans Thompson (1877-1963); both bur.

---

[1] Carroll Co., Tenn. Deeds, Bk. K, p. 537, recorded 23 OCT 1854, witnessed by John Norwood and W.R. Poll.
[2] The 1830 Federal census for Carroll Co., Tenn. shows a daughter under age 5 and a daughter between the age of 10-14 years.

Foster Cem.

    1511.   VERA BELLE ALLEN, b. 1908, d. 1994.

   152.   ISAAC RICHMOND ALLEN, furniture dealer, b. 24 JUL 1873 in Ennis, Tex., d. 14 DEC 1941 in Ennis, Ellis Co., Tex., bur. Myrtle Cem. of Ennis, Tex., m. Nannie Alice Kendall, b. 1875, d. 1957.

   153.   LEVI JAMES ALLEN, b. 21 JUN 1871, d. 4 JAN 1888 in Ellis Co., Tex.

   154.   JESSE H. ALLEN, b. 14 OCT 1879, d. 11 JUN 1884 in Ellis Co., Tex.

   155.   ROBERT GREEN ALLEN, b. 29 JAN 1886, d. 23 OCT 1950 in Ellis Co., Tex., bur. Myrtle Cem., m. Juliette Davenel, b. 1898, d. 1932.

   156.   VERA FOSTER ALLEN, b. after 1880.

16.   ELIZABETH JUNE ALLEN, b. 1 MAR 1830 in Carroll Co., Tenn., d. 4 AUG 1894.

17.   ISAAC THOMAS ALLEN, b. 12 JUN 1832 in Carroll Co., Tenn., d. intestate 27 FEB 1911 in Ennis, Tex.,[1] bur. Myrtle Cem., m. c.1855 to MARY ANN HICKS, b. JAN 1839 in Ga., d. 23 DEC 1910 in Ennis, Tex., dau. of John W. Hicks and Caroline Harrison, *q.v.* Issue:

   171.   AURELIA BEATRICE ALLEN, b. 23 OCT 1859 in Ennis, Tex., d. 15 AUG 1943 in Stamford, Tex., m. (1) 17 JUL 1896 in Ellis, Tex. to Henry Clay Lobban, b. 1857, d. 1892, she m. (2) L.R. Bird, res. Fisher Co., Tex.

   172.   WILLIAM THOMAS ALLEN, grocer, b. 5 DEC 1861, d. 1 JUN 1937 of colon cancer, bur. Myrtle Cem., m. 6 SEP 1896 in Ellis, Tex. to Anna E. Wills.

   173.   CHARLES LEE ALLEN, judge, attorney, b. 25 JUL 1865 in Decatur, Tex., d. 15 SEP 1942 of myocarditis at 3216 Beverly Dr., Highland Park, Tex., bur. Myrtle Cem., m. 16 OCT 1887 in Ellis Co. to Lydia C. Smith, res. Dallas Co., Tex. Four children.

   174.   MINNIE MAUDE ALLEN, b. 1 DEC 1871, d. 9 MAY 1944 in Ennis, Tex., m. 18 DEC 1889 to Charles Paul Kendall, son of Thomas Kendall and Martha Jester. Two children.

   175.   CAROLYN ALLEN, m. William Leonard Foster, son of William Foster and Ararat Dunn.

   176.   MARY ELIZABETH ALLEN, m. 6 JAN 1886 in Ennis, Tex. to William Leonard Foster, son of William Foster and Ararat Dunn, res. Sterling Co., Tex.

18.   MARTHA ALLEN, b. c.1835 in Tenn., not listed on the 1860 census.

19.   ARAMINTA PINK "Minta" ALLEN, b. 1838 in Marshall Co., Miss., d. 1873 in Decatur, Wise Co., Tex.

1(10).   GEORGE WASHINGTON ALLEN, b. 12 JUL 1840 in Marshall Co., Miss., d. 20 MAR 1912 in Navarro Co., Tex., served in Civil War, bur. Hopewell Cem., Navarro, Tex., m. 11 OCT 1865 in Ennis, Tex. to Susan Alice Sheets (1846-1925). Child:

   1(10)1.   TAPLEY GREEN ALLEN, b. 30 AUG 1868 in Ellis, Tex., d. 2 MAY 1939 in Navarro, Tex., bur. Hopewell Cem., m. Hattie Beulah Dearmore, b. September 1871, d. 1905.

---

[1] Ellis Co., Tex. Probate Packets, #1510.

6. Thomas Allen
(1800-c.1893)

Thomas Allen (my ancestor), was a farmer. He was born in late 1800, perhaps in Montgomery County, North Carolina, and died about 1893 in Washington County, Arkansas.

Carroll County, Tennessee was formed in 1821 from Chickasaw Indian Lands, also called "The Western District." Thomas Allen heads a household (as does his brother Isaac Allen) in Carroll County on the 1830 Federal census [page 156]. On 7 DEC 1832, Thomas Allen sold to Robert Stokes a 100-acre tract of land on Allen's Creek on the west side of Sandy River in Carroll County, Tennessee.[1]

He is enumerated on the Federal census in 1840 for Carroll County, Tennessee [page 165]. He is enumerated on the Federal census on 7 SEP 1850 for DeSoto County, Mississippi [family 93; page 319], with wife Lucy, born c.1803 in North Carolina. On the 1860 Federal census for Hunt County, Texas, Precinct #9, with wife Ruth (perhaps Bell[2]), born c.1806 in North Carolina [family 130; page 345; post office Greenville]. Some researchers propose that Ruth and Lucy are the same person, allowing for the common range of ages found on census records. The 1860 Federal agricultural census shows Thomas Allen owned 126 acres in Hunt County, Texas.

In October 1860, Thomas Allen bought 80 acres of land from Samuel Denton (a portion of Denton's 640-acre patent) in Hunt County, Texas.[3] In October 1867, Thomas and Lucy Allen sold to Walker Fore, two parcels in Hunt County, and presumably thereafter moved to Arkansas.[4] Enumerated on the Federal census in August 1870, for Washington County, Arkansas (Marr's Hill Township), next to the family of S.A. [Sarah Ann] Hicks [page 28].

On 29 SEP 1871, Thomas Allen bought land from Denton D. Stark in Washington County, Arkansas.[5] On the Federal census taken 11 JUN 1880 he resided with son Samuel G. Allen in Washington County, Arkansas [family #154, page 18], where both of Sam's parents are shown as born in North Carolina, and where Thomas's father is born in Virginia and mother in North Carolina. This would indicate Samuel Allin, late of Carroll County, Tennessee was from Virginia.

---

[1] Carroll Co., Tenn. Deeds, Bk. C, p. 51, recorded December session 1832, registered 28 FEB 1833. The deed is signed by Thomas Allen only and there is no evidence of a wife releasing her right to the property.

[2] The Texas death certificate for his son Andrew Jackson Allen, d. 17 DEC 1916, gives parents Joe Allen and Lucy Larene Bell. Some have speculated that Lucy and Ruth were the same person named Lucy Ruth Bell.

[3] Hunt Co., Tex. Deeds, Bk. H, p. 101, dated 12 OCT 1860, located on the waters of cowlick fork [Cow Leach] of Sabine River, southeast of Greenville, Tex.

[4] Hunt Co., Tex. Deeds, Bk. K, p. 62, dated 15 OCT 1867, for 80 acres on Cow Lick [Leach] fork of Sabine River (formerly Denton's), and 100 acres (formerly Fry).

[5] Washington Co., Ark. Deeds, Bk. V, p. 285, for multiple parcels 17 acres, three acres, and 100 acres.

Children of Thomas Allen and Lucy or Ruth (perhaps Bell):

61.   JOHN B.[1] ALLEN, farmer, b. 14 DEC 1828 in Tenn., d. 1863 in Hunt Co., Tex., m. 18 MAR 1857 in Hunt Co., Tex. to Margaret R. Brown, b. 21 SEP 1839 in Ill., d. 1 MAR 1864 in Hunt Co., dau. of Richard Brown[2] and Talitha C. Miller. Enumerated in 1860 for Greenville, Hunt Co., Tex., Precinct #9 [family 131; page 346]. In August 1861, John B. and Margaret mortgaged to Patrick Sullivan the same 80-acre parcel that Thomas Allen purchased in 1860.[3] Children:

611.   JAMES MADISON ALLEN, b. 1858 in Tex.
612.   TILITHA A. ALLEN, b. 1860 in Tex.
613.   WILLIAM P. ALLEN, b. 1862, laborer, living with grandmother Talitha Brown in 1880 Federal census for Hunt Co., Tex.
614.   ELIZABETH ALLEN, made a ward of Samuel Gillion Allen in 1866.[4]

+ 62.   SAMUEL GILLION ALLEN, farmer, b. 15 AUG 1829 in Carroll Co., Tenn., d. 3 JAN 1913 in Rhea's Mill, Washington Co., Ark., m. 1 MAR 1876 [perhaps to his second wife] in Washington Co., Ark. to MARY ANN HICKS, *q.v.*

63.   SARAH ANN ALLEN, b. c.1827/1833 in Carroll Co., Tenn., d. c.1868, m. 15 JUN 1866 in Hunt Co.,[5] Tex. as the second wife of SAMUEL ROBINSON HICKS, q.v.

64.   JOSEPH ALLEN, b. c.1838 in Tenn., not found on the 1860 census.

65.   SUSANNAH M. ALLEN, b. c.1840 in Tenn.

66.   ANDREW JACKSON ALLEN [photo], farmer, farm laborer in 1860, b. 12 MAR 1843 in Carroll Co., Tenn., d. 17 DEC 1916 of pneumonia in Eliasville, Stephens Co., Tex., bur. Allen-Horton Cem. northeast of Ivan, Stephens Co., m. c.1877 to Tabitha A. Delong, b. 25 JUN 1860, d. 5 MAY 1940 of myocarditis in Eliasville, Young Co., Tex., bur. Hill Cem., dau. of Elias DeLong and Malissa Kimball.   Children:

Figure 8 - Andrew J. Allen and Tabitha A. DeLong

661.   NANCY ANN ALLEN, b. 24 FEB 1878, d. 17 DEC 1961 in Dickens Co., Tex., m. (1) Walter Eugene Fletcher, and m. (2) Harry Nance Patton.
662.   LUCY B. ALLEN, b. 2 DEC 1879, d. 3 AUG 1880, bur. Allen-Horton Cem.

---

[1] Perhaps stands for Bell or Burton.
[2] On 30 OCT 1865, Richard Brown was bonded in Hunt Co., Tex. to be the guardian of his grandchildren: James Madison Allen, Telitha A. Allen and William P. Allen. See Probate Packet #A063 and A063 regarding the guardianship.
[3] Hunt Co., Tex. Deeds, Bk. I, p. 82, dated 20 AUG 1861.
[4] Hunt Co., Tex. Probate Packets, #A063A, petition filed 7 DEC 1865, bond dated 2 JAN 1866.
[5] Hunt Co., Tex. Marriages, Bk. A, p. 182.

663.   CARRIE ALLEN, b. 6 JAN 1882, d. 15 APR 1959, m. Frank Rubenkoenig.

664.   JAMES HARRISON ALLEN [photo], b. 9 DEC 1884, d. 26 FEB 1977, bur. Llano Cem., Amarillo, Potter Co., Tex., m. (1) Attie B. Gilmore, div., m. (2) Ellen Marie Smith.

665.   THOMAS HENRY ALLEN, b. 21 FEB 1886, d. 4 FEB 1974 in Oklahoma City, Okla., m. 10 MAR 1940 to Lily V. Gatewood Prosser, b. 1895, d. 1976; both bur. Moore Cem., Cleveland Co., Okla.

666.   HATTIE FRANCES ALLEN, b. 6 JAN 1889, d. 14 DEC 1975, m. Eugene Milam, b. 1881, d. 1970.

667.   WILLIE ELIAS ALLEN, b. 6 JAN 1891, d. 13 NOV 1969 in Lubbock, Tex., m. Alta Roy Walker.

668.   DOUGLAS ALLEN, b./d. 15 DEC 1892.

669.   Infant ALLEN, b./d. 22 JAN 1893.

66(10).   GROVER CLEVELAND ALLEN, b. 27 FEB 1894 in Stephens Co., d. 16 NOV 1918 in Stephens Co., m. 6 OCT 1915 to Charlotte Thelma McGlamery, who m. (2) 4 SEP 1921 in Young Co., Tex. to Willie Thomas Whitehead.

66(11).   FRED ALLEN, b. 15 OCT 1896, d. 9 APR 1970, bur. Breckenridge Cem., Stephens Co., Tex.

66(12).   OSCAR EARL ALLEN, b. 11 MAR 1899 in Ivan, Tex., d. 1 DEC 1971 in Breckenridge, Tex., m. Audra Hokett, b. 1899, d. 1980.

Figure 9 - James Harrison Allen and Ellen Marie Smith

67.   WINCY J. ALLEN, b. c.1846 in Carroll Co., Tenn., d. 29 JAN 1896 in Stephenville, Erath Co., Tex., bur. in Oak Dale Cem., m. 3 NOV 1878 in Washington Co., Ark.[1] to ROBERT W. HICKS, *q.v.*

68.   THOMAS J. ALLEN, b. c.1847 in Tenn.

69.   JAMES W. ALLEN, b. May 1850 in DeSoto Co., Miss.

6(10).   MARY E. ALLEN, b. c.1854 in Hunt Co., Tex.

---

[1] Washington Co., Ark. Marriages, Bk. E, p. 336.

62. Samuel Gillion Allen
(1829-1913)

From records kept in the Allen Family and provided to me by my grandmother, it is known that Samuel Gillion Allen was born on Saturday, August 15, 1829. This is confirmed by the date on his tombstone in the Rhea Cemetery (formerly Rhea's Mill). By census records, he was born in Carroll County, Tennessee.

In October 1862, S.G. Allen bought 25 acres of land in Hunt County, Texas.[1] In May 1862, Samuel G. Allen enlisted for a period of 3 years as a private in Company A, First Battalion (Burnett's) Texas Sharp Shooters, at Greenville, Hunt County, Texas. He was sick in April 1863 and at the hospitals in Jackson and Port Hudson, Louisiana.[2] Grandmother said he was a chuck wagon driver in the Confederate Army. In 1866, S.G. Allen was appointed guardian of Elizabeth Allen, minor heir of his late brother John B. Allen, in Hunt County, Texas.[3]

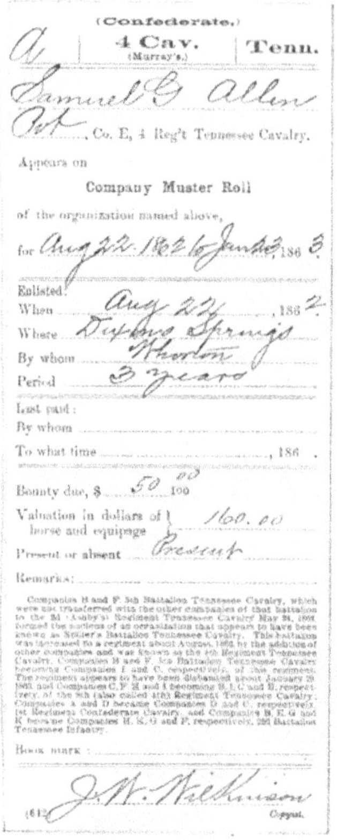
(Confederate.)
A | 4 Cav. (Murray's.) | Tenn.
Samuel G. Allen
Pvt, Co. E, 4 Reg't Tennessee Cavalry.
Appears on
Company Muster Roll
of the organization named above,
for Aug 22 1862 to Jan 1 1863
Enlisted:
When Aug 22, 1862
Where
By whom
Period 3 years
Last paid:
By whom
To what time , 186 .
Bounty due, $ 50 00/100
Valuation in dollars of horse and equipage 160.00
Present or absent Present
Remarks:
Book mark:
J.W. Wilkinson
(612) Copyist.

Figure 10 - Enlistment record for S.G. Allen for service in the war

In September 1868, Samuel G. Allen of Hunt County, Texas, sold to Marshall Fore, a parcel on Cow Lick [Leach] Fork of Sabine River, being the north half of an 89-acre tract deeded to Allen by William Gunter on 2 DEC 1861, containing 44½ acres.[4]

From a receipt found in family records we know that on 23 NOV 1874, S.G. Allen paid school taxes of $10.90 at Greenville, Hunt County, Texas. Before his son Homer J. Allen died in 1973, Sam apparently told his son Vance Allen that he had been married twice and did not return home after the Civil War—somewhere in Tennessee—where he left a wife and four boys.[5] According to Loyd Crawford, when Sam Allen's family came from Texas through Oklahoma they were attacked by Indians. The Allens were rescued by infantry and taken to Ft. Gibson where they remained two weeks before moving to Rhea's Mill, Washington County, Arkansas.[6] Sam Allen bought his property directly from the government and, until it was sold, his family was the single owner.[7]

On Wednesday, 1 MAR 1876, Samuel G. Allen was married in Washington County, Arkansas to Miss MARY ANN HICKS, from Stephenville, Erath County, Texas, the daughter of Samuel Robinson Hicks (see mention elsewhere). Part of the marriage record of Washington County says:

---

[1] Hunt Co., Tex. Deeds, Bk. I, p. 365, recorded 1 NOV 1862.
[2] Military records are online at *Fold3.com* via the Library of Virginia and other sources.
[3] Hunt Co., Tex., Probate Packets, #A063A, petition for guardianship dated 7 DEC 1865, bond dated 2 JAN 1866.
[4] Hunt Co., Tex. Deeds, Bk. K, p. 246, dated 3 SEP 1868.
[5] Letter to Wesley E. Pippenger from Mrs. Vance (Sally) Allen of Overland Park, Kansas, dated March 1980.
[6] Telephone conversation with Loyd Crawford, June 25, 1986, (602) 455-0159, mailing address 5001 S. Hickory Tree #242, Broken Arrow, OK 74011.
[7] Letter from Loyd Crawford.

Page 516, State of Arkansas, County of Washington.

"You are hereby commanded to solemnize the rights and publish the bonds of matrimony between S.G. Allen, aged 40 years and M.A. Hicks, aged 22 years, according to law and do you officially sign and return this license to the parties herein named. Witness my hand and official seal, this 25th day of February 1876, Signed R.R. Smith, Clerk."

Hence, Sam and Mary Ann were married by John Clements, Minister of the Gospel, whose credentials are recorded at Bentonville, Arkansas.

On 27 AUG 1877, S.G. Allen bought 40 acres of land from Francis M. Bowyer, it being located as the southwest quarter of the northwest quarter of Section 32, Township 16, 32 West, in Washington County, Arkansas.[1]

On 16 APR 1878, S.G. Allen paid taxes on the Southwest and Northwest parts of Section 32, Township 16, Range 32, 40 acres, for a sum of $7.71 to the County of Washington, State of Arkansas. Other receipts that have been found in the family records indicate that he paid dues on April 6, 1887 to the Independent Order of Odd Fellows (I.O.O.F.), Lodge 265, Viney Grove, Arkansas.

In June 1880, S.G. Allen headed a household near Rhea's Mill, Marr's Hill Township, Washington County, Arkansas, with wife Mary Ann and three sons. Neighbors included the Crawford, Phillips, Woodruff, and Hicks families.

Mary Ann (Hicks) Allen kept a memorandum book[2] where she recorded various events, including deaths of neighbors, family accounting information, and things important to her. Below are several entries of interest:

> I got my shoes Dec. 20, 1911
> Roy & Homer got their suits Dec. 20, 1911
> I got my buggy December the 20, 1918
> Got the clock 7 Jan. 1926
> We got our phone the 19 of March 1914
> March the 22 is the day to sow cabbage seed
> I went to Musko[gee] the 12 day of April, came home the 6 day of May.

In 1890, S.G. Allen was taxed in Washington County, Arkansas, for his 40-acre tract he purchased in 1877.

In 2 JUN 1900, Samuel G. Allen headed a household in Rhea's Mill Township of Washington County, Arkansas, with wife Mary A. The place of birth for both his parents is North Carolina, and Mary A.'s parents is Georgia.

In April 1910, Samuel G. Allen headed a household in the same location, and the birthplace for Mary A.'s parents is mistakenly noted as Alabama. The family of Leonidas E. Crawford is nearby.

---

[1] Washington Co., Ark. Deeds, Bk. Z, p. 574.
[2] This was a small advertising booklet, with blank pages inside. On the cover is printed "Dr. Porter's Memorandum Book." I will refer to this hereafter as Mary Allen's memorandum book.

Sam Allen died at his home in Washington County, Arkansas on January 3, 1913, and was buried in the Rhea Cemetery nearby.

On 12 JUL 1915, Mary Allen applied to the state of Arkansas for a pension based on the Civil War service of her deceased husband S.G. Allen. She declared he served in Company A, Burnett's Regiment of infantry from the state of Texas, and was honorably discharged on or about 26 MAY 1865. The application also states he died 3 JAN 1915, yet we have many records to prove the correct year is 1913. Mrs. Allen's application was notarized by S.F. Allen whose commission as a notary expired February 9, 1919. This is undoubtedly her son Samuel Frank Allen. As proof of service for S.G. Allen, Messrs. M.L. Pasley and J.B. Matthews, citizens of Rhea, Arkansas, declare in 1915 that they knew S.G. Allen for 30 years and that he was a confederate soldier who served from 1861 to 1865. This statement is also notorized by S.F. Allen. Contained in the pension application papers is a torn and incomplete slip of paper which bears the following statement:

> "I, S.G. Allen, Co. A Burnett's ___ do solemnly swear that I will not again bear arms against the Govt. of the united states nor aid or a _ _ _ the Enemy of said Govt. until ____ Exchanged. In testimony whereof hereunto set my hand.
>   S.G. Al _ _ _ _
> Therein and subscribed to before ___ 24th day of May A.D. 1868.
>   Edward ___ "

This paper appears to be something used merely to document the above statements, for across one end in a different handwriting appears the following, seemingly unrelated statements:

> " _ _ _ _port? of Alexandria, June 1, 1865, H _ _ _, ___ bearer to his home in Texas. By order of Mayor Franklin H. Clark, com _ _ _(year?), Ferg _ _ _, adj." and a statement "Transportation furnish _ _ from Alex.(andria?) to Shreveport, La., (signed) T.R. Hearst, May (year?)."

According to the provisions of the Act of the General Assembly of the State of Arkansas, dated March 11, 1901, Mary Allen was granted a pension of $100.00 (period not stated) which was last paid in February 1931 just before her death on 11 MAR 1931. I presume this pension was monthly, and if so, this was a reasonable sum for that era.

From notes in Mary Allen's memorandum book we know that the family barn was built in 1918 and roofing was put on the smoke house on 1 JAN 1920. In Mary Allen's notes we also find that her brother Jeff Hicks and family visited Rhea on 27 AUG 1927.[1] An obituary for Mary Allen appeared in the *Prairie Grove Herald* newspaper:[2]

<u>Mrs. Mary Allen Passes at Rhea on March 11</u>

      Funeral services for Mrs. Mary Allen, 76, who died Mar. 11 at her home near Rhea, Ark., where she had lived for 56 years, were held from the M.E. church at Rhea, March 12. Rev. Wm. Sherman, pastor of the M.E. church, Fayetteville, who was her pastor when he

---

[1] Mary Allen's memorandum book.
[2] Taken from *Prairie Grove Herald* Newspaper, Volume 29, No. 11, dated 19 MAR 1931.

served his first pastoral charge, officiated, assisted by Rev. E.E. Stevenson of Prairie Grove, and Rev. J.C. Snow, her pastor.

Pallbearers were: Luther Pasley, Jeff David, Orlan Crawford, A.V. Pasley, Lloyd Crawford and Horace Carter.

Mrs. Allen was born in Erath County, Texas, October 5, 1854, married to S.G. Allen March 1, 1876, who died in Jan. 1913.

Surviving children are Robert E. Allen and Homer Allen of Kansas City, Mo., Elmer Allen of Lubbock, Texas, S.F. Allen of DeQuincy, La., Roy Allen of Muskogee, Okla., and Clara Allen of Rhea.

The oldest child died at the age of four, and Maud, who married Loyd Crawford, died Dec. 1, 1924. Other surviving relatives are a brother and sister in Texas, 13 grandchildren. All of the children were with her during her last illness and were present at the funeral except Elmer.

In 1984, James H. Crawford and Vance Allen initiated proceedings to sell the property on which Sam Allen's home stood. A petition listed all 27 identifiable descendants who were notified of their respective interests in the matter. The 40 acres of S.G. Allen and his wife Mary Ann were sold on April 18, 1985 for the sum of $11,000.00. Grandmother Davison's portion received was $666.53, paid on April 19, 1985 by a check from the Washington County Circuit Clerk, Alma Kollmyer and drawn on McIlroy Bank and Trust of Fayetteville, Arkansas.

Figure 11 - Samuel Gillion Allen and wife Mary Ann Hicks, c.1910

Figure 12 - Fragmented page from the Family of Bible of Samuel Gillion Allen and Mary Ann Hicks

Children of Samuel Gillion Allen and Mary Ann Hicks (all born in Rhea's Mill, Arkansas):

621.   LAFAYETTE JEFFERSON ALLEN, b. Thurs., 14 DEC 1876, never married, and d. young on Sat., 26 AUG 1882. His place of burial has not been located.

+ 622.   ROBERT EDWARD ALLEN,[1] b. Fri., 17 JAN 1879, m. Mary Ellen Lewis in Fayetteville, Arkansas. See mention later.

+ 623.   WILLIAM ELMER ALLEN, b. Fri., 12 AUG 1881, m. in Stephenville, Erath Co., Tex. to Hattie Mollie Cook. See mention later.

+ 624.   SAMUEL FRANK ALLEN, b. Tues., 10 FEB 1885, m. in Rhea's Mill, Ark. to Laura Edmiston. See mention later.

625.   CLARA BELLE ALLEN, b. Fri., 30 SEP 1887, near Rhea's Mill, was never married. She went to Kansas City, Mo. on 21 AUG 1910 and came back to Rhea on 29 NOV 1911.[2] An entry in her mothers memorandum book says that Clara "commenced work for Neal, May 6, 1922", and we know that she had a social security account. Clara d. Tues., 14 NOV 1972 in Fayetteville, Ark. and was bur. Thurs., 16 NOV 1972 in Rhea Cem. Grandmother remembered the day of Clara's funeral, where as the cows were mooing, Clara's casket was carried from the church across the street to the cemetery. Her residence was then at Lincoln, Ark. Clara B. Allen's funeral bulletin says that pallbearers were Ray Tucker, Leon Tucker, Travis Beaty, Tommy Tucker, Milton Sparks, and Charles Branchcomb, with the Rev. Van Hooker presiding. Funeral expenses were charged to Homer Allen of Lincoln, Ark. Clara was really the last of the Allen Family to be active in the Rhea's Mill church. Several family papers were found in "Aunt Clara's trunk."

Figure 13 - Loyd Crawford

626.   MYRTLE MAY ALLEN, possibly a twin, b. 30 SEP 1887.[3] When I asked my grandmother about this she said she had never heard of such a person. It may have been an infant. The only other suggestion I have to this entry is that it was a name later changed to Clara B. Allen.

627.   MAUD ELIZABETH ALLEN, b. Wed., 25 FEB 1891. According to Mary Allen's memorandum book, Maud came down with the measles on 25 JUL 1910. She was m. on Wed., 27 SEP 1916[4] in Fayetteville, Ark. to Loyd [or Lloyd] Crawford. Mr. Crawford had brothers named Leon and Orland Crawford. Loyd was b. 12

---

[1] My mother, Zora Eileene (Davison) Pippenger claims her grandfather's full name was Robert E. Lee Allen, but I have found no record to verify this.
[2] Mary Allen's memorandum book.
[3] Taken from papers found in the Hicks Family Bible.
[4] Mary Allen's memorandum book, and Loyd Crawford.

JAN 1896 at Rhea's Mill, son of Oscar Crawford (d. in.Tulsa, Okla) and "Petie" Victoria Cowan. About 1922, Loyd and Maud moved from Rhea to live in Fayetteville, Ark., but by 1930 he was enumerated in Tulsa, Okla. where they rented a home. She d. 1 DEC 1923 in Fayetteville Hospital after an illness of nearly 3 months, and was bur. Sun., 2 DEC 1923 in the Rhea Cem. Her funeral at the Methodist Church was performed by her former pastor Rev. W.A. Downum. Loyd Crawford m. (2) to Maud Summers, dau. of Edward R. Summers., res. Tulsa, Okla. Children:

6271.   IVAN CRAWFORD, b. 9 AUG 1916 in Ark.

6272.   JAMES H. CRAWFORD, b. 1920 in Ark., res. Tulsa, Okla.

6273.   MARY LUCILLE CRAWFORD, b. 1922 in Okla., m. Mr. Bell, of Tex.

628.   LEROY BENTON ALLEN, b. Sat., 23 JUN 1894 on the family farm in Rhea's Mill. He came down with the measles on 28 JUN 1910. He went to North Platte, Lincoln Co., Neb., to work for the railroad, and was trained as a telegrapher. He was m. (1) there 10 OCT 1917 to Nelly Matthews. In late 1922, Roy moved Muskogee where he worked for M.K.&T Railroad as a car inspector. During World War I he came back to Rhea's Mill, from Camp Pike, Ark. on 1 JAN 1919.[1] Nellie Matthews, dau. Joseph B. and Betty Matthews, was b. 20 FEB 1895, d. in a hospital in Muskogee on 23 JAN 1933, and is bur. in Prairie Grove Cem. At age 36, Roy m. (2) on 2 MAY 1934 by I.W. Fulgham, Baptist minister, in Wagoner, Okla. to Alice Schwarz, age 26. When I contacted Alice she would not help at all with family history. Lois Beverage indicated that Alice Allen lived in Union Gap, Wash. Roy Allen lived in Muskogee, Okla. from about 1923 to 1974 when at age 80 he moved to Prairie Grove, Ark. He d. 23 JUL 1980 in Washington Regional Medical Center Hospital of Fayetteville, Ark. of cardiac arrest. He was bur. in the Prairie Grove Cem. on 26 JUL 1980. Roy Allen's niece, my grandmother, was not notified about his death until many days after his burial. We learn from Roy Allen's death certificate that he had social security account and records for this account show it was issued to Benton Roy Allen whose father was Samuel George Allen; so that data is a bit messed up. Roy served in the domestic Army during World War I. He was a Shriner and a Mason, and once belonged to the Lodge in Muskogee, Okla. His residence at the time of death was 607 North Lewis Street, Prairie Grove, Ark. I wrote a letter to Roy in 1979, asking for assistance on the Allen family history. I got a response, saying that Homer and Vance got all the family information and he couldn't help.[2] Children:

6281. LOIS JUANITA ALLEN, b. January 18, 1921 in North Platte, Lincoln Co., Neb., m. 28 APR 1944 in Muskogee, Okla. to Beryl Beverage. Children:

62811.   BEVERLY SUE BEVERAGE, b. 29 JAN 1947 in Muskogee, m. (1) 26 AUG 1967 to Jeff Carrillo, div. 1980. Beverly m. (2) 12 APR 1981 to Ronald Waters. Children:

628111.   NICOLE LYNETTE CARRILLO.

---

[1] Mary Allen's memorandum book.

[2] This three-sentence response was obviously not in the handwriting of an aged Roy Allen, and typical of his second wife Alice. I presume that he never saw my letter asking for assistance on the Allen family history. A similar one was written to grandmother in March 1980, that "Homer, Georgia & Vance got everything. Clara had even the family Bible & records. Roy & Lois got nothing."

628112. JOHNATHAN EDWARD CARRILLO.
628212.   BERL ALLEN BEVERAGE, b. 13 AUG 1950 in Muskogee.
6282. SAMUEL JOSEPH ALLEN (named after both his grandfathers), b. 21 JAN 1933, lived only 1 day,[1] bur. Greenhill Cem. of Muskogee.

+ 629. HOMER JOHNSON ALLEN, b. Mon., 27 FEB 1899. Like his brother Roy and sister Maud, Homer came down with the measles on 26 JUL 1910. He was m. on Wed., 6 SEP 1922 in Fayetteville, Ark. to Georgia May Miller. See mention later.

Figure 14 - Homer Johnson Allen

---

[1] Information provided to Lois Allen Beverage by Clara Allen.

Deaths and Marriages Recorded in
Mary Ann (Hicks) Allen's Memorandum Book[1]

Birdy Norwood departed this life August 11, 19.10
Mrs. Leroy Rhea departed this life April 24th, 19.11
Mrs. Jacob died March 19.11
Sarra Mathews departed this life February 19.12
Ina Crawford was married Sept. the 27, 19.11
Betty Stephin was married Oct. 30, 19.11
Rose Cammel and Deney (sic.) the 2 November 19.11
Pleane Jacobs married March the 20, 19.12
Mrs. Pearson departed this life March the 23, 19.13
Mrs. Liza Frazier departed this life Oct. the 27, 19.13
Mr. Edmiston departed this life April the 8, 1915
Frank Mathews was married Aug. 25, 19.15
Maud was married the 27 of Sep., 19.16
Elmer and Edna was married Feb. 21, 19.17
Alley and Rella the Feb. 21, 19.17
Girty Rhea died April the 28, 1924?
Homer Allen was married Sep. 6, 19.22
Edna Ezell departed this life July 24, 1924
Mrs. Templeton departed this life Jan. 6, 1911
S.G. Allen departed this life Jan. the 3, 19.13
Brother Will Hicks departed this life Feb. the 16, 19.16
Robert William Hicks departed this life Feb. the 16th 19.16 [recorded twice]
R.E. Allen was married August 30 (1900)
Elmer Allen was married Oct. 22, 19.5
Frank Allen was married Nov. 5, 19.5
Maud Allen was married Sept. 27, 19.16
Roy Gregory was married Dec. 1922 to Mr. Clent Davis
Aunt Maggie Powell departed this life Jan. 16, 19.23
Lois Allen was born Jan. 1 _?, 19.21
Dellavan Printas Allen was born Feb. the 2th (sic) 19.10
Ivan Estell was (sic) August the 9, 19.17
Homer Allen was married Sept. 5, 19.22
Roy Allen was married the 10 of Oct. 19.17
Patsy was boarn March 28, 1922

---

[1] Notice she records the year by placing a period between the second and third digit, i.e. "19.11."

HICKS FAMILY

The first clue as to the ancestry of Mary Ann, wife of Samuel G. Allen, was given to me by Georgia May (Miller) Allen. Even though her mind was failing when I spoke with her during the summer of 1979, Georgia remembered a few things, and HICKS was one thing that she was quick to spout off—the maiden name of Sam Allen's wife. Subsequently, I found that there existed an old family Bible from the Hicks Family. Although it was largely damaged by mice, we were able to salvage the family information pages. From these pages, a transcript was made.

Mary Ann Hicks was a daughter of Samuel Robinson Hicks and wife Grizzel Ann Brison. It appears as though the marriage date of S.R. Hicks and Grizzel Ann Brison is recorded in the Bible pages as April 28, 1844.[1] From the Federal census of Crawford County, Georgia we know that S.R. Hicks had an older brother John W. Hicks. Samuel R. Hicks is enumerated in the 1860 Federal census:

1860 U.S. Census—Erath County, Texas, Beat #1, page 14, July 4, 1860, Post Office: Stephenville, Texas.

Family	Head	Age	Occupation	Birthplace
81	HICKS, Sam R.	39	Farmer & City	Tennessee
	, Gizell A.	35	Officer	South Carolina
	, John H.	15	Farmer	Georgia
	, Robert W.	13		Georgia
	, Margaret M.J.	10		Georgia
	, Mary Ann	5		Texas
	, Joseph L.	1		Texas

We also find that S.R. Hicks is enumerated in the 1850 Federal Census for Chattooga County, Georgia, wherein the birthplace of his son Robert W. Hicks is recorded as Alabama. Other possibly related Hicks families are clustered together nearby.

1850 U.S. Census - Chattooga County, Georgia, Seminole District, pages 383-4, taken October 14, 1850.

Family	Head	Age	Occupation	Birthplace
1	HICKS, John W.	37	Farmer	Tennessee
	, Caroline	30		Alabama
	, William	13		Georgia
	, Mary A.	12		Georgia
	, Frances	7		Georgia
	, James	4		Georgia
	, Lafayette	1		Georgia
3	HICKS, S.R.	30	Farmer	Tennessee

---

[1] Date confirmed by information written by Clara Allen, however she wrote 1824, which is an obvious error. Also see Chattooga Co., Ga. Marriages, Bk. 1, p. 50, for Samuel R. Hicks to G.A. Bryson.

	, Ann	25		South Carolina
	, John	6		Georgia
	, Robert W.	3		Alabama
	, Margaret	6/12		Georgia
5	HICKS, Davis	48	Farmer	Georgia
	, Mary	49		Georgia
	, Davis	20	Farmer	North Carolina
	, Henry	18		North Carolina
	, Mary	16		North Carolina
	, Elizabeth	12		North Carolina
	, James C.	7		Georgia
7	HICKS, Sarah	60		Georgia
	, Margaret	25		Georgia
	, Andy	8		Georgia
	, Jasper	2		Georgia
	, Newton	2		Georgia
9	HICKS, James	38	Farmer	North Carolina
	, Martha	32		Virginia
	, Mary A.	9		North Carolina
	, Permelia A.	7		North Carolina
	, Elizabeth	6		North Carolina
	, Susan C.	4		North Carolina
	, Sarah A.	1		Georgia

From these records it appears that at least some of this clan of Hicks Family moved from Georgia to North Carolina, to Tennessee and maybe some back to Georgia. It may be that the Sarah Hicks, age 60, is mother to many of these.[1] I also notice that in the family of John W. Hicks, a son is named Lafayette Hicks. This is the name given the first son born to Samuel Gillion Allen and Mary Ann Hicks.

We find that in Texas, S.R. Hicks was elected as Erath County Treasurer on August 6, 1860.[2] This would explain why the Federal census for earlier that year indicated he was a city officer. This shows that he was either elected to an additional term, or served in a different capacity previous to his election to County Treasurer. S.R. Hicks was also the first sheriff of Erath County after its organization. Several of our Hicks Family members are buried in the Oak Dale Cemetery, located on Highway 108 north of Stephenville, Erath County, Texas.

---

[1] The newspaper obituary for R.W. Hicks indicates he moved with his father from Georgia to Arkansas, then to Texas.
[2] Taken from Homer Stephen, *History of Erath County, Texas* (Stephensville, Tex.: By the Author, 1950), page 5.

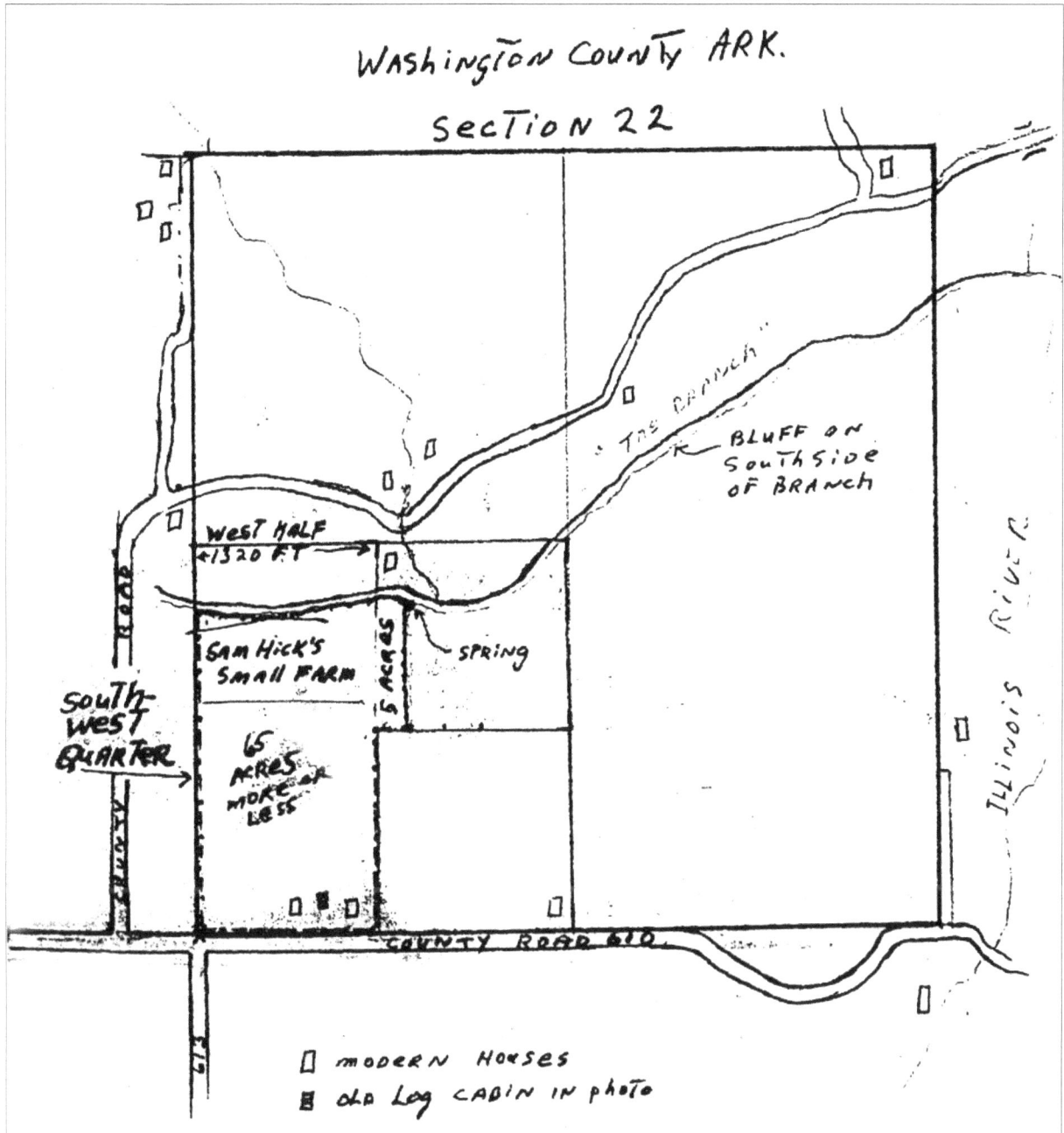

Figure 15 - Diagram of the Farm of Samuel R. Hicks, Washington County, Arkansas

Early Hicks Family

With the preliminary research above, further investigation draws attention to the estate of William Nelson Hicks who died in 1848 in Chattooga County, Georgia. We know John W. Hicks was appointed administrator. Both John W. Hicks and his brother Samuel Robinson Hicks appear as heads of household on the 1850 Federal census for Chattooga County. Also found there is a household headed by Sarah Hicks who is perpahs the widow of William Nelson Hicks and thus the mother of John and Samuel.

Samuel Robinson Hicks
(1820-1867)

Samuel Robinson[1] Hicks, was born 3 SEP 1820 in Tennessee and perhaps a son of William Nelson Hicks who died in 1848 in Chattooga County, Georgia. Sam was a cattle rancher and farmer. S.R. Hicks was married on 28 APR 1844[2] in Chattooga County, Georgia, to Grizzel Ann Brison [or Bryson], born 14 JUN 1825, perhaps in Laurens Couunty, South Carolina who died 3 NOV 1865 in Hunt County, Texas. One claim is that Grizzel was the daughter of Hugh Brison (1770-1835) and his wife Margaret (1784-1863).

He appears on the 1850 Federal agricultural census for Seminole District of Chattooga County, Georgia, having no land but owning farm equipment and a horse. His entry is next to that of J. Hicks who owns land and multiple farm animals.

On 14 OCT 1850, the family is enumerated on the Federal census for Seminole District of Chattooga County [family #3; page 383a], with two Bryson families as neighbors. S.R. Hicks was a private in Company C of the 3rd Tennessee Infantry for the Confederate States Army.

Widower S.R. Hicks married second on 15 JUN 1866 in Hunt County, Texas to SARAH ANN ALLEN, q.v., sister of Samuel Gillion Allen.

The following story came to me in 2009 from Brad Adams:

> After the birth of the last child Frances Caroline Hicks, mother Grizzel was never well again, and lived until November 3rd of that year and died of child bed fever. To forget this grief and get a new start, Sam decided to go to Oregon. He loaded his heavy old wagon with his household goods and sold his farm to a new settler. He left the two slaves, who were now free anyway, for lack of room. Little "Fannie" was the charge of Mary, the 12-year old. Little Jeff was now 2 years old. Malinda was the cook. Will rode the horse. On the way to Oregon, they circled back through Arkansas, probably to miss the Indian Territory which later became Oklahoma, and also intending to pick up the Oregon Trail in Missouri. While going through Arkansas, they stopped at Rhea's Mill to visit some distant relatives, and to rest a while. Sam had a carbuncle on his neck which was very painful and he finally decided to have it removed. It proved to be a malignant tumor and Sam knoew he could no longer go West. He bought a small farm, married his friend's sister, Sarah Allen, and lived about 2 years.

> Samuel Roberson Hicks died in Rhea's Mill, Arkansas on November 9, 1867. Will, the oldest son, had joined another wagon train and gone to Oregon, where he remained two years before returning to Stephenville via Rhea's Mill, Arkansas, where he stopped for a visit with his stepmother's family. Little Jeff said when he grew up, he too was going back to Texas, which he did. Mary, a dark-haired, black-eyed lass, married one of the settlers, Sam Allen, at Rhea's Mill. Jeff, later sent for his step-mother and his little sister, Fannie, to come to Texas. Magnolia remembers when she was a little girl, her "step-Grandma and Aunt Fannie came to live with us." Magnolia is the first daughter and second child of "little Jeff." She was born in 1892. Step-Grandma and aunt Fannie must have come to live with Jeff and his family about 1895 or '96. Magnolia remembers the funeral when Step-Grandma died and the wedding when Aunt Fannie married and went west. (She eventually settled at DeMoine, New Mexico).

---

[1] Researcher Brad Adams has his name as Samuel Roberson Hicks.
[2] A date found in the Hicks Family Bible, believed to be his marriage. Records of Chattooga Co., Ga. provide date 24 APR 1844. See Chattooga Co., Ga. Marriages, Bk. A, p. 50.

Malinda stayed at Rhea's Mill until 1870, when a young man she knew at Stephenville, Texas came and married her and took her back to her old home town. The young man was Samuel Wesley Johnson. They were married Sept. 1, 1870. He sold his horse, bought an ox wagon and headed for Texas with his bride. The trip home took six or seven weeks. While camped in a clearing one evening, they heard a noise and upon looking out of the wagon they saw seven Indians riding up. Sam told Lindy to pretend to be asleep and to pray a lot, which they did. The Indians rode up, looked in the wagon, grunted, and rode off, after they had let the oxen loose. Sam only had one gun and he wanted to leave it with Lindy while he rounded up the oxen and she insisted he take it for his protection. It is not known how this argument was settled. Back in Texas, after one Indian raid, Sam and Lindy went to check on their neighbors and found all dead except a baby boy who was unharmed, but was crawlilng around in the cow lot.

S.R. Hicks died 9 NOV 1867, and the administration of his estate was granted 2 MAY 1868 in Washington County, Arkansas to Andrew E. Edmiston.[1] Final settlement of his estate was filed by A.E. Edmiston on 12 AUG 1870. Thomas Allen filed a claim on 2 FEB 1869 for $27.50 against S.R. Hicks' estate.[2] Widow S.A. Hicks headed a household near Rhea's Mill, Marr's Hill Township of Washington County, Arkansas in August 1870.

Children Samuel Robinson[3] Hicks and his first wife Grizzel Ann Brison:

1. JOHN HUGH HICKS, b. 20 JAN 1846 in Chattooga Co., Ga., perhaps served in the Confederate States Army, d. 1863.

2. ROBERT[4] WILLIAM "Will" HICKS, b. 5 JUL 1847 in Ala., and d. Wed. morning at 7:30, 16 FEB 1916 of Bright's disease in Oak Dale, Erath Co., Tex., bur. in the Oak Dale Cem., near Stephenville, Tex. At his death he resided 4 miles north of Stephenville, Tex., and was a member of the M.E. Church South. R.W. Hicks was married (1) on 3 NOV 1878 to WINCY J. ALLEN, q.v., who d. 7:15 p.m. Wed., 29 JAN 1896 in Stephenville, Tex., age 48, bur. 4 p.m. on 30 JAN 1896 in Oak Dale Cem. near Stephenville. R.W. Hicks m. (2) on 9 MAY 1897 in Washington Co., Ark.[5] to Mary (unknown), b. 1874 in Stephenville, Tex. R.W. Hicks served in the C.S.A.[6]

3. MARGARET MALINDA JANE "Maggie" HICKS, b. 15 FEB 1850 in Chattooga Co., Ga., d. 3 SEP 1930 of senility at the farm home of her daughter in the Oak Dale community, m. 1 SEP 1870 in Ark. to Rev. Samuel Wesley Johnson, a pioneer Methodist circuit rider. S.W. Johnson, b. 20 APR 1848, d. 26 FEB 1885 in a train accident in Alexander, Erath Co., Tex. Both were bur. in Oak Dale Cem. near Huckaby, Erath Co., Tex. Children:
   31. JOSEPH ALONZO JOHNSON, b. 19 JUL 1871 in Stephenville, d. 19 JUN 1927 in Plainview, Hale Co., Tex., bur. Llano Cem., Amarillo, Tex., m. 28 MAR 1895 in Stephenville to Lula Thomas Williams, b 1876, d. 1960. 10 children.

---

[1] Washington Co., Ark., Bk. E, pp. 56, 210, 480. On 30 APR 1869, Andrew E. Edmiston became guardian for minor heirs Mary, Jefferson, Fanny and Malinda Hicks.
[2] Washington Co., Ark., Wills, Bk. E, p. 173.
[3] See Crosby County Historical Commission, *A History of Crosby County [Texas], 1876-1977* (Taylor Publishing Co., 1978), p. __, article on Jefferson Davis Hicks Family, gives the name of his father as Samuel Roberson Hicks.
[4] Researcher Brad Adams has this man as Rathal William Hicks, b. JUL 1848.
[5] Mary's application for a widow's pension indicates her place of marriage was Erath Co., Tex.
[6] He was granted a pension for his C.S.A. service; record copies at the Texas State Library; widow Mary applied File #25046, rejected.

32.   MARY ELLEN JOHNSON, b. 4 APR 1876 in Oak Dale, Erath Co., Tex., d. 11 AUG 1957, bur. Llano Cem.

33.   ERIE LULA JOHNSON, b. 21 MAR 187[8], d. 16 MAY 1964, bur. Oak Dale Cem., m. 1 OCT 1898 to John S. Birdwell, b. 13 JUN 1866, d. 19 OCT 1939. Issue:

    331. CARL BIRDWELL, res. Bryan, Tex.

34.   MARY ELLA JOHNSON, b. 27 DEC 1873, d. 3 JUL 1957 in Waco, McLennan Co., Tex., m. Rev. Charles Vachel Bailey, b. 29 JAN 1862 in Clinton Co., Mo., d. 24 JAN 1953 in Waco, Tex., bur. Oakwood Cem., Waco, Tex.

35.   MYRTLE EFFIE JOHNSON, b. 23 OCT 1883 in Stephenville, Tex., d. 24 JAN 1944, bur. Live Oak Cem., Brady, McCulloch Co., Tex., m. Robert Otis Andrews, b. 27 NOV 1883, d. 30 JAN 1935.

36.   ANNIE LAURA JOHNSON, b. 11 FEB 1878 in Erath Co., Tex., d. 29 APR 1944 in Carnegie, Caddo Co., Okla., m. (1) NOV 1899 at Stephenville to Andrew Thomas Kerr, d. 27 OCT 1906, m. (2) 15 JUL 1917 in Stephenville as the second wife of William Whitson Rutherford, b. 17 AUG 1869 in Ellis Co., Tex., d. 13 MAR 1949 in Oklahoma City, Okla., bur. Alfalfa Cem., Caddo Co., Okla., son of J.W. (1840-1919) and Hessabell (1844-1928) Rutherford. Issue:

    361.   GRACE ERIE KERR, b. 12 SEP 1901, d. 25 SEP 1959, m. Guy Martin Hockman (1893-1963), bur. Carnegie Cem., Carnegie, Caddo Co., Okla. Issue:

    3611. CHARLES NEDWIN HOCKMAN, b. 1921, d. 2009.

    3612. BEN DUANE HOCKMAN, b. 1923, d. 1946.

    362.   COY KERR, of Port Arthur, Tex.

    363.   INA FAYE RUTHERFORD, m. Alton Burditt, of Gulfport, Miss.

37.   CLARA BELLE JOHNSON, b. 21 NOV 1880 in Oak Dale, Tex., d. 31 JUL 1962 in Lubbock, Tex., m. D.R. Williams, res. Lubbock, Tex.

  4. SAMUEL RECTOR HICKS, b. 4 JUL 1853, d. in Stephenville, Erath Co., Tex. on 9 OCT 1853.

+ 5. MARY ANN HICKS (our ancestress), b. 5 OCT 1854 in Stephenville, m. 1 MAR 1876 in Washington Co., Ark.[1] to SAMUEL GILLION ALLEN, q.v. She d. 11 MAR 1931 at her residence near Rhea's Mill, Ark., bur. 12 MAR 1931 in Rhea Cem.

  6. JOSEPH LAFAYETTE HICKS, b. 28 JAN 1859 in Erath Co., Tex., d. 25 JAN 1863.

  7. JEFFERSON DAVIS HICKS, farmer, b. 18 JAN 1862 in Erath Co., Tex., d. 6 AUG 1931 of apoplexy in Crosbyton, Crosby Co., Tex., and bur. 8 AUG 1931 in the Oak Dale Cem. near Huckaby, Erath Co., Tex., m. 8 SEP 1889 in Erath Co. to Sarah J. McKinney, b. 18 AUG 1870 in Tenn., came to Erath Co. in 1880, d. 7 APR 1944 of diabetes, in Lubbock General Hospital, Lubbock, Tex.,[2] and bur. next to her

---

[1] Washington Co., Ark. Marriages, Bk. D, p. 516.
[2] *Stephenville Empire-Tribune*, 14 APR 1944.

husband. She was a dau. of W.H. McKinney and Amanda Ross of Knoxville, Tenn., and lived in Clay Co., Tex. after 1910, then removed to Crosbytown, Tex. Issue:

71. BENJAMIN FRANKLIN HICKS, b. 5 JUL 1890, d. 18 MAY 1972, bur. Resthaven Memorial Park, Lubbock, Tex.

72. CLINTON ELLIS HICKS, res. Houston, Tex., d. 1973 in Houston, Tex., m. Mable (unknown), d. 1963.

73. BERNICE RAY HICKS, b. 22 OCT 1898, d. 3 OCT 1972 of a heart attack, bur. Resthaven Memorial Park, Lubbock, Tex.

74. SAMUEL R. HICKS, farmer, cattle rancher, m. Bertha Lassiter, res. Odessa, Tex. Issue:

    741. JIMMY HICKS, m. Lynn (unknown).

    742. TOMMY HICKS.

75. MAGNOLIA HICKS, 12 JUN 1892, d. 16 NOV 1986, bur. Resthaven Memorial Park, m. 1920 to W.E. Busby, res. Lubbock, Tex. Issue:

    751. WILLIAM R. BUSBY, b. 14 DEC 1923 in Tarrant Co., Tex., d. 10 AUG 1949 in a car accident in Colo., bur. Resthaven Memorial Park.

76. BONNYE HICKS, teacher, b. 13 APR 1901, d. 3 JAN 1987, bur. Resthaven Memorial Park, m. 1924 to Spurgeon G. Stewart, Sr. Issue:

    761. SPURGEON G. STEWART, JR., b. 22 JUN 1927, d. 1 MAY 2009, bur. Woodlawn Cem., Houston, Tex., m. Lilly B. (unknown), b. 1929, d. 2000.

    762. WILLIAM HICKS STEWART, killed in action in Korea in 1951.

77. RUTH HICKS, b. 6 NOV 1904, d. 2 OCT 1982, bur. Resthaven Memorial Park, m. (1) Milford Harkins, and m. (2) in 1944 to Edgle Dee Wheeler, d. 1977, res. Crosbyton, Tex. Issue:

    771. SAMMY R. HARKINS.

8. FRANCES CAROLINE "Fannie" HICKS, b. 28 JAN 1864/5 in Tex. If she lived, she never knew her mother who died 9 months later.

John W. Hicks
(c.1813-after 1900)

John W. Hicks, perhaps a son of William Nelson Hicks who died in 1848 in Chattooga County, Georgia. He is a brother to Samuel Robinson Hicks, was born c.1813 in Tennessee. He was first married in the early 1830s in Georgia, and married second on 10 NOV 1844 in Chattooga County, Georgia to Caroline Harrison,[1] born in 1812 or 1820 in Alabama. Chattooga County was formed in 1838 from parts of Floyd and Walker counties.

On 5 SEP 1848, John W. Hicks is appointed administrator of the estate of William Nelson Hicks, late of Chattooga County, Georgia.[2] It may be that William was John's father.

---

[1] Chattooga Co., Ga. Marriages, Bk. A, p. 57. Online marriages state same day in Chatham Co., Ga. Also, the 1880 Federal Census gives that Caroline was b. 1820 in Ga., with both her parents from S.C.

[2] Chattooga Co., Ga. Probate Records, loose originals, 1856-1915, file William N. Hicks.

He appears on the 1850 Federal agricultural census for Seminole District of Chattooga County, Georgia, owning land and multiple farm animals. His entry is next to S.R. Hicks who does not own land but has some farm equipment and a horse.

On 11 OCT 1850, the family was enumerated on the Federal census in Seminole, Chattooga County, Georgia [family #1; page 383], with John as a farmer with five children all born in Georgia.

In 1860, they resided in the Western District of Upshur County, Texas. On the 1870 Federal census, they resided in Precinct 4 near Calloway, Upshur County, Texas. In 1880, John and Caroline reside in Ellis, Texas with their daughter Mary Ann (Hicks) Allen. John and Caroline are enumerated on the 1900 Federal census for Ellis, Texas, and the record show his parents were both born in Tennessee, her parents were both born in Georgia.

Children of John W. Hicks and his first wife (name unknown)

   1. WILLIAM HICKS, b. c.1836 in Ga.

+ 2. MARY ANN HICKS, b. 17 JAN 1837 in Ga., d. 16 MAR 1920 in Tex., m. ISAAC THOMAS ALLEN, *q.v.*

   3. FRANCES HICKS, b. 1843 in Ga.

Children of John W. Hicks and his second wife Caroline Harrison:

   4. JAMES T. HICKS, farmer, b. 31 AUG 1846 in Ga., m. Mattie (unknown), b. 1847 in Ga., d. 2 JUN 1927 of heart trouble, bur. Ennis, Tex. Issue:
      41.   CHARLES HICKS, b. JAN 1873 in Tex.
      42.   JAMES HICKS, b. MAR 1880 in Tex.
      43.   MATTIE HICKS, b. AUG 1883 in Tex.

   5. LAFAYETTE E. HICKS, b. 1849 in Ga., m. Mary E. (unknown). Issue:
      51.   JOHN ARTHUR HICKS, b. 1869 in Tex.

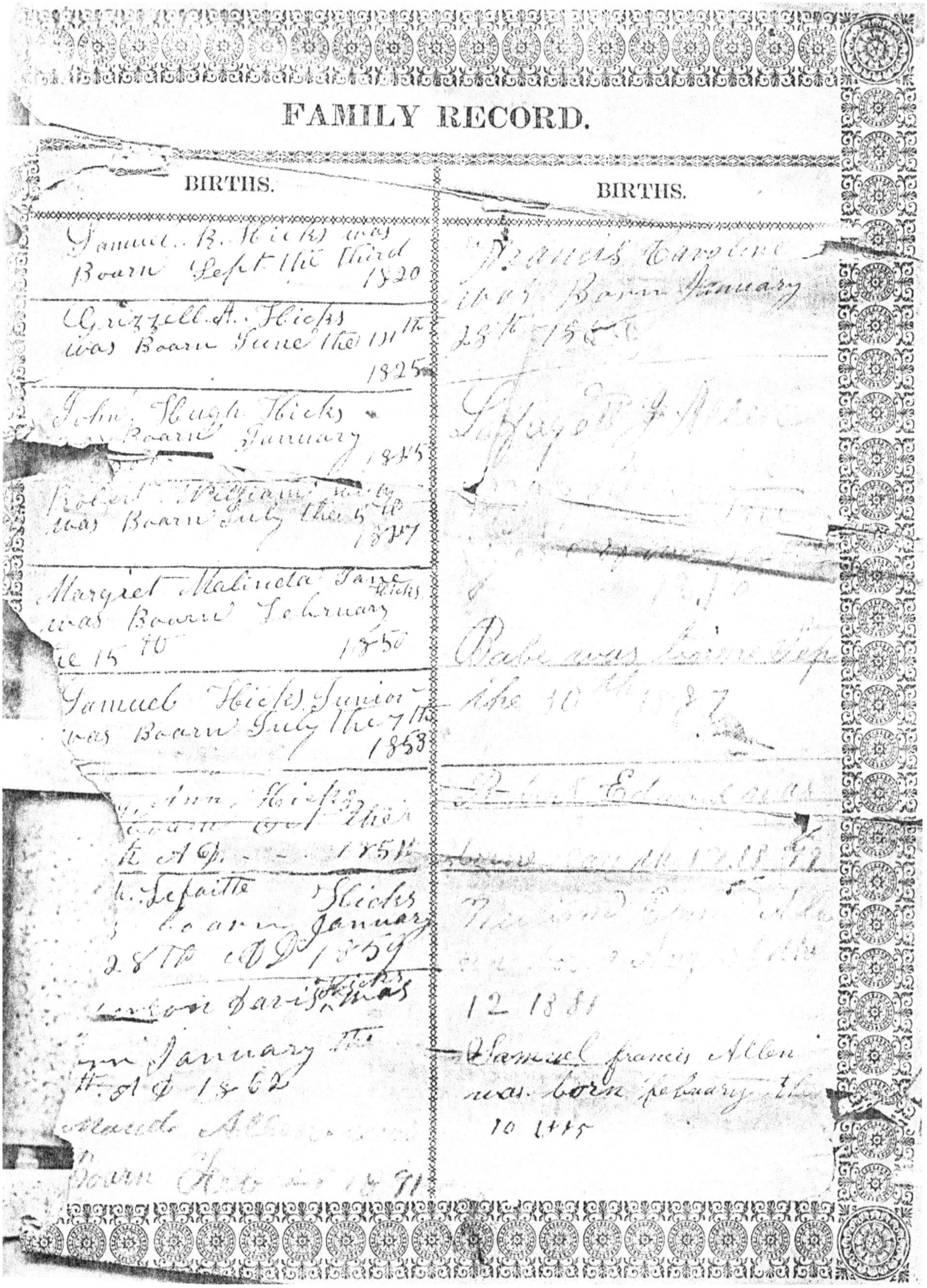

FAMILY RECORD.

BIRTHS.	BIRTHS.
Samuel B. Hicks was Boarn Sept the third 1820	Francis Caroline was Boarn January 23th 185_
Grizzell A. Hicks was Boarn June the 13th 1825	Siffagon A Allen
John Hugh Hicks Boarn January 1845	
Robert William was Boarn July the 5th 1847	
Margret Malinda Jane Hicks was Boarn February the 15th 1850	Babe was born Sep the 10th 1882
Samuel Hicks Junior was Boarn July the 7th 1853	
_ Ann Hicks _ born Oct the _ A D _ 1856	Robert Edwin _
_ Lefaitte Hicks boarn January 28th A D 1859	_ Allen
_ son Davis Hicks _ January _ A D 1862	12 1881
_ Allen Boarn Aug _ 1871	Samuel francis Allen was born february the 10 1845

Figure 16 - A mutilated page from the Hick Family Bible

Hicks Bible Insert

Below is a transcription of a ragged sheet found in the Hicks Family Bible. All writing with the exception of an entry for Roy E. Allen, is the same: a fine script in black ink. It seems that originally the page was for recording family births.

Roy E. Allen, married October 22, 1905
Lafayette J. Allen, Dec. 14, 1876
Robert E. Allen, Jan. 17th, 1879
William E. Allen, Aug. 12th, 1881
Samuel F. Allen, Feb. 10th (12th written over), 1885
Myrtle May Allen, 1887, Sep. 30th

In the margin of the paper is written: "believe me dress can not improve the charm that first awoke my love" and "friend ship is something to be proved"

Turn this above paper over and the following things are written in the same handwriting: "remember me when this you see, so may a mild apart live be", "Fannie Hicks may", and if practicing, "Fannie Hicks" is written three times.

MRS. YOUNG, FAYETTEVILLE. ARK.

Figure 17 - Robert Edward Allen

Hicks Family Record
Transcribed from the Hicks Bible

The family record, as well as the entire bible, was so badly damaged, that a photocopy of the information is not very satisfactory for reproduction. Following is a transcription of what is contained.

Births

Samuel R. Hicks was boarn Sept. the third 1820
Grizzell A. Hicks was boarn June the 14th 1825
John Hugh Hicks was boarn January ( ) 1885
Robert William Hicks was boarn July the 5th 1887
Margret Malinda Jane Hicks was boarn February the 15th 1850
Samuel Hicks Junior was boarn July the 7th 1853
Mary Ann Hicks (was) boarn Oct. the (5t)h A.D. 1854
(Josep)h Lefaitte Hicks (wa)s boarn January 27th A.D. 1859
(Jeffer)son Davis Hicks was (boa)rn January the ( )th A.D. 1862
Maud Allen was Boarn Feb. 25, 1891
Francis Caroline (Hicks) was Born January 28th 1865
Lafayett J. Allen was borned Dec. the (14th) year ( ) 1876
Babe was borne Sep. the 30th 1887
Robert Edward (Allen) was borne Jan. the 17, 1879
William Elmer Allen was borne August the 12, 1881
Samuel Francis Allen was born february the 10, 1885

Deaths

Samuel Hicks Junior Died October the 9th 1853 Joseph Lefayett Hicks Departed this Life January the 25th A.D. 1863

Grizzell A. Hicks Departed this life November the 3rd 1865 Samuel R. Hicks Departed this Life November the 9th 1867

Marriage?[1]

From the copy I received from Sally Allen (late of Cookson, Oklahoma), we find "Aprile the 28(th), 1844" on the end of the copy for deaths. It is upside down, as showing through a page on the reverse. I believe this could be the marriage date of Samuel R. Hicks and Grizzel Ann.

---

[1] I was not provided a specific page for marriages by Sally Allen.

Allen Family *(continued)*

622. <u>Robert Edward Allen</u>
(1879-1958)

Robert E. Lee Allen,[1] the second son of Samuel Gillion Allen and his wife Mary Ann Hicks, was born on Friday, 17 JAN 1879, on the family farm near Rhea's Mill, Washington County, Arkansas. We have an early photograph of him taken about 1897 by Mrs. Young, Photographer, of Fayetteville, Washington County, Arkansas.

Robert E. Allen of Rhea, Arkansas, aged 21 years, was married on 30 AUG 1900 in Washington County, Arkansas, to Miss MARY ELLEN LEWIS of Wheeler,[2] aged 19 years, as performed by N.M. Thompson, Justice of the Peace. Mary Ellen Lewis was the daughter of William (M. or F.) Lewis and Sarah Elizabeth Adair, born Monday, 18 OCT 1880 at Pocahontas, Columbia Township, Randolph County, Arkansas.[3]

On one occasion, Robert E. Allen's visit back home to his mother in Rhea, Arkansas was recorded in Mary Allen's memorandum book as "Bob and Mary visited on April 28, 1910." In 1913, Robert corresponded with his

Figure 18 - Mary E. Lewis and Robert E. Allen, wedding, 1900

brothers Frank and Elmer regarding settlement of their father's affairs in Arkansas. Frank felt Robert benefitted financially and remained quite upset about it, and was mad about the disposal of a buggy that belonged to Mr. Lewis.

The 1918 city directory for Kansas City, Missouri lists Robert E. Allen, laborer for Coen Building Materials Company, residence at 1927 Mercington Street.

Mr. Allen played the fiddle for local dances, on an instrument which is now in my possession. Before her death, Mary E. (Lewis) Allen gave the fiddle to her daughter Pearl (Allen) Davison. For a time it hung on the wall in the home of Janice L. (Davison) Giese where it fell off and was broken. It was restored in Denver, Colorado in 1980.

---

[1] According to my mother, Z. Eileene (Davison) Pippenger.
[2] According to the 1900 Arkansas Business Directory (Southern Directory Company, Little Rock and Ft. Smith: 1900, p. 402.) Wheeler, Arkansas is the "county seat bank and shipping point, Fayetteville 10 miles (away), population 50, mail daily." Since we know today Fayetteville is the county seat of Washington County, I assume Wheeler was the "county center" for banking and not the county seat. I haven't seen that the county seat of 'government' has ever changed.
[3] Randolph Co., Ark. was formed in 1835 from Lawrence Co. The county seat is Pocahontas.

On August 22, 1950 a Kansas City newspaper announced that Robert E. Allen would hold an open house to celebrate his 50th wedding anniversary, an event held from 3 to 7 p.m. at their home at 4441 Bales Avenue, Kansas City, Missouri. The article states that the couple was married in Fayetteville, Arkansas and have lived in Kansas City forty two years.

Mary Ellen (Lewis) Davison died 30 APR 1960 at 12 noon after suffering a stroke at the home of her son-in-law Chester L. Davison at 8421 Blue Ridge Extension, Kansas City, Missouri. She was buried 2 MAY 1960 in Memorial Park Cemetery of Kansas City, Missouri. She suffered an earlier stroke in 1951 which left her unable to move about freely.

According to his death certificate, Robert E. Allen died 7 MAY 1958 of terminal uremia at the Krestwood Medical Center in Kansas City, Mo., at 12:25 p.m.; his residence being at 4441 Bales St. in Kansas City. A newspaper obituary states he had lived in Kansas City 55 years, and retired from the park department two years previous, where he had been employed for nearly 15 years. He was a member of the Aldersgate Methodist Church. His sister Clara Allen is listed as living in Lincoln, Ark. The funeral service was handled by Wilks Funeral home, the service being held in the chapel at 2315 Linwood St., Kansas City—the same facilities that would handle burial arrangements for his wife. Burial took place on Fri., 9 MAY 1958 at the Memorial Park Cemetery.

Figure 19 - Mary E. Lewis and Robert E. Allen

Children of Robert Edward Allen and Mary Ellen Lewis:

+   6221.   VELMA PEARL ALLEN, my grandmother, b. Sat., 3 MAY 1902, near Springtown (Flint Twp.), Benton Co., Ark.[1] She always used the name Pearl. I have a small new testament Pearl was sent for Christmas 1912 by her uncle Martin Luther "Lute" Lewis. It is addressed to 3700 E. 19th St., Kansas City, Mo. and has a one cent postage stamp inside the front cover. Pearl was m. 11 OCT 1922 at the courthouse in Olathe, Johnson Co., Kan., to CHESTER LELAND DAVISON of Kansas City, Mo., as witnessed by William and Edith Antoine. Grandmother d. 14 JUL 1990 of cancer, testate, in Kansas City and was buried in Memorial Park Cem. After residing for short periods at two different assisted care facilities, Chester d. 30 MAR 1991 of heart failure in Kansas City, Mo., and was bur. in Memorial Park Cem. See Davison Family.

---

[1] Public birth records were not kept in Arkansas for this period, and I remember that grandmother loved to tell the story that she and her mother had to appear in court to swear she was born when she was standing right there.

+ 6222. SAMUEL WAYNE ALLEN, b. Sat., 16 DEC 1905, in Stephenville, Erath Co., Tex. He was m. three times, and d. 12 MAY 1969 in Tucson, Ariz. See mention later.

Figure 20 - Velma Pearl Allen, graduation

Figure 21 - Velma Pearl and Samuel Wayne Allen

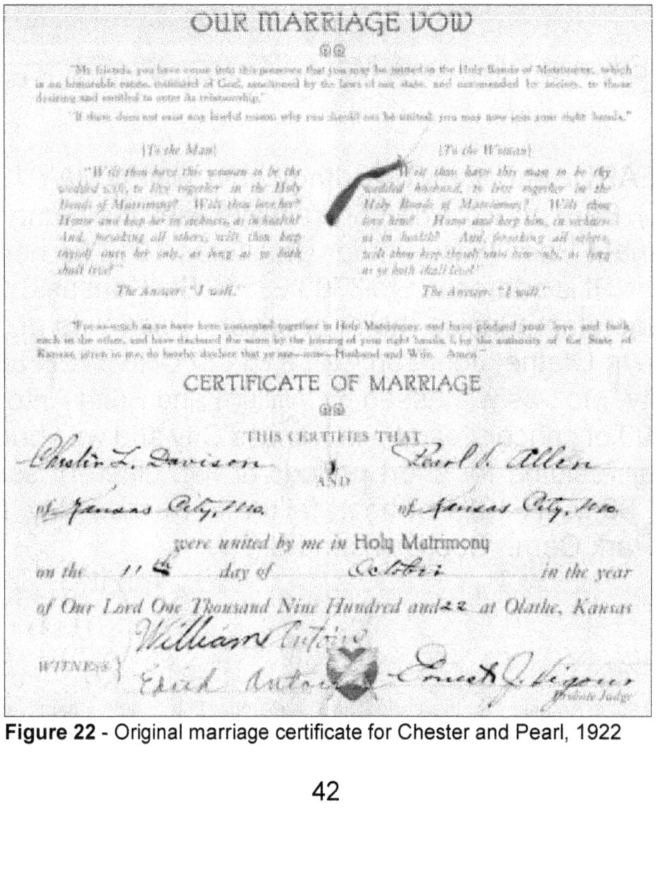

Figure 22 - Original marriage certificate for Chester and Pearl, 1922

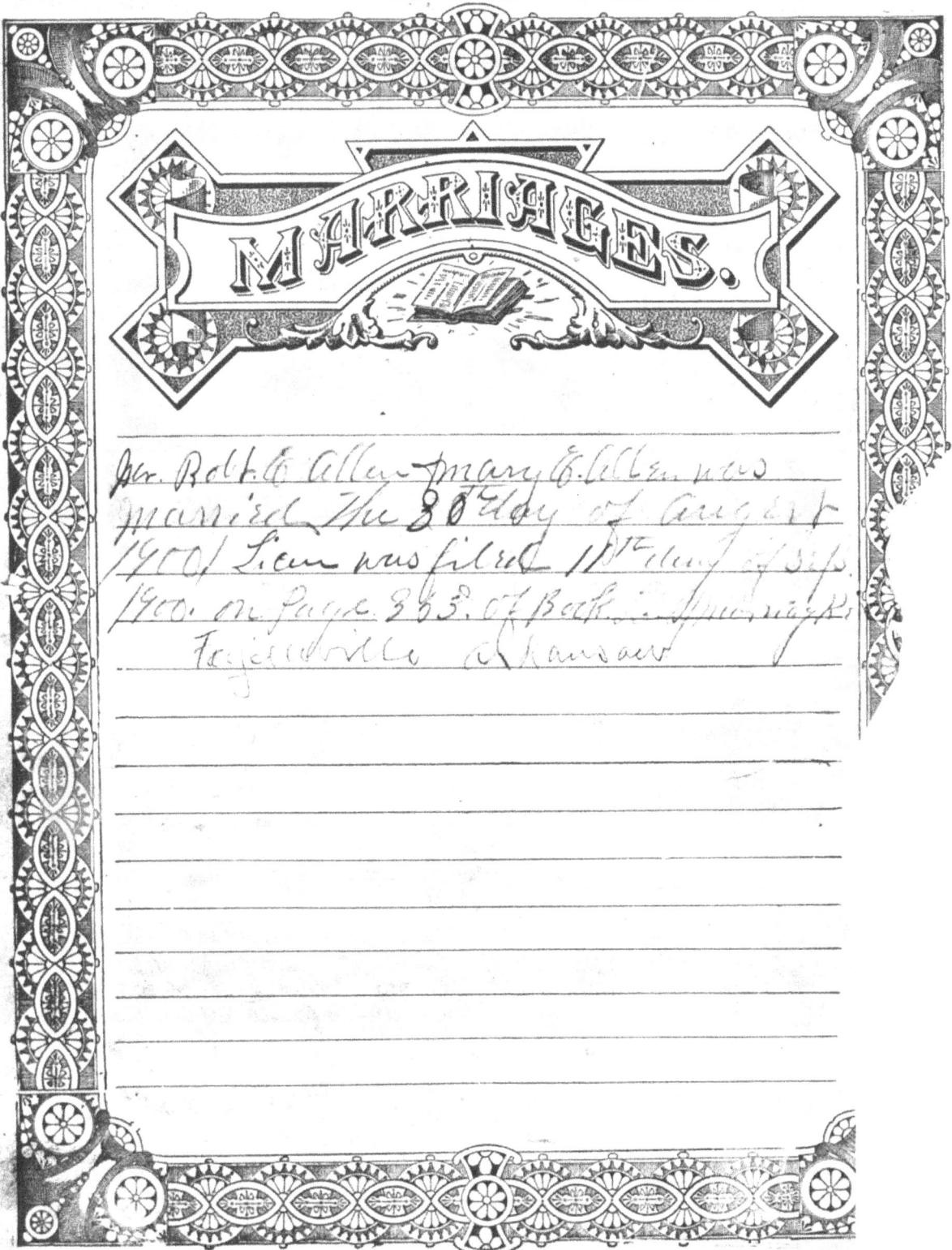

Figure 23 - A surviving page from the Family Bible of Robert E. Allen

6222. <u>Samuel Wayne Allen</u>
(1905-1969)

Samuel Wayne Allen, only son of Robert Edward Allen and Mary Ellen Lewis, was born 16 DEC 1905 in Stephenville, Erath County, Texas at 2:00 p.m. His delayed birth certificate is certified by Mrs. Betty Henning of Jackson County, Missouri. His sister called him Wayne while his son called him Sam. As mentioned earlier, he was married three times. The first marriage of "Wayne" Allen was circa 1923 to Zora Decker, later Zora Heckart of Apache Junction, Arizona.[1] In a letter from Dorothy Jean (Allen) Lytch[2] is found that her mother [Zora] passed away in her sleep on 3 JAN 1984 and was cremated 3 days later. Her ashes were to be spread over Superstitious Mountain in Arizona Saturday the 14th. Her husband's ashes are there. Sam put an article in the "Personals" section of the Kansas City newspaper (no date other than September) which read: "NOT responsible for debts contracted by my wife Mrs. Zora Allen after this date. S.W. Allen, 4340 Bales."

Figure 24 - Samuel Wayne Allen

After Sam and Zora were divorced, Sam Allen married second about 1932 to Ruth Izora Gooch. I spoke with Ruth on the telephone on 4 JUL 1986 and she was living alone with her three poodles and three cats. She said that she and Wayne eloped for their marriage; they were visiting her oldest brother and sister in Clinton, Illinois, and decided to get married there. Ruth Gooch's folks lived at the bottom of the hill on Bales Street in Kansas City, Missouri, and she and Sam lived on Mercington Street soon after they were married. Both of her children [Sam, Jr. and Marlene] were born in a Kansas City hospital nearby. Information that I obtained regarding Ruth Gooch's family included a story she told about her being born a 7-month twin. "My older sister May said we looked like rats that mother kept in a shoebox behind the heating stove."

Figure 25 - Wayne Allen, 1944

Ruth Izora Gooch was born 2 MAR 1912 in Little Rock, Arkansas as one of six children born to Edgar Franklin Gooch and his wife Sarah Emma (Battonfield) West. Sarah had been married previously to William Arthur West, so Ruth Gooch had half-brothers and sisters: namely Annie May West who married Carl Britton; William Arthur West; and Andrew Edward West. Sarah E. West remarried Edgar F. Gooch and had children: May Gooch,

---

[1] My mother Zora Eileene Davison was named after her.
[2] Letter to Pearl and Chester Davison, dated January 12, 1984.

who had Parkinson's disease and lived in a rest home in Tucson, Arizona, and had married three times; Charlie (unknown) who was a bricklayer; Roy Iree and Ruth Izora Gooch (twins); Emery Gooch; Armour Gooch, buried in Memorial Park Cemetery of Kansas City, Missouri; and Lillian Gooch who died as an infant. Sarah E. Gooch died in Kansas City, Missouri and she and her husband Edgar F. Gooch were buried in Memorial Park Cemetery of Kansas City, Missouri.

Figure 26 - Sam and Ruth Allen

Sam Allen remarried third on 15 MAR 1957 in Lordsburg, Hidalgo County, New Mexico by C.L. Brown, Justice of the Peace, to Mrs. Dorothy Mae (Elliott) Barnaby, born 26 NOV 1923 in Kevil, Ballard County, Kentucky (west of Paducah), who was a daughter of Hubert Joseph Elliott and Lola Mae Young. Lola, from Calloway County, Kentucky, died at the age of 79, and for a number of years lived in Michigan.

According to Dorothy Mae (Elliott) Allen, Samuel Wayne Allen served several terms with the U.S. Navy. During World War II he was a warrant officer with the CB's when he was severely wounded with shrapnel. He recovered from his injuries and hearing loss in Honolulu, Hawaii. The records of Sam's first term of Navy Reserve service indicate he enlisted 14 AUG 1924 at Kansas City, Missouri and was honorably discharged 13 AUG 1928 at Great Lakes, Illinois. Sam's military papers for a later term indicate he enlisted again on 30 JUN 1943 at Tucson, Arizona and was honorably discharged from the U.S. Naval Hospital in Seattle, Washington on 27 OCT 1944. His height was about 5 foot 6 inches, weight about 130 pounds, blue eyes, brown hair, and a "ruddy" complexion. According to his military papers, he had several identifying marks, and a tatoo on his forearm. Sam Allen's occupation during both terms of service was an electrician, and he had his own shop in Tucson. Samuel Wayne Allen died 12 MAY 1969 in Tucson, Arizona.

Child of Samuel Wayne Allen and his first wife Zora Decker:

62221.   DOROTHY JEAN ALLEN, m. Seth Lytch, res. in Morongo Valley, Calif. then Chanutte, Kan.

Children of Samuel Wayne Allen and his second wife Ruth Izora Gooch:

62222.   SAMUEL WAYNE ALLEN, JR., b. 10 AUG 1935 in Kansas City, Mo., was nicknamed "Bud." He m. Nonette (unknown), and res. in Norco, Calif. When I spoke with his mother Ruth, she indicated he worked for the military and was temporarily on duty in South America.

62223.   PHYLLIS MARLENE ALLEN, b. 18 APR 1932 in Kansas City, Mo., was m. four times. When I spoke with her on 4 JUL 1986 she said she met James M. Yarding, b. 28 FEB 1929 in Kaukabee, Ill., while in grade school in Tucson, Ariz., to whom she was m. (1) on 11 JUN 1950 by Probate Judge R.R. Gale in

Lordsburg, N.M. Marlene described her Jimmy as short, and an electrician. They div. c.1952 in Tucson. "We are still friends." Marlene m. (2) on 6 JUN 1952 in Lordsburg, Hidalgo Co., N.M. to Harley Yoder, b. 10 JAN 1930 in LaGrange, Ind. This marriage was witnessed by Mrs. Ruth Allen.[1] Marlene described Harley as a real short person who worked with her dad Samuel Wayne Allen. She and Harley div. c.1955 in Tucson, Ariz. Marlene m. (3) in January 1957 in Alamagordo, N.M. to Jose Munoz, Jr. She described him as a "tall and domineering Mexican." They div. c.March 1970 in Las Cruces, N.M. Marlene m. (4) to William F. Dark-Miller, a "cowboy" she met at her church of Jehovah's witnesses. Children:

622231. JAMES "Jimmy" WAYNE YARDING, b . 15 MAR 1951 in Kaysville, Utah, a military base, and d. 6 JAN 1972 in Tucson, Ariz., bur. in Evergreen Cem., Tucson.

622232. DAVID RUSSELL YODER, b. 16 NOV 1953 in Tucson, Ariz. He m. Susan (unknown). Children:

   6222321. JENNIFER YODER.

   6222322. JEREMY JOSEPH YODER.

622233. JOSE "Joey" MUNOZ, III, b. 8 SEP 1957 in Las Cruces, N.M., m. 7 OCT 1978 in Las Cruces to Yolanda Flores. Children:

   6222331. CELINA MARLENE MUNOZ.

   6222332. MARCO JOSE MUNOZ.

622234. THOMAS "Steven" MUNOZ, b. 25 SEP 1958 in Las Cruces, res. in Tule Rosa, N.M.

622235. RANDOLPH "Randy" GEORGE MUNOZ, b. 8 NOV 1961 in Las Cruces, served in the U.S. Army, and was stationed in Colorado.

622236. DENISE MUNOZ, b. 25 JUL 1960 in Las Cruces.

Child of Samuel Wayne Allen and his third wife Dorothy Mae Elliott:

62224. STANLEY WADE ALLEN, b. at 8:35 a.m. on 3 NOV 1965 in Tucson Medical Center, Tucson, Pima Co., Ariz., m. (1) 19 JAN 1987 to Christina Lee Johnstone, div. 6 JUL 1990, m. (2) bef. 1994 to Tamara Y. Stout, div., res. Alexandria, Va. Children:

622241. NATHANIEL WAYNE ALLEN, d. 7 days after birth.

622242. RYAN WADE ALLEN, b. 8 JUL 1988 in Tucson, Ariz.

622243. SHELDON WADE ALLEN, b. 8 JAN 9194 at K.I. Sawyer Air Force Base, Mich.

622244. JACOB MICHAEL ALLEN, b. 10 SEP 1995 at Scott Air Force Base, Ill.

622245. SARAH YUVONNE ALLEN, b. 29 OCT 1999 at Andrews Air Force Base, Md.

622246. JACI MAELYNN ALLEN, b. 27 FEB 2006 in Alexandria, Va.

---

[1] Information from marriage certificate.

623. William Elmer Allen
(1881-1947)

Wiliam Elmer Allen, son and third child of Samuel Gillion Allen and Mary Ann Hicks, was born on Friday, 12 AUG 1881 in Rhea's Mill, Washington County, Arkansas. He lived most of his life in parts of Texas, and it is there where we find much about his family. Elmer married on Sunday, October 22, 1905 in Stephenville, Erath County, Texas to Miss Hattie Mollie Cook. His occupation was a building contractor. Marjorie Ruth (Allen) Fowler writes of her father that "he was never blessed with this world's 'possessions' but he was an honest, hard working man that provided the very best for us that he could. No children ever had a finer Mother and Daddy than we had."[1]

From Hattie Allen's death certificate we know that informant Prentiss D. Allen indicated that Hattie was the daughter of J.D. Cook of Alabama, and his wife Judy Fenell. We have a letter from Hattie and the kids, when she is was in Goodnight, Texas, writing a letter back to Rhea, Arkansas to Elmer Allen. Apparently they went to visit family and appears that it may have been for the funeral of a Grandfather Strickland. According to the *Columbia Lippincott Gazeteer of the World* (1961), Goodnight, Texas is a village roughly 300 persons, "located in Armstrong County, in the extreme north part of Texas on the edge of the high plains of the panhandle, 20 miles west north west of Clarendon; retail center in cattle and grain."

In March 1942, Hattie Allen was involved in an automobile accident, and was sent to St. Anthony Hospital in Amarillo, Potter County, Texas where she died of a skull fracture on Tuesday, 3 MAR 1942. She was buried the next day in the Lubbock Cemetery of Lubbock, Texas.

William Elmer Allen died of a heart attack on 18 MAR 1947 in West Texas Hospital of Lubbock, Texas. The cause of death on his death certificate was carcenoma. He was buried on 20 MAR 1947 in the Lubbock City Cemetery.

Children of William Elmer Allen and Hattie Mollie Cook:

6231. MARJORIE RUTH ALLEN, b. Mon., 21 AUG 1916, m. in Lubbock, Tex. on Sun., 11 AUG 1940 to Arch Terry Fowler. According to a letter I received from Ruth (Allen) Fowler, her husband was b. Sat. 5 AUG 1916, and d. 30 AUG 1981 of a heart attack in the Methodist Hospital of Lubbock, Tex., bur. in Resthaven Memorial Park of Lubbock, Texas. From A.T. Fowler's obituary we know he was a native of Brownfield, Tex., graduating from the Texas Technological College in 1937 with a bachelor of science degree and a masters degree (1939) in horticulture. Mr. Fowler served in the U.S. Marine Corps for four years during World War II, in the Pacific arena and attained rank of major. He retired in 1975 from the U.S. Department of Agriculture's Home Administration. Mr. Fowler was active in the Oakwood Baptist Church where he and his family had been members since 1966. Pallbearers were Clinton Kennedy, Jay Havens, Ralph Griffiths, Rayford Tanner, Marvin Harvey, Dr.

---

[1] Letter from Ruth (Allen) Fowler to me, dated March 18, 1980.

Ted Allen, Don Allen and Ron Allen. Children:

62311.   JOE DEAN FOWLER, b. Thurs., 13 JUN 1946 who has lived in Snyder, Tex.

62312.   LINDA KAY FOWLER, b. Thurs., 13 APR 1950 who has lived in Arlington, Tex.

6232. PRENTISS DELEVAN ALLEN, b. Wed., 2 FEB 1910, d. Wed., 22 NOV 1972, was m. Sun., 25 MAY 1941 to Mary Roberta Curd, b. 16 SEP 1904, d. 7 SEP 1991. Both bur. Lubbock Cem. No children.

6233. CARROLL BURTON ALLEN,[1] b. Mon., 29 APR 1912, d. 25 DEC 1991, bur. Lubbock Cem., m. Thurs., 11 JAN 1934 to Bernice Ione Hooker, b. Sun., 19 OCT 1913, d. 7 FEB 1997, bur. Lubbock Cem., dau. of L.H. and Lilly Ola Hooker. Children:

62331.   DON GELIN ALLEN, b. Tues., 2 FEB 1937. Child:

623311. KENT ALLEN.

62332.   TED WAYNE ALLEN, b. Sat., 2 SEP 1939.

62333.   RONNIE RAY ALLEN, b. Wed., 18 AUG 1943.

62334.   ROBERT BURTON ALLEN, b. Wed., 21 NOV 1934, d. 14 AUG 1936.

---

[1] I find this name very interesting, and speculate it may be a clue to the Allen Family genealogy. His grandfather, Samuel Gillion Allen, was from Carroll Co., Tenn. Sam's grandfather Samuel Allin died there in 1827. Also, there is a Burton Allen who died testate in Carroll Co. in 1851, leaving a wife Rebecca [Windsor], and two sons and two daughters. The eldest son Alfred Windsor Allen died in 1895 in Clay Co., Ark. I have not linked Burton Allen to our family.

624. Samuel Francis "Frank" Allen
(1885-1958)

Samuel Francis Allen was born in Rhea's Mill, Washington County, Arkansas on Tuesday, 10 FEB 1885, a son and fourth child of Samuel Gillion Allen and his wife Mary Ann Hicks. "Frank" Allen was married at the bride's home in Rhea's Mill, by Reverend G.B. Griffin, on Sunday, 5 NOV 1905 to Mary Launa Edmiston, daughter of John Smith Edmiston and Emily West. Mary L. Edmiston was born 4 FEB 1883 in Rhea's Mill.

Vera (Allen) Ford wrote that "John Edmiston, my grandfather, married Emily West and had four children: Launa, Annie, Sam and Tom Edmiston. Emily West died when my mother was 2 years old (c. 1885). John Edmiston then married [c.1885] to Nina [Elizabeth] Dunlap (don't know the date) who had 2 sons: Homer and Fred. John and Nina Edmiston had two children: J.D. and Watson Edmiston. All are deceased."

Mary Edmiston's father died on Wednesday, 8 APR 1915 and she died in the City Hospital of Fayetteville, Washington County, Arkansas on 18 SEP 1957. Funeral services were held from the Prairie Grove Methodist Church, with the Reverend W.A. Downum of Fort Smith, Arkansas presiding. She was buried in the Prairie Grove Cemetery, Washington County, Arkansas on Friday, 20 SEP 1957.

Facts learned from Mary L. Allen's obituary include that she was a long time resident of Westville, Oklahoma where the Allens sold their farm on Highway 62 east of town and moved to Prairie Grove. Mary was a member of the Methodist Church in Westville, and was an active member in the Woman's Society of Christian Service. Mr. S.F. Allen is the notary who signed when Mary Allen (his mother) applied for a pension based on the service in the Confederate States Army of his father S.G. Allen.

In a historical society publication[1] we see that Frank Allen had his own Star mail route outside of Rhea's Mill, Arkansas c.1934, and so did Tom Edmiston.

Frank Allen died enroute to the hospital near Prairie Grove on Sunday, 23 FEB 1958, and was buried in the city cemetery on 25 FEB 1968. A lengthy obituary appearing in the Westville, Oklahoma newspaper provides much information on his life.

Children of Samuel Francis Allen and Mary Launa Edmiston:

6241. MARGARET VERA ALLEN, b. in Rhea's Mill on Sat., December 26, 1908, was m. in DeQuincy, Calcasieu Co., La., on 27 JUN 1937 to James Miller Ford who d. May 11, 1982. In the 1980s she lived in Hemet, Calif. In a letter I received from Vera Ford[2], we find that two children were born to this couple:

   62411. MARGARET ANNE FORD, b. 24 APR 1937 in Lake Charles, La., who was m. 2 JUN 1956 to Larry Brian Kennedy. Children:

   624111. ANNE EILEEN KENNEDY, b. 2 MAY 1959.

[1] *Washington County, Arkansas Historical Society Bulletin*, Volume 14, (Fayetteville, AR: 1964), page 22.
[2] Letter to the author from Vera Ford, dated May 6, 1980.

624112.   BRIAN FORD KENNEDY, b. 16 DEC 1961.
624113.   KAREN LEIGH KENNEDY, b. 29 MAY 1964.
624113.   LYNN KENNEDY, b. 5 DEC 1966.
62412.   MARY LOU FORD, b. 5 APR 1940 in Lake Charles, Calcasieu Co., La., m. 3 JUN 1960 to Edwin B. Nettleton. Children:
625121.   MARK NETTLETON, b. 29 OCT 1963.
625122.   ANDREW NETTLETON, b. 25 FEB 1965.
625123.   BRADLEY NETTLETON, b. 13 AUG 1970.
625124.   SARAH NETTLETON, b. 25 MAY 1971.

6242. ANNIE LUCILLE ALLEN, b. Tues., 20 JUN 1911 in Rhea's Mill, d. c.31 OCT 1987 in Sulphur, La., m. in November 1940 in Sulphur, Calcasieu Co., La., to Edward Pearson Cabaniss who died in May 1976. He was bur. on his birthday, 22 MAY 1976. They had no children. From a family Christmas card address book we see that in 1965 she was living at 616 W. Kent St., in Sulphur, La.

6243. MARY GERALDINE ALLEN, b. Tues., 17 NOV 1914 in Rhea's Mill, d. Tues., 27 MAY 1969 in Memphis, Tenn., bur. Perkins Cem. of DeQuincy, La., m. (1) to David W. Smith, and m. (2) 7 NOV 19__ to Marion E. Hill who d. 7 NOV 1966. They had no children. Res. in Memphis, Tenn. in 1957.

6244. JAMES DELMAS ALLEN, b. Sun., 21 APR 1907 in Rhea's Mill, d. 5 AUG 1953 in DeQuincy, Calcasieu Co., La., bur. Perkins Cem., m. Elizabeth Freeman. We have a baby picture believed to be Delmas Allen. Children:

62441.   BETTY LOU ALLEN, of DeQuincy, La., m. Harvey Brown. Children, including:
624411.   SCOTT BROWN, in 1983 was a pitcher for the Kansas City Royals baseball team.
62442.   JIMMY DALE ALLEN, m. Pat (unknown). 3 children.

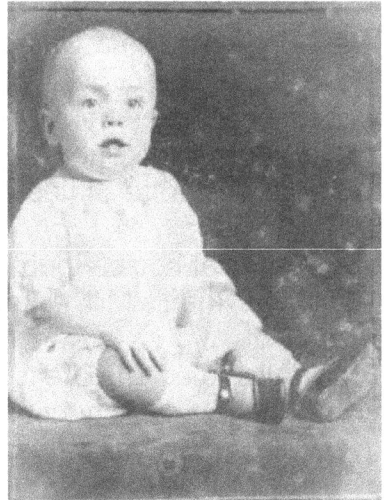

Figure 27 - Delmas Allen

629. <u>Homer Johnson Allen</u>
(1899-1974)

The ninth and youngest child of Samuel Gillion Allen and his wife Mary Ann Hicks was Homer Johnson Allen, born on Monday, 27 FEB 1899 near Rhea's Mill, Washington County, Arkansas. Homer Allen was married in Fayetteville, Washington County, Arkansas on Wednesday, 6 SEP 1922 to Georgia May Miller, daughter of Robert Baker Miller and his wife Rachel O. Johnson. "Georgie" was born 23 MAY 1903 in Clarkville, Oklahoma. The county record for the marriage of Homer J. Allen and Georgia M. Miller reads that Miss Georgia Miller was age 19 and of Summers, Washington County, Arkansas. They were married by W.B. Smith, Justice of the Peace.

Mr. and Mrs. Allen lived in Lincoln, Arkansas in about 1963, then moved to Bonner Springs, Kansas two months before Homer died. Homer died on Monday, 2 SEP 1974 and was buried on Wednesday in the city cemetery of Bonner Springs, Kansas. According to the funeral bulletin, pallbearers were Dale Allen, Mark Allen, Chris Allen, Thomas Durrie, Kenneth Coonfield, and Tommy Ray Tucker. Mr. Allen was a member of the Bonner Springs Masonic Lodge No. 366.

By talking with Georgia (Miller) Allen for a brief time, I was able to get enough clues to proceed a few steps further on her immediate family history. Robert Baker Miller was born on Friday, 4 MAY 1883. From information given by John A. Johnson on the death certificate for Robert's wife, Rachel Ollie (Johnson) Miller, we find that she was born in Newton County, Arkansas on Sunday, 22 FEB 1885. Rachel was the daughter of John A. Johnson of Rome County, Tennessee and his wife Arzona Robinson of Carroll County, Arkansas. Rachel died in the Elizabeth Hospital near Dutch Mills (Township), Washington County, Arkansas, of coronary occlusion at 6:05 p.m. on Saturday, August 17, 1938. She was buried in White Rock, Washington County, Arkansas. It is through this Allen Family lineage which many existing family papers and documents were preserved and located.

Georgia May Miller Allen died 25 AUG 1988 at Kaw Valley Manor, 501 E. Morse St., Bonner Springs, Kansas. Her death notice indicates she was a sales clerk for Watson Brothers Drug Store in Bonner Springs for 20 years and retired in 1962. She was a member of the Bonner Springs United Methodist Church. Burial was in Bonner Springs Cemetery.

Children of Homer Johnson Allen and Georgia May Miller:[1]

6291. VANCE CAMERON ALLEN, b. Mon., 20 AUG 1923 at 4447 Bales St., Kansas City, Jackson Co., Mo., m. Thurs., 10 JUL 1952 in Bentonville, Ark. to Sally Lou Wasson, dau. of Charles Wasson and Hester Mae Mise.[2] Res. Cookson, Okla. Children:

    62911. CHRISTOPHER LYNN ALLEN, b. 14 JUN 1953.

    62912. CARLA CELINE ALLEN, b. 1 APR 1956, m. 6 AUG 1977 in Overland Park,

---

[1] Some information taken from a letter I received from Mary Ann Allen of Bonner Springs, Kansas, dated 1 NOV 1977.
[2] In Mary Ann (Hicks) Allen's memorandum book we see that a "Grandmother Wasson" died 25 JUL 1940. Her relationship has not been identified.

Kan. to Bill Porter.

6292. FRANCIS EUGENE ALLEN, b. Mon., 16 MAY 1928 in Muscogee, Okla., was m. Sat., 16 APR 1949 to Mary Ann Coonfield, dau. of Kenneth Coonfield and Virginia Wasson, b. 16 AUG 1929. Res. Tonganoxie, Kan. Children:

62921. TERESA ANN ALLEN, b. Fri., 18 JUL 1952, m. 9 JUL 1977 to Theodore Wallace Ellis, Jr., b. 26 OCT 1953.

62922. DALE EUGENE ALLEN, b. Wed., 22 JUN 1955, m. 23 JUL 1976 to Shelley Trumbull, b. 8 SEP 1956.

6293. RICHARD EARL ALLEN, b.Thurs., 28 AUG 1930 in Kansas City, Mo., m. 4 JUL 1953 in Bonner Springs, Kan. to Virginia Loux. Children:

62931. MARK RICHARD ALLEN, b. Sat., 15 MAY 1954.

62932. MARGO CATHERINE ALLEN, b. Thurs., 15 DEC 1955.

62933. MICHAELYN YVONNE ALLEN, b. Sun., 29 DEC 1968.

LEWIS FAMILY

For some reason, the life history of William Lewis, husband of Sarah Elizabeth (Adair) Lewis, and father of Mary Ellen (Lewis) Allen, has been nearly a complete mystery. We can not locate either where he was born (other than Arkansas) nor where and when he died. Grandmother is certain he died about 1905 and was buried in old Union Cemetery of Kansas City, Missouri. I have been at this cemetery several times and closely examined their records for the period 1900 through 1920, and we still can't find a clue to confirm he was buried there. The 1890 City Directory for Kansas City has the entry: "Lewis, Sarah E., widow of William, residence 1932 N. 14th." This means he was dead by 1890.

Grandmother remembers just a plain concrete slab identifying the grave, and never knew why her mother didn't have a tombstone made. A William M. Lewis is involved in the estate of Mary E. (Sweazea) Adair, mother of Sarah E. (Adair) Lewis, about 1868 in Randolph County, Arkansas.

Part of the mystery may be resolved if we analyze a marriage record in Randolph County, Arkansas where a William F. Lewis was married in 1873 to Jane Adair. I believe the record is incorrect and the bride was our Sarah Elizabeth Adair. Women of the time often were known by their nickname (for example, "Polly" or in this case possibly "Jane"), and because of this, many marriage records are recorded with a nickname or family calling; and in some cases some are wrong all together. Our Sarah E. Adair did have a sister Jane Adair. Further research will prove this point. Also, I have kept in mind that at least two sets of my own grandparents have marriage certificates recorded with the wrong names. Considering this, I feel we have another case with recording the marriage of William Lewis and Sarah Adair where Sarah Adair is recorded as Jane Adair.

Presuming that this is the case, our Lewis ancestry is recorded in *Pioneer Lewis Families*, by Michael Cook—a truly encyclopedic genealogy of the Lewis Family which contains over 5,000 pages of data.

According to a history book about Randolph County, Arkansas[1], the Lewis Family has resided there since at least 1858, being members of the "One Hundred Club." A John Lewis and his son settled in Davidsonville, Davidson Township.[2] The Allen and Lewis families were residents of Pitman's Ferry, Little Black Township; the old town of Pittman being located on the river quite a distance northeast of the present post office of Pittman.[3] It was located near the state line with Missouri and was at the edge of what is now Clay County. Ripley County, Missouri is just across the state line, and a few family marriages are found in the records there.

---

[1] *History of Randolph County, Arkansas*, 1st ed., (Democrat Printing and Lithographers Company, Little Rock), page 107. Book not dated on the title page, but mentions time of print on page 157 as July 31, 1946).
[2] Ibid., page 175.
[3] Ibid., page 211.

Lewis Family Lineage

Whether our Lewis Family is of English or Welch origin is uncertain. Our lineage is as follows:

A.   DAVID LEWIS, born 14 DEC 1695 in Charles County, Maryland, died 11 NOV 1773 in Carteret County, North Carolina, married c.January 1719 to Mary Crawford, born c.1690 in Virginia. In 6 JUN 1738, David Lewis acquired about 60 acres in Frederick County, Virginia from John Smith. In the 1740s, he bought 200 more acres in Frederick County from Andrew Hampton and John Brooks.[1] In 1751, David purchased 184 acres from William Hiatt where "Lewis now lives," and got a land grant from Lord Fairfax for 400 acres at the mouth of Mill Creek.[2] In 1756, David and Mary sold 150 acres of Smith's 420 patent to back William Hiatt,[3] and were by this time living in South Carolina. In 1768, David sold 145 acres of his 400-acre Lord Fairfax grant to Dr. John Briscoe.[4] 10 children, of whom:

+ B.   JOHN LEWIS,[5] born 11 APR 1720 in *Oak Grove*, Frederick County, Virginia, died 10 JUN 1802 in Hillsboro, Randolph County, North Carolina, was married (1) 16 OCT 1745 in Frederick County to Priscilla [Elizabeth] Brooks, and married (2) to Elizabeth McGrath. 8 children, of whom:

+ C.   DAVID LEWIS, eldest son of John Lewis and Priscilla Brooks, born 21 MAR 1747 in Berkeley County, Virgnia,[6] died 23 JUN 1822 in Anderson County, South Carolina, and was buried in the Old Stone Church Cemetery. He was married (1) 30 JAN 1768 in Guilford County to Ann Beeson, married (2) in 1813 to Penelope (unknown). 13 children, of whom:

+ D.   ISAIAH LEWIS, SR., born 3 SEP 1769 in Guilford County, North Carolina, died testate 25 JAN 1837 in Vigo County, Indiana,[7] buried in the Smith Family Cemetery in Vigo County, Indiana. He was married to Nancy Julian, born in South Carolina, died in Lawrence County, Illinois. 11 children, of whom:

+ E.   ISAIAH LEWIS, JR., born 1808 in Warren County, Kentucky, died testate before 26 MAR 1850 in Randolph County, Arkansas, was married c.1821 in Warren County

---

[1] Cecil O'Dell, *Pioneers of Old Frederick County, Virginia* (Marceline, Mo.: Walsworth Publishing Co., 1995), p. 145, citing the Hite/Fairfax Lawsuit, British copy, p. 143.

[2] Virginia Northern Neck Land Grants, Bk. H, p. 266, dated 21 SEP 1751, to David Lewis, 400 acres, whereon he now lives, adjacent to that of Jacob Brooks and Mill Creek. Adjacent to this was a parcel of 164 acres taken out by his son David Lewis, Jr. in 1753.

[3] Frederick Co., Va. Deeds, Bk. 4, p. 170, dated 1 SEP 1756.

[4] Frederick Co., Va. Deeds, Bk. 12, p. 491, dated 1 AUG 1768.

[5] Sources conflict as to the father of John Lewis, whether it was John Lewis of Brecon, Wales, or David Lewis who d. c.1773 in Cartaret Co., N.C. and married Mary Crawford. As the first born son of John Lewis was named David one might speculate that he was named for his paternal grandfather, making David Lewis the likely father of John Lewis.

[6] Also see Michael L. Cook, *Pioneer Lewis Families* (Evansville, Ind.: Cook Publications, 1978), Vol. 1, pp. 117-120, 125, 155, 167. LDS records show he was born in Guilford Co., N.C. Problem: Guilford County was not created until 1770. Other sources give place of birth has Hanover Co., Va. Various biographical sketches written in the 19th and 20th century in Lawrence Co., Ill. state that David Lewis was born in Virginia, and was a son of John Lewis of County Donegal, Ireland.

[7] Vigo Co., Ind., Complete Record No. 2, p. 140, will dated 18 JAN 1837, proved 13 FEB 1837.

to Mary "Polly" Wright, daughter of William Wright and Frances Campbell.[1] 11 children, of whom:

+   F.   JOAB[2] LEWIS, born 26 DEC 1833 in Carroll County, Tennessee, died in 1886. He was married (1) 11 JUL 1852 by E.D. Pitman, J.P. in Randolph County, Arkansas to Martha Ann Kelly, born c.1834 in Arkansas. 14 children, of whom:

+   G.   WILLIAM M. [or F.] LEWIS, born 23 MAY 1855 in Lawrence County, Arkansas, died in Kansas City, Missouri (date unknown), was married 2 OCT 1873 in Randolph County, Arkansas to SARAH ELIZABETH ADAIR, *q.v.* 7 children, of whom:

+   H.   MARY ELLEN LEWIS, born 18 OCT 1880 in Randolph County, Arkansas, died 30 APR 1960 in Kansas City, Missouri, was married 30 AUG 1900 in Washington County, Arkansas to ROBERT EDWARD ALLEN, *q.v.*

B. John Lewis
(1720-1802)

John Lewis (my ancestor), born 11 APR 1720 in *Oak Grove*, Frederick County, Virginia, was first married 16 OCT 1745 in Frederick County to Priscilla [Elizabeth] Brooks, born 16 JAN 1725, died after 1797 in Randolph County, North Carolina, daughter of Jacob Brooks and Elizabeth Warren. Just when the couple left Virginia is not known, so the birthplace of their first children is uncertain. Also, county formation changes affect the locations given. Some researchers have claimed this John Lewis was married second c.1754, perhaps in Rowan County, North Carolina to Elizabeth McGrath; however the wording of his family Bible does not support this, as John and Priscilla are stated the parents of eight children.

The couple moved to Rowan County, North Carolina where they lived on Pole Cat Creek. The county lines changed over time, with Anson County (1750) becoming Rowan, and in turn parts it were taken to form Guilford (1770) then Randolph County (1779). In 1771, John Lewis purchased land from Solomon Allred near what is today Ramseur, Randolph County, North Carolina.

John Lewis died testate on 10 JUN 1802[3] in Hillsboro, Randolph County, North Carolina. He and his wife Priscilla were buried at Centers Meeting House Cemetery of Randolph County, North Carolina.

The children of John Lewis and his first wife Priscilla Brooks:[4]

+   1.   DAVID LEWIS (my ancestor), b. 21 MAR 1747 in Berkeley Co., Va. or Anson Co.,

---

[1] Many researchers have that this Isaiah Lewis married in 1828 in Vigo Co., Ind. to Mary "Polly" Smith and that he is the same Isaiah Lewis is found on the 1830 and 1850 census for Vigo Co., Ind. See discussion elsewhere.
[2] His name Joab is sometimes seen as Jacob in records.
[3] Randolph Co., N.C. Wills, Bk. 2, p. 100, proved August Term 1802.
[4] Birthdates are found in a Lewis Family Bible, that was posted by *cdloftin@charter.net*.

N.C., d. 23 JUN 1822, m. Ann Beeson. See below.

2. JACOB LEWIS, b. 24 MAY 1750 in Berkeley Co., Va. or Anson Co., N.C., d. 23 NOV 1812 in Wilkes Co., Ga., m. 1 JAN 1769 perhaps in Frederick Co., Md. to Sarah Avery Noland, b. 16 JAN 1750 in Cecil Co., Md., d. 20 NOV 1841 in Ridgeville, Butler Co., Ala., dau. of Pierce Noland. He was a private in the N.C. militia at Fort Pitt. Children:
21. DAVID LEWIS, b. 25 FEB 1770.
22. JOHN AVERY LEWIS, b. 3 SEP 1771, d. 1849 in Butler Co., Ala., m. Jane Hurley.
23. MARY MARIAH LEWIS, b. 25 FEB 1773, d. 12 FEB 1855 in Hancock Co., Ga., m. Mansel Womack, b. 4 JUN 1770 in Prince Edward Co., Va., d. 11 DEC 1826 in Hancock Co., Ga.
24. PEARCE AUDREY LEWIS, b. 4 OCT 1774, d. 1853 in Russell Co., Ala., m. Phebe Langdon.
25. ROSANNAH LEWIS, b. 17 OCT 1776.
26. JACOB LEWIS, b. 25 MAY 1778, d. 1850, m. Sarah Mills.
27. GEORGE NOLAND LEWIS, b. 2 JAN 1780, d. 1841, m. Katherine Brooke.
28. ABRAHAM LEWIS, b. 8 NOV 1783.
29. SARAH AVERY LEWIS, b. 10 APR 1786, d. 1862, m. December 1805 in Warren Co., Ga. to John Womack, b. 1780, d. 1832. 12 children.
2(10). NOLAND RICHARD LEWIS, b. 21 SEP 1791, m. 1818 to Sally Miller Gibson.

3. ROSANNA LEWIS, b. 5 JAN 1752 in Anson [later Rowan then Randolph] Co., N.C., d. 1818 in Floyd Co., Va., m. 1769 in Stony Creek, Orange Co., N.C. to Isaac West, b. 1741 in Pa., d. testate September 1814 in Montgomery Co., Va.[1] 10 children.

4. JEAN LEWIS, b. 15 JUL 1755 in Rowan Co., N.C., d. c.1825, m. John Campbell, d. 16 OCT 1825. 8 children.

5. STEPHEN LEWIS,[2] b. 4 JUN 1757 in Rowan Co., N.C., d. testate 1792[3] in Randolph Co., N.C., m. Susanna (unknown). A family story here is that in 1786, Stephen Lewis raped Lydia Allred, niece of Solomon Allred, and on another occasion was shot by his brother Richard Lewis. 6 children, of whom:
51. DAVID LEWIS, inherited from his father a 150-acre tract that formerly belonged to Richard Wright in Randolph Co., N.C.

6. RICHARD LEWIS, b. 22 JUL 1759 in Rowan Co., N.C., d. 21 SEP 1826 in New Albany, Floyd Co., Ind., bur. Scott Cem., served in the Revolutionary War, m. c.1782 in N.C. to Lydia Fields, b. 19 JUN 1762 in Rowan Co., N.C., d. 9 JAN 1852 in New

---

[1] Montgomery Co., Va. Wills, Bk. 2, p. 236; also a copy in Floyd Co., Va. CF1839-002.
[2] Stephen Lewis and was reportedly shot by his brother Richard Lewis. The story goes that Stephen Lewis had been beating his wife and his brother Richard was quite upset about it. He helped Stephen's wife to escape to live with others. Susanna eventually returned to Stephen and admitted that it was Richard who had helped her. Stephen vowed to kill him and went looking. Richard, anticipating as much, shot and wounded Stephen when he appeared. Knowing Stephen would return, Richard went to Stephen's house and killed him. See *Randolph Legends and Stores*, Randolph County Heritage, Vol. 1 (1993).
[3] Randolph Co., N.C., Superior Court Wills, Bk. 1, p. 112, dated 4 DEC 1791, proved March Term 1792.

Albany, Ind. 11 children.

7. SARAH LEWIS, b. 15 JAN 1763 in Rowan Co., N.C., d. 23 JAN 1785 in Randolph Co., N.C., m. 28 OCT 1780 in Guilford Co., N.C. to Isaiah Ruckman, b. 9 JAN 1759 in Bucks Co., Pa., d. 1816 in Barren Co., Ky.,[1] son of Joseph Ruckman and Sarah White. 6 children.

8. JOHN LEWIS, b. 9 MAR 1765 in Rowan Co., N.C., d. 5 MAY 1848 in Wayne Co., Ind., m. 15 MAR 1781 in N.C. to Sarah Ruckman. 12 children, of whom:
    81.   RICHARD LEWIS, b. 6 AUG 1784.

<u>Last Will and Testament of John Lewis</u>
Randolph County, North Carolina, 1797

In the Name of God Amen! The fifth day of May, in the year of our Lord one thousand seven Hundred & ninety- seven. I **John Lewis**, of the County of Randolph & State of No. Carolina, being weak in body but of perfect mind and memory, thanks be given unto God! Therefore calling unto mind, the mortality of the body & knowing that it is appointed, for all men once to die, do make & ordain this My Last Will & Testament. In the manner & form following, viz. that principally & first of all, I give & recommend my soul into the Hands of God who gave it, & my Body to the Earth to be decently Buried according to the direction of my Executors hereafter named; nothing doubting, but at the General [Re]surrection. I shall receive the same again by the Mighty Power of God, And as touching such worldly Estate as it hath pleased God to bless me with, I give & Dispose of the same as followeth, after my last debts is paid & Funeral Expenses —

   I give to my son **John Lewis** my Home Plantation, containing of two hundred acres of Land, the same being in two Surveys, the old survey contains One Hundred and Forty acres, the new Survey contains Sixty Acres. Item, I give to my son **David Lewis** Five Shillings. Item, I give to my son **Jacob Lewis** ten shillings. All my moving effects is to be sold & twelve months credit given to the Purchaser. The money to be divided in the following manner, viz.: Between my Wife, my son **Richard**, my Daughter **Rosannah West**, my Daughter **Jane Campbell**, & my Daughter **Sarah Ruckman**; But if they should decease then the surviving Party to divide equally. My wearing apparel not to be sold, but to be divided between **John & Richard**. Last of all I do constitute & appoint **Richard Lewis** and **John Lewis** & **John Campbell** my whole & sole Executors of this my Last will and Testament. And I do hereby disallow, revoke & disannul all & every other Testament, will & Legacies, requests, & Executors any way before named, willed & Bequeathed, & confirming this & no other to be my last Will & Testament. In witness hereof, I have hereunto set my hand & seal the day & year above written.

   Signed, sealed & published & pronounced
to be the sd. J. Lewis' Last Will & Testament   [signed] **John Lewis** [seal]
in the presence of:
W.C. Knight
Jeremiah Todd   The above Will was proven in open Court by Thomas Lamb & ordered to
Thomas Lamb   be recorded.   Copy Test. J. Harper, Clk.

Figure 28 - Transcript of Will for John Lewis, 1797

---

[1] Also see *A Memorial and Biographical Record of Iowa*, p. 882.

C. David Lewis
(1747-1822)

David Lewis (my ancestor), son of John Lewis and Priscilla Brooks, was born 21 MAR 1747, perhaps in Berkeley County, Virginia or Anson County, North Carolina. He was first married 30 JAN 1768[1] in Rowan County to Ann Beeson, daughter of Benjamin Beeson and Elizabeth Hunter, who was born 30 MAY 1749 near Hopewell Meeting House, Frederick County, Virginia. History books about Randolph County describe David Lewis as tall, athletic man. He was a farmer and a merchant.

According to a Beeson Family genealogy by Henry Hart Beeson (1968), Benjamin Beeson, who died 14 JUN 1794, was a son of Richard Beeson (b. October 1674, d. 1 JAN 1777) and Charity Grubb (b. 20 SEP 1687, d. 27 NOV 1761). Charity Grubb was a daughter of John Grubb and Frances Vane, while Richard Beeson was a son of Edward Beeson and Rachel Pennington, the former of whom died in Nottingham, Chester County, Pennsylvania about 1712. The Beeson Family was Quaker,[2] and because Ann married a Presbyterian on 30 JAN 1768 she was dropped from the Quaker Meeting House.[3]

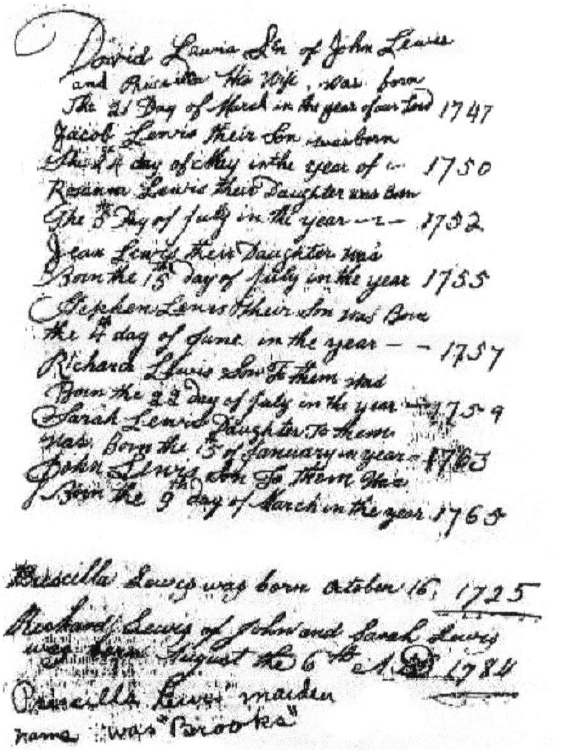
David Lewis Son of John Lewis
and Priscilla His Wife, was born
The 21 Day of March in the year of our Lord 1747
Jacob Lewis their Son was born
the 4 day of May in the year of 1750
Rosanna Lewis their Daughter was born
the 3 Day of July in the year 1752
Jean Lewis their Daughter was
Born the 15 day of July in the year 1755
Stephen Lewis their Son was Born
the 4 day of June in the year 1757
Richard Lewis Son to them was
Born the 22 day of July in the year 1759
Sarah Lewis Daughter to them
was Born the 13 of January in year 1763
John Lewis Son to them was
Born the 9 day of March in the year 1765

Priscilla Lewis was born october 16, 1725
Richard Lewis of John and Sarah Lewis
was born August the 6th A.D. 1784
Priscilla Lewis maiden
name was "Brooks"

Figure 29 - David Lewis Family Bible Record

David and his parents fled from Virginia to North Carolina at the beginning of the French and Indian War. Between April 1781 and April 1782, Isaiah's father, grandfather and three uncles fought with the 10th Regiment, North Carolina Militia during the Revolutionary War.[4] David served as a private in the regiment for Benjamin Bailey's Company of the North Carolina military, and joining on 12 APR 1781 to serve with Colonel Abraham Shephard, was discharged 12 APR 1782.[5] Upon return from the war, David acquired land in Pendleton County, South Carolina based on his service in the war.

After Ann Lewis died 7 DEC 1812 in the Pendleton District (now Anderson County), South Carolina and was buried at nearby Old Stone Church Cemetery, David married second in

---

[1] Number 8L100 in *Pioneer Lewis Families*, by Michael L. Cook.
[2] *A Short History of the Lewis Family in Lawrence County*, by Q. Lewis (Lawrenceville, Ill.: 1940). Used as a source for many tidbits on Lawrence Co., Ill.
[3] Minutes of the New Garden Quarterly Meeting, Guilford Co., N.C. Also *Combined History of Edwards, Lawrence and Wabash Counties, Illinois* (Philadelphia, Pa.: J.L. McDonough & Co., 1883), p. 329.
[4] Also see Lawrence County Historical Society, *Lawrence County, Illinois Commemorative Edition* (Paducah, Ky.: Turner Publishing Co., 1995), p. 246, biographical sketch Isaiah Lewis.
[5] North Carolina Records, Vol. XVI, p. 1106.

1813 to Penelope (unknown), who is named in his will. Penelope died c.1816.[1]

David died 23 JUN 1822 in Pendleton District of Anderson, Pickens County, South Carolina, and left a will in Anderson County that mentions his eldest son Isaiah Lewis.[2] David was buried with wife Ann in Old Stone Church Cemetery located on Highway 76 between Clemson and Pendleton, South Carolina.

Children of David Lewis and Ann Beeson:[3]

+ 1.   ISAIAH LEWIS, SR. (my ancestor), b. 3 SEP 1769 in the part of Rowan Co. that later became Guilford and Randolph cos., N.C., d. 25 JAN 1837 in Vigo Co., Ind., bur. Smith Cem. in Vigo Co., Ind., m. Nancy Julian. See mention later.

2.   PRISCILLA LEWIS, b. 4 SEP 1770 in newly-formed Guilford Co., N.C., d. 19 JAN 1822, m. c.1789 in prob. N.C. to Thomas Field, b. c.1761, d. after 1830.

3.   JACOB LEWIS, b. 14 JAN 1772 in Guilford Co., N.C., d. testate[4] 4 AUG 1838 in Pickens Co., S.C., bur. Lewis Cem. of Pickens, S.C.,[5] m. 22 FEB 1792 in Guilford Co., N.C. to Ailisie Leonard, b. 11 OCT 1771, d. 24 OCT 1857, bur. Lewis Cem. After the death of his father in 1822, he moved to Pickens Co. along Twelve Mile Creek, and was there a farmer, grist mill owner and a Baptist minister at Secona Church. Shown on the 1850 Federal agriculture census for Pickens Co. [page 399]. Children:[6]

31.   DAVID LEWIS, b. 10 JAN 1793 in Randolph Co., N.C., d. 1865 in Cass Co., Ga., m. Nancy Williams.

32.   JOSEPH LEWIS, b. 17 NOV 1794 in Randolph Co., N.C., rem. to Gordon Co., Ga.

33.   ABNER LEWIS, b. 8 FEB 1797 in Randolph Co., N.C., d. 24 SEP 1885 in Sonora, Gordon Co., Ga., bur. Bethlehem Baptist Church Cem., m. Mary Breazeale Gibson, b. 1804 in N.C., d. 1877 in Ga., dau. of Absalom Gibson and Fanny Alexander. 10 children.

34.   MARY LEWIS, b. 20 MAY 1799 in Randolph Co., N.C., d. 24 APR 1877 in Pickens Co., S.C., m. Richard Brown Baker, b. 1793 in Ga., d. after 1860 in Pickens Co., S.C. 5 children.

35.   JOAB LEWIS, farmer, b. 22 JAN 1801 in Randolph Co., N.C., d. 12 MAR 1881 in Pickens Co., S.C., bur. Old Pickens Presbyterian Cem., m. (1) c.1822 to Elizabeth House, b. 6 APR 1800 in S.C., d. 5 AUG 1855 in Grayson Co., Tex., bur. Lewis Cem., Grayson Co., m. (2) 26 APR 1857 in S.C. to Vilanta Gibson Cobb, b. 5 JUL 1812 in S.C., d. 17 MAR 1901 in Pickens Co., S.C., dau. of Absalom Gibson and Fanny Alexander, bur. Old

---

[1] At least one researcher has claimed that Ann Beeson and Penelope Lewis are the same person, as Penelope Ann Beeson. However, I support the evidence that David Lewis had two wives because of the wide gap in the birth of children between 1789-1814.
[2] Anderson Co., S.C. Wills, Bk. A, p. 270, dated 19 JAN 1822.
[3] Also see Letter, 23 OCT 1988, from Helen Legate Campbell, of Murfreesboro, Tenn.
[4] Will dated 4 MAY 1837, wit. by Jacob Guyton, Micajah Alexander and Mary Wood.
[5] The cemetery is located off of Highway 39-142, Nine Times Rd., south of Route 11.
[6] Birthdates of children taken from the Jacob Lewis Bible record, copied in 1931 by Katherine Lewis Childress, in possession of Ernest Lewis of Pickens Co., S.C.

Pickens Presbyterian Cem. 6 children.

36. ANN BEESON "Annie" LEWIS, b. 13 DEC 1803 in Pickens Co., S.C., d. 1 NOV 1889 at the res. of her dau. Mrs. L.L. Bennett in Sonoraville, Gordon Co., Ga., bur. Bethlehem Baptist Church Cem., Sonoraville, m. William Alexander (b. 1794 in N.C., d. testate 27 FEB 1845 in S.C.[1]), son of Daniel and Mary Alexander of Pendleton, later Pickens, S.C.[2], moved to Gordon Co., Ga. 10 children.

37. ELIZABETH LEWIS, b. 7 SEP 1805 in Pickens Co., S.C., d. 7 JUL 1884 in Oconee Co., S.C., bur. Mount Grove Baptist Church Cem., Pickens Co., S.C., m. in 1829 to Anthony Stewart, son of Robert Stewart and Elizabeth Burroughs, b. 21 JAN 1810 in Pendleton District, S.C., d. 5 JUN 1894 in Oconee Co., S.C. 10 children.

38. JAMES E. LEWIS, b. 26 JAN 1807 in Pickens Co., S.C., d. 26 MAR 1883 in Pickens Co., S.C., m. 28 DEC 1828 to Mary Stewart, dau. of Robert Stewart and Elizabeth Burroughs, b. 11 OCT 1811 in Pickens Co., S.C., d. 26 MAR 1883 in Pickens Co. 13 children.

39. CATHERINE LEWIS [photo], b. 7 OCT 1810 in Pickens Co., S.C., d. 14 FEB 1894 in Collin Co., Tex., m. James Alexander (1806-1891), son of Thomas Alexander (d 1856) and Kesiah Watson. 12 children.

3(10). JACOB LEWIS, b. 29 APR 1813 in Pickens Co., S.C., d. 6 APR 1888 in Pickens Co., S.C., m. Katherine Stewart, b. 6 FEB 1814, d. 11 NOV 1890. 11 children.

Figure 30 - Catherine Lewis Alexander

4. JOAB LEWIS, b. 23 DEC 1773 in Guilford Co., N.C., d. 23 AUG 1887 in Simpson Co., Ky., bur. Lewis Cem., Franklin, Simpson Co., Ky., m. (1) c.1796 to Phelba Barton, and m. (2) Catharine Leonard (1775-1830).

41. LEONARD LEWIS.

5. ABNER LEWIS, b. 22 SEP 1775 in Guilford Co., N.C.

6. NERIAH FREDERICK LEWIS, farmer, b. 25 JUN 1778 in Guilford Co., N.C., d. 27 NOV 1843 in Macoupin Co., Ill., bur. Carlinville City Cem., Shaw's Point, Ill., m. 4 MAR 1800 in Anderson Co., S.C. (near the Georgia border) to Mary Moss, b. 29 OCT 1775, d. 16 JAN 1846 during the Navuvoo Exodus, dau. of Samuel Moss (1739-after 1800) and Rachel Julian. About 1809 rem. to a tract about 3 miles east of Franklin, Simpson Co., Ky. By 1838, Neriah obtained land in Lawrence Co., Ill.[3] Children, the first six born in the Pendleton District of Anderson Co., S.C.:

61. ANN LEWIS, b. 21 DEC 1800 in Pendleton District, S.C., d. 1876, m. 24 FEB 1824 in Simpson Co., Ky. to Ellis Wilcox (1789-1890).

---

[1] Pickens District, S.C. Wills, Bk. 1, p. 106, dated 20 FEB 1845, prov. 6 JUN 1845, wit. by Jordan Rice and his brother Thomas Alexander.

[2] This is the ancestral line of Virginia (Wood) Alexander, co-author of the well-known books *Alexander Kin*.

[3] Lawrence Co. Ill. Land Grants, Sec. 14 T3N, Range 12W.

62. MARTHA LEWIS, b. 6 MAR 1802 in Pendleton District, S.C., d. 3 MAY 1842, m. c.1826 in Sangamon Co., Ill. to Travis Moore. 4 children.

63. BENJAMIN FRANKLIN LEWIS, b. 22 APR 1803 in Pendleton District, killed 30 OCT 1838 at Haun's Mill, Caldwell Co., Mo., bur. Haun's Mill Cem., m. 27 JAN 1826 in Simpson Co., Ky. to Joannah Ryon. Several children rem. to Utah.

64. TARLTON LEWIS, carpenter, b. 18 MAY 1805 in Pendleton District, d. 22 NOV 1890 in Teesdale, Wayne Co., Utah, m. 27 MAR 1828 to Malinda Gimlin (1811-1894).

65. JOHN MOSS LEWIS, b. 19 MAY 1807 in Pendleton District, d. MAR 1891, m. 15 AUG 1839 in Morgan Co., Ill. to Elizabeth Woods.

66. BEASON LEWIS, b. 23 FEB 1809 in Pendleton District, d. 22 JAN 1888 in Richmond, Cache Co., Utah, m. (1) 6 FEB 1846 to Elizabeth Ryon, m. (2) 24 FEB 1854 in Salt Lake City to Elizabeth Almira Pond.

67. SAMUEL LEWIS, b. 1 NOV 1810 in Franklin, Simpson Co., Ky., d. 1882 in Ill., m. Rebecca Wright.

68. ELIZABETH LEWIS, b. 25 JUN 1812 in Simpson Co., Ky., d. 5 NOV 1843.

69. DAVID LEWIS, b. 10 APR 1814 in Simpson Co., Ky., d. 2 SEP 1855, m. 23 NOV 1834 in Simpson Co., Ky. to Duritha Trail, m. (2) 4 AUG 1854 in Salt Lake City to Elizabeth Carson.

6(10). NERIAH LEWIS, b. 29 APR 1816 in Simpson Co., Ky., d. 22 JUL 1890 in Richmond, Cache Co., Utah, m. (1) 5 JAN 1836 in Ky. to Rebecca Hendricks, m. (2) 28 MAR 1857 in Salt Lake City to Martha Catherine Youngblood.

6(11). HIRAM LEWIS, b. 11 FEB 1818 in Franklin Co., Ky., d. 11 FEB 1858, m. 3 DEC 1838 to Cecelia Harris.

6(12). MARY M. LEWIS, b. 25 NOV 1820 in Franklin Co., Ky., d. 1888, m. Jonathan B. "Jay" Blackburn.

7. BENJAMIN LEWIS, b. 26 MAY 1781 in Guilford Co., N.C.

8. ELIZABETH ANN LEWIS, b. 21 SEP 1783 in Randolph Co., N.C., d. 4 OCT 1840 in Pickens Co., S.C., m. c.1802 as the first wife of Micajah Alexander, b. 8 MAY 1778 in Va., d. 27 DEC 1877 in Pickens Co., son of Daniel Alexander (1760-1850) and Mary White; both bur. Parrott Family Cem., Pickens Co. Micajah m. (2) to Mary Atkinson. Children:

81. DANIEL D. ALEXANDER, b. 29 JUL 1803 in Pickens Co., S.C., d. 10 NOV 1853, m. Lavina Rice, b. 10 OCT 1805, d. 2 JAN 1880; both bur. Alexander Cem. of Oconee Co., S.C. 10 children.

82. [LUCY] ANNA ALEXANDER, b. 1807, d. 1869, m. c.1830 to Jeremiah Roberts, b. 1807 in S.C., d. 1858 in Dalton, Ga., son of Isaac Roberts and Elizabeth Davis. 6 children.

83. DAVID ALEXANDER, b. 1809, d. 1859 in Harrison Co., Tex., m. Sarah Ann Youngblood (1820-1880). 6 children.

84. MARY ALEXANDER, b. 1809, d. 1855, m. Moses Levi Cantrell, b. 1809, d. 1880.

85. MELVINA ALEXANDER, b. 1810, d. 9 OCT 1865 in Greenville, S.C., m. David Roberts, b. 1804, d. 1854. 10 children.

86. JOHN BAPTIST ALEXANDER, b. 1811, d. November 1887, m. Elizabeth J. Stansell (1827-1891). 7 children.

87. ELISHA RICKMAN ALEXANDER, b. 1814, d. 1878 in Pickens Co., S.C., m. Amanda Rice, b. 1816, d. 1878, dau. of Isaac Rice. 13 children.

88. ELIZABETH ALEXANDER, b. 1820, d. 20 JUN 1891 in Pickens Co., S.C., bur. Bethel Church Cem., Pickens Co., S.C., m. Caleb B. Murphree, b. 1818, d. 11 FEB 1863 in Pontotoc Co., Miss., served in C.S.A. 9 children.

89. MALINDA "Millie" ALEXANDER, b. 7 JAN 1823 in Pickens Co., S.C., d. 10 MAR 1910 in Pickens Co., S.C., bur. Antioch Baptist Church Cem., Pickens, S.C., m. Jeremiah Sylvester Parrott, b. 5 JUL 1821 in S.C., d. 2 JUL 1903 in S.C. 10 children.

8(10). MICAJAH M. ALEXANDER, b. 1824, d. 21 SEP 1869.

8(11). ELIZA LOUISA "Lucy" ALEXANDER, b. 18 MAR 1827/8, d. 19 OCT 1912 in Pickens Co., S.C., m. 14 NOV 1845 to Ephraim Gilstrap, b. 10 NOV 1821, d. 10 FEB 1905; both bur. Parrott Cem. 11 children.

9. COSBI "Casley" LEWIS, b. 17 JUL 1785 in Randolph Co., N.C., m. John Woodall.

(10). TARLETON LEWIS, b. 11 AUG 1787 in Pendleton Dist., Pickens Co., S.C., d. c.1866 in Bartow Co., Ga., bur. Lewis-Bagwell Cem., near Glexatile, Ga., m. c.1807 to Rachel Williams, b. 1789, d. 1870. In 1837, Tarleton Lewis sold two parcels of land to William Alexander in Pickens Co., it being part that belonged to his father David Lewis, and which Tarleton obtained from his brother Benjamin Lewis.[1] Children:

(10)1. JAMES W. LEWIS, b. Fri., 13 NOV 1807 in Pendleton District, S.C. or Ga., d. 5 JAN 1884 in Bartow Co., Ga., bur. Lewis-Linn Cem., Bartow Co., Ga., m. Adeline Louisa Duff, b. 1812, d. 1892.

(10)2. ANN BEESON LEWIS, b. Thurs., 10 JAN 1810, d. 5 JUL 1848 in Ga., m. Joshua Holden.

(10)3. RUTH WELLS LEWIS, b. Mon., 7 OCT 1811 in Fairmont, Ga., d. 31 JUL 1896 in Wichita Falls, Tex., bur. Riverside Cem., m. 14 MAY 1831 to William Ray Duff, b. 12 APR 1803, d. 15 OCT 1855 in Sarepta, Miss.

(10)4. MARGARET H. LEWIS, b. Fri., 27 JAN 1815 in Calhoun, Gordon Co., Ga., d. 20 JAN 1862 in Calhoun, Ga., bur. L.P. Owens Farm, Gordon Co., Ga., m. James Madison Field, b. 1816, d. 1888.

(10)5. DAVID F. LEWIS, b. Fri., 7 OCT 1818, d. 11 SEP 1852, bur. Bagwell-Lewis Cem., Bartow Co., Ga.

(11). HANNAH LEWIS, b. Fri. morning, 2 OCT 1789 in Pickens Co., S.C., d. 22 JUL 1869 in Johnson Co., Mo., bur. Centerview Cem., m. (1) c. 1804 in N.C. to Ezekiel Harlan, and m. (2) c.1821 to Silas Perry. Child:

(11)1. NATHAN WASHINGTON PERRY, b. 17 APR 1830, d. 18 MAY 1891, bur. Centerview Cem.

---

[1] Pickens Co., S.C. Deeds, Bk. C-1, p.285, dated 4 JAN 1837, one tract of 277 acres, another of 237 acres; wife Rachel releases dower.

Children of David Lewis and Penelope (unknown):

(12).   DAVID LEWIS, b. 24 JAN 1814.

(13).   ROSANNAH LEWIS, b. 26 OCT 1815 in Anderson, Pendleton Dist., Pickens, S.C.

Isaiah Lewis, Sr.
(1769-1837)

Isaiah Lewis, Sr. (my ancestor), son of David Lewis and Ann Beeson, was born 3 SEP 1769 in part of Rowan County, North Carolina (which became Guilford and later Randolph County).[1] He was married about 1786 in Guilford County to Nancy Julian, who was of Huguenot descent and a daughter of Peter Julian, Jr. and Ruth Pugh. She was born about 1774 in South Carolina. Isaiah Lewis was a wheelwright. It has also been said that he operated a freighting business to transport merchandise by river and wagon between Tennessee and the Carolinas. After moving to Kentucky in 1804 he was a cotton farmer.

Peter Julian, Jr. was married about 1771 to Ruth Pugh, daughter of Azariah Pugh and Hannah Beals, who was born 26 FEB 1746 near the Hopewell Friends Meeting House of Frederick County, Virginia. Peter's father, Peter Julian, Sr. was born about 1712 and died about 1806. The father was married perhaps four times. His father, Rene Julien (St. Julien) was of Bohemia Manor, Cecil County, Maryland, and was born about 1660 in Vitre, Brittany, France, and married Mary Bullock of the Isle of Bermuda. Rene died after 1774, perhaps in Frederick County, Virginia, and was buried in the old Opuequon Cemetery near Winchester, Frederick County, Virginia.

After residing in Guilford County, North Carolina immediately following marriage, Isaiah and Nancy removed, about 1799, to Pendleton District of Pickens County, South Carolina where they stayed 7 years before moving on to Warren County, Kentucy. They moved about 1816 to Edwards County, Illinois where he obtained a 160-acre tract (in the name of his son Peter Lewis), located on the south side of the St. Louis Tract. This tract was about 3 miles west of Lawrenceville, and on the old State road. Here Isaiah Lewis became a teacher, and after his cotton farm failed he planted a fruit orchard and started a nursery. On 16 JUN 1824, Lawrence County was established from Edwards County. Isaiah assisted John Dunlap in surveying the town of Lawrenceville.

On 10 JUN 1825, Isaiah sold his farm to his son Philip Lewis and moved to Vigo County, Indiana where he bought land. In February 1836, Isaiah Lewis and wife Nancy [Julian] of Vigo County, Indiana, sold 160 acres to Andrew York.[2]

---

[1] Also see *Illinois Historical and Lawrence County Biographical* (Chicago: Munsell Publishing Co., 1910), p. 705, in a biographical sketch of Harley V. Lewis, it is stated that Isaiah Lewis was a native of Virginia and a wheelwright by trade, and his wife Ann Beeson was a native of Virginia as well.
[2] Vigo Co., Ind., Deeds, Bk. 8, p. 315.

While raising a large family, Isaiah took an active part in the early history of Lawrence County, serving on the first petit jury and acting as an early school teacher. He also assisted John Dunlap in surveying the village of Lawrenceville and was elected county commissioner in 1829 to serve one term. At the conclusion of his term as commissioner, he moved to Vigo County, Indiana where he died on 25 JAN 1837 at the home of his daughter. He was buried in Smith Cemetery near Bloomtown, Vigo County, Indiana.

Nancy returned to Lawrence County where she made her home with her son David Lewis and his wife, and died 28 JUN 1845 due to the "black tongue [cholera]," and was buried at night in Collins Graveyard, which was opposite the old Hollister Family farm on Route 1, 3 miles south of Lawrenceville, Lawrence County, Illinois.

Children of Isaiah Lewis, Sr. and Nancy Julian, order uncertain:

1. REBEKAH LEWIS, b. c.1787 in Randolph Co., N.C., d. in the 1880s, bur. Smith Cem. near Bloomtown, Vigo Co., Ind., m. 2 JAN 1809 in Ky. to Eli Noel, res. in Logansport, Ind.

2. DAVID LEWIS, b. c.1788 in Randolph Co., N.C., d. 14 JUN 1845 in Lawrence Co., Ill., bur. Collins Cem., 3 miles south of Lawrenceville, Ill., m. 17 JUN 1813 to Elizabeth Hendricks. By 1838 he obtained land in Lawrence Co., Ill.[1]

3. PETER LEWIS, b. c.1790 in Randolph Co.,[2] N.C., d. 1 SEP 1821 [or 5 SEP 1825] in Vandalia, Ill., m. 31 MAY 1819 to Mahala Spencer, daughter of Col. Wilson Spencer who fought in the Revolutionary War and was active in the county militia. He was known to have established the first nursery in Lawrence Co., Ill. Child:
   31. JAMES ALLEN LEWIS, raised by his grandparents, b. 16 NOV 1820 in Lawrence Co., Ill., d. 7 MAY 1898 in Galveston, Cass Co., Ind., bur. Galveston Cem., m. Gennetta C. (unknown), b. 10 APR 1822, d. 21 SEP 1903, bur. Galveston Cem.

+ 4. PAUL LEWIS (twin), b. 21 JAN 1800 in Pendleton District, Pickens Co., S.C., d. February 1872 in Randolph Co., Ark., bur. Pitman's Ferry of Randolph Co., Ark., m. (1) 15 MAR 1820 to Ann Stewart, and he m. (2) 22 FEB 1854 in Randolph Co., Ark. to Mary "Polly" (Wright) Lewis, widow of his brother Isaiah, Jr.

+ 5. PHILIP LEWIS (twin), b. 21 JAN 1800 in Pendleton District, Pickens Co., S.C., d. 4 FEB 1873 in Lawrence Co., Ill., bur. Pleasant Hill-White House Cem. of Lawrence Co., Ill., m. (1) 13 NOV 1823 in Lawrenceville, Ill. to Mary "Polly" Craven, daughter of John Craven and Mary Kennedy.

6. JACOB LEWIS,[3] b. 27 JAN 1802 in Pendleton District, Pickens Co., S.C., m. 5/6 MAY 1824 in Edwards Co., Ill. to Rebecca Louisa James, b. 16 FEB 1804, d. 25 JUL

---

[1] Lawrence Co. Ill. Land Grants, Sec. 14 T3N, Range 12W.
[2] Randolph Co. was formed in 1779 from Guilford Co., N.C., and named for Peyton Randolph, the first president of the Continental Congress.
[3] Also see *Lawrence County, Illinois Commemorative Edition* (Lawrence County Historical Society), p. 248, biographical sketch.

1865, bur. White House Cem.[1] He homesteaded c.1824 in Edwards Co., Ill. Jacob set out the first orchard in Petty Twp. and may have used trees from his brother Peter's nursery. He d. suddenly 15 MAR 1889 while in Vandalia, Richland Co., Ill. to buy Government land, and was bur. in Pleasant Hill-White House Cem. Children, of whom:

61. WILLIAM LEWIS, d. 1887, m. Mary Elizabeth Smith, d. 1885. Children:

    611. SAMUEL LEWIS, raised by his uncle Paul Lewis in Lawrence Co., Ill., m. Lucy Spencer, dau. of Lafayette Spencer and Mary Pettit.

    612. GERTRUDE LEWIS.

    613. GEORGE LEWIS.

7. JOHN LEWIS, b. 31 JAN 1804 in Warren Co., Ky., d. 12 SEP 1841 in Lawrence Co., Ill., age 37y 7m 13d, bur. Bluffs Cem. there, m. 15 MAR 1825 in Lawrence Co., Ill. to Matilda Stewart, d. 8 APR 1866, age 59y 3m 1d, bur. Bluffs Cem. 9 children, of whom:

75. JOSEPHUS McCORKLE LEWIS, b. 18 OCT 1832 in Ill., d. 26 JUL 1909 in Lawrence Co., bur. Bluffs Cem., m. 6 JAN 1857 in Lawrence Co., Ill. to Elizabeth A. Burget, b. 20 FEB 1840, d. 11 SEP 1913, bur. Bluffs Cem.

8. WILLIAM MILTON [or Melton] LEWIS, b. 23 AUG 1806 in Warren Co., Ky., d. 19 JAN 1861 in Lawrence Co., Ill., bur. Pleasant Hill-White House Cem., m. 29 MAY 1828 in Lawrence Co., Ill. to Martha Craven, b. 15 OCT 1813, d. 5 NOV 1878, bur. White House Cem., dau. of John Craven and Mary Kennedy. 8 children.

9. ANN LEWIS, b. 1808 in Warren Co., Ky., m. 3 JUL 1822 in Lawrence Co., Ill. to Andrew R. McMahon.

+ (10). ISAIAH LEWIS, JR. (my ancestor), b. 1808 in Warren Co., Ky., d. testate 1850 in Randolph Co., Ark., m. 13 MAR 1828 in Vigo Co., Ind. to Mary "Polly" Wright.[2]

(11). MARY LEWIS, b. 1811 in Warren Co., Ky., d. 8 JUN 1852 in Vigo Co., Ind., m. 7 JUN 1827 in Vigo Co., Ind. to Hugh Scott, rem. in 1830s to Terre Haute, Vigo Co., Ind., then in 1856 to Jasper Co., Iowa. Hugh, b. 15 NOV 1799 in Fleming Co., Ky., d. 16 SEP 1882, son of Thomas Scott and Hannah Reid. 9 children, including:[3]

    (11)1. HENRY CLAY SCOTT, b. 16 MAY 1836 in Warren Co., Ky., rem. to Van Zandt Co., Tex., d. 12 JAN 1892, m. Sarah Elizabeth Smith (1841-1923), bur. Scott-Johnson Cem., Wills Point, Van Zandt Co., Tex.

---

[1] *History of Edwards, Lawrence and Wabash Counties, Illinois* (Philadelphia, Pa.: J.L. McDonough & Co., 1883), p. 317.

[2] She is easily confused with a Mary "Polly" Smith who was b. c.1807 in N.C., m. 13 MAR 1828 in Vigo Co., Ind. to an Isaiah Lewis (also b. 1808 in Ky.) who is found on the Federal census there in 1830 and in 1850. Enumerated in 1850 with Isaiah and Mary are the following children: Orlando Lewis (age 17), Marion (age 15), Sarah (age 9), Dennis (age 8), John (age 6), all b. in Ill., and William (age 4 months, b. in Ind.). The correct Mary Wright was married between 1821 and 1824, probably in Simpson Co., Ky., to Isaiah Lewis. The latter seems more likely because by 1830, our Isaiah Lewis was in Carroll Co., Tenn., then Randolph Co., Ark. by 1840 where also followed by Mary's brother Philemon W. Wright. Our Isaiah Lewis, Jr. was dead by 1850. By 1854, Mary (Wright) Lewis is named in the probate of her father's estate in Benton Co., Tenn. After Isaiah's death his widow Mary was m. 22 FEB 1854 to Paul Lewis, and she is more likely Mary Wright Lewis and not Mary Smith Lewis.

[3] See *Past and Present of Jasper County, Iowa*, Vol. 1, pp. 443-44.

4. <u>Paul Lewis</u>
(1800-1872)

Paul Lewis, a twin son of Isaiah Lewis, Sr. and Nancy Julian, was born 21 JAN 1800 in Pickens County, South Carolina. He was first married 15 MAR 1820 in Edwards County, Illinois to Ann Stewart, daughter of James P. Stewart and Margaret Witherspoon, who was born c.1802 in Tennessee. Ann's sister Methel was married to Daniel Payne of Lawrence County, Illinois, who operated a water grist mill on the Ambraw River in Lawrenceville, which he had purchased from the DuBois Brothers.

About 1820, moved to Edwards County, Illinois (which in 1825 was in part formed into Lawrence County). By 1838, he obtained land in Lawrence County.[1]

Paul Lewis was known to have operated the first linseed oil mill in Lawrence County, Illinois, and it was perhaps the only one that existed, and did so until about 1860. It was then operated by oxen, the tread being 60 feet in diameter. Paul was interested in books and collected quite a large library for his time. This family was found on the 1830 [page 262] and 1840 Federal census for Lawrence County, Illinois, then were known to be in Hot Springs, Arkansas about 1846 where they had moved to benefit Mrs. Lewis' health.

By the time of the 1850 Federal census, they were enumerated in Jefferson Township, Independence County, Arkansas [page 313], and then moved back to Lawrence County, Illinois by the time of the 1860 Federal census [page 226].

Paul Lewis, of Izzard County, was married second on 22 FEB 1854 in Randolph County, Arkansas[2] to Mary "Polly" (Wright) Lewis, the widow of his brother Isaiah Lewis, Jr.

Paul was listed on the 1870 Federal census for Little Black Township of Randolph County, Arkansas [page 50]. He died in February 1872 at the home of his brother Joab Lewis near Pitman's Ferry, Randolph County, Arkansas.

On 18 JUN 1880, Mary "Polly" (Wright) Lewis Lewis [sic] is shown on the Federal census [page 45] as living with her son Joab Lewis in Little Black Township of Randolph County, Arkansas. It shows her father was born in South Carolina and her mother was born in Virginia.

Children of Paul Lewis and Ann Stewart:

41.	PERRY LEWIS, farmer and mill builder, b. 30 MAR 1821 in Lawrence Co., Ill., d. Fri. night, 19 JAN 1912 in Lawrenceville, Ill., bur. Pleasant Hill Cem., Bridgeport, Ill., m. 8 FEB 1846 there to Mary Jane Musgrave, b. 31 MAR 1827 in Jeromesville, Ohio, dau. of John Musgrove of Ire., d. 23 SEP 1910 at the home of her daughter Mary Spencer in Lawrence Co., Ill. Perry worked closely with his uncle David Lewis in the building of a water mill at Lawrenceville, later becoming foreman, and was especially

---

[1] Lawrence Co. Ill. Land Grants, Sec. 36, Township 4N, Range 13W.
[2] Randolph Co., Ark. Marriages, Bk. 1, p. 205, Paul is age between 50 and 80, and Mary is age between 45 and 90.

gifted in the framing of large timbers and did so in building barns and bridges. He was the first boat builder of Lawrence Co., Ill., active in politics, and a Mason in the Bridgeport Lodge in 1864. Children:

411.   LYDIA ANN LEWIS, b. 15 DEC 1846 in Lawrence Co., Ill., d. 15 MAY 1921 in Lawrence Co., bur. Lawrenceville City Cem., m. as second wife of Elkanah B. Price,[1] rem. to Seattle, Wash. Children:

    4111.   ALLEN G. PRICE, b. 1883, d. 1885.

    4112.   GUY C. PRICE, b. 1886, d. 1887, bur. Lawrenceville City Cem.

412.   JOSEPH BATTENFIELD LEWIS,[2] b. 4 FEB 1850 in Lawrence Twp., Lawrence Co., Ill., d. 24 MAR 1929 in Bridgeport, Ill., bur. Pleasant Hill Cem., was a carpenter on the first Big Four Railroad Bridge and the first Big Four Depot in Lawrenceville, Ill., between 1874 and 1875, m. 1 FEB 1880 to Mary Ellen Lake, b. 17 DEC 1853, d. 3 JAN 1927, dau. of Abner Lake. Seven children, of whom:

    4121.   BYRON RAY LEWIS,[3] b. 18 NOV 1880 near Bridgeport, Ill., d. 29 JAN 1979, bur. Pleasant Hill Cem., m. 6 JUL 1916 to Luella Eaton, b. 7 MAY 1878, d. 18 OCT 1962.

413.   JOHN PAUL LEWIS, b. 24 DEC 1847 in Lawrence Co., Ill., d. 19 JUN 1915 in Pony, Mont.

414.   JAMES POTTS PAINE LEWIS, b. 24 MAR 1852 in Lawrence Co., Ill., d. 29 OCT 1872 in Lawrence Co., Ill.

415.   MARY MALVINA LEWIS, b. January 1856 in Ill., d. 1935, bur. Pleasant Hill Cem., m. 18 FEB 1894 in Lawrence Co., Ill. to Charles Spencer, b. 1855, d. 1926.

416.   GEORGE MARSHALL LEWIS, b. 6 SEP 1858 in Lawrence Co., Ill., d. 8 MAR 1941 in Lawrence Co., Ill., bur. Pleasant Hill Cem.

417.   EDWIN MORRISON LEWIS, b. 12 DEC 1860 in Lawrence Co., Ill., d. 30 JUN 1942 in Lawrence, Ill., bur. Lawrenceville City Cem., m. Ann Black, b. 1864, d. 1935.

418.   CORNELIUS ELMER LEWIS (twin), b. 11 FEB 1864 in Lawrence Co., Ill., d. 27 OCT 1889 in Lawrence Co., Ill., bur. Pleasant Hill Cem.

419.   CORNELIA ELANOR LEWIS (twin), b. 11 FEB 1864 in Lawrence Co., Ill., d. 24 JAN 1953 in Lawrence Co., Ill., bur. Lawrenceville City Cem., m. Thornton Combs, b. 1854, d. 1929. Child:

    4191.   LEWIS COMBS, b. 1891, d. 1943, bur. Lawrenceville City Cem.

41(10).   SARAH ELIZABETH LEWIS, b. 30 NOV 1867 in Lawrence Co., Ill., d. 2 DEC 1867 in Lawrence Co., Ill.

41(11).   JAMES P. LEWIS, a telegrapher at the railroad depot in Lawrenceville, Ill., d. there of typhoid in 1872.

41(12).   ALICE MATILDA LEWIS, b. 14 JUN 1871 in Lawrence Co., Ill., d. 28 SEP 1951 in Greencastle or Kokomo, Ind., m. (1) Granville Theodore Haltom, b. 2 MAR 1858, d. 31 AUG 1901, m. (2) Thomas Justin Haltom, b. 28 SEP 1876 in Putnam Co., Ind., d. 19 FEB 1915 in Greencastle, Ind.

---

[1] His first wife was Mildred M. who d. 6 OCT 1876, age 22y 10m, bur. in Lawrenceville City Cem.

[2] Also see *Illinois Historical and Lawrence County Biographical* (Chicago: Munsell Publishing Co., 1910), p. 706, biographical sketch, and see *Lawrence County, Illinois Commerative Edition* (Lawrence County Historical Society), p. 246, biographical sketch.

[3] Also see *Lawrence County, Illinois Commerative Edition* (Lawrence County Historical Society), p. 246, biographical sketch.

42. JAMES STEWART LEWIS, b. 1823 in Lawrence Co., Ill., d. May 1898, m. Angeline Watson, b. 1823, d. 1900.

43. MATILDA ANN LEWIS, b. c.1824 in Lawrence Co., Ill., m. 17 MAR 1843 to Asa Mayes.

44. PHILIP HOWARD LEWIS, b. 8 FEB 1826 in Lawrence Co., Ill., d. 26 JAN 1893 in Seattle, King Co., Wash., bur. Lake View Cem., m. Hester L. Brown.

45. MARGARET LEWIS, b. c.1831 in Lawrence Co., Ill.

46. VOLTAIRE LEWIS, b. 1834 in Lawrence Co., Ill., d. 1840, bur. Lewis Cem., located in Sect. 29 of Petty Twp., Lawrence Co., Ill.

47. JOHN LEWIS, b. c.1836 in Lawrence Co., Ill., d. 23 APR 1846.

48. MARY E. LEWIS, b. c.1837 in Lawrence Co., Ill., d. c.1865 in Ark., m. 16 OCT 1853 in Batesville, Independence Co., Ark. to John McElmurry, b. 1830, d. 1896.

49. NANCY LEWIS, b. c.1838 in Lawrence Co., Ill., d. 21 AUG 1839.

4(10). MARTHA SARAH LEWIS, b. 1 AUG 1840 in Lawrence Co., Ill., d. 20 FEB 1919, bur. Lewis Cem., Hillsboro, Tex., m. as the fourth wife of (10)2. WILLIAM MARTIN LEWIS, of Randolph Co., Ark., *q.v.*

4(11). JANE LEWIS, b. c.1842 in Lawrence Co., Ill.

4(12). PAUL ALEXANDER LEWIS, b. c.1844 in Lawrence Co., Ill., d. 1872.

5. Philip Lewis
(1800-1873)

Philip Lewis, a twin son of Isaiah Lewis, Sr. and Nancy Julian, was born 21 JAN 1800 in Pendleton District, Pickens County, South Carolina.[1] He moved with his father's family from Kentucky then in 1814 to Lawrence County, Illinois. He was first married 13 NOV 1823 in Lawrenceville, Illinois to Mary "Polly" Craven, born 25 AUG 1784, who was a daughter of John Craven and Mary Kennedy. Polly died 25 FEB 1850 and was buried in the White House Cemetery.

Philip purchased his father's lands and built a fine residence which was later the home of Dr. J.C. Barr in Lawrenceville, Illinois. Philip was a blacksmith and wagon maker (wheelwright), and mined some of the earliest coal that was produced in Lawrence County

---

[1] Also see *Illinois Historical and Lawrence County Biographical* (Chicago: Munsell Publishing Co., 1910), p. 705, in a biographical sketch of his son Harley V. Lewis, it states Philip was born in 1800 in Virginia.

for use in his blacksmith shop. He followed the Universalist faith.

Philip Lewis was married second on 15 DEC 1850 in Lawrence County to a neighbor, Mrs. Julia Hester Dunlap McCleave (1813-1853), widow of Benjamin McCleave, Jr. Hester Lewis died 18 NOV 1853. Philip married third on 2 AUG 1855 to Martha Ann Harris (1808-1888). Philip's family was enumerated on the 1850 Federal census for Crawford County, Illinois [page 376].

On 6 JAN 1860, Philip Lewis sold his farm to his son-in-law John H. Griggs and moved with his wife Martha to Randolph County, Arkansas to visit his twin brother Paul. He remained there for one year but returned to Illinois when it appeared that the Civil War was imminent. He then bought an 80-acre farm in Bridgeport, Illinois, where he followed the trade of a wheelwright in conjunction with farming.

Philip Lewis died 4 FEB 1873 in Lawrence County, Illinois and was buried in the White House Cemetery nearby.

Children of Philip Lewis and Mary "Polly" Craven:

51.　ELIZABETH LEWIS, b. 23 DEC 1824 in Ill., d. 10 JUL 1880 in Lawrence Co., Ill., m. 31 JAN 1847 to William Neal, b. 3 OCT 1818, d. 10 APR 1904, both bur. Pleasant Hill Cem., Bridgeport, Ill. Children:
　511.　MARY LOUISA NEAL, b. 1848 in Ill.
　512.　ELBERT L. NEAL, b. 1851, d. 1866, bur. Pleasant Hill Cem.
　513.　JAMES ALLEN NEAL, b. 1854, d. 1855, bur. Pleasant Hill Cem.
　514.　ALICE NEAL, b. 1856 in Ill.
　515.　ADALINE NEAL, b. 1859, d. 1860, bur. Pleasant Hill Cem.
　516.　WILLIAM E. NEAL, b. 1862, d. 1950, m. Dora Heath, b. 1860, d. 1936, both bur. Pleasant Hill Cem.

52.　LOUISA LEWIS, b. 20 AUG 1826 in Lawrence Co., Ill., d. 26 DEC 1888 in Dennison, Grayson Co., Tex., m. 28 JUL 1842 in Lawrence Co., Ill. to John Henry Bruffey, b. 15 AUG 1811 in Lewisburg, Greenbrier Co., Va. [now W.Va.], d. 7 DEC 1888 in Dennison, Tex., both bur. Oakwood Cem. of Dennison, Tex. 11 children.

53.　WILLIAM MILTON LEWIS, carpenter, and grain and hardware merchant, b. 17 JUL 1828 in Lawrence Co., Ill., d. 2 FEB 1882, m. (1) 9 DEC 1852 in Lawrence Co. to Amanda White, and m. (2) 16 APR 1854 in Lawrence Co. to Catherine Emma "Kate" Eaton, b. 25 DEC 1836 in Lawrence Co., Ill., d. 4 NOV 1899 in Bridgeport, daughter of Caius Marius Eaton and Lucy Payne. C.M. Eaton was a millwright and came from Vermont. After going to Arkansas in 1857 with his father, he returned and bought a 160-acre tract in Lawrence Co. William was very active and an industrious citizen of Bridgeport, Ill. With the building of the Ohio and Mississippi Railroad, he became carpenter foreman in the building of stations, and built the first depot in Bridgeport where he served as station master. He had the first hardware store in Bridgeport and was an early grain dealer. William was also active in the building of the Christian Church. Children:

531. Dr. HARLIE VERNON LEWIS,[1] b. 9 JAN 1859 in Bridgeport, Ill., d. 11 FEB 1939 in Bridgeport, m. 5 OCT 1881 to Hettie Harvey Ray, daughter of Dr. Thomas Ray. H.L. Lewis began his early practice in Bridgeport, Ill., and continued there until he moved to Lawrenceville, Ill. about the turn of the century. He was interested in gathering biographical sketches of physicians of the county, and left the work incomplete at his death. He was educated at a medical college in Cincinnati, Ohio. Seven children.

532. MARY MOLLIE LEWIS, b. 1857, d. bef. 1883.

533. HENRY H. LEWIS.

534. SIGEL DURWARD LEWIS, b. 1862 in Ill., d. 1899, m. 28 AUG 1889 in Lawrence Co., Ill to Elizabeth Ellen Seed.

535. UDOLPHUS S. LEWIS, b. 1864 in Ill.

536. Dr. CAIUS MARIUS LEWIS,[2] physician and postmaster, b. 22 JAN 1867 in Bridgeport Twp., Ill., d. 26 JUL 1960 in Bridgeport, Ill., bur. Lawrenceville City Cem., m. (1) 16 OCT 1895 to Bertha Benefiel, b. 1872, d. 31 MAY 1901, dau. of Jesse B. Benefiel (1833-1908), m. (2) 24 JUN 1903 to Anna McNeill (1877-1962), dau. of George McNeill. His home was burned in 1913 in the great fire in Bridgeport. Children:

    5361. CHESTER DELVEY LEWIS, b. 1899 in Bridgeport, d. 1936 of tuberculosis in Ft. Bayard, N.M., m. 1930 to Ruth Tracy (1904-1970). Widow Ruth m. in 1944 to Lloyd Hancock (1904-1980).

    5362. WILLIAM M. LEWIS, was killed by lightning during his senior class picnic

54. PRISCILLA LEWIS, b. 17 MAY 1830 in Lawrence Co., Ill., d. 25 APR 1852 in Lawrence Co., m. 18 MAR 1851 in Lawrence Co. to George M. Whitaker.

55. MARY ANN LEWIS, b. 7 JUN 1832 in Lawrence, Ill., d. 7 SEP 1883.

56. ERWIN LEWIS, b. 20 MAY 1834, d. 22 DEC 1855.

57. FRANKLIN LEWIS, b. 7 NOV 1836 in Lawrence Co., Ill., d. 29 OCT 1908 in Vincennes, Knox Co., Ind., m. (1) 24 MAR 1868 in Lawrence Co., Ill. to Ann Keller, b. 1838, d. 1879, he m. (2) to Angeline Doan. Children, of whom:

    571. HARRY ALBERT LEWIS, fiddle player and vegetable farmer, b. 12 MAR 1869 in Lawrence Co., m. 4 JAN 1894 to Margaret Jane Brown, dau. of Leander Brown and Josephine Lake. 5 children.

58. CYNTHIA E. LEWIS, b. 23 DEC 1838 in Lawrence Co., Ill., d. 14 JUN 1904 in Bridgeport, Ill., m. 24 MAY 1855 to James Eaton, b. 11 MAR 1831, d. 27 FEB 1920, both bur. Mount Zion Cem., Lawrence Co., Ill.

59. MARTHA LEWIS, b. 11 FEB 1841 in Ill., d. 26 FEB 1902, m. 29 NOV 1865 in

---

[1] Also see *Illinois Historical and Lawrence County Biographical* (Chicago: Munsell Publishing Co., 1910), p. 704, biographical sketch.

[2] Also see *Illinois Historical and Lawrence County Biographical* (Chicago: Munsell Publishing Co., 1910), p. 704, biographical sketch.

Wabash, Ill., to Samuel Coles Besley, farmer, b. 10 APR 1824, d. 19 JAN 1923, son of James Besley (1804-1888). Martha and Samuel bur. Friendsville Cem., Wabash Co., Ill. 9 children.

5(10). ELEANOR LEWIS, b. 6 MAY 1843, d. 22 MAR 1877 in Lawrence, Ill., m. 30 JAN 1862 to John H. Griggs.

5(11). PERRY COMMODORE LEWIS, b. 20 JUL 1845 in Lawrenceville, Ill., d. 5 FEB 1898, m. (1) 22 JUL 1863 to Lydia L. Hamilton, and m. (2) 4 DEC 1882 in Lawrence Co., Ill. to Jane "Jennie" Moore.

5(12). JULIAN LEWIS, b. 18 MAY 1848 in Lawrence Co., Ill., d. 13 OCT 1848.

5(13). CAROLINE LEWIS, b. 9 FEB 1850 in Lawrence Co., Ill., d. 5 NOV 1867.

Children of Philip Lewis and second wife Hester Dunlap McCleave:

5(14). SAMUEL DUNLAP LEWIS, b. 6 APR 1852 in Lawrence Co., Ill., m. 17 JAN 1876 to Maggie Lane.

5(15). LEVI LEWIS, b. 7 NOV 1853, d.12 SEP 1854.

Children of Philip Lewis and third wife Martha Ann Harris:

5(16). JOHN BUCHANAN LEWIS, b. 9 MAY 1856 in Lawrence Co., Ill., d. 3 NOV 1927, m. 24 NOV 1878 to Alzina Cummins, b. 12 OCT 1859, d. 6 JUN 1935, both bur. Pleasant Hill Cem.

5(17). JAMES LEWIS,[1] operated a saw mill and a threshing machine, b. 1 OCT 1858 in Lawrence Co., Ill., d. 31 MAY 1952, removed to Petty Twp., m. (1) on 3 OCT 1884 to Mary Jane Bickell, b. Crawford Co., Ill, dau. of John Bickell. James m. (2) 14 NOV 1913 to Orilla Ayers, b. 1878, d. 1953, both bur. Lawrenceville City Cem. Eight children.

5(18). PHILIP (a.k.a. Robert Milton) LEWIS, b. 21 SEP 1860 in Ark., d. 8 DEC 1934, bur. West Chapel Cem., Clinton Co., Ohio, m. 23 DEC 1880 to Minnie Lake.

10. Isaiah Lewis, Jr.
(1808-1850)

Isaiah Lewis, Jr. (my ancestor), was a son of Isaiah Lewis, Sr. (1769-1837) and Nancy Julian, and born in 1808 in Warren County, Kentucky. He came with his parents to what would become Lawrence County, Illinois in 1814,[2] and may have removed with them to

---

[1] Also see *Illinois Historical and Lawrence County Biographical* (Chicago: Munsell Publishing Co., 1910), p. 706, biographical sketch.
[2] Lawrence Co. was formed in 1821 from parts of Crawford and Edwards counties.

Vigo County, Indiana about 1825.

Many researchers show that Isaiah was married 13 MAR 1828 by George Malcain, J.P., in Vigo County, Indiana to Mary "Polly" Smith who was born in North Carolina. However, it is more likely that he married instead about 1821 in Warren County, Kentucky to Mary Wright,[1] born c.1803 in Warren County, Kentucky, daughter of William Wright (b. 14 DEC 1774 in Laurens, S.C., d. November 1854 in Benton Co., Tenn.) and Frances Campbell (1778-1860). See later that the 1880 Federal census shows for Joab Lewis that both of his parents were born in Kentucky.

In 1830, the family is found on the Federal census for Carroll County, Tennessee [page 183].

On 1 OCT 1839, Isaiah Lewis, Jr. obtained a land patent for 40 acres in Randolph County, Arkansas.[2]

As Isak Lewis [sic], he is enumerated in 1840 on the Federal census for Little Black Township of Randolph County, Arkansas [page 148], with 5 children (plus one male of age to be a brother), no slaves, with four persons being employed in agriculture.

In 1847, Isaiah Lewis, Jr. and William Adair purchased items from the estate of William Watson, late of Randoph County, Arkansas. The administrator was James Isaacs.

Isaiah Lewis, Jr. died in Randolph County sometime after the date of his will 7 DEC 1849 and before it was proved there on 26 MAR 1850. The testator named his wife Polly and son Joab Lewis,[3] and does not name other younger children.

In 14 OCT 1850, Mary Lewis heads household 153 in Fayette Township of Randolph County, Arkansas, and it shows she was born about 1801 in Kentucky. Widow Mary (Wright) Lewis was remarried 22 FEB 1854 in Randolph County, Arkansas to Paul Lewis, her brother-in-law.

Possible children of Isaiah Lewis, Jr. and Mary "Polly" Wright:

(10)1.   CHARLES WESLEY LEWIS, carpenter, b. 1826 in Carroll Co., Tenn., d. after 1880 in Warm Springs, Randolph Co., Ark., m. (1) 6 FEB 1845 in Randolph Co.,[4] Ark. to Louisa Burton, b. c.1827 in Tenn., d. c.1868 in Ark., he m. (2) 2 MAR 1871 in Randolph Co.[5] to Mrs. Jennetta Jane Lacy Goliher [or Gallahar], b. 1834 in Randolph Co., d. 1924, bur. Jane Cem., McDonald Co., Mo., daughter of Valentine Lacy and Mary Lavina Waddle, widow of John H.

---

[1] On 22 FEB 1854, in Randolph Co., Ark., Mary, widow of Isaiah Lewis, was m. to Paul Lewis. Paul Lewis and wife Mary are involved in the settlement of estate for William Wright, dec., in Benton Co., Tenn. in 1860.
[2] Arkansas Land Patents, Randolph Co., Vol. AR0500.168, doc. #2081, NW NW Sec. 12, Twp. 21N, Range 2E.
[3] Randolph Co., Ark. Wills, Bk. 1, p. 343, dated 7 DEC 1849, proved 25 MAR 1850, witnessed by James B. White and William M. Lewis.
[4] Randolph Co., Ark. Marriages, Bk. 1, p. 72.
[5] Randolph Co., Ark. Marriages, Bk. 2, p. 442.

Goliher. He owned 80 acres in Randolph Co.[1] Enumerated on 13 AUG 1860 on Federal census for Piney Fork Twp., Lawrence Co., Ark., post office Evening Shade [family 800; page 226]. On the 1880 Federal census for Warm Springs, Ark. Children:

(10)11.   TALITHA ANN LEWIS, b. 1 SEP 1846,[2] d. April 1928, bur. Elm Springs Cem., Washington Co., Ark., m. 17 SEP 1871 in Randolph Co., Ark.[3] to Jefferson Lafayette Brown, b. 1848, d. 1939, bur. Elm Springs Cem. Enumerated in 1880 in Springdale, Ark., and 1900 in Elm Springs, Washington Co., Ark.; and 1910 and 1920 in Harmon, Washington Co., Ark. 8 children.

(10)12.   ISAIAH LEWIS, b. 1848 in Ark.

(10)13.   CATHERINE LEWIS, b. 1849 in Randolph Co., Ark.

(10)13.   WILLIAM W. LEWIS, b. 1851 in Randolph Co., Ark.

(10)14.   ANDREW LEWIS, b. 1853 in Ark.

(10)15.   PHILEMINA W. LEWIS, b. 1857 in Ark.

(10)16.   SARAH JANE LEWIS, b. 1858 in Ark.

(10)17.   MAHALA LEWIS, b. 1862 in Ark.

(10)18.   CHARLES C. LEWIS, b. 1865 in Ark.

(10)19.   LOUISA LEWIS, b. 1868 in Ark.

(10)1(10).   PERRY VINSON LEWIS, b. 17 DEC 1871 in Randolph Co., Ark., d. 24 MAY 1901, bur. Jane Cem., McDonald Co., Mo.

(10)1(11).   ISAAC LEE LEWIS, b. 14 MAR 1874 in Pocahontas, Ark., d. April 1941, Rocky Mount, McDonald Co., Mo., m. Martha Elizabeth Ross, b. 1878, d. 1965.

+ (10)2.   WILLIAM MARTIN LEWIS, b. 3 OCT 1827 in Carroll Co., Tenn., d. 3 DEC 1888 in Randolph Co., Ark., bur. Shiloh Cem., Randolph Co., m. (1) 3 AUG 1848 to LOUCINDA ELIZABETH BIGGER, *q.v.*, and m. (2) Mary Jane Hassell, and m. (3) Miss Fowler, and m. (4) to 4(10). MARTHA SARAH LEWIS, *q.v.* Granddaughter Herma Lewis Hawley thought William moved to near Hardy, Sharp Co., Ark. during the Civil War, and returned to Randolph Co., Ark.

+ (10)3.   CATHERINE C. LEWIS, b. 22 AUG 182[9], d. June 1882, bur. Shiloh Cem., m. (1) 11 AUG 1849 in Randolph Co., Ark. to 3241. JOHN G. BIGGER, *q.v.*, b. 1829, d. 1863, and m. (2) to William T. Breeding.

+ (10)4.   JOAB LEWIS (my ancestor), farmer, b. 26 DEC 1833 in Carroll Co., Tenn., d. 1886 in Randolph Co., Ark., m. (1) Martha Ann Kelly, and m. (2) in 1866 to Vehemia "Beatrice" Cavendar.

  (10)5.   MARY LEWIS, b. c.1838 in Randolph Co., Ark.

---

[1] Arkansas Land Patents, Randolph Co., Vol. AR0730.315, doc. #15266, W NE Sec. 14, Twp. 21N, Range 2E.
[2] Her tombstone is in error with birth year 1844.
[3] Randolph Co., Ark. Marriages, Bk. 2, p. 38.

(10)6.   JAMES LEWIS, b. c.1841 in Randolph Co., Ark.

(10)7.   JOHN LEWIS, b. c.1843 in Randolph Co., Ark.

(10)2. William Martin Lewis
(1827-1888)

William Martin Lewis, son of Isaiah Lewis, Jr. and Mary "Polly" Wright, was born 3 OCT 1827/8 in Carroll County, Tennessee. He was married (1) 3 AUG 1848 in Randolph County, Arkansas[1] to LOUCINDA ELIZABETH BIGGER, q.v. He was married (2) 23 JUL 1856 in Lawrence Co., Ark.[2] to Mary Jane Hassell, b. c.1839, and married (3) Miss Fowler, and married (4) by 1865 to 4(10). MARTHA SARAH LEWIS, daughter of Paul Lewis and Ann Stewart, q.v.

In the 1850, William moved his family to near Hardy, Sharp County, Arkansas where they stayed during the Civil War, and returned to Randolph County, Arkansas. In 1856, he obtained a patent for 80 acres in Randolph County.[3]

Enumerated on 11 AUG 1860 in Piney Fork Township, Lawrence County, Arkansas, post office Evening Shade [family 795; page 225], near the households of his older brother Charles W. Lewis and his younger brother Joab Lewis.

On 9 SEP 1870, the family is on the Federal census for Little Black Township, Randolph County, Arkansas [page 50]. He was a close neighbor of Paul Lewis.

On 21 JUN 1880 he was enumerated on the Federal census for Demun Township in Randolph County. That record notes his parents were both born in Kentucky.

William Martin Lewis died 3 DEC 1888 and was buried in Shiloh Baptist Cemetery in Randolph County without a headstone (added later). About 1900, widow Martha moved with her siblings to Hill County, Texas. Martha smoked a pipe.

Children of William Martin Lewis and first wife Loucinda Elizabeth Bigger:

(10)21.   JAMES NORRIS LEWIS, b. 26 AUG 1849 near Pocahontas, Randolph Co., Ark., d. 6 JAN 1931, bur. Shiloh Cem., m. 2 APR 1874 by William F. Roach in Davidson Twp. of Randolph Co.[4] to Mary Susan McIlroy, daughter of Andrew Jackson McIlroy[5] and Sarah Ann Davies, b. 12 SEP 1848 in Ark., d. 26 APR 1916, bur. Shiloh Cem. In 1894 he obtained land in Randolph Co. through the

---

[1] Randolph Co., Ark., Marriages, Bk. 1, p. 122, by Elisha Landers, M.G. of the Missionary Baptist Church, with consent of their parents.
[2] Lawrence Co., Ark. Marriages, Bk. B, p. 184.
[3] Arkansas Land Patents, Randolph Co., Vol. AR0590.328, S NW Sec. 28, Twp. 20N, Range 1E.
[4] Randolph Co., Ark. Marriages, Bk. C, p. 32.
[5] The Andrew McIlroy family was number 343 on the 1860 Federal census for Davidson Twp., Randolph Co., Ark. Andrew McIlroy and Sarah Ann Davies were bur. with their family in Ross Cem. of Randolph Co., Ark. Also see Goodspeed's *History of Northeast Arkansas*, pp. 411, 413.

Homestead Act.[1] Children:

(10)211. WILLIAM A. LEWIS, b. 4 JUL 1875, d. 22 JUL 1879 of diphtheria, bur. Shiloh Cem.

(10)212. JAMES FRANK LEWIS, b. 1 MAY 1877, d. 31 AUG 1879 of diphtheria, bur. Shiloh Cem.

(10)213. LELA J. LEWIS, b. 2 JAN 1879, d. 5 AUG 1879 of diphtheria, bur. Shiloh Cem.

(10)214. JOHN NEWTON LEWIS, b. 2 DEC 1881 in Eleven Points, Ark., d. Colorado Springs, Colo., m. 1905 to Ethel Durham. In 1917 the family moved to Oklahoma City, Okla., both bur. Evergreen Cem., Colorado Springs, Colo. Child:

(10)2141. MAXINE VALENTINE LEWIS.

(10)215. EVERETT MARION LEWIS, b. 12 FEB 1886, d. January 1931 in Tulsa, Okla., bur. Ark., m. (1) Marie Hidden, m. (2) name unknown.

(10)22. WILLIAM FRANKLIN LEWIS, merchant and farmer, hotel keeper in Maynard,[2] b. 25 DEC 1851 in Randolph Co., Ark., d. 28 AUG 1913, bur. Maynard Cem. of Randolph Co., m. 31 DEC 1874 there[3] to Eliza "Emily" M. Richardson, b. November 1855 in Mo., daughter of J.H. Richardson and Eliza A. Wadsworth who was from Pike Co., Ill.[4] William had two stores and farmed on the side. His family was enumerated in Siloam Twp., Randolph Co., on the 1900 Federal census [ED 112, S7 L16], and were recorded as family 46 in Richardson Twp. on the 1910 Federal census for Randolph Co. Children:

(10)221. JOHN J. "Jack" LEWIS, attorney, b. October 1878 in Ark., d. in Fullerton, Calif., m. in Little Rock, Ark. to Ida Long. Child:

(10)2211. Infant LEWIS, son, b./d. 11 AUG 1905, bur. Maynard Cem.

(10)222. CHARLES PERRY LEWIS, b. September 1880 in Ark., d. Carthage, Mo., m. Essie (unknown).

(10)223. ALFRED JACOB LEWIS, b. 29 AUG 1882 in Ark., d. 13 OCT 1944 near Pocahontas, Ark., bur. Masonic Cem., m. (1) 4 DEC 1906 in Randolph Co., Ark. to Ada Virginia Kibler, b. 30 MAY 1885, d. 17 SEP 1923, and m. (2) to Hassel Odom Lindsay. Children:

(10)2231. PAUL KIBLER LEWIS, b. 15 OCT 1907, d. 9 SEP 1967, bur. Masonic Cem. of Pocahontas, Ark., m. Mary E. (unknown), b. 26 NOV 1908, d. 16 JUN 1978, bur. Masonic Cem.

(10)2232. WILLIAM McDOWELL LEWIS.

(10)2233. MARY VIRGINIA LEWIS.

(10)224. GEORGE W. LEWIS, b. November 1884 in Ark., m. Ana Polen, res. Riverside, Calif. Child:

(10)2241. WOODROW W. LEWIS, b. Walnut Ridge, Ark.

---

[1] Arkansas Land Patents, Randolph Co., Vol. AR0430.34, doc. #7293, SW NE Sec. 27, Twp. 20N, Range 1W and SE NW Sec. 27, Twp. 20N, Range 1W for 80 acres..

[2] See photo of the Old Lewis Hotel at Manard, 1904, in *Randolph County, Arkansas: A Pictorial History* (Morley, Mo.: Acclaim Press), p. 152. Members of the Lewis Family pictured are "Uncle Bill" Lewis, Mrs. Emily Lewis, Ida (Mrs. J.J.) Lewis, Alf Lewis, George Lewis, Tommie Lewis, and Herma Lewis.

[3] Randolph Co., Ark., Marriages, Bk. 3, p. 58, by Rev. Hardin Smith, M.G. who was from Independence, Mo.

[4] See Goodspeed's *History of Northeast Arkansas*, p. 423.

OLD LEWIS HOTEL AT MAYNARD, 1904

The Old Lewis Hotel was operated by "Uncle Bill" Lewis and his wife at Maynard in 1904. The wooden sidewalks at the right which ran beside the hotel were known as "Lovers Lane," and led to the Ouachita Maynard Academy, which can be seen in the background. Professor Rorex was in charge of the academy at the time the picture was made. On the downstairs porch of the hotel are, standing from left: teacher Miss Alberta Bass, Cady Scates, unknown, "Uncle Bill" Lewis, Mrs. Emily Lewis, Mrs. Rorex, Professor Rorex, Ida Lewis (Mrs. J.J.), J.J. Lewis, Lantie Martin, next two unknown, Raymond Reynolds and Ben Woodall. Standing upstairs from the left are: Alf Lewis, George Lewis, unknown, Ora Ford, Bush Kirkpatrick, Tommie Lewis, Herma Lewis, Minnie Woodall, Lura Phipps and Bess Marsh. Standing at the right outside the gate is Elvis Abbott and an unknown boy. There was a big spring at the back of the hotel. Students of the academy stopped to drink at this spring and they would hide notes under the rocks. Rules were very strict, but romance always found a way. Old Ouachita Maynard Academy is said to have dispensed a "lot of learning."

Figure 31 - Old Lewis Hotel at Maynard, Arkansas, 1904

(10)225. TOMMY RUTH LEWIS, b. December 1890 in Ark., bur. Inglewood Cem., Calif., m. 24 MAR 1912 in Randolph Co.,[1] to Nathan Deaton.

(10)226. MARION LEWIS, m. Mr. Stephenson.

(10)227.-29. Four Infants.

(10)23. BENJAMIN WILEY LEWIS, b. c.1854 in either Randolph or Lawrence Co., Ark., m. 5 SEP 1884 in Randolph Co.,[2] to Vicey Wilson. He worked for the railroad, and disappeared from family contact c.1890.

---

[1] Randolph Co., Ark., Marriages, Bk. 17, p. 112.
[2] Randolph Co., Ark., Marriages, Bk. 6, p. 267.

Children of William Martin Lewis and his second wife Mary Jane Hassell:

(10)24.   THOMAS MARION LEWIS, b. 29 APR 1856 in Pocahontas, Randolph Co., Ark., d. 16 JUN 1919 in Hillsboro, Tex., and perhaps bur. in Shiloh Cem., unmarked, m. (1) 21 JAN 1875 in Randolph Co.,[1] to Frances Catherine Pratt, daughter of Matthew Young Pratt and Phoebe Jane Stout, b. 29 MAY 1856, d. 14 AUG 1894 of birth complications in Pocahontas, bur. Shiloh Cem. After Frances died he m. (2) 31 JUL 1895 in Randolph Co. to Nancy Catherine Flannery, b. 30 NOV 1870, d. 1 FEB 1959 in Dallas, Tex. Children:

(10)241.   MATTIE W. LEWIS, b. 26 NOV 1874, d. 8 SEP 1889, bur. Shiloh Cem.

(10)242.   JAMES M. LEWIS, b. 17 JUL 1876, d. 12 AUG 1878, bur. Shiloh Cem.

(10)243.   ROBERT NEWTON LEWIS, b. 11 MAR 1880 in Pocahontas, d. 22 SEP 1961 in Hillsboro, Tex., m. 20 OCT 1901 in Randolph Co. to Arkie Matilda Mondy, b. 1884, d. 1960, both bur. Peoria Cem., Hill Co., Tex.

(10)244.   FRANK LEWIS.

(10)245.   THOMAS S. LEWIS, b. 5 DEC 1882, d. 26 OCT 1918, bur. Peoria Cem.

(10)246.   EDGAR "Everett" LEWIS, b. 9 AUG 1894, d. 28 AUG 1899, bur. Shiloh Cem.

(10)247.   LAURA LEWIS, m. Jeff Brice.

(10)248.   ELLA LEWIS.

(10)249.   CHRIS E. LEWIS, b. 24 DEC 1897, d. 3 MAR 1985 in Overton, Tex.

(10)25.   MARY K. LEWIS, b. 7 FEB 1859 in Randolph Co., Ark., d. 12 FEB 1881, m. 15 FEB 1875 in Randolph Co., to James William Ford, Jr., b. 20 OCT 1855, d. 11 JAN 1895, both bur. in Shiloh Cem. Children:

(10)251.   WILLIAM M. FORD, b. October 1875, d. 22 OCT 1911, bur. Shiloh Cem.

(10)252.   MANUEL FORD, b. 22 OCT 1877, d. 28 JUL 1879, bur. Shiloh Cem.

(10)253.   HATTIE JANE FORD, b. 4 JUL 1879, d. 21 OCT 1901, m. Charles C. Warner.

(10)26.   ELIZABETH LEWIS, b. c.1860 in Ark.

(10)27.   JOAB LEWIS, b. 1861 in Ark. (age 19 in 1880), farm worker.

(10)28.   JOSEPH A. LEWIS, b. c.1863 in Lawrence Co., Ark., d. 1895 at the home of Sam McIlroy, m. 11 AUG 1889 in Randolph Co. to Sarah Ellen Pratt, b. 2 JUN 1871, d. 1897, daughter of Matthew Young Pratt and Phoebe Jane Stout. Herma (Lewis) Hawley remembered her mother died of kidney infection and was buried in Fender Cem. near O'Kean, Ark. Sarah m. (2) 20 DEC 1896 in Randolph Co. to Samuel Mullins, bur. Fender Cem. Children:

(10)281.   HERMA JANE LEWIS, b. 14 JUL 1890 at Five Mile Spring in Randolph Co., m. 28 FEB 1913 in Houston, Tex. to Joseph Robert Hawley. On the 1900 Federal census she was residing with her uncle William Franklin Lewis. Children:

(10)2811.   ROBERT LEWIS HAWLEY, b. 11 MAR 1915 in Christ Hospital of Cincinnati, Ohio.

---

[1] Randolph Co., Ark., Marriages, Bk. 3, p. 56.

(10)2812.   MARY ELIZABETH HAWLEY, b. 5 JUN 1916 at 886 Washington Ave., Memphis, Tenn.

(10)282. CLYDE LEWIS, d. inf.

Children of William Martin Lewis and his fourth wife Martha Sarah Lewis:

(10)29.   PAUL MARTIN "P.M." LEWIS, truck driver, b. 17 MAR 1865 in Ark., d. 27 DEC 1928 in Childress, Tex., m. 17 OCT 1886 in Randolph Co., to Clara Frazier, b. 5 OCT 1866 in Ark., d. 21 FEB 1952, both bur. Childress Cem. Children:

(10)291. LULA MAY LEWIS, b. 26 OCT 1887, d. 11 APR 1891, bur. Shiloh Cem.

(10)292. WILLIAM MARTIN LEWIS, b. 11 JAN 1888 in Ark., d. 11 JUN 1953, bur. Childress Cem.

(10)293. LEOTA ISABELLE LEWIS, b. 21 FEB 1890 in Ark., d. 15 DEC 1973, bur. Childress Cem.

(10)294. GROVER LEWIS, b. September 1893 in Ark.

(10)295. PEARL LEWIS, b. 13 OCT 1896 in Tex., d. 14 DEC 1986, m. William Bert Allen, Sr., b. 18 AUG 1889, d. 30 AUG 1956, both bur. Childress Cem.

(10)2(10).   AMANDA C. "Mandy" LEWIS, b. 3 OCT 1866 in Ark., d. 15 MAY 1944, m. 11 OCT 1883[1] in Randolph Co. to Samuel Benjamin McIlroy, son of John A. McIlroy and Mary Ann Jones, b. 27 OCT 1860, d. 9 FEB 1910. Children:

(10)2(10)2. I.V. McILROY, b. 1 OCT 1886, d. 12 AUG 1963.

(10)2(10)2. ESSIE McILROY, b. 2 APR 1890, d. 11 MAR 1956.

(10)2(10)3. DALLAS McILROY, b. 13 JUN 1892, d. 1965.

(10)2(10)4. LEWIS McILROY, b. 13 JUN 1892, d. 1975.

(10)2(10)5. SAMUEL BENJAMIN McILROY, b. 9 APR 1904 in Hill Co., Tex., d. 1968, m. 12 AUG 1923 to Lenna Hooker.

(10)2(11).   PHILIP H. LEWIS, b. March 1868 in Pocahontas, Ark., d. 28 DEC 1928, bur. Childress Cem., Childress, Tex., m. 19 JAN 1887 near Pocahontas to Ella Cassie Walker, b. August 1866 in Tenn., d. 1938. Shortly after 1892 they moved to Hillsboro, Hill Co., Tex. where they were enumerated on the 1900 Federal census [District 36, page 1]. Children:

(10)2(11)1. LULA MAY LEWIS, b. 26 OCT 1887 in Ark., d. 11 APR 1891 in Randolph Co., Ark.

(10)2(11)2. ERNEST SOULA LEWIS, b. 10 JUN 1889 in Ark., d. 15 DEC 1970 in Arkansas Pass, Tex., m. Minnie Elizabeth Ryan, b. 6 NOV 1889 in Prentiss, Miss., d. 18 SEP 1990 in Refugio, Tex., daughter of Charles Alonzo Ryan (1863-1952) and Cora Estella Apperson (1869-1905).

(10)2(11)3. PHILIP EARL LEWIS, b. 10 MAY 1892 in Randolph Co., Ark., d. 27 DEC 1928, m. Nell McCleland.

(10)2(11)4. DANIEL VAUGHN LEWIS, b. 1 MAR 1899 in Tex., d. 16 AUG 1944 in Chlidress, Tex., m. in Childress Co., Tex. to Anne Sheehan.

(10)2(11)5. CARL RALPH LEWIS, b. 1901 in Hillsboro, Tex., d. 1983, m. Artie (unknown).

---

[1] Another researcher has Amanda C. Lewis, b. 3 OCT 1887, m. James Franklin Bradshaw. 6 children.

(10)2(11)6.   MAZZIE ELLA LEWIS, b. 6 JUN 1902 in Hillsboro, Tex., d. 25 JAN 1965, m. (1) in Childress Co., Tex. to Rev. Gerald Sheehan (1885-1931), m. (2) 1940 to Doc Blankinship.

(10)2(12).   JEFF D. LEWIS, b. 1869 in Randolph Co., Ark.

(10)2(13).   BLANCH LEWIS (twin?), b. August 1870 in Randolph Co., Ark. Not listed in the 1880 census.

(10)2(14).   LUCY LEWIS (twin?), b. 1870 in Randolph Co., Ark., m. Mr. Taliaferro.

(10)2(15).   MARTHA "Myrtie" LEWIS, b. 13 NOV 1873 in Randolph Co., Ark., d. 15 NOV 1889, bur. Shiloh Cem.

(10)2(16).   PERRY LEWIS, b. August 1876 in Randolph Co., Ark., m. Lottie Ford, and res. in Tex. Lottie m. (2) Mr. Marshall. Children:
    (10)2(16)1.   EVERETT LEWIS.
    (10)2(16)2.   HERBERT LEWIS.
    (10)2(16)3.   HAZEL LEWIS.

(10)2(17).   ALICE E. LEWIS, b. 17 AUG 1878 in Randolph Co., Ark., d. 17 SEP 1890 in Randolph Co., bur. Shiloh Cem.

(10)21. James Lewis – Declaration

I, James Lewis, of the County of Lawrence and State of Illinois, do hereby certify that the data herein is freely and voluntarily given and for the purpose of assisting members of the family in establishing their connections.

I was born in the aforesaid County and State on October first 1858, the son of Philip Lewis and Martha Ann Black. This was the third marriage of Philip Lewis, and I was the second son born of this marriage. My full brother John B. was older than I and my younger brother, Robert, sometimes called "Bob" or [Philip], are now deceased. I am now the sole living child of Philip Lewis.

My father was the son of Isaiah Lewis and Nancy Julian who had a large family and came to this county from Kentucky and the Carolinas several years before Lawrence County was formed and settled on land bought from the government and located about three miles west of Lawrenceville and recorded in the records of the County. My father when first married went to housekeeping on his father's farm and it was not long until he purchased the farm and his parent moved near Terre Haute, Indiana. The date of the purchase of the farm may be obtained from the deed records of the County and would be the approximate date when Isaiah Lewis left it. On this farm my father lived up to near the time of the Civil War and on this farm all his children were born except the youngest, Robert who was born in Arkansas. I was the last of his children born on the farm. When I was a small child my father sold the farm, took his wife and smaller children to Arkansas to visit his brother Paul and with the possibility of locating near him but war appeared to be coming and he returned to Illinois and purchased the farm where I now live and one and one half miles west of the above mentioned farm where I was born and the farm long after the family left it was known as the Philip Lewis farm and is now known as the Barr Farm or Barr Orchard. I have lived approximately eight years on the farm where I now live.

My father Philip was born in the Carolinas in 1800, the exact day and month can be had from his monument in the White House Cemetery one and one half miles west of my home. This monument was erected about seventy years ago and I have cared for it. Byron R. Lewis, of Bridgeport, Illinois is a Trustee of the White House Cemetery and can give in information about the many members of the family buried there.

My father Philip was a twin brother of Paul Lewis and from what my father told us children had a great liking for him. The two lived but a short distance apart and were frequently together until Paul had to move on account of his wife's health. Both believevd in and preached Universalism. Perry Lewis who bought his father Paul out and lived to be more than ninety years of age knew my father as his uncle and us children as his cousins. My oldest half brother William M. Lewis and Perry Lewis were two of the ablest and best known business men of their day, were close together and knew each other as first cousins. Besides the brothers Paul and Philip who remained in the County after their father Isaiah moved away were my uncles David, Jacob, John and William. My other uncles and aunts lived near Terre Haute. Dr. Harley V. Lewis, a nephew and near my own age, gathered much information about the family many years ago and some of it is published in the county histories.

Not only am I the last of the children of Paul Lewis but I believe I am the last living grandchild of Isaiah Lewis who came here as much as one hundred and thirrty years ago.

Given under my hand and seal at Bridgeport, Illinois, this 20th day of March, 1946.

James Lewis [seal]

(10)4. **Joab Lewis**
(1833-1886)

Joab Lewis (my ancestor) was a son of Isaiah Lewis, Jr. and Mary "Polly" Wright and was born in 26 DEC 1833 in Carroll County, Tennessee. He is mentioned in the 1849 will of his father. He married first on 11 JUL 1852 by E.D. Pitman, J.P. in Randolph County, Arkansas[1] to Martha Ann Kelly, born c.1834 in Arkansas. Joab was a farmer and a Southern Baptist.

Figure 32 - Joab Lewis

He is found in the Federal census for 14 OCT 1850 in Randolph County, Arkansas, with his mother Mary, born in Kentucky, as head of household [family 153; no page number].

Enumerated on 13 AUG 1860 on the Federal census for Piney Fork Township, Lawrence County, Arkansas, post office Evening Shade [family 799; page 226], near his older brothers Charles W. Lewis and William Martin Lewis.

Joab Lewis, age 32, was married second on 24 MAY 1866 by W.J. Johnson, J.P., in Randolph County, Arkansas[2] to Vehemia "Beatrice" Cavendar, born 1845 in Tennessee. They had five children.

On the Federal census for 22 AUG 1870, Joab Lewis heads household 26 [pages 459 and 482] near Pocahontas post office in Randolph County, with wife Behamia [sic].

Joab Lewis, age 46, married third on 29 AUG 1879 in Ripley County, Missouri to Nancy Jane (Dennis) Harris, age 38,[3] and had two children.

On the Federal census for 18 JUN 1880 in Little Black Township, Randolph County, Arkansas [page 45], we find Joab Lewis with wife Nancy Jane, age 39. This entry also shows Nancy's children by former marriage: Sarah B. Harris (age 12) and Arthur Harris (age 10), and his mother Mary (Wright) Lewis, age 78, born in Kentucy. Also significant is that the family is living next door to that of Philemon and Charity Wright, the brother of Mary Wright (who married first Isaiah Lewis, Jr. and second to Paul Lewis), who was Joab's uncle. Mary Lewis's father was born in South Carolina and her mother in Virginia.

In 1886, Joab Lewis was assessed real estate taxes for the following properties: E-1/2 of the NE-1/4 in Sect. 11, Twp. 21, Range 2E (80 acres); NW-1/4 of NE-1/4 in Sect. 11, Twp. 21, Range 2E (40 acres); and the W-1/2 of NW-1/4 in Sect. 12, Twp. 21, Range 2E (80 acres).

---

[1] Randolph Co., Ark. Marriages, Bk. 1, p. 225.
[2] Randolph Co., Ark., Marriages, Bk. 2, p. 184.
[3] Ripley Co., Mo., Marriages, Bk. D, p. 169, by J.H. Witt, M.G.

Joab died after 30 JUL 1886 in Pitman, Randolph County, Arkansas. He was buried in an unmarked grave near his home on the hill off Military Road.

Children of Joab Lewis and first wife Martha Ann Kelly:

(10)41.   PERMELIA [or Pernessa] JANE LEWIS, b. 2 JUL 1853 in Lawrence Co., Ark., d. 5 DEC 1930 in Corning, Clay Co., Ark., bur. Ingram Cem. near Maynard, Randolph Co., Ark., m. (1) December 1873 in Randolph Co.[1] to James Powell, m. (2) 3 MAR 1878 as the third wife of William Perry Green Johnston (b. 3 DEC 1833, d. 26 JUL 1896, a C.S.A. soldier), and m. (3) J.W. Ingram. Children:

(10)411.   CHARLES ANDREW JOHNSTON, b. 13 FEB 1879 in Randolph Co., d. 31 MAY 1937 in Rogers, Ark., m. 1 FEB 1900 in Randolph Co. to Minnie L. Spencer, b. 27 MAR 1883, d. 22 APR 1970, both bur. Johnston Cem., Reyno, Randolph Co., Ark.

(10)412.   HORACE A. JOHNSTON, b. 1880 in Randolph Co.

(10)413.   MARY ARENA JOHNSON, b. 1882 in Randolph Co., d. 1925 in Kansas City, Wyandotte Co., Kan.

(10)414.   IDA BELLE JOHNSTON, b. 30 MAR 1884 in Randolph Co., d. 24 OCT 1873 at Rogers, Ark., m. 3 JAN 1904 in Randolph Co. to Samuel Joseph Williamson, b. 1881, d. 1966, both bur. Johnston Cem., Reyno, Ark. Child:

(10)4141.   LEON WILLIAMSON, res. Pocahontas, Ark.

(10)415.   JOAB JOHNSTON, b. 1886 in Randolph Co., Ark.

(10)416.   AMANDA ELIZABETH JOHNSTON, b. 7 AUG 1888 in Little Black Twp., Randolph Co., Ark., d. 21 DEC 1949 in Corning, Ark.

(10)417.   WINNIE LEOTA JOHNSTON, b. 1892 in Randolph Co., Ark.

(10)418.   JESSE LEMAN JOHNSTON, b. 27 APR 1893 in Randolph Co., d. FEB 1974 in Cape Girardeau, Mo.

(10)419.   PAUL MARTIN JOHNSTON, b. 24 MAR 1895 in Randolph Co., Ark.

(10)42.   WILLIAM MARTIN [or F.[2]] LEWIS (my ancestor), b. 23 MAY 1855[3] in Lawrence Co., Ark., d. in Kansas City, Mo. (perhaps by 1904), m. 2 OCT 1873 by D.A. Presley, M.G., in Columbiana Twp., Randolph Co., Ark., to SARAH ELIZABETH [Jane] ADAIR,[4] daughter of Watson M. Adair and Mary Elizabeth "Polly" Sweazea, q.v., b. 12 JUN 1853 in Randolph Co., Ark., d. 19 DEC 1935 of acute pulmonary edema at the home of her daughter Mary at 1927 Mercington in Kansas City, Mo., bur. in Grinter Chapel Cem. of Kansas City, Kan. Enumerated on the 1880 Federal census for Columbiana Twp., Randolph Co. [page 3]. The family moved to Kansas City about 1904. Children:

(10)421.   THOMAS M. LEWIS, b. 1876 in Ark. No further information.

---

[1] Randolph Co., Ark., Marriages, Bk. C, p. 13, date of marriage is blank. Filed 31 DEC 1873.
[2] Grandmother's records give William F. Lewis, but county and Federal census records often give William M. Lewis. There are muliple persons named William M. Lewis living at the same time in Randolph Co., Ark. It is William M. Lewis as a child of Joab Lewis on the 1860 Federal census for Lawrence Co., Ark.
[3] Birthdate comes from papers of Joab Lewis that are in the possession of granddaughter Helen Legate Campbell.
[4] Randolph Co., Ark., Marriages, Bk. C, p. 11, gives bride's name as Jane Adair, same date.

(10)422.   NANCY J. "Nannie" LEWIS, b. c.1878 in Ark., d. 11 JUN 1939 in Benton Co., bur. Oakley Chapel Cem., located on the south side of Route 71, 3 miles west of Rogers, Ark., m. 25 JAN 1903 in Benton Co., Ark. to Mansell Alexander Downey, of Mason Valley, b. 20 MAR 1882 in Ark., d. 9 FEB 1956 of coronary thrombosis in Hocomo, Mo., bur. Free Union Cem. of Leota, Howell Co., Mo., brother to James B. Downey and son of Eli Downey and Cynthia Philpott. Child:

(10)4221.   EULA IDELLA DOWNEY, b. 1908 in Rogers, Ark., d. 5 APR 1969 at the St. James Hotel in Philadelphia, Pa., bur. Forest Hill Cem. of Kansas City, Mo. She was a short person in appearance, and generally dressed quite nicely. When we would be seated looking through old photographs, my grandmother would talk often about her friendship and adventures with Eula Downey. Eula's funeral expenses were charged to a John P. Jordan of Philadelphia, Pa. No relation has been identified with this person. Eula's obituary in the Kansas City newspaper reads: "Miss Eula I. Downey, 60, Philadelphia, formerly of Kansas City, died Saturday in Philadelphia. She was born in Rogers, Arkansas. She was a retired accountant. She leaves a cousin Pearl Davidson, Kansas City. Graveside services will be at 11 o'clock Friday at Forest Hill cemetery here."

Figure 33 - Eula I. Downey

Figure 34 - Mansell and Nancy Downey

83

+   (10)423.   MARY ELLEN LEWIS (my ancestor), b. 18 OCT 1880 in Columbiana Twp., Randolph Co., Ark., d. 30 APR 1960 in Kansas City, Mo., bur. 2 MAY 1960 in Memorial Park Cem., Kansas City, Mo., m. 30 AUG 1900 in Fayetteville, Washington Co., Ark. to ROBERT EDWARD ALLEN, *q.v.*

Figure 35 - Betty E. Lewis Dill Miller and husband Charles E. Henning

(10)424.   BETTY ELIZABETH LEWIS, b. 12 MAR 1882 in Ark., d. 4 JUN 1966 of arterio-sclerosis in St. Mary's Hospital of Kansas City, Mo., bur. in Forest Hill Cem. She m. (1) 17 DEC 1899 in Washington Co. to Edward Dill, m. (2) Mr. Miller, and m. (3) 18 JUN 1918 by Rev. William F. Jones in Kansas City, Mo. to Charles Earl Henning, b. 19 MAY 1887 in York, Nebr., son of Edward Hickman Henning (b. 6 MAR 1854 in Halifax, Pa., d. 1 MAR 1942 at York, Nebr.) and Inez Mae Martin (d. 13 JAN 1903), d. 14 SEP 1961 of coronary thrombosis in Baptist Memorial Hospital of Kansas City, Mo. He served in the Army during World War I, worked for the Burlington Railroad, and belonged to Trinity Methodist Church, Masonic Lodge, and the Veterans of Foreign Wars. As indicated by his newspaper obituary (1961), he had brothers Edward Henning of Alhambra, Calif., Jay Henning of Cheyenne, Wyo., and a sister Fay Henning Class of Denver, Colo.[1] As a child, I attended a birthday party grandmother held for "Aunt Betty," at the Davison Family home at 8421 Blue Ridge Extension. We have several belongings in the Pippenger Family, one of which is well known as "Aunt Betty's pan." We always used this handled dutch oven to carry water when camping, and it is still used today for making large pots of soup and chili. Children:

    (10)4241.   EDWIN EARL DILL, b. 1904, d. 5 FEB 1918 of mitral insuffiency,

---

[1] Based on this information, I called (telephone (307) 634-7466), and located Mrs. Jay R. Henning of 2021 Bradley Avenue, Cheyenne WY 82001 who was the widow of Charles E. Henning's brother Jay. She indicated that the Hennings were from York, Nebr., and she was from Lodgepole, Nebr. Charles E. Henning's brothers and sisters were: Fred Henning, who had a son Dick; Ed Henning; Frank Henning who died young; and Jay Henning. Jay R. Henning of Cheyenne, Wyo. retired in 1974 from the Cheyenne Light and Power Co. after 40 years service, and died at the age of 76. I have been provided a small history of the Henning Family.

bur. Forest Hill Cem. Earl was one of grandmothers favorite cousins.

(10)4242. Daughter MILLER, res. in Little Rock, Ark.

(10)425. MEOMA ANNA LEWIS,[1] b. 7 APR 1888 in Rogers, Benton Co., Ark., d. 18 FEB 1966 in Hocomo, Howell Co., Mo., bur. Army-Union Cem. at West Plains, Hocomo Co., Mo., m. (1) 19 DEC 1904 in Monnette, Barry Co., Mo., to James Curry Ross, Sr., b. 25 FEB 1878 in Rogers, Ark., d. 15 MAR 1924 in the Veterans Hospital at Leavenworth, Kan., bur. beside his mother Elizabeth Ann Ross in Grinter Chapel Cem. near Kansas City, Kan. Ross served in the Spanish-American War, in Co. F, 1st Ark. Inf. Oma m. (2) 1 DEC 1928 in Kansas City, Mo. to Thomas Luther Rhoads, b. 12 MAR 1889, d. 13 NOV 1969 in the Veterans Hospital at Poplar Bluff, Mo., bur. Army-Union Cem. Children:

Figure 36 - John F. Fritz and wife Ina May Ross

(10)4251. INA MAY ROSS, b. 20 APR 1906 in Rogers, Ark., d. 13 MAR 1964 in Tucson, Ariz., bur. Evergreen Memorial Park, m. 15 APR 1928 to John F. Fritz, b. 25 AUG 1905, d. December 1964.

(10)42511. BOBBY FRITZ, who retired on June 30, 1985 after 34 years with the International Guard.

(10)42512. LoRITA MAY FRITZ, b. 27 AUG 1931 in Kansas City, Mo., m. 31 JAN 1948 to Harold Tucker Kennedy, Sr. Children:

(10)425121. MICHAEL J. KENNEDY, b. 17 NOV 1948, res. in D.C., d. 17 JUN 1968 in Vietnam, Republic of China.

(10)425122. ROBERT M. KENNEDY, b. 5 DEC 1950. Children:

(10)4251221. LYDIA L. KENNEDY.

(10)4251222. RICHARD KENNEDY.

(10)425123. HAROLD TUCKER KENNEDY, JR., b. 24 JUL 1953. Child:

(10)4251231. MICHAEL J. KENNEDY.

(10)42513. CAROL JOANNE FRITZ, b. 26 OCT 1939 in General Hospital of Kansas City, Mo., m. (1) 5 APR 1957 to David L. Ballard, m. (2) 21 APR 1979 to Richard R. Lane. Res. Tucson, Ariz. Children:

(10)425131. LORITA LYNN BALLARD, b. 3 FEB 1958 in Community Hospital of Smithville, Mo. Child:

(10)4251311. VENISE MARIE BALLARD FECAROTTA, b. 5 APR 1982.

---

[1] Many dates originally came from the bible record of Oma Lewis, now in the possession of her grandson Bobby Fritz, Tucson, Arizona.

(10)425132.   PATRICIA KAY BALLARD, b. 22 JUN 1959 in Community Hospital.

(10)4252.   JAMES CURRY ROSS, JR., b. 12 FEB 1909 in Rogers, Ark., d. 24 NOV 1980 in Tucson, Ariz., bur. Lakeside Cem., m. (1) 9 APR 1931 to Jean Skaggs, m. (2) Nadine (unknown).

(10)4253.   RUTH ELIZABETH ROSS, b. 13 NOV 1913 in Kansas City, Mo., d. 13 JAN 1989 of a heart attack, m. (1) 15 JUN 1929 to Eugene Wood, m. (2) 25 DEC 1938 at Ott, Ark. to Paul Henry McCormack. Children:

(10)42531.   EUGENE J. WOOD, m. Sue (unknown), res. Issaquah, Wash.

(10)42532.   JIM McCORMACK, m. Nancy (unknown), res. Gamaliel, Ark.

(10)4254.   LEWIS EARL ROSS, b. 20 NOV 1920 in Muncie, Johnson Co., Kan., d. NOV 1979 in Springfield, Mo., bur. Army-Union Cem. of Howell, Mo., married and divorced. Children:

(10)42541.   LARRY EUGENE ROSS.

(10)42542.   GARY DEAN ROSS.

(10)42543.   PATRICIA ANN ROSS.

(10)4255.   THOMASINA RHOADS, b. 16 FEB 1930 in Kansas City, Mo., m. 30 APR 1950 at West Plains, Hocomo Co., Mo. to Danny Dale Surritte. Children:

(10)42551.   BENITA DALENE SURRITTE, b. 29 JUN 1953, m. Mr. Wells.

(10)42552.   KENNETH LAYNE SURRITTE, b. 11 JUL 1956.

Figure 37 - Thomasina Rhoads

Figure 38 - Ina, Johnny and Bobby Fritz

(10)426. WILLIAM FRANKLIN "Bud" LEWIS, cabinet maker, b. 4 JUL 1888 in Ark., d. 16 AUG 1946 of acute alcoholism in Truman General Hospital of Kansas City, Mo., bur. Memorial Park Cem., m. (2) 14 MAY 1910 by Kirk Prather, probate judge, in Kansas City, Wyandotte Co., Kan., to Hattie Goodman, b. 14 OCT 1889 on a farm near Summerfield, Osage Co., Mo., daughter of David H. Goodman and Sarah Ann Keeney who were m. 1 MAY 1875 in Osage Co.

Figure 39 - Jack and Hattie Lewis, his father Bud, and granny Sarah

Bud worked for Consumer Ice Co. at 22nd and Campbell Streets in Kansas City, Mo., and then for American Ice Company at 47th and Tracy. He met his wife Hattie when he delivered ice to her house, and asked her on a date to Paramount Park. Hattie m. (2) to Ira V. Rees who is bur. at Mount Moriah Cem. Hattie d. 4 MAY 1988 in Baptist Medical Center in Kansas City, and was a member of Antioch Baptist Church. Child:

(10)4261. HERBERT LEROY "Jack" LEWIS, b. 6 JAN 1912 at his grandfather David H. Goodman's farm near Summerfield, Mo., d. 30 JUN 1989 in Kansas City, Mo., m. 18 MAR 1933 in Liberty, Clay Co., Mo. to Beryl Sanders, b. 24 SEP 1910 in Triplett, Mo., daughter of Robert Lee Sanders and Dessa Jury. Res. in Calif.

(10)427. MARTIN LUTHER "Lute" LEWIS, b. 17 NOV 1898 in Monette, Barry Co., Mo., d. 4 MAY 1959 of coronary occlusion at 4447 Bales, Kansas City, Mo., bur. Mount Olivet Cem., m. (1) 23 OCT 1916 by C.H. Clark, J.P., to Mernice A. Trapp, age 18, in Kansas City, Mo., m. (2) Mrs. Sophia Fritts, divorced,[1] m. (3) 3 JUN 1950 in Kansas City, Mo.[2] to Grace M. (Braim) Lewis, a divorcée, daughter of Eugene Braim and Elizabeth Kramer, b. 22 SEP 1906 in Quincy, Ill., d. 9 APR 1958 of cervical cancer, bur. Mount Olivet Cem. Lute Lewis had an excellent mind for remembering numbers, and operated a telegraph office for Western Union at 8th and Delaware Streets in Kansas City. His mother accidentally washed his hair in lye, so he lost it all forever. According to Beryl (Sanders) Lewis, Lute *wore a toupée[3] and looked just like Charlie McCarthy.* Some of his hair pieces were made from my great-grandmother's hair, Mary Ellen (Lewis) Allen.

---

[1] Also on file in Kansas City, Missouri is a marriage for a Martin L. Lewis to Nina Payne, on 28 JUN 1922.
[2] Jackson Co., Mo. Marriages, Bk. 175, p. 430.
[3] Grandmother notes that it was made from her mother's (Maryl Ellen Lewis) hair.

(10)43.   MARY E. "Mollie" LEWIS, b. 17 MAY 1857 in Randolph Co., Ark., m. 26 NOV 1882 in Randolph Co., Ark. to Daniel Joseph Scates, b. 1856 in Carroll Co., Tenn., d. 1900. Children:

(10)431.   JOHN ROBERT SCATES, b. 8 NOV 1884 in Ark., d. 19 JAN 1945 in Almeda, Calif.

(10)432.   MAUDE L. SCATES, b. 7 MAR 1889 in Ark., d. Oklahoma City, Okla.

(10)433.   EDGAR LEE SCATES, b. 28 FEB 1892 in Pitman, Ark., d. 3 OCT 1948 in Jackson, Mo., bur. Mount Pleasant Cem. of Pitman, Ark., raised by Birdie Lewis Legate.

(10)434.   HERBERT OLIVER SCATES, b. 17 SEP 1894 in Doniphan, Mo., d. 2 JUL 1971 in Jackson, Mo., bur. New Lorimier Cem., Cape Girardeau, Mo., m. Claire Kassell, b. 19 JAN 1897, d. 2 DEC 1995. Children:

Figure 40 - Lute and Grace Lewis

(10)4341.   JEAN ANN SCATES.

(10)4342.   MARGARET SCATES.

(10)4343.   DANA CLAIRE SCATES, b. 2 JUL 1933, d. 17 SEP 1933.

(10)434.   MARGARET SCATES, m. Charlie Mathis, res. Oklahoma City, Okla.

(10)44.   CHARLES WESLEY LEWIS, carpenter, farmer, b. 1 FEB 1859 in Randolph Co., Ark., d. 15 OCT 1936 of pulmonary edema in a hospital at Corning, Clay Co., Ark., bur. Pitman Cem., m. 2 APR 1882 in Randolph Co., Ark. to Ada Z. Cunningham, daughter of David and Amanda Cunningham of Tenn., b. 3 AUG 1866 in Tenn., d. 1933, bur. Pitman Cem. The Federal census shows his household in 1880 and 1900 in Little Black Township of Randolph Co. In 1886, he was appointed the guardian of his younger siblings Birdie and John Edward Lewis.[1]   He was mayor of Success, Ark. Children:

(10)441.   BEULAH Z. LEWIS, b. 26 SEP 1884 in Ark., d. MAR 1973 in Memphis, Tenn., m. Thomas Shannon "Huck" Reed, of Corning, Ark., b. 1877, d. 1959. 5 children.

(10)442.   JOSEPH CURTIS "Curt" LEWIS, b. 12 JAN 1886 in Pitman, Ark., d. in the late 1970s in Success, Clay Co., Ark., m. (1) Miss Smith, and m. (2) Alma Faye Bryant, b. 1895, d. APR 1987. Children:

(10)4421.   CURTIS GAGE LEWIS.

(10)4422.   JOSEPH CRAYTON LEWIS, res. Success, Ark.

(10)4423.   DOROTHY FAYE LEWIS, m. Mr. Manning.

(10)443.   MARVIN FLEMING LEWIS, b. 5 FEB 1888 in Ark., d. 11 MAR 1968 in Brownsville, Tex., m. 18 OCT 1938 in Randolph Co. to Elizabeth Catherine Baltz, res. Oklahoma City, Okla.

(10)444.   AMY I. LEWIS, b. 1 APR 1892 in Ark., d. 25 JAN 1991, m. 18 DEC 1910

---

[1] Randolph Co., Ark. Guardian Bonds, p. 417, filed 16 OCT 1886, C. Wesley Lewis principal with W.P.G. Johnston and D.F. Cunningham as securities.

in Success, Ark. to Robert Elmo Riggs, b. 1887, d. 1948, res. Sullivan, Mo., bur. Rolla Cem., Rolla, Mo.

(10)445.   LESTER LAWRENCE "Buck" LEWIS, b. 1 FEB 1898 in Pitman, Ark., d. 3 AUG 1952 in Driscoll, Tex., m. 9 OCT 1918 in Randolph Co. to Edith Greer, b. 1898, d. 1996, both bur. Rolla Cem., Rolla, Mo.

(10)45.   PAUL A. "P.A." LEWIS, b. 28 SEP 1860 in Randolph Co., Ark., d. intestate in September 1896 in Little Black Twp., Randolph Co., m. (1) 7 FEB 1886 in Randolph Co., to Henrietta Love Shemwell, bur. Pitman Cem., m. (2) in 16 DEC 1890 to Lula S. Witt, who after the death of Paul m. (2) 30 OCT 1902 in Randolph Co. to W.C. Odom. This family was found on both the 1870 [page 460] and 1880 Federal census for Little Black Twp., Randolph Co., Ark., and Paul was taxed for property there in 1890. Children:

(10)451.   HENRY "Carson" LEWIS, b. (1) to Dorenda Elizabeth Spencer, div., m. (2) (unknown), and d. in Tenn. Elizabeth d. 1946 in Randolph County Hospital, Pocahontas, Ark. Children:

  (10)4511.   WILLIAM "Bill" LEWIS, m. Esther (unknown), and he was raised by Mr. Harold Shamble.

  (10)4512.   TEULA MAE LEWIS, b. 25 JUN 1907 in Randolph Co., d. 26 FEB 2003, bur. Maynard Cem., m. 29 MAR 1929 there to Abe Wellington Mock, b. 1904, d. 1975, son of Wellington Lafayette Mock. She raised her family in Los Angeles, Calif. but moved to Bartlett, Tenn. Children:

    (10)45121.   WENDALL MOCK, res. Pocahontas, Ark.

    (10)45122.   WELLINGTON LEWIS MOCK, res. Memphis, Tenn.

  (10)4513.   WENDELL DEMPSEY LEWIS, b. 18 OCT 1912 in Supply, Ark., d. 17 JUL 1977 in Poplar Bluff, Mo., bur. 20 JUL 1977 in Ingram Cem., "PFC U.S. Army, WWII." He m. 1946 in Randolph Co. to Esther McCauley, b. 10 FEB 1917, d. 2009.

  (10)4514.   GENEVA LEWIS, m. 2 DEC 1927 to D.H. Caldwell.

(10)452.   TULA LEWIS, m. (1) in 26 OCT 1905 in Randolph Co. to Demp Powell, m. (2) (unknown), and d. c.1981 in Los Angeles, Calif.

Children of Paul Lewis and second wife Lula S. Witt:

(10)453.   MARY ETTA LEWIS, b. 8 AUG 1891, d. 7 JUL 1974, unmarried, bur. Maynard Cem. of Randolph Co., Ark.

(10)454.   BLANCHE LEWIS, b. 1893, m. 5 APR 1910 in Randolph Co. to Arlie [or Orley] Parker.

(10)455.   PAUL ANDREW LEWIS, b. 28 FEB 1897, d. 30 SEP 1975, m. 18 FEB 1921 to Bessie Louise Murphy, b. 22 JAN 1898, d. 11 NOV 1983, both bur. Maynard Cem.

(10)46.   JOSEPH H. LEWIS, b. 19 JAN 1863 in Ark. Not on the 1880 census.

(10)47.   RANSOM M. LEWIS, b. 22 MAY 1865 in Ark. Not on the 1870 census.

Children of Joab Lewis and second wife Vehemia "Beatrice" Cavendar:

(10)48. CATHERINE REBECCA[1] LEWIS, b. 12 FEB 1867 in Pitman, Randolph Co., Ark., d. 3 APR 1947 in Ripley Co., Mo., bur. Towle's Cem. near Doniphan, Ripley Co., m. John Ferdinand Ruff, b. 1849, d. 1925. She was reportedly a tall, proud woman who walked straight as if she had an iron rod down her back.[2] Children:

(10)481. JENNIE RUFF, b. 18 APR 1885 at Current View, Ark., m. Edward G. Athy.

(10)482. REDMAN RUFF, sheriff at Corning, Ark. for several years, b. 14 JAN 1894, d. 7 AUG 1955, bur. Cantwell Cem., Corning, Ark.

(10)49. GEORGE FRANKLIN LEWIS, b. 6 OCT 1868 in Little Black Twp., Randolph Co., Ark., d. 23 MAR 1899, bur. Pitman Cem., m. 31 JUL 1892 in Randolph Co. to Mary Bateman.

(10)4(10). AMANDA L. LEWIS, b. 17 JAN 1872 in Randolph Co., Ark., taught school, bur. near Doniphan, Mo.

(10)4(11). [Rev.] ROBERT L. LEWIS, b. 3 MAY 1874 in Pitman, Randolph Co., Ark., d. 28 SEP 1940 of heart failure at his home at 2609 Whittier Blvd., Whittier, Calif., bur. in Rose Hills Memorial Park Cem., m. 31 OCT 1897 in Randolph Co., to Jennie Malone. He taught school and was a judge at Piggott, Ark. before moving to Calif. Children:

(10)4(11)1. ORVILLE ROBERT LEWIS, b. 18 NOV 1901, d. 4 MAR 1986 in Orange Co., Calif., bur. Forest Lawn Memorial Park Cem.

(10)4(11)2. CYRUS JOAB LEWIS, b. 1904, res. Lake Havasu, Ariz.

(10)4(11)2. MARY MILDRED LEWIS, b. 1909.

(10)4(12). HATTIE LEWIS, b. 9 OCT 1876.

Children of Joab Lewis and third wife Nancy Jane (Dennis) Harris:

(10)4(13). BIRDIE LEWIS, b. 23 SEP 1881 in Pitman, Randolph Co., Ark., ward of her brother Charles Wesley Lewis in 1886, d. 24 MAY 1955 at her home near Maynard, bur. Pitman Cem., m. 15 NOV 1896 in Randolph Co., to Robert Hilton Legate, b. 4 JAN 1875 at Big Sandy, Tenn., d. 26 JAN 1965, bur. Pitman Cem. Enumerated in 1900 in Little Black Twp., and listed as family 153 in Little Black Twp. on the 1910 Federal census for Randolph Co. Children:

(10)4(13)1. EMERY J. LEGATE, b. 22 NOV 1897, d. 21 MAR 1989, m. 7 MAY 1920 to Zella Reeves, b. 1900, d. 1987, both bur. Pitman-Mount Pleasant Cem., Randolph Co., Ark.

(10)4(13)2. DENNIS HARLEY LEGATE, b. 29 MAY 1900 in Randolph Co., d. 1

[1] Also seen as Rebecca Catherine Lewis.
[2] Letter, 23 OCT 1988, from Helen Legate Campbell, of Murfreesboro, Tenn.

DEC 1987, bur. 3 DEC 1987 in Pitman-Mount Pleasant Cem.

(10)4(13)3. CLARENCE LEGATE, b. 1902, d. 1976.

(10)4(13)4. CHARLIE LEGATE, b. 1905, d. 1989, m. 2 DEC 1922 to Beulah Reeves, b. 1903, d. 1996, both bur. Pitman-Mount Pleasant Cem.

(10)4(13)5. LEO LEGATE, b. 1907, res. Logansport, Ind.

(10)4(13)6. HELEN LEGATE, b. 9 SEP 1918 in Randolph Co., m. Doyle Douglas Campbell, d. February 1988.[1]

(10)4(14). JOHN EDWARD LEWIS, b. 19 MAR 1883 in Pitman, Ark., ward of her brother Charles Wesley Lewis in 1886, d. 12 DEC 1951, bur. Hollywood Cem., McComb, Pike Co., Miss., m. (1) (unknown) in Doniphan, Ripley Co., Mo., and m. (2) in La. to Linda Kerlin, b. 1887, d. 1956. Children:

(10)4(14)1. J.E. LEWIS.

(10)4(14)2. RUBY LEWIS, m. Mr. Ellis, res. McComb, Miss.

(10)4(14)3. AGNES LEWIS, m. Mr. Allen, res. Lake Charles, La.

(10)4(14)4. DOROTHY LEWIS, m. Mr. Thomas, res. Mo.

(10)4(14)5. CORNELIA LEWIS, d. c.1983.

---

[1] I have a number of letters written to me by Helen (Legate) Campbell.

ADAIR FAMILY

The mother of Robert Edward Allen's wife Mary Ellen Lewis, was Sarah Elizabeth (Adair) Lewis, who was born on Sunday, 12 JUN 1853 in Randolph County, Arkansas. Sarah E. Adair was married on 2 OCT 1873 in Randolph County, Arkansas to William Martin (or F.) Lewis.[1] She was one of at least five children born to Watson M. Adair and his wife Mary Elizabeth Sweazea.

Sarah E. "Granny" Lewis died of acute pulmonary edema in Kansas City, Missouri on Thursday, 19 DEC 1935 and was buried in the Grinter Chapel Cemetery, Muncie, Kansas (now part of Kansas City, Kansas), on 21 DEC 1935.

In an undated 1984 letter I have from Grandmother Davison, she wrote that Sarah "passed away here in Kansas City at 1927 Mercington, I think Janice and Eileene were about 6 and 11 years old. The reason she was buried in Kansas was Aunt Oma and her husband Jim Ross lived out there at Grinter Heights, Kansas and his mother passed away, and he bought lots out there for her. He always said one of them was for Grandma Lewis—so he passed away and is buried in the same place."

I started obtaining clues to the ancestry of Sarah E. Adair from Randolph County, Arkansas marriage records and the Federal census. The county clerk from Randolph County was very helpful in the 1980s in sending copies documents she found that contained our family names. From year 1850 we see the following census record:

1850 Federal Census - Randolph County, Arkansas, Page 36A.

Family	Head	Age	Occupation	Birthplace
526	ADAIR, Mahala	40		Tennessee
	, Thomas	17		Arkansas
	, Sarah C.	14		Arkansas
	, George W.	7		Arkansas
	, John H.	4		Arkansas
527	SWEERZA, Johnston	19		Arkansas
530	ADAIR, Watson M.	26		Tennessee
	, Mary E.	22		Arkansas
	, Thomas W.	3		Arkansas

1860 Federal Census - Randolph County, Arkansas, Current River Township, Post Office - Cherokee Bay, Arkansas.

Family	Head	Age	Occupation	Birthplace
951	ADAIR, Huldy	50	widow/hsekpr	Tennessee
	, George W.	17		Arkansas
	, John H.	13		Arkansas
952	WATSON, Sherrod	25	farmer	Arkansas
	, Sarah	23	housekeeper	Arkansas
	, Selah A.	2		Arkansas

---

[1] Randolph Co., Ark. Marriages, Bk. C, p. 11, gives marriage as William Lewis to Miss Jane Adair, same date.

Watson M. Adair is mentioned as an heir in the estate of William Adair, administered in February 1848, who was lately a Justice of the Peace, of Randolph County, Arkansas. This William Adair, is undoubtedly the father of our Watson M. Adair.

William Adair
(c. 1805[1]-1848)

Early information about William Adair is unknown. Sometime before 1824 he was married to Mahala/Mahuldah "Huldy" Womack, born before 1810 in Tennessee, daughter of John L. and Nancy Womack, who died 15 FEB 1848 in Randolph County, Arkansas. Mahala's sister Lucy Ann Womack was married 21 MAR 1840 in Randolph County to Peter Watson. This connection may explain the name of William's eldest son Watson M. Adair. John L. Womack patented land in Lawrence County, Arkansas on 1 NOV 1834 in what is today in Clay County. He had a brother Larkin Womack and was perhaps a son of David Womack.

No Adair families are found in Lawrence District of Arkansas Territory for the 1830 Federal census. There is a William Adair family in 1830 for White County, Tennessee, but the parents appear too old to be William and Huldy. Our William Adair is shown on the 1831 [page 7], 1833 [age 13], 1834 [age 11], and 1835 [page 14] tax lists for Current River Township of Lawrence County, Arkansas. Even though William Adair is shown on the tax lists he is not found in deed records for acquiring any land. He may have been a renter during these times. In 1835, part of Lawrence County[2] was used to form Randolph County. Randolph County deeds begin in 1836. On 16 AUG 1838, William Adair patented land in Randolph County.

It is not known whether William Adair was related to Margaret Jane Adair, born c.1790 in South Carolina, who died 28 JUN 1860 in Randolph County, and was married c.1808 in Tennessee to Elias F. McNabb, born c.1785 in South Carolina, and died 23 JUN 1857. These was a proximity between the Adair and McNabb families for some time. One claim is that Margaret was a daughter of James Adair who was born 15 MAY 1760 in Duncan's Creek, Laurens County, South Carolina, and was married to Eleanor Holland Erwin (1760-1796).

On 17 JAN 1839, William Adair and wife Huldah, of Randolph County, sold to Robert Smith of Lawrence County, Arkansas, for $67.95, 40 acres in Randolph County, being the NW-1/4 of the SW-1/4 of Section 27 in Township 20 North of 3 East.[3] Randolph Couunty court records in the 1840s, show William Adair as a justice of the peace.

William Adair died 16 FEB 1848 in Randolph County, Arkansas without making a will. His grave is in the Nelson-Clay Family Cemetery of Reyno, Clay County, Arkansas.[4] On 16 FEB 1848, William Jarrett was appointed in Randolph County to administer William Adair's

---

[1] Many researchers attribute his birth year as 1810, but that seems highly likely if he is to be fathering children as early as 1824.
[2] In 1815, Lawrence Co. was formed from part of New Madrid Co., Mo., which was an original district in Mo. since 1812.
[3] Randolph Co., Ark. Deeds, Bk. A, p. 127.
[4] Located on County Road 107 (south of County Road 114), south of Datto, Ark. and east of Reyno, Ark.

estate. Jarrett informed the court that Adair's estate was worth more than $300.

The 1850 [page 36A] and 1860 Federal census for Randolph County, Arkansas show a different name for the wife of William Adair, but they may indeed be the same person. We see her as what appears to be "Huldy," and also as "Mahuldah." She is head of household on the 1860 Federal census for Current River Township of Randolph County, Arkansas [family 951, page 364].

A Huldy Adair died 18 DEC 1861 in Randolph County, Arkansas. Her estate was administered by her son-in-law Sherrod W. Watson who was bonded 11 JAN 1862 in Randolph County Court.[1]

Children of William Adair and wife Mahala Womack:

+   1.   WATSON M. ADAIR, b. 1824 in Tenn., d. before 1858, probably in Randolph Co., Ark., m. 13 FEB 1845 in Randolph Co., Ark.[2] to 4. MARY ELIZABETH "Polly" SWEAZEA, b. 1824, d. JAN 1868 in Randolph Co., *q.v.*

    2.   MARY LEE ADAIR, b. 1825 in Tenn., perhaps White Co., m. 11 APR 1844 in Randolph Co., Ark.[3] by Isham Jones, J.P., to Hezekiah B. Copeland, b. 1813 in Tenn., d. 1861. Enumerated 21 AUG 1850 on Federal census for Bates Co., Mo. [District 6, page 232]. On 15 JAN 1858 in Warsaw, Mo., Hezekiah B. Copeland of Vernon Co., Mo. was granted a warrant for 40 acres in Vernon Co. Children:
         21.   DAVID COPELAND, b. 1845 in Ark.
         22.   RHODA COPELAND, b. 1847 in Ark.
         23.   REBECCA JANE COPELAND, b. 1 FEB 1848 in Ark., d. 15 JUL 1905, m. 22 JAN 1867 in Benton Co., Ark. to Jesse Newton Adams, b. 6 MAR 1845 in Tenn., d. 15 JUL 1905 in Arkansas City, Ark.
         24.   SARAH COPELAND, b. 1849 in Mo.

---

[1] Randolph Co., Ark. Probate Records, Vol. 6, pp. 90-1, bond filed 25 JAN 1862.
[2] Randolph Co., Ark. Marriages, Bk. 1, p. 67.
[3] Randolph Co., Ark. Marriages, Bk. 1, p. 58.

Figure 41 - Benjamin Franklin Copeland Family

25. BENJAMIN FRANKLIN COPELAND [photo], b. 3 JAN 1854 in Mo., d. 11 SEP 1930 of heart disease in Hittle, Tazewell Co., Ill., m. Mary Catherine Wilson, b. 14 MAR 1860, d. 21 OCT 1926; both bur. Sunnyside Cem., Caney, Montgomery Co., Kan. 8 children.

3. THOMAS ADAIR, b. c.1834 in Lawrence Co., Ark., alive in 1868, bur. Nelson-Clay Cem., Reyno, Clay Co., Mo.

4. SARAH CAROLINE ADAIR, b. 11 MAY 1837[1] in Randolph Co., Ark., d. 18 MAY 1876 in Clay Co., Ark., bur. Richwoods Cem. near Corning, Clay Co., m. (1) 20 DEC 1857 in Randolph Co., Ark.[2] by James M. Reynolds, J.P., to Sherad W. Watson, b. 1835 at Reyno, Ark., d. 13 DEC 1862, son of Peter Watson who m. (2) in 1840 to Lucy Ann Womack. Enumerated on the 1850 Federal census for Current River Twp. Enumerated on the 1860 Federal census for Current River Twp. [family 952; page 364]. Sarah m. (2) 20 MAR 1864 to Robert Newton Vinson, b. 3 MAR 1845, d. 27 DEC 1904, son of Elijah Vinson, bur. Thompson Cem., Randolph Co. Children:

41. CELIE ANN WATSON, b. 19 SEP 1858 in Ark., d. after 1882.

42. GEORGE WASHINGTON SHERAD WATSON

Figure 42 - Robert N. Vinson

---

[1] Her tombstone gives an incorrect birth date of 28 OCT 1826.
[2] Randolph Co., Ark. Marriages, Bk. 1, p. 302.

[photo], b. 13 DEC 1862 in Randolph Co., Ark., d. 14 OCT 1942 in Heelstring, Clay Co., Ark., m. 4 AUG 1895 to Ursley Almeda Sharpe, b. 1859, d. 1904. Child:

421.　MAE OMA WATSON, b. 1900, d. 1927.

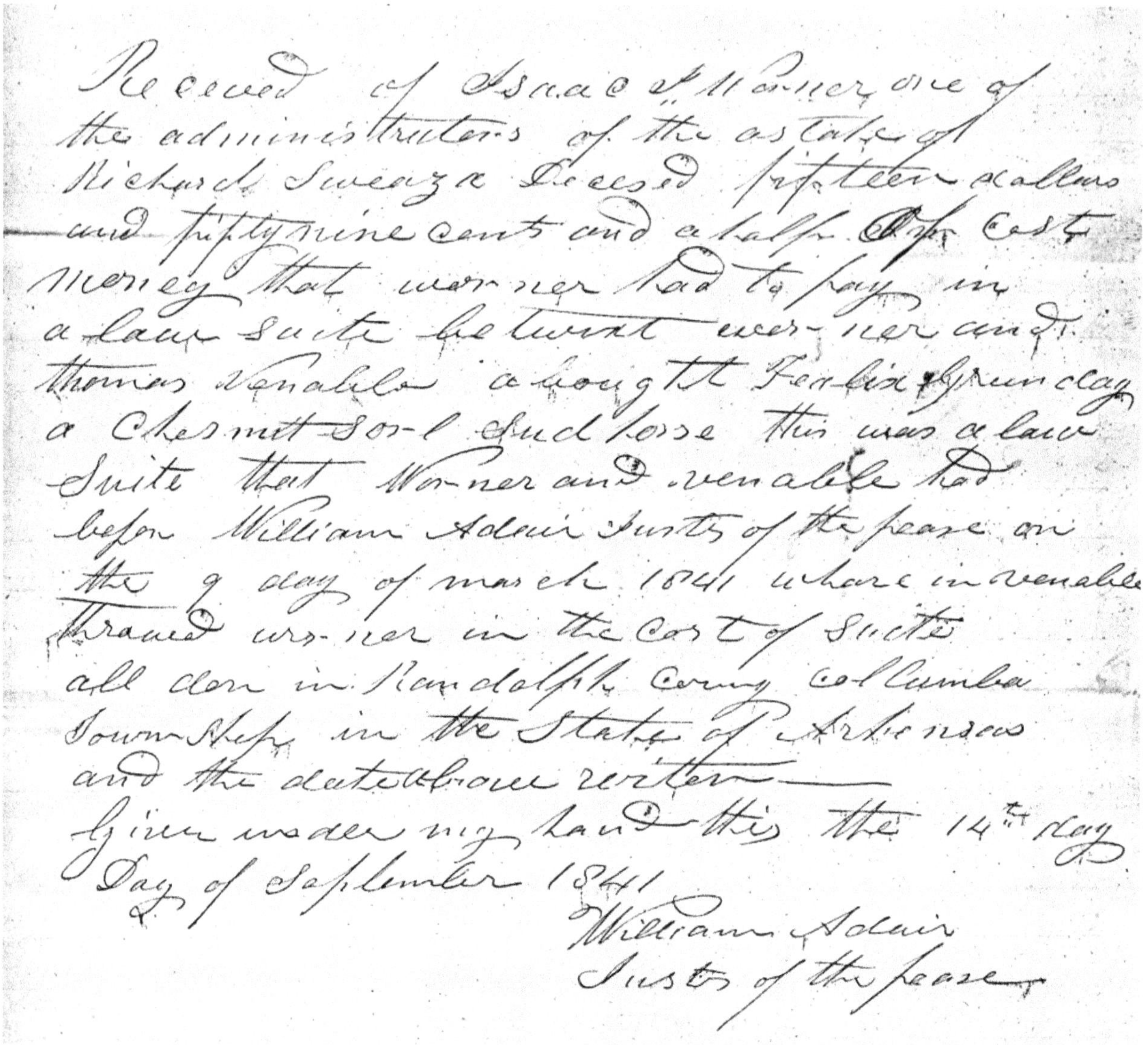

Figure 43 - Receipt from the estate papers of Richard Sweaza, 1841, showing signature of William Adair, J.P.

5.　GEORGE W. ADAIR, farmer, b. c.1845 in Arkansas. Enumerated on the Federal census for 28 JUN 1860 in Current River Twp., Randolph Co., Ark. Alive in 1862, perhaps bur. in Nelson-Clay Cem., Reyno, Clay Co., Mo.

6. JOHN H. ADAIR, b. 5 MAR 1847 in Arkansas, is probably the same John H. Adair who was m. Sun., 19 MAR 1871 in Randolph Co., Ark.[1] by Elder Peter Watson to Lucy Wood. He is listed as living alone on the 1870 Federal census for Randolph Co. [family 192, page 427], age 25, a farmer with real estate valued at $500, and personal property valued at $350. There are no other Adair families listed in this county for the 1870 Federal census.

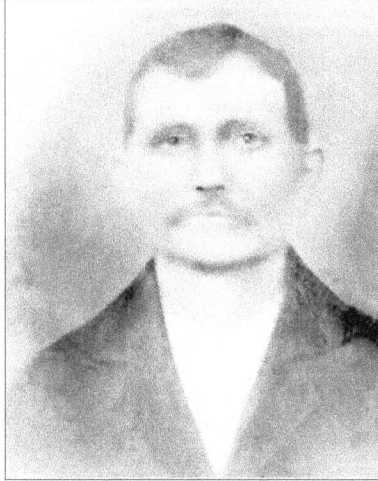

Figure 44 - George W.S. Watson

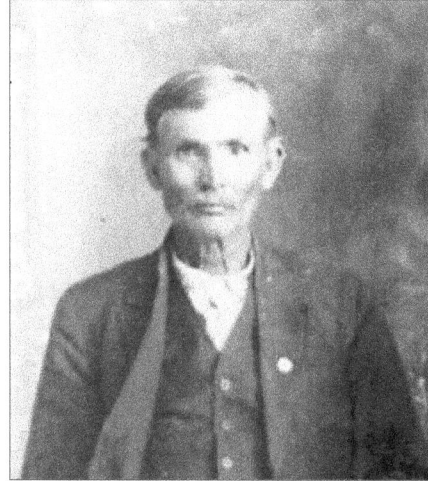

Figure 45 - George W.S. Watson

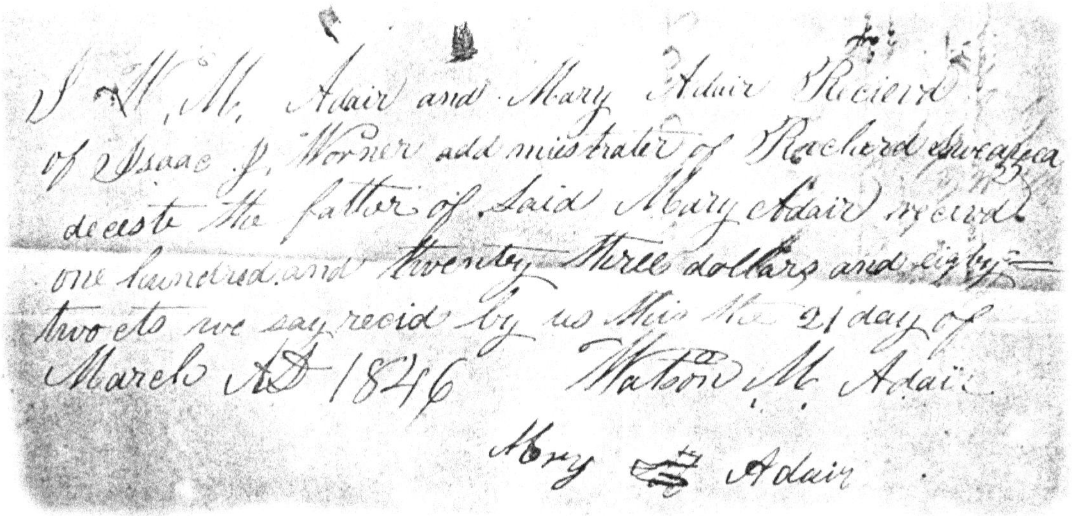

I W. M. Adair and Mary Adair Recieved
of Isaac J. Worner addministrater of Rachard Sweazea
deceste the father of said Mary Adair received
one hundred and twenty three dollars and eighty
two cts we say recd by us this the 21 day of
March AD 1846 Watson M. Adair
Mary her mark Adair

Figure 46 - Receipt from the estate papers of Richard Sweazea, 1846, showing signatures of Watson M. and Mary Adair

[1] Randolph Co., Ark. Marriages, Bk. 2, p. 450.

1. Watson M. Adair
(1824-c.1858)

Watson M. Adair (my ancestor), son of William Adair and Mahala Womack, was born in 1824 in Tennessee, perhaps White County. He died some time before 1858, probably in Randolph County, Arkansas, and was buried in the Nelson-Clay Family Cemetery, at Reyno, Clay County, Arkansas.

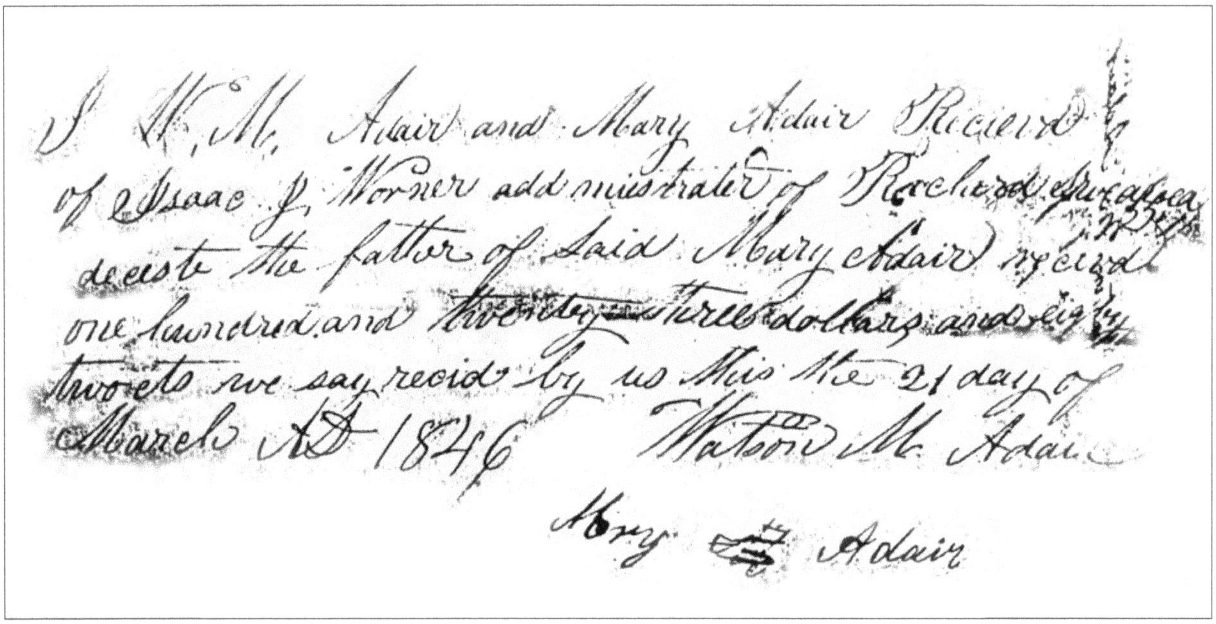
I W. M. Adair and Mary Adair Recieved of Isaac J. Worner addministrator of Richard Sweazea decest the father of said Mary Adair received one hundred and twenty three dollars and sixty two cts we say recid by us this the 21 day of March AD 1846 Watson M. Adair

Mary (her mark) Adair

Figure 47 - Receipt signed by Watson M. and Mary Adair in the estate of Richard Sweazea, 1846

Watson was married 13 FEB 1845 in Randolph County, Arkansas[1] by Mordicai Hallaburton, Minister of the Gospel, Sect of the United Baptists, to 4. MARY ELIZABETH SWEAZEA, *q.v.*, born 1824 in Arkansas, who died in January 1868 in Randolph County. In July 1849, Watson M. Adair and wife Mary sold multiple parcels totaling 160 acres in Randolph County, and a lot on Broadway Street in the town of Pocahontas, to Randolph Cook.[2]

The couple is enumerated on the 1850 Federal census for Randolph County [family 53; page 36B]. Widow Mary was married second on 27 JUN 1858 at the residence of Mary Adair in Randolph County to Joseph Vinson,[3] born in 1839, from whom she was divorced in 1867 in Randolph County.

Mary Adair died in 1871, and a bond was granted 14 OCT 1871 to Thomas W. Adair to

[1] Randolph Co., Ark. Marriages, Bk. 1, p. 67.

[2] Randolph Co., Ark. Deeds, Bk. C, p. 177, filed 18 JUL 1849; being the SW¼ of the SW¼ of Section 27, and the west half of the SE¼ of Section 27, also the NW¼ of the NW¼ of Section 34, all in Township 30, north of the base lines in Range 1 East of the 5th principal meridian, all containing 160 acres; also a lot of ground in the town of Pocahontas that is described on the town plat as Lot 5 in Block 34 east of Broadway Street, and bounded on the north by Lot 4 in the said block and on the east by Marr Street, on the south by Lot 6 and on the west by Lot 2 in the said block, which lot was conveyed by the county Commissioners to Richard Sweazea by deed of 15 OCT 1839. That Sweazea died leaving seven children and heirs at law: Deborah, Mary, Caroline, James, Nancy Jane, Richard and Francis Marion, of whom Mary, wife of Watson M. Adair, is one.

[3] Randolph Co., Ark. Marriages, Bk. 1, p. 320, by Martin Grider, J.P. Joseph Vinson was a minor when he was married here, so consent was obtained from his mother as his only living parent.

administer her estate.[1] One of the appraisers was William M. Lewis.

Children of Watson M. Adair and Mary Elizabeth Sweazea:[2]

11. THOMAS W. ADAIR, b. 23 FEB 1847 in Randolph Co., Ark., d. 26 MAR 1878, bur. Bigger Cem., located on old Bellview Rd., about 5 miles north of Pocahontas, Randolph Co., Ark. He served in Reeve's Cavalry from June 1863 to June 1865 in the C.S.A., and widow Mary was granted a pension of $100 a month.[3] Thomas W. Adair was m. 17 MAR 1867 at the residence of Allis Benson in Randolph Co., Ark.[4] to Mary Ellen Revil/Bevil, b. 9 SEP 1848 in Tenn., d. 31 JAN 1927, bur. Masonic Cem. Ellen heads a household on the Federal census for 26 JUN 1880 in Demun Twp., Randolph Co. [family #212; page 32]. Enumerated 18 JUN 1900 in Pocahontas, Ark., showing only 4 of her 7 children are alive. Children:

111. THOMAS ADAIR, b. 1868 in Ark.
112. ISABELLE ADAIR, b. 1870 in Ark.
113. RICHARD ADAIR, b. 1870 in Ark.
114. MINNIE ADAIR, b. 1872 in Ark., m. 4 MAY 1890 in Randolph Co. to Thomas S. Rowen, b. 1861.
115. JOHN WILLIAM ADAIR, carpenter, b. 6 APR 1874 in Ark., d. 13 FEB 1957 in Sedalia, Mo., bur. Masonic Cem.
116. FRANK E. ADAIR, b. December 1874 in Ark., d. 2 JUN 1965, bur. Masonic Cem.
117. BERTHA G. ADAIR, b. July 1882 in Ark.

12. MATILDA JANE ADAIR, b. JAN 1850 in Ark., apparently died as an infant, for we do not see that name again in this family.

+ 13. SARAH ELIZABETH ADAIR (my ancestor), b. 12 JUN 1853 in Randolph Co., Ark., m. 2 OCT 1873 in Randolph Co. to (10)42. WILLIAM MARTIN (or F.) LEWIS, *q.v.*

14. JAMES M. ADAIR, farmer, b. January 1855 in Ark., m. 5 JAN 1874 in Randolph

Figure 48 - Sarah E. Adair, "Granny Lewis"

---

[1] Randolph Co., Ark. Administrator Bonds, p. 406, dated filed 17 OCT 1871, with Richard Sweeza and Samson Golaher as securities.
[2] From the estate papers of Mary Adair, deceased, c. 1871, the administrator was son Thomas W. Adair.
[3] Confederate Pensions, application #24312 of Mary E. Adair, widow of Thomas W. Adair, late of Randolph Co., Ark.
[4] Randolph Co., Ark. Marriages, Bk. 1, p. 237.

Co.[1] to [Winiford] Mary Windfordham, b. May 1863 in Ark. Enumerated on the Federal census for 18 JUN 1880 in Demun Twp., Randolph Co. [family #171; page 25], and 1 JUN 1900 in Demun Twp., renting his farm. Res. in Manna, Ark. Children:

141. MARY J. "Mollie" ADAIR, b. January 1875 in Ark., m. 15 APR 1905 in Randolph Co. to Arthur Samuel Moore. 3 children.

142. JOHN W. ADAIR, b. 5 FEB 1879 in Ark., d. 6 JAN 1901, bur. Clearview Cem. of Pocahontas, Randolph Co., Ark.

143. PETER M. ADAIR, b. April 1883 in Ark.

144. THOMAS ADAIR, b. February 1885 in Ark.

145. JOSEPH ADAIR, b. May 1890 in Ark., m. 3 DEC 1910 to Belle Hackworth, b. 1891.

146. JAMES ADAIR, b. January 1895 in Ark.

147. BURLEY ADAIR, b. 28 FEB 1897 in Ark., d. 6 DEC 1897, bur. Clearview Cem.

148. LELIA ADAIR, b. March 1899 in Ark., m. 5 SEP 1917 in Lawrence Co., Ark. to Homer Tinker.

15. SUSAN VINSON, b. c.1859 in Ark. It appears that on 2 NOV 1872 Sarah Adair and Susan Vinson were not of age when both parents were deceased, and came under the guardianship of a their uncle Richard Sweazea.[2]

---

[1] Randolph Co., Ark. Marriages, Bk. 3, p. 16.
[2] Randolph Co., Ark. Guardian Bonds, p. 213, granted to Richard Sweeza [sic].

SWEAZEA FAMILY

The parents of Sarah Elizabeth (Adair) Lewis were Watson M. Adair and Mary Elizabeth Sweazea, daughter of Richard Sweazea, who were married in Randolph County, Arkansas. The spelling or origin of the surname is uncertain, yet in a sketch which appears in a book on northeastern Arkansas, we learn that Richard Sweazea may be of French origin.[1]

The Sweazea Family of Arkansas may have come from Elbert County, Georgia. Elbert County was formed in 1790 from Wilkes County, Georgia. Lineage:

A.   MATHIAS SWAZY (Swayze), b. 1699 in Southhold, Suffulk Co., N.Y., m. (1) Eunice Case, daughter of Theophilus Case and Hannah Young, d. 22 DEC 1725, and he m. (2) 1 JUL 1728 to Elizabeth Tinker. Son:

B.   MATHIAS SWEEZEY, SR., b. 1725 in New York, he was involved in a suit of Nicholas Albertson, millwright, and declared bankrupt in 1768[2] in Bethlehem Twp., Hunterdon Co., N.J.,[3] d. after 1792 in Cumberland Co., Pa., m. c.1745 in Hunterdon Co., N.J. to Sarah (unknown). In 1787, he sold his land in Cumberland Co., Pa. to his son John Sweezey. At least 4 children, of whom:

C.   MATHIAS SWEEZEY, JR., second son, b. 1750 in Morris Co., N.J., served in the Revolutionary War, d. 8 JUL 1786 in a duel with John Earl Baylis in Rutherford Co., N.C., m. (1) to Nancy Jane Coulter, b. 1750 in Rye Twp., Cumberland Co., Pa., d. c.1783 in Rutherford Co., N.C., dau. of Richard Coulter. Mathias m. (2) to Rachel Burnett, dau. of Joseph Burnett. The Sweezey Family moved with the Coulter Family to Wilkes Co., Ga., then Elbert Co., Ga., then the Coulter Family moved on to Blount Co., Tenn. by the early 1800s. Son:

D.   RICHARD SWEAZEA, b. c.1770 in Rye Twp., Cumberland Co., Pa., d. 1828 in Wayne Co., Mo., m. c.1790 to Jane Johnston, b. 1776, d. 8 SEP 1832 in Lawrence Co., Ark. Children:
   1. Mary "Polly" Sweazea, b. c.1790[4] in Elbert Co., Ga., d. 1 JAN 1843, m. 11. JAMES [W.] BIGGER [later Biggar], *q.v.*, bur. Shelbyville, Tex.
   2. Margaret Sweazea, b. c.1792 in Elbert Co., Ga., d. Lawrence Co., Ark., m. William Balance.
   3. William G. Sweazea, b. c.1795 in Elbert Co., Ga., d. 11 OCT 1840 in Randolph Co., Ark., m. (unknown). 4 children.
   4. Nancy Sweazea, b. c.1798, m. 17 MAY 1808 in Roane Co., Tenn. to Benjamin or Adam Draper.
   5. RICHARD G. [or J.] SWEAZEA (my ancestor), b. 1795 in Elbert Co., Ga., m. 113. MATILDA CAROLINE BIGGER, *q.v.*
   6. John M. Sweazea, b. 1805 in Elbert Co., Ga., d. bef. 1870 in Bollinger Co., Mo., m.

---

[1] *Biographical and Historical Memoirs of Northeast Arkansas, Illustrated.* (Chicago, Ill.: The Goodspeed Publishing Company, 1889), page 434.
[2] *The Pennsylvania Journal*, 19 MAY 1768.
[3] *Genealogical Magazine of New Jersey*, Vol. 67 No. 1.
[4] The dual tombstone for her and her husband in Bigger Cem., Shelbyville, Tex. appears to be a modern one, and thus the dates are subject to argument. It reads: BIGGAR / JAMES / 1775-1836. / MARY S. / 1785-1843.

Christina (unknown). 9 children.

7. Johnston Sweazea, b. 4 FEB 1806, d. 1846,[1] m. 1 MAY 1834 in Lawrence Co., Ark. to Polly Eleanor Balance.

8. Rebecca Sweazea, b. 1808 in Elbert Co., Ga., d. Wayne Co., Mo., m. (1) Johnston Solomon Sharp, m. (2) Levi P. Richardson.

E. RICHARD G. SWEAZEA, son of Richard Sweazea and Jane Johnston, born 20 JAN 1801 in Elberton, Georgia.

The division of the estate of Jane Sweeza/Swezee was made in 1832 in Lawrence County, Arkansas, among the heirs: William Balance (husband of Margaret), Nancy Draper, Rebecca Sharp, and William, John, Richard and Johnston Swezee.[2]

Richard G. Sweazea
(1795-1840)

Richard G. [or J.] Sweazea was born c.1795, perhaps in Elbert County, Georgia, and was a son of Richard Sweazea and Jane Johnston. He was married to MATILDA CAROLINE BIGGER, *q.v.*, on 15 JAN 1821, perhaps in Wayne County, Missouri. She was a daughter of James W. Bigger [later Biggar], born 1 JAN 1770 in Tennessee who died 1 MAR 1833 in Shelbyville, Texas.[3]

In the 1830 U.S. Census for Columbia Township, Lawrence County, Arkansas we see a Richard Sweezer on page 5. This is no doubt our ancestor. Randolph County was created from Lawrence County on 29 OCT 1835.

On 16 AUG 1838, a Richard Sweazea obtained a land patent for 40 acres in Randolph County, Arkansas.[4] On 15 OCT 1839, Richard Sweazea purchased from the Commissioners of Randolph County, Lot 5 in Block 34 west of Broadway in the town of Pocahontas.[5] Many records show his name as Richard Sweeza.

Richard died 11 OCT 1840 without making a will. In November 1840, Matilda Sweazea, widow of Richard, and Isaac J. Warner, heir-at-law, estimated that Richard Sweazea's estate was worth about $3,000. In today's money this would be at least $100,000. A bond for Matilda and Isaac as administrators was dated 30 OCT 1840 and witnessed by

---

[1] On 25 SEP 1846, Joseph Spikes is bonded as the administrator of the estate of Johnston Sweazea, dec., in Randolph Co., Ark.
[2] Lawrence Co., Ark. Probate and Wills, 1817-1834, p. 182, on 8 SEP 1832, Richard Sweazea and Johnson Sweazea applied for letters of administration of her estate and reported she had lately died without making a will.
[3] Daughter of James W. Bigger [later Biggar] who died in 1833 in Shelbyville, Tex., bur. in Bigger Cemetery there. There are two signs: Biggar (on the gate), and Biggers Cemetery on a sign post. Sources (1) Freda Roberts, 4112 NW 15th, Oklahoma City OK 73107, (2) Thomas F. Bigger, Joaquim, Texas. It appears that this James Bigger was a son of William C. Bigger who d. ante 1790, a veteran sergeant of the VA Continental Line in the Rev. War, captured at Charleston and d. while being held prisoner of war. However, according to another source: [Margie G. Brown, *Genealogical Abstracts Revolutionary War Veterans, Scrip Act 1852* (Decorah: The Anundsen Publishing Co., 1990), p. 196],James was one of ten children of John Bigger, Sr. who d. testate 1814 in Prince Edward Co., and wife Elizabeth (perhaps Cary). John Bigger's will dated 6 JAN 1814, prov. 20 JUN 1814 in Prince Edward Co., Will Book 4, p. 386.
[4] Arkansas Land Patents, Randolph Co., Vol. AR0490.266, doc. #169.
[5] Randolph Co., Ark. Deeds, Bk. A, p. 190, filed 15 DEC 1839. Commissioners appear to be Daniel List, G.B. Croft and George W. Drope. Ten years later, and after Richard Sweazea's death, daughter and heir Mary, wife of Watson M. Adair, sold this to Randolph Cook.

Ambrose Bigger and Johnston Sweazea. Apparently Warner died and left Sweazea's estate unsettled, so in April 1848, William Cook was appointed administrator.[1]

After Richard Sweazea's death, his widow Matilda Sweazea was married second on 27 NOV 1844 by William Adair, J.P., to Randolph Cook, *q.v.*, possibly at the residence of Matilda Sweazea in Randolph County, Arkansas.[2]

On 16 OCT 1844, James N. Bigger was appointed guardian of Mary E. (over age 14), Frances M. (under 21 years), Matilda (under age 21), Richard (under age 21) and Nancy Jane (under age 21) by Probate Judge James Martin in Randolph County, Arkansas. William Cook was discharged as administrator *de bonis non* of Richard Sweazea in July 1848.[3]

Randolph Cook was appointed guardian of Nancy J., Richard and Frances M. Sweazy on 24 JUL 1854. Richard Sweazea (Jr.) was appointed guardian of Sarah Adair and Susan Vinson,[4] heirs-at-law of Mary Vinson deceased, on 2 NOV 1872. Sarah and Susan signed and had requested his guardianship on 30 OCT 1872 in the Probate Court of Randolph County, Arkansas (statement). This Richard Sweazea signed as witness to papers of administration where Thomas W. Adair was appointed administrator of the estate of Mary Adair, deceased, at Pocahontas, Arkansas on 14 OCT 1871.

One very helpful note found among the administration papers was a receipt whereby Watson M. Adair claimed he and Mary Adair received $123.82 from Isaac J. Warner, administrator of the estate of Richard Sweazea, deceased, the <u>father of said Mary Adair</u>.

Children of Richard G. Sweazea and Matilda Caroline Bigger:

1. MARY E. "Polly" SWEAZEA, b. 1817, d. 1852, m. 17 JUN 1847 by William Adair, J.P., in Randolph Co., Ark. to William S. Fericks/Fedricks/Fredric/Federicks, farmer, b. 1820, d. 1897. In October 1847, Mary Fredericks was summoned into Randolph Co. Court to testify in the suit of William Adair versus Joseph Spikes, Administrator of her uncle Johnston Sweazea. They are enumerated on the Federal census of 18 AUG 1860 in Little Black Twp., Randolph Co., Ark. Widower William S. Fedricks m. (2) in 4 MAR 1862 in Randolph Co. to Mary E. Downey, and m. (3) 13 NOV 1863 in Randolph Co. to Christina Jones. Children:
   11. WILLIAM N. FEDRICKS, b. 1851 in Ark.
   12. RICHARD B. FEDRICKS.

2. JAMES SWEAZEA, b. and d. inf. 1821, perhaps in Wayne Co., Mo.

3. DEBORAH SWEAZEA, b. 20 SEP 1823, d. 1860, m. 1840[5] in Randolph Co., Ark.

---

[1] Randolph Co., Ark. Wills, Bk. 1, p. 299, bond dated 12 APR 1848.
[2] Randolph Co., Ark. Marriages, Bk. A, p. 73.
[3] Randolph Co., Ark. Probate Records, Vol. 1, p. 419, dated 1 JUL 1848, suit of James G. Russell, surviving administrator of James Bigger against William Cook, administrator *de bonis non* of Richard Sweazea, the court orders that Cook is discharged.
[4] I propose Mary Adair remarried Vinson in 1858.
[5] Statement certified by William Adair, says "I. Russell married Deborah Sweazea and Isaac J. Warner in 1840," filed 1843. Per Randolph Co., Ark. Wills, Bk. 1, p. 44, she was married by 3 NOV 1840.

to Isaac J. Warner, b. 1814 in Mo. Enumerated on the 1850 Federal census for Columbia Twp., Randolph Co., Ark. Children:

31.   MARY J. WARNER, b. 1843 in Ark.

32.   JAMES R. WARNER, b. 1844 in Ark.

33.   JOHN S. WARNER, b. 1850 in Ark., m. 20 DEC 1874 in Randolph Co. to America E. Hurn.

+ 4.   MARY ELIZABETH SWEAZEA (my ancestor), b. 1824 in Ark., appointed as a ward of James N. Bigger on 16 OCT 1844 in Randolph Co., d. JAN 1868, m. (1) 13 FEB 1845 in Randolph Co., Ark. to 1. WATSON M. ADAIR, *q.v.*, and m. (2) 1858 to Joseph Vinson, div.

5.   JOHNSTON A. SWEAZEA, b. 4 DEC 1825, d. June 1858 in Randolph Co.,[1] m. (1) 31 JAN 1847 in Randolph Co., Ark. to Margaret Jarrett.[2] He m. (2) 30 OCT 1853 to Jane Bridges, sister of Wiley J. Bridges who d. 17 OCT 1856 in Randolph Co. I find a Johnston A. Sweezy, age 19, living with Henry Jarrett, age 22, and next door to the family of Mahala Adair in Randolph Co. on the 1850 census [family #527; page 36]. On 10 NOV 1853, Mary Adair sold to J.A. Sweazea her rights to land in Section 23 of Randolph Co., Ark.

6.   MATILDA CAROLINE SWEAZEA, b. between 1826-1830, d. 1859, appointed as a ward of James N. Bigger on 16 OCT 1844 in Randolph Co.,[3] m. 31 OCT 1844 at "the bride's home" in Columbia Twp., Randolph Co., Ark. by Rev. William Adair,[4] to William Cook. They are enumerated on the Federal census for 14 SEP 1860 in Demun Twp., Randolph Co., Ark. Children:

61.   MARTHA P. COOK, b. 1847 in Ark.

62.   DELIA [or Deborah] J. COOK, b. 1850 in Ark.

63.   WILLIAM R. COOK, b. 1853 in Ark., d. 1885 of pneumonia. He left minor heirs had appointed James T. Ellis their guardian in 1887:[5]

    631.   JAMES M. COOK, b. after 1873.

    632.   WILLIAM DALLAS COOK, b. after 1873.

64.   JAMES COOK, b. 1855 in Ark., m. 3 MAR 1888 in Randolph Co. to Sarah "Sallie" Vinson, b. 1865 in Ark. Enumerated on the 1900 Federal census for Demun Twp., Randolph Co. Children:

    641.   KIBLER COOK, b. 2 MAR 1883, d. 8 MAR 1965, bur. Masonic Cem., m. 27 JUL 1905 in Randolph Co. to Myrtle Barnett. 13 children.

    641.   LENA COOK, b. August 1890 in Ark.

    642.   SALLIE B. COOK, b. June 1893 in Ark.

    643.   EUGENE R. COOK, b. October 1896 in Ark.

    644.   PAUL PYATT COOK, b. December 1897 in Ark.

65.   MARY C. COOK, b. 1858 in Ark.

---

[1] Randolph Co.,. Ark. Administration Bonds and Letters, 1852-1886, p. 313, bond for administration of his estate to Isaac L. Jarrett.

[2] Randolph Co., Ark. Marriages, Bk. A, p. 104.

[3] Randolph Co., Ark. Probate Records, Vol. 1, p. 168, stating that Matilda is over the age of 14 years.

[4] Randolph Co., Ark. Marriages, Bk. A, p. 73.

[5] Randolph Co., Wills, Bk. 10, pp. 222, 228.

7. JAMES SWEAZEA, b. 1831, mentioned in the proceedings of his father's estate settlement in November 1840.

8. REBECCA SWEAZEA, b. 1832 in Wayne Co., Mo.

9. NANCY JANE SWEAZEA, b. 11 OCT 1834, appointed as a ward of James N. Bigger on 16 OCT 1844 in Randolph Co., d. 4 DEC 1921 in Pocahontas, Randolph Co., Ark., bur. Thomas Cem. at Attica, Ark., m. (1) on 27 NOV 1857 in Randolph Co., Ark. to Abram N.M. Bridges, a farmer from Tenn. They are enumerated on the Federal census of 21 AUG 1860 for Columbia Twp. in Randolph Co. Nancy m. (2) 14 DEC 1865 in Randolph Co. to Joseph Gray Thomas, Sr., b. 1843 in N.C., d. 1913. Family is in the 1910 directory for Columbia Twp., Randolph Co., where he is a farmer with three children, on 120 acres hill and 65 acres in cultivation. Methodist. Children:

   91. MARCIA THOMAS, b. 1866 in Ark., d. before 1900, m. 3 SEP 1890 in Randoph Co. to Jesse H. McCoy.

   92. ESTHER M. THOMAS, b. 1867, d. before 1900.

   93. JOHN WILLIAM THOMAS, b. 3 NOV 1868, d. 2 NOV 1955 in Attica, Ark., m. three times.

   94. MATILDA J. THOMAS, b. 1871, d. before 1900.

   95. JOSEPH GRAY THOMAS, JR., b. November 1873, d. 9 APR 1960 in Attica, Ark., bur. Thomas Cem., m. 19 MAR 1903 to Georgie Purdy.

   96. LEOTA ELIZABETH THOMAS, b. June 1875 in Ark., d. 17 JUN 1973 in Dallas, Tex., m. 17 NOV 1891 in Randolph Co. to S. Peter Foster.

(10). RICHARD SWEAZEA (see sketch below), farmer and blacksmith, b. 1 FEB 1837 in Randolph Co., Ark., appointed as a ward of James N. Bigger on 16 OCT 1844 in Randolph Co., served at Camp Price from 1862-1864 in the 8th Ark. Inf. of the C.S.A. and in 1864 served in the Army east of the Mississippi River,[1] d. 3 FEB 1900, bur. Oak Grove Cem. near Attica, Randolph Co., Ark., m. (1) 29 NOV 1865 at the home of Thomas S. Simington in Randolph Co. to Louisa Jane (Russell) Bigger. Jane Sweazea d. in November 1869 of consumption in Roanoke, Randolph Co., age 28.[2] Richard m. (2) 1873 to Sarah Angeline Russell, b. 14 DEC 1834 in Lincoln Co., Tenn., widow of Marion Russell, res. in 1907 in Attica, Ark., who d. 5 FEB 1912 in Randolph Co. Sarah A. Sweazea applied in 1907 and received a widow's pension based on Richards's service in the C.S.A.

(11). FRANCIS MARION SWEAZEA, b. 6 OCT 1839, appointed as a ward of James N. Bigger on 16 OCT 1844 in Randolph Co., enumerated twice in 1860: residing in the household of Randolph Cook, and in the household of William S. Fedrick.

---

[1] See the Last Will and Testament of his step-father, Randolph Cook, in Randolph Co., Ark., in 1864.
[2] Arkansas Mortality Schedule, 1870, Randolph Co., line 31.

The following subject of this biographical sketch is Mary E. (Sweazea) Adair's uncle Richard, but ties us directly to the family ancestry.

<u>History of Arkansas—Randolph County</u>

"Richard Sweeza. In giving a history of Randolph County, Ark., the name of Mr. Sweeza deserves honorable mention, for he has always been industrious and enterprising, and has ever aided enterprises which tend to the interests of the county. He was born near where he now lives, on the 1st of February, 1837, and is one of two surviving members (the other survivor being Nancy Jane, the wife of Joseph Thomas, a farmer of the county) of a family of nine children born to Richard and Matilda (Bigger) Sweeza, both of whom were born in Missouri, former's birth occurring in Carter County. They were reared to maturity and married in that State, and after the celebration of their nuptials they resided in Carter County several years, then came to Randolph County, Ark., being among the very first settlers of the county. The country was full of Indians and wild animals at that time, but Mr. Sweeza began to clear a farm, an followed this occupation in connection with blacksmithing throughout life, accumulating thereby a large amount of property. He died in 1841, when a comparatively young man, his widow afterward becoming the worthy companion of Randolph Cook, of Illinois, and her death occurred in that State in 1855. Both Mr. and Mrs. Sweeza were members of the Methodist Episcopal Church South, and he was of French descent. Richard Sweeza, the immediate subject of this sketch, received his early education at home, and made his home with his stepfather, Mr. Cook, until the opening of the Rebellion, when he enlisted in Company C, of the Eighth Arkansas Infantry, Confederate States Army, and was on active duty east of the Mississippi River until the close of the war. He was in twenty-three regular engagements, among which were the battles of Shiloh, Murfreesboro, Chickamauga, Perryville, Atlanta, Nashville, Missionary Ridge and many others. He was wounded by a musket ball in the upper lip, at Atlanta, and also at Ringgold Gap by a shell striking the lock of his gun and bursting. At Atlanta he was taken prisoner, but was retaken by his friends ten minutes later, and in this engagement his whole command was captured with the exception of twenty men. He saw some very hard service, and after the war he returned home with the consciousness of having been a brave and faithful soldier. Like his father before him he has always been engaged in farming and blacksmithing; and although he commenced life for himself with little or no means, he has succeeded well, and now owns 200 acres of excellent land. In 1867 he was united in marriage to Mrs. Louisa Jane (Russell) Bigger, a daughter of Col. James G. Russell, and the widow of Ransom Bigger, who was killed during the war. She died in 1870, an earnest member of the Methodist Episcopal Church South, and three years later Mr. Sweeza wedded Mrs. Sarah A., the widow of Marion Russell. She was born in Lincoln County, Tennessee, December 14, 1834, and both are now members of the Methodist Episcopal Church, he being a steward in the same. He is a Democrat politically, and is one of the interprising men of the county."

Figure 49 - Biographical Sketch of Richard Sweeza

BIGGER FAMILY

Origin of the Bigger Family is unknown. The name appears as Bickers, Bigger, Biggers and Biggar. One early group of the Bigger Family ended up in Prince Edward County, Virginia,[1] where we find a John Bigger, Sr., who in 1755 was compensated for building a bridge over Spring Creek.[2] In 1760, John Biggars was involved in land processioning near the Sandy River.[3] In 1777, he was part of a militia company in Prince Edward County.[4]

A John Bigger died intestate in Prince Edward County in 1782.[5] Another John Bigger, died testate in Prince Edward County, where his will was dated 6 JAN 1814, which was proved 20 JUN 1814. He was married to Elizabeth (perhaps Cary[6]).

Another early family group lived in Hanover County, Virginia as early as the 1730s where we later find David, John, and William Bigger transferring property after the Revolutionary War. Louisa County was formed in 1742 from Hanover County. Most of the records from Hanover were destroyed in the Richmond evacuation fire in April 1865.

The earliest land record I found is for a William Bigger who on 17 AUG 1725 obtained a patent for 400 acres in St. John's Parish of King William County, described as being on the north side of the North Anna River and beginning at the land he bought of Dolphus Hendrick.[7] There is obviously multiple generations with a person named William Bigger.

Bickers Family

It appears that the Bigger surname is mixed with the Bickers[8] Family, and as such is connected to Robert Bickers who obtained several land patents along the North Anna River, sometimes in what is now Orange County, Virginia. Another link of the surname is through Macon Biggirs [sic] and John Bickers, brothers, who witnessed a deed in 1794 in Orange County, Virginia, to William Edwards who was son-in-law of Robert Bickers, Sr.[9] One family history states that Nicholas Bickers is the emigrant who came from Scotland to Orange County then Louisa County, Virginia.[10]

A Robert Bickers, planter, was born c.1708, perhaps in Suffolk County, England, and was married 6 JUN 1732 to Elizabeth Collins, perhaps in Spotsylvania County. The same day he leased to John Collins of Caroline County a 200-acre tract in St. Mark's Parish that was

---

[1] Prince Edward Co., Va. was named in honor of Edward Augustus, son of Prince Frederick Louis, and was formed in 1753 from Amelia Co., Va. Amelia Co., Va. was formed in 1734 from parts of Prince George and Brunswick counties, Va.
[2] Bradshaw, p. 30.
[3] Herbert Clarence Bradshaw, *History of Prince Edward County, Virginia* (Richmond: Dietz Press, 1955), p. 47.
[4] Bradshaw, pp. 118, 120.
[5] Clayton Torrence, *Virginia Wills and Administrations*, p. 35; inventory filed there as well.
[6] See *William and Mary College Quarterly*, Second Series, Vol. 25, p. 144.
[7] Virginia Land Patents and Grants, Patent Bk. No. 1, p. 251.
[8] Bickers in German loosely translates to "church."
[9] Orange Co., Va.. Deeds, Bk. 20, p. 340, dated 21 OCT 1794, between Francis Taylor and Benjamin Taylor, executors of George Taylor, dec., and William Edwards, a 410-acre tract in Orange Co., adjacent to Francis Taylor, Charles Taylor, Francis Taliaferro, Lewis Wills and Mildred James.
[10] Lyon Gardiner Tyler, ed., *Encyclopedia of Virginia Biography* (New York: Lewis Historical Publishing Co., 1915), Vol. 5, p. 589.

part of 1,000 acres granted by patent to Bickers[1] on 28 SEP 1728. Elizabeth released her dower right.[2] In 1736, Robert Bickers, of St. Mark's Parish, Orange County, leased to Jeremiah Deer, a 200-acre portion of a 1,000 acre tract formerly granted to Bickers and relapsed from him by John Bryant of Hanover County, and 500 acres part thereof sold to Bickers by Bryant, located on the southwest side of the north fork of the Beaverdam Run, a branch of Pamunkey River.[3] In 1738, John Bryant, of Hanover County, leased to Robert Bickers of St. Mark's Parish, Orange, County, a 500-acre tract that was taken up in copartnership between Joseph Hawkins and Robert Bickers and by Bryant lapsed, adjoining lands of Samuel Smith and Nathaniel Clayborne, on both sides of a branch of Pamunkey River called Beaverdam Run.[4]

In 1741, Robert Bickers obtained a patent for 244 acres in Orange County on the heads of the branches of the North Fork of the North Anna River, adjacent to land of Augustine Smith.[5] That year, Robert Bickers, of St. Thomas Parish, Orange County, leased to John Seayres of Essex County, 145 acres at the head of the branches of the north fork of North Anna River, adjacent to Augustine Smith.[6]

In 1749, Robert Bickers obtained a land patent for 100 acres in Orange County on the branches of the Pamunkey River adjacent to himself.[7] He acquired yet another 220 acres in the same area that was adjacent to himself and a patent granted to Isaac Waters.[8]

In 1751, Robert Bickers, planter, and wife Elizabeth, of St. Thomas Parish, Orange County, conveyed a 229-acre portion of his 1749 patent to James Bickers, Sr. In 1756, Robert Bickers added another 137 acres to his Pamunkey River tract,[9] and added another 170 acres by the southwest mountain road.[10] In 1757, Robert Bickers, Sr. conveyed to his sons William Bickers and Robert Bickers, Jr., 200 acres in Orange County, located at a branch of Berry's Run, adjacent to Jeremiah Dear, James Smith (now of Andrew Shepherd).[11]

Son Robert Bickers, Jr. died intestate in 1762 in Orange County.[12] In 1758, Robert Bickers and wife Elizabeth, sold 75 acres of the Pamunkey tract to Jeremiah Dear of Albemarle County.[13] In 1762, Robert Bickers and wife Elizabeth conveyed 140 acres of land in Spotsylvania County to John Collins.[14] In 1763, Robert Bickers and wife Elizabeth sold 110

---

[1] Spotsylvania Co., Va. Deeds, Bk. B, p. 296, lease dated 6 JUN 1732, released the next day. This deed refers to Virginia Land Office Patent Book 13, p. 437, dated 28 SEP 1728, for 1,000 acres adjacent to Samuel Smith.
[2] Spotsylvania Co., Va. Orders, Bk. 1730-1732, p. 124, court held 6 JUN 1732.
[3] Orange Co., Va. Deeds, Bk. 3, p. 24, dated 27 OCT 1738.
[4] Orange Co., Va. Deeds, Bk. 1, p. 284, dated 21 APR 1738, wit. by Jeremiah Dear and Rebeckah Dear and others.
[5] Virginia Land Patents and Grants, Patent B. No. 19, p. 945, for importation of 5 persons: William Hawkins, Matthew Stanton, Thomas Walker, Henry Kendall and Solomon Ryan.
[6] Orange Co., Va. Deeds, Bk. 6, p. 186, dated 23 SEP 1741, lease and release.
[7] Virginia Land Patents and Grants, Patent Bk. No. 27, p. 96, dated 10 FEB 1748/9, for importation of two persons: Edward Green and James Hopkins.
[8] Virginia Land Patents and Grants, Patent Bk. 28, p. 721, dated 5 SEP 1749, for importation of four persons: William Cooper, Robert Thomson, Elianor Cross and Sarah Thurston.
[9] Virginia Land Patents and Grants, Patent Bk. 33, p. 220, dated 16 AUG 1756, for importation of three persons: Matthew Tibbit, Hannah Drake and Andrew Mannen.
[10] Virginia Land Patents and Grants, Patent Bk. 33, p. 420, dated 10 NOV 1757, adjacent to Thomas Smith, John Taliaferro and Robert Taliaferro's orphans, and that George Taylor failed to pay quit rents and cultivate and make improvements, granted to Bickers after suit.
[11] Orange Co., Va. Deeds, Bk. 12, p. 399, dated 23 JUN 1757.
[12] Orange Co., Va. Wills, Bk. 2, p. 330, inventory presented.
[13] Orange Co., Va. Deeds, Bk. 12, p. 447, dated 27 APR 1758.
[14] Orange Co., Va. Deeds, Bk. 13, p. 231, dated 25 MAR 1762.

acres on both sides of the road from Orange Courthouse to Fredericksburg, bounded by Taliaferro and [George] Taylor, to Andrew Shepherd.[1]

In 1771, Robert Bickers and wife Elizabeth conveyed 150 acres in Orange County to William Edwards,[2] adjacent to land of Thomas Gulley, John Mallory and Joseph Bickers. In 1791, Charles Medearis, of Middlesex County, conveyed to Francis Taliaferro, 100 acres bounded by William Bickers, Jeremiah Dear, William Edwards, Robert Bickers, and Hay Taliaferro.[3] In 1796, William Edwards and wife Hannah, conveyed to Robert Biggers, a tract in Orange County, adjacent to Joseph Bickers, Francis Taliaferro, Thomas Mallory, Nicholas Bickers.[4]

Robert Bickers died testate in Orange County in 1808, and his will names his elder son William Bickers, son-in-law William Edwards, and younger son Joseph Bickers.[5]

Probable children of Robert Bickers and Elizabeth Collins, order uncertain:

a. William Bickers, b. 1732 in Orange Co., Va., d. 1798, m. Margaret "Peggy" Pines. 7 children.
b. Robert Bickers, b. 1734, d. intestate 1762 in Orange Co.
c. John Bickers, b. 1735, d. by 1801,[6] m. (1) Sarah (unknown), m. (2) 5 NOV 1788 in Orange Co. to Ann "Nancy" Landrum. In 1796, John and Sarah conveyed 100 acres in Orange Co., Va. to George Scott.[7] In 1799, John and Nancy conveyed 108 acres in Orange Co. to John Daniel.[8] Child:
    1. William B. Bickers, b. 1784, d. 1851, m. Nancy Evans.
d. Thomas Bickers, b. 1740 in Orange Co., d. 1835, m. Elizabeth (unknown). Son:
    1. William P. Bickers, b. 1766, d. 1855 in Jasper Co., Ill., m. (1) 3 JUN 1794 in Orange Co. to Sally Leathers, and m. (2) 1823 to Nancy Todd in Ky.
e. Hannah Bickers, b. c.1742, d. 1836, m. William Edwards, b. c.1750, d. 1815. 6 children.
f. Joseph Bickers, b. 1748, d. testate 1817 in Orange Co.,[9] m. Agnes Long, who d. testate 1835 in Orange Co.[10] Heirs named in the will of Agnes Bickers:
    1. Caleb Bickers, b. 1772.
    2. Elizabeth Bickers, b. 1780, m. William Long. 4 children.
    3. Matilda Bickers, b. 14 DEC 1785, d. 1861 in Louisa Co., m. 23 JUL 1804 in Orange Co. to Philip B. Smith, son of Mathias Smith. 7 children.
    4. Abner Bickers, b. 1786, m. 23 FEB 1829 in Orange Co. to Nancy Scott.
    5. Susan Bickers, b. 1788, d. 1875, m. 23 DEC 1811 at the residence of Joseph Bickers in Orange Co. to John Jones, son of Elijah Jones, b. 1780, d. 1865. John

---

[1] Orange Co., Va. Deeds, Bk. 13, p. 220, dated 20 MAR 1762.
[2] Orange Co., Va. Deeds, Bk. 15, p. 420, dated 28 NOV 1771.
[3] Orange Co., Va. Deeds, Bk. 20, p. 30, dated 5 MAY 1791.
[4] Orange Co., Va. Deeds, Bk. 21, p. 89, dated 22 FEB 1796.
[5] Orange Co., Va. Wills, Bk. 4, p. 277, dated 29 MAR 1775, prov. 26 SEP 1808.
[6] Orange Co., Va. Deeds, Bk. 22, p. 247, dated 22 MAR 1801, between William C. Webb and the heirs and legal representatives of John Bickers, dec., convey rights to deed from Bickers to Webb in 1798.
[7] Orange Co., Va. Deeds, Bk. 21, p. 52, dated 25 APR 1796.
[8] Orange Co., Va. Deeds, Bk. 21, p. 497, dated 19 AUG 1799.
[9] Orange Co., Va. Wills, Bk. 6, p. 284, dated 25 APR 1816, prov. 22 SEP 1817, recorded 24 OCT 1825.
[10] Orange Co., Va. Wills, Bk. 8, p. 89, dated 1 OCT 1831, prov. 23 FEB 1835.

Jones got bounty land for his service with Capt. Isaac Willis of Culpeper Co. He d. 18 MAR 1867/8 at his residence in Orange Co. Children:

51. James Newton Jones, b. 15 OCT 1812, d. 31 DEC 1894 in Corinth, Miss., m. Mary Blandina Gordon.
52. Elizabeth Jones.
53. Churchill Jones, b. 1823, d. 1907, m. 19 OCT 1837 in Orange Co. to Keziah Pates.
54. Mary Frances Jones.
55. John Burton Jones, b. 18 MAR 1826.

6. Nancy Aley Bickers, b. 1792, m. 26 DEC 1816 in Orange Co. to Sanderson Brown.
7. Alexander Bickers, b. 1796, d. 4 AUG 1875, m. 27 SEP 1830 in Orange Co. to Mary Jones.
8. Joseph Bickers, b. 1802, m. 4 OCT 1836 in Orange Co. to Ellen Lloyd.
9. Joshua Bickers.
10. Brumfield Bickers.

g. Nicholas Bickers, b. 16 AUG 1744 in Orange Co., served in the Virginia line of the Continental Army during the Revolutionary War, d. testate 1836 in Orange Co.,[1] m. Jane (perhaps Carty or McCarty). Children:

1. Joel Bickers, m. 19 MAR 1805 in Orange Co. to Rosanna Atkins, dau. of John Atkins.
2. Benjamin Carty Bickers, b. 1782, d. 1847, m. 26 SEP 1815 in Orange Co. to Joannah Martin.
3. Polly Bickers, b. 1783, m. 16 MAR 1802 in Orange Co. to Benjamin Hawkins.
4. Joanna Bickers, b. 1795, m. 3 AUG 1815 in Orange Co. to Coleman Marshall.
5. Moses Bickers, b. 1799.
6. William Henry Bickers, b. 1804, d. 1881, m. Elizabeth Hawkins.

William Bigger
(c.1714-1785)

This William Bigger (my ancestor) may be have been born in what is now Goochland County,[2] and a son of another William Bigger (1680-1768), and grandson of yet another William [or John] Bigger (c.1650-1680) who was married to Martha Woodward,[3] daughter of William Woodward and widow of both Gideon Macon of New Kent County[4] and Nathaniel West. William Bigger is likely a brother of John Bigger (d. 1814) who lived in Prince Edward County, Virginia.[5] A William Bigger had a daughter Susannah

---

[1] Orange Co., Va. Wills, Bk. 8, p. 212, dated 17 MAR 1825, prov. 27 JUN 1826.

[2] Goochland Co., Va. was named for Sir William Gooch, lieutenant governor of Virginia, and was formed in 1728 from Henrico Co., Va.

[3] Clayton Torrence, *Winston of Virginia and Allied Families* (Richmond, Va.: Whittet & Shepperson, 1927), p. 279, indicates that Martha Woodward m. M. Biggers, a Scotchman.

[4] John Frederick Dorman, ed., *Adventurers of Purse and Person*, 4th Ed. (Baltimore, Md.: Genealogical Publishing Co., Inc., 2007), Vol. 3, p. 491, cites that Nathaniel West (d. after 1723), m. Martha (Woodward) Macon, dau. of William Woodward and widow of Gideon Macon of New Kent Co., who m. (3) _____ Biggers; citing King William Co., Va. Record Bk. 1, pp. 109, agreement in division of Woodward Lane on 20 JUL 1703.

[5] Prince Edward Co., Va. Deeds, Bk. 8, p. 255, dated 15 OCT 1790. I also note that in 1790, a William Biggar, late of King William Co., but now of Prince Edward Co., purchased land from Mary Davidson of Fayette Co.; that Mary's late husband Richard Davidson died possessed of land in Prince Edward Co. and she sold her dower. Also see *The Southside Virginian*, Vol. 2 No. 2 (January 1984), p. 66.

who was married to John Bibb who left a will in Goochland County in 1769.[1] Another daughter of William was perhaps married to John Watson, and she had a brother John Bigger who was living with John Bibb in 1749.

In 1735, Capt. Thomas Carr, then of Caroline County, Virginia, conveyed to William Bigger, Jr., carpenter, a lease for 158 acres on the south side of Little Rockey Creek in Hanover County, Virginia, which was part of a 3,770-acre patent granted to Thomas Carr, Gent., of King William County on 22 FEB 1727.[2] On 3 SEP 1736, Carr also conveyed to William Bigger, Jr., a 400-acre tract in Hanover County.

Sometime about 1740, William Bigger was married to Martha Pollard,[3] daughter of Richard Pollard and granddaughter of William Fleming of St. Paul's Parish, Hanover County, Virginia. She is named in Fleming's will that was proved 4 OCT 1744 in Hanover County.[4]

In 1744, William Biggars, Jr. and wife Martha Pollard of Louisa County, Virginia conveyed 50 acres on the west side of the Little Mountains to Stephen English, and 350 acres to Samuel Brockman of Orange County, Virginia, being a part of 400 acres that were conveyed to Biggars by William Carr and recorded in Hanover County, Virginia.[5]

In 1747, William Bigger obtained a land patent for 400 acres in Louisa County that was on both sides of Bunches Creek and adjacent to John Tait.[6] In 1751, William Biggar and William White were ordered to procession all the lands from Hiccory Creek to Rogers Branch between the North Anna River and the ridge road that leads to Gibson's Ford in Fredericksville Parish of Louisa County.[7] In 1770, William Biggars, Sr. of Trinity Parish, sold to William Biggars, Jr. a 100-acre parcel near William White's plantation.[8]

In 1777, Andrew Trible and wife Sarah conveyed to John Bigger a 140-acre tract in Louisa County, Virginia.[9] The same year, David Bigger was commissioned a second lieutenant to serve in the Louisa County Militia for the Revolutionary War.[10] In 1778, William Harris and wife Elizabeth conveyed 100 acres on the south side of the North Anna River to David Bigger.[11]

---

[1] Goochland Co., Va. Wills, dated 24 MAY 1769, prov. 17 JUL 1769.

[2] Hanover Co., Va. Court Records, 1733-1735: Deeds Wills and Inventories, p. 325, dated 3/4 SEP 1735; Mary Carr relinquishes her dower. Virginia Land Patents and Grants, Patent Bk. 13, p. 210.

[3] See Janice Luck Abercrombie, *Louisa Co., Va., Judgments, 1766-1790* (Athens, Ga.: Iberian Publishing Co., 1998), p. 112; citing Reel 138 Frame 002, Will of William Fleming of Hanover Co., prov. 4 OCT 1744, devises to his grandchildren, including "Martha Pollard who married Biggars." Also see Louisa Co. CF1771-002. This William Biggers died testate in Louisa Co., will proved. 14 FEB 1785, naming wife Martha, and naming children John, James and Sarah Biggers, and Mary Maddison. Also names David Bigger, Macon Bigger, Eleanor Terry, and grandson William Bigger. In 1785, a Martha Bigger, dau. of William, was young enough to need a guardian in Louisa Co.

[4] Louisa Co., Va. Chancery Causes, #1771-002.

[5] Louisa Co., Va. Deeds, Bk. A, pp. 134-35, dated 12 MAR 1733/4, adjacent to Stephen English, Benjamin Hensley and William Maab. Most early records of Hanover Co., Va. have been destroyed.

[6] Virginia Land Patents and Grants, Patent Bk. 28, p. 21, dated 12 JAN 1746/7.

[7] Fredericksville Parish Vestry Book, 1742-1787, p. 37, session of 23 SEP 1751.

[8] Louisa Co., Va. Deeds, Bk. D½, p. 192., dated 12 MAR 1770.

[9] Louisa Co., Va. Deeds, Bk. E, p. 134, dated 3 FEB 1777, adjacent to John Thomson, David Tomson, William Linney, William Harris, Arthur Nash, William Douglass and John Maddison.

[10] Louisa Co., Va. Orders, Bk. 1774-1782, p. 173, dated 11 AUG 1777.

[11] Louisa Co., Va. Deeds, Bk. E, p. 238, dated 9 MAR 1778, adjacent to Parson Douglass, William Harris, Thomas Graves and Thomas Harris.

In 1784, William Bigger and wife Martha, of *White House*, sold 245 acres of their land in Louisa County, Virginia to William White, Jr.[1]

William Bigger, Sr. died by 14 FEB 1785 when his will was recorded in Louisa County. It names wife Martha and children John, James and Sarah Bigger, Mary Maddison, and David and Macon Bigger, and Eleanor Terry, and grandson William Bigger. Martha was bonded as executrix of his estate.[2]

Possible children of William Bigger and Martha Pollard:

+ 1. WILLIAM [C.] BIGGER, JR. (my ancestor), b. c.1750, perhaps in Louisa Co., Va., d. 1812 in Mecklenburg Co., N.C., m. 13 OCT 1781[3] to Martha Richardson.

   2. MACON BIGGER, b. 1752 in Louisa Co., Va., wit. a deed in 1794 in Orange Co., Va.,[4] d. testate[5] 7 SEP 1811 in Maysville, Mason Co., Ky., m. 22 JUL 1779 by Rev. William Douglas[6] after bond of 20 JUL 1779 in Louisa Co. to Christian Grissage Poindexter, b. 1863, d. 1825. Children, of whom:
       21. HULDAH BIGGER, b. 17 MAY 1783, bapt. 3 SEP 1785, m. 6 DEC 1799 in Orange Co. to Gabriel King.
       22. BETSIE SMITH BIGGER, b. 22 APR 1785, bapt. 3 SEP 1785, m. 29 DEC 1808 in Orange Co. to Thornton Tucker.
       23. PHEBE BIGGER, m. 17 JAN 1810 in Orange Co. to Hamlet Sanford.

   3. DAVID BIGGER, b. c.1754, d. intestate by July 1804 in Louisa Co., Va., m. before 1776 to Elizabeth Fergusson.[7] Children:
       31. WILLIAM A. BIGGER, b. 5 MAY 1776 in Louisa Co., d. 30 SEP 1842 in Ralls Co., Mo., m. 16 JUN 1807 in Montgomery Co., Ky. to Matilda Harrison.
       32. MARY "Polly" BIGGER, b. 1779.
       33. FERGUSON BIGGER, b. 2 MAR 1781, bapt. 11 SEP 1783.
       34. MILES SPOTSWOOD BIGGER, b. 4 FEB 1786, bapt. 4 FEB 1787.

   4. MARY BIGGER, b. c.1756, m. before 16 AUG 1785 to John Maddison,[8] d. 27 APR 1833 in Amherst Co., Va. At least 8 children, including:
       41. SALLY MADDISON, m. by bond 3 NOV 1794 in Louisa Co. to Gideon Gooch, res. *Duckinghole Plantation*,[9] Orange Co., Va. soon after marriage.
       41. NANCY MADDISON, b. 6 AUG 1785, bapt. 16 APR 1786.

---

[1] Claudia Anderson Chisholm and Ellen Gray Lillie, *Old Home Places of Louisa County* (Louisa: Louisa County Historical Society, 1979), p. 173.
[2] Louisa Co., Va. Wills, Bk. 3, pp. 52, 53.
[3] W. Mac Jones, Ed., *The Douglas Register: Being a detailed record of Births, Marriages and Deaths together with other interesting notes, as kept by the Rev. William Douglas, from 1750 to 1797* (Richmond, Va.: J.W. Fergusson & Sons, Printers and Publishers, 1928), p. 99.
[4] Orange Co., Va. Deeds, Bk. 20, p. 340, dated 21 OCT1794, between the executors of George Taylor, dec., and William Edwards.
[5] Mason Co., Ky. Wills, Bk. C, p. 160, dated 21 MAR 1811, prov. 9 SEP 1811; names his wife but does not name any children.
[6] *The Douglas Register*, p. 12.
[7] *The Douglas Register*, p. 99, the earliest date of birth of a child in the Register.
[8] Louisa Co., Va. Wills, B k. 3, p. 52, dated 25 OCT 1780. See also *The Douglas Register*, p. 125, which gives the earliest date of birth of a child in the Register.
[9] Duckinghold Creek flows north from the North Anna River in Louisa Co., Va.

5. JOHN BIGGER, b. c.1758, d. testate by 1824, m. 14 JUN 1779 in Louisa Co. [wit. by John Maddison] to Mildred Ferguson,[1] who d. testate by 1835 in Louisa Co.[2] In 1788, a John Bigger sold to William Linney a 190-acre parcel in Louisa Co. near land of William Bigger and adjacent to that of David Bigger.

6. SARAH "Sally" BIGGER, b. c.1760 in Louisa Co., Va., d. bef. 1796, m. 11 SEP 1783 by Rev. William Douglas, after bond of 21 JUL 1783 in Louisa Co. to George Morris, with consent of her father William Bigger, and surety her brother James Bigger. George, b. 29 MAR 1764 in Hanover Co., d. 15 MAY 1853. Child:
   61.   PATSY OLIVER BIGGER, b. 2 JUL 1784, bapt. 1 DEC 1784.

7. ELEANOR "Nelly" BIGGER, b. c.1763, m. before 14 JAN 1786[3] to David Terrie or Terry. Children, of whom:
   71.   CATIE TERRY, b. 24 FEB 1777, bapt. 29 MAY 1783.
   72.   NELLY TERRY, b. 3 MAR 1783, bapt. 29 MAY 1783.
   73.   CHAMP TERRY, b. 14 JAN 1786, bapt. 6 NOV 1786.

8. JAMES BIGGER. No further information.

9. MARTHA BIGGER, b. c.1771 in Louisa Co., Va., d. 1855 in Clark Co., Ky. In September 1785, John Maddison was appointed guardian to Martha Bigger, daughter of William Bigger.[4] She was married by Rev. William Douglas after bond of 27 AUG 1791 in Louisa Co. to Samuel Morris, b. 28 OCT 1768 in Louisa Co., d. intestate March 1862 in Clark Co., Ky.,[5] son of Davis Morris and Elizabeth Guthrey.[6] Marriage bond had surety John Maddison. Children:
   91.   GUTHRIE MORRIS, b. 1799, d. 1837, m. 1819 to Frances Allen.
   92.   POLLY MORRIS.
   93.   WASHINGTON MORRIS.
   94.   MINERVA MORRIS, b. 14 DEC 1810 in Clark Co., Ky., d. 21 JUL 1884 in McLean Co., Ill., m. 9 JAN 1827 in Clark Co. to William Dooley.

Unconnected:

JOHN BIGGER, JR., b. c.1740, d. testate before 20 AUG 1782, m. 4 MAY 1769 in Amelia Co., Va. to Martha Booker. Possible children:
11.   SUSANNA BIGGER, m. by bond 29 DEC 1772 in Prince Edward Co., Va. to Richard Carter.
12.   JOSEPH BIGGER, b. c.1767, d. 1822 in Montgomery Co., Ala., m. 10 JAN 1787 in Amelia Co., Va. to Elizabeth Macon.

[1] Louisa Co., Va. Deeds, Bk. F, p. 459, dated 14 SEP 1788.
[2] Louisa Co., Va. Wills, Bk. 9, p. 256, will of Mildred Bigger; Bk. 6, p. 422, will of John Bigger..
[3] *The Douglas Register*, p. 125, the earliest date of birth of a child in the Register.
[4] Louisa Co., Va. Guardian Bonds, Inventories and Accounts, 1767-1814, p. 142, dated 12 SEP 1785.
[5] Clark Co., Ky. Settlements and Wills, Bk. 17, p. 297, inventory dated 27 MAR 1862.
[6] John W. Pritchett, *Southside Virginia Genealogies* (2007), p. 1029.

John Bigger
(-1814)

John Bigger was a brother of William Bigger (d. 1785). A John Biggers obtained a land patent in 1763 for 400 acres in Prince Edward County that was located between Briery and Buffalo rivers.[1] He is listed on the 1800 tax list for Prince Edward County, Virginia,[2] and his household includes three white male tithables over age 16, seven horses, and ten slaves. John Bigger, died testate in Prince Edward County, where his will was dated 6 JAN 1814 and proved 20 JUN 1814. He was married to Elizabeth (perhaps Cary[3]). Elizabeth Bigger heads a household on the 1820 Federal census for Prince Edward County.

Perhaps related here is a John Bigger who obtained in 1749 a land patent of 400 acres in Amelia County on the south side of the south fork of Buffalo River, adjacent to Woodson.[4]

Possible children of John Bigger and Elizabeth (perhaps Cary), order uncertain:

1. JAMES BIGGER, b. c.1758. He is listed on the 1800 tax list for Prince Edward Co., Va., with two white males over the age of 16, seven horses, and seven slaves. Enumerated on the 1810 and 1820 Federal census for Prince Edward Co. Perhaps he had the following children:
    11.   BETSY COLEMAN BIGGER, b. 20 JAN 1780 in Prince Edward Co., Va., d. 1851 in Smith Co., Tenn., m. 12 JAN 1803 in Prince Edward Co.[5] to Simon P. Hughes, b. 26 JAN 1778, d. 1858 in Smith Co., Tenn.
    12.   SUSANNAH BIGGER, m. 19 MAR 1807 in Prince Edward Co. to Thomas Rice.
    13.   MARY "Polly" BIGGER, m. 15 APR 1806 in Prince Edward Co. to John Carter [or John Carter Prince].

2. SUSANNAH BIGGER, perhaps b. 1760 in Prince Edward Co., Va., d. 11 JAN 1840 in Lexington, Oglethorpe Co., Ga., m. 1780 in Prince Edward Co. to William Watson Patmon, b. c.1760 in Henrico Co., Va., who d. testate 1821 in Oglethorpe Co., Ga. 11 children, of whom:
    21.   POLLY PATMON, m. Samuel Weaver.[6]

3. SALLY H. BIGGER.

4. ELIZABETH H.C. BIGGER, b. c.1768, m. by bond 18 NOV 1806 in Prince Edward Co., Va. to Samuel Scott,[7] of Montgomery Co., Va. Child:
    41.   SARAH SCOTT, m. Archer Jones, Jr.

---

[1] Virginia Land Grants and Patents, Patent Bk. 35, p. 192, dated 23 MAY 1763, adjacent to Messrs. Anderson, Flournoy, Wimbish and Biggers.
[2] *The Virginia Genealogist*, Vol. 49 No. 4 (October-December 2005), p. 286.
[3] See *William and Mary College Quarterly*, Second Series, Vol. 25, p. 144.
[4] Virginia Land Patents and Grants, Patent Bk. 27, p. 216, dated 25 JUL 1749.
[5] Prince Edward Co., Va. Marriages, James Bigger consents for marriage of his daughter, and surety is Jeremiah Whitworth.
[6] *William and Mary College Quarterly Historical Magazine*, Vol. 25 (July 1916), p. 144.
[7] William Scott consents to the marriage, with John Bigger as surety.

5. JOSEPH BIGGER. No further information.

6. THOMAS "Tommy" BIGGER. 8 children, including:
    61.   LUCY S. BIGGER, m. by bond 19 JAN 1807 in Prince Edward Co., to George W. Bell.

7. ANDREW BIGGER. No further information.

8. MARY "Polly" BIGGER, *dau. of John Bigger, Sr.*, b. c.1787, perhaps in Goochland Co., Va., m. by bond 4 FEB 1803 when underage in Prince Edward Co., Va. to William Steger,[1] b. 1777, d. 1830, son of William H. Steger. Children:
    81.   ANN CARY STEGER, b. 1813 in Va., d. 13 JAN 1892 in Mills, Tex., m. 23 SEP 1828 in Ky. to William D. Fletcher Harrison. 3 children.
    82.   WILLIAM H. STEGER, b. 1819, d. 1859.

1. William [C.] Bigger, Jr.
(c.1750-1812)

William [C.] Bigger, Jr. (my ancestor), son of William Bigger, Sr. [or John] and Martha Pollard, was born about 1750 in perhaps Louisa County, Virginia. He was married sometime in the mid 1770s to Martha Richardson. Evidence of his marriage is found in *The Douglas Register*, wherein the date of 13 OCT 1781 is given for the birth of the earliest child found in that record.[2] Martha was a daughter of Landie Richardson as proved in a deed in Louisa County in 1779.[3]

William C. Bigger, Jr. served as sergeant in the Virginia Continental Line during the Revolutionary War, and was known to be captured at Charleston, S.C. during the War of 1812, and died while being held a prisoner of war. In 1784, William Biggers was appointed administrator to the estate of Charles Stewart in Spotsylvania County, Virginia, with Macon Bigger as surety.[4]

Information in Application File 730 of the 1853 Scrip Act[5] reveals three sons Joseph, James and Thomas Bigger. In 1787, a William and Martha Bigger, of Louisa County, Virginia sold 100 acres whereon they both lived on the banks of Goldmine Creek.[6]

He and his wife are enumerated on the 1810 Federal census for Mecklenburg County, North Carolina, with two children.

---

[1] Prince Edward Co., Va., marriages show that William Steger m. Polly Bigger, daughter of John Bigger, Sr. who consents to the marriage. Surety was Wiltshire Cardwell.
[2] *The Douglas Register*, p. 99, the earliest date of birth for a child in the Register, and not the date of marriage.
[3] Louisa Co., Va. Deeds, Bk. H, p. 37, dated 1 JAN 1779, from Landie Richardson to his daughter Martha and her husband William Bigger.
[4] Spotsylvania Co., Va. Wills, Bk. E.
[5] Margie B. Brown, *Genealogical Abstracts, Revolutionary War Veterans, Scrip Act 1852* (Decorah, Ia.: The Amundsen Publishing Co., 1990), p. 196. Also, there are some researchers that state the William Bigger who m. Martha Richardson was a son of William Bigger and Martha Pollard, and that Martha was b. 17 MAR 1759 in Goochland Co., Va., a dau. of Landie Richardson and Sarah Underwood, and d. in 1810 in Ky.
[6] Louisa Co., Va. Deeds, Bk. F, p. 160, dated 8 JAN 1787, adjacent to the line of David Biggers, and John and William White.

William Bigger died in 19 DEC 1812 in what is now Union County, North Carolina. Union County was formed in 1842 from parts of Anson and Mecklenburg counties.

Children of William [C.] Bigger, Jr. and Martha Richardson:

11. JAMES [W.] BIGGER (my ancestor), b. c.1775 in Va., perhaps Louisa Co., Va., prob. d. 1833 in Shelby Co., Tex.,[1] perhaps m. (1) c. 1796 to Jane Stewart in Williamson Co., Tenn., and m. (2) c.1816 in Wayne Co., Mo. to D1. MARY "Polly" SWEAZEA, *q.v.*, b. c.1790 in Elberton, Elbert Co., Ga., dau. of Richard Sweazea and Jane Johnston. She d. by 1 JAN 1843 and Richard Sweazea Bigger was appointed administrator of her estate in Shelby Co., Tex., bur. Bigger Cem. on the old Jim Bigger farm just outside of Shelbyville, Tex. James and family moved via Williamson Co., Tenn. to Wayne Co., Mo., and to Lawrence Co., Ark. about 1827. In 1830 he obtained a land patent for 80 acres in what is now Randolph Co., Ark.[2] In Texas the surname is often spelled Biggar. Proposed children of James W. Bigger and his first wife Jane Stewart:

    111. JOSEPH BIGGER, perhaps b. 18 APR 1797 in Williamson Co., Tenn., d. 26 JAN 1833, m. Mary (unknown), d. 27 NOV 1873, age 76y 26d; both bur. in Bigger Cem. of Owen Hill, Williamson Co., Tenn.

    112. AMBROSE C. BIGGER, b. 1801 in Williamson Co., Tenn., d. 1848 in Randolph Co., Ark., m. 18 OCT 1838 in Randolph Co., Ark. to Mary Ann McDonald, daughter of Isaac McDonald and Mary Ivy who were m. in 1807 in Jackson Co., Ga. Children:

        1121. LUCINDA BIGGER, b. 1840 in Randolph Co., Ark., m. Thomas Tyler.

        1122. JAMES BIGGER, b. 1842 in Ark.

        1123. MARY "Polly" BIGGER, b. 1843 in Ark.

        1124. CALVIN S. BIGGER, b. c.1845, d. 1899, m. Elizabeth Condit.

        1125. JEFFERSON BIGGER, b. 1849, d. 1852.

        1126. WILLIAM BIGGER, b. 1853 in Ark.

        1127. NETTIE BIGGER, b. 1856.

    113. MATILDA CAROLINE BIGGER (my ancestor), b. 1802 in Williamson Co., Tenn., d. 1 JAN 1855 in Ill., m. (1) 15 JAN 1821 in Wayne Co.,[3] Mo. to RICHARD SWEAZEA (1795-1840), *q.v.*, and m. (2) c.1844 in Randolph Co., Ark. to [William] Randolph Cook, b. 1816 in Tenn., d. testate in June 1864 in Randolph Co.[4] Children, of whom:

        1131. MARY ELIZABETH SWEAZEA (my ancestor), b. 1824, d. 1868, m. 13 FEB 1845 in Randolph Co., Ark. to 1. WATSON M. ADAIR, *q.v.*

        1132. WILLIAM R. COOK, b. 14 DEC 1846,[5] d. 18 APR 1868, bur. Bigger Cem., Attica, Ark.

---

[1] One researcher's claim is that this James Bigger died between 1833 and 1835 in Shelby Co., Tex., bur. Bigger Cem. near Shelbyville, Tex. However, I find that in January 1837, Richard Sweazea is bonded in Randolph Co., Ark. as administrator of the estate of James Bigger, dec. On 13 JAN 1841, Ambrose C. Bigger and James G. Russell are appointed administrators of the estate of James Bigger, dec. [Probate Records, Vol. 1, p. 64], and that they are summoned by court of Randolph Co., Ark. in April 1843.

[2] Arkansas Land Patents, Randolph Co., Vol. AR0470.354, doc. #442.

[3] Wayne Co., Mo. was created in 1818 from Cape Girardeau Co., Mo.

[4] Randolph Co., Ark., Administration Bonds and Letters, 1852-1886, p. 364, will dated 7 JUN 1864, prov. 24 JAN 1866, devising all his lands to be divided between son William R. Cook and step-son Richard Sweazea.

[5] He is in the household of William and Caroline Cook on 14 SEP 1860 in Randolph Co., Ark., but with age 7.

114. LUCINDA BIGGER,[1] b. 1 JAN 1804 in Williamson Co., Tenn., d. 1851 in Reynolds Co., Mo., m. Arnold Mann/Mahn, rem. to Reynolds Co., Mo. where he d. 1869. Children:

1141. ISAAC MANN.

1142. LUCINDA MANN.

1143. PHOEBE MANN.

1144. CLARK MANN, b. 1841 in Reynolds Co., Mo., m. (1) Jane Copeland, d. 1877 in Reynolds Co., m. (2) 29 FEB 1880 to Lucinda M. Wallis, and m. (3) to Missouri McFadden. 8 children.

1145. MARTHA ANN MANN, b. 1843 in Reynolds Co., Mo., m. Andrew A. Duncan.

115. JAMES NORRIS BIGGER, farmer, b. 1810 in Williamson Co., Tenn., d. 1872 in Randolph Co., Ark., m. in Mo. to Lucretia Parrish, b. 1812, d. 1874 in Randolph Co. In 1859 he secured a land patent for 40 acres in Section 33 of Randolph Co., Ark.[2] Enumerated 9 NOV 1860 for Randolph Co., and on the Federal census for 23 AUG 1860 in Columbia Twp., Randolph Co., Ark. [family 64]. Children:

1151. JOHN G. BIGGER, farmer, b. 1829 in Lawrence Co., Ark., d. intestate in May 1863 in Randolph Co., Ark.,[3] bur. behind the Methodist Church, m. 3 AUG 1848 to (10)3. CATHERINE C. LEWIS, daughter of Isaiah Lewis, Jr. and Mary "Polly" Wright, b. 22 AUG 182[9] in Randolph Co., Ark. (1860 census), d. JUN 1882, bur. Shiloh Cem., located near Five Mile Spring about ½ mile from Highway 90. Enumerated on the Federal census for 28 JUN 1860 in Current River Twp., Randolph Co., Ark. [family 938; page 362]. Widow Catherine m. (2) William T. Breeding.

11511. MARY F. BIGGER, b. 1850 in Randolph Co., Ark., d. inf.

11512. BENJAMIN FRANKLIN BIGGER, hotel keeper,[4] namesake of the town of Biggers,[5] b. October 1851 in Pocahontas, Randolph Co. Ark., d. testate 14 MAY 1917 in Biggers, Ark.,[6] bur. Masonic Cem., m. 5 APR 1874 in Ripley Co., Mo. to Ida Josephine Simington, b. 17 JUL 1857, d. 7 APR 1940, bur. Masonic Cem., daughter of Thomas S. Simington (1822-1897) and Emily Russell (1833-1897),[7] bur. Oak Grove Cem. Children:

115121. LUTE BIGGER, b. 6 FEB 1878, d. 7 APR 1899, bur. Bigger Cem., Attica, Randolph Co., Ark.

115122. THOMAS BIGGER.

115123. CATHARINE "Kate" BIGGER, m. Mr. Harrison.

---

[1] Another Lucinda Elizabeth Bigger was married to William Lewis on 3 AUG 1848 in Randolph Co., Ark.

[2] Arkansas Land Patents, Randolph Co., Vol. AR0690.039, doc. 13442, for part of the NW, NW of Sect. 33, Twp. 20N, Range 1E.

[3] Randolph Co., Ark. Administrator Bonds, p. 153, administration of the estate of John G. Bigger, late of Randolph Co., Ark. was granted by bond of 16 MAY 1863 to James M. Casey; again at p. 236, for bond dated 23 APR 1866 to James M. Casey.

[4] The old Bigger Hotel and livery (formerly belonging to Eli Heavener), established in 1881 in Pocahontas, burned 23 DEC 1921, and is pictured in the *Pocahontas Star Herald*, 26 SEP 1956.

[5] In 1889, B.F. Bigger bought land and established a ferry crossing the Current River. He built a distillery. The town of Biggers was a stop on the Southern Missouri and Arkansas Railroad that went to Poplar Bluff, Mo. Biggers quickly developed as a lumber mill town.

[6] Randolph Co., Ark. Wills, Bk. 3, p. 570, wil dated 20 OCT 1904 with codicil 6 APR 1906, sets up trust.

[7] Randolph Co., Ark. Deeds, Bk. 13, p. 313, dated 9 MAR 1881, T.S. and Emily Simington sold property to trustees of the Methodist Episcopal Church South in Randolph Co., Ark. to establish Oak Grove United Methodist Church. History of the church is found in the *Pocahontas Star Herald*, 4 JUN 1981.

115124. GEORGE W. BIGGER, b. 3 NOV 1885, d. 10 MAY 1917, bur. Masonic Cem.

115125. ELLA BIGGER.

115126. MAY BIGGER.

11513. JOHN P.M. BIGGER, b. 1853 in Randolph Co., Ark., d. 31 OCT 1912 in the war, m. 25 OCT 1874 in Randolph Co. to Isabella Margaret McNabb.

11514. RANSOM MARION BIGGER, b. 4 MAR 1857 in Randolph Co., Ark., d. 18 DEC 1908, bur. Oak Grove Cem., m. (2) 12 AUG 1877 in Ripley Co., Mo. to Alice Isabel Russell, b. 10 FEB 1860 in Randolph Co., Ark., d. 13 FEB 1903, bur. Oak Grove Cem. Nine children, of whom:

    115141. BENJAMIN FRANKLIN BIGGER, m. Myrtle Frances Mayes.

11515. LUCRETIA HARRIET JANE BIGGER, b. 16 MAR 1859 in Randolph Co., Ark., d. 24 DEC 1933, m. 7 FEB 1880 in Randolph Co. to James Mike Rooffener.

11516. Walter Lucas Breeding.

1152. LUCRETIA H. JANE BIGGER, b. 17 AUG 1830 in Lawrence Co., Ark., d. in 1864 in Mo., m. 15 DEC 1853 in Randolph Co. to Jacob Foster, b. 1831, d. 1911. 5 children.

1153. RANSOM MARION BIGGER, farmer, b. 1836 in Randolph Co., Ark., d. December 1865[1] in the Civil War in Ga., m. 14 MAR 1861 in Randolph Co., Ark.[2] to Louisa Jane Russell, daughter of James Goldsby Russell and Parthenia Bridges. Widow "Jane" m. (2) in 1865 to Richard Sweazea, *q.v.*

1154. JAMES BIGGER, farmer, b. 1840 in Randolph Co., Ark., d. in 1864 in Ga.

1155. CAROLINE BIGGER, b. 1841 in Randolph Co., Ark., d. 1921 by burning to death, m. 1 OCT 1887 in Randolph Co. to Arthur Barham, b. 1813.

1156. MATILDA EVELYN BIGGER, b. 1842 in Randolph Co., Ark., d. 1869.

1157. MARY ANN BIGGER, b. 1844 in Randolph Co., Ark., d. 1869, m. 12 FEB 1863 in Randolph Co., Ark. to John Praytor.

1158. FRANKLIN PAYNE BIGGER, b. 1846 in Randolph Co., Ark., d. 1880, m. 28 DEC 1870 in Randolph Co., Ark. to Charlotte Ann "Lotta" McKee. She m. (2) to Chesterfield Bigger, b. September 1847 in N.C. Children:

    11581. WILLIAM CHESTERFIELD BIGGER, b. 25 JUN 1874 in Ark., d. 2 DEC 1964, bur. Masonic Cem., m. 14 MAR 1897 to Mattie Lou Sago, b. 4 FEB 1877, d. 27 NOV 1969. Seven children.

    11582. JOHN MacDOWELL BIGGER, b. 4 SEP 1876, d. 14 MAY 1974, bur. Masonic Cem., m. 11 MAR 1897 in Randolph Co. to Hattie Dora Abernathy, b. 1878, d. 1952.

1159. THALIA BIGGER, b. 26 AUG 1848 in Randolph Co., Ark., d. 8 MAR 1884 in Randolph Co., bur. Foster Cem., m. 21 JUN 1866 in Randolph Co. to Jacob Foster after her sister Lucretia died, b. 17 AUG 1830, d. 11 JUL 1911, bur. Foster Cem. 7 children.

115(10). WILLIAM R. BIGGER, b. 1 JAN 1850 in Attica, Randolph Co., Ark., d. 2

---

[1] Randolph Co., Ark. Administrator Bonds, p. 194, dated 27 DEC 1865 for James N. Bigger to administer the estate of Ransom M. Bigger.

[2] Randolph Co., Ark. Marriages, Bk. 2, p. 27, by minister Mahlon McNabb.

JAN 1908 in Randolph Co., bur. Bigger Cem. at Attica, m. 29 JUL 1880 there to Laura McKee, b. 1855 in N.C., dau. of John McKee; members of the Methodist Episcopal Church South.

115(11). EMMA HAYS BIGGER, b. 1854 in Randolph Co., Ark., m. 25 MAR 1875 in Randolph Co., to Martin Vanburen Seagraves, b. 18 SEP 1847, d. 18 NOV 1921, bur. Sanders Cem.

115(13). CHESTERFIELD BIGGER, farmer, b. 1856 in Randolph Co., Ark., d. by suicide, m. 1891 to Mrs. Charlotte Ann (McKee) Bigger, widow of his brother Franklin Payne Bigger. 4 children.

115(14). JOSEPHUS A. BIGGER, b. 1856, d. 1857.

116. JOSIAH BIGGER, b. 1815, m. Martha (unknown). Children:
- 1161. FRANK BIGGER, b. 1848.
- 1162. MARY BIGGER, b. 1852.
- 1163. EMILY BIGGER, b. 1854.
- 1164. JOHN C. BIGGER, b. 1855.

Children of James W. Bigger and his second wife Mary "Polly" Sweazea:

117. RICHARD SWEAZEA BIGGER, b. 1817 in Mo., went to Tex. and d. 1864 in the Civil War, m. Delilah Runnels, b. 1818, d. 1903, bur. Bigger Cem., Shelbyville, Tex. Children:
- 1171. BENJAMIN FRANKLIN BIGGER, b. 1844, d. 12 SEP 1862.
- 1172. LORIE BIGGER, b. 1846, d. 1859.
- 1173. MARGARET E. BIGGER, b. 1 JAN 1847, 24 JUL 1925, m. John Adams. 7 children.
- 1174. JAMES C. BIGGER.
- 1175. CHRISTOPHER COLUMBUS BIGGER, b. 19 FEB 1852, d. 29 APR 1929 in Shelby Co., Tex., m. Mollie Creech. 3 children.
- 1176. RICHARD MORGAN BIGGER, b. 2 JAN 1860, d. 29 DEC 1924 in Center Ridge, Shelby Co., Tex., m. Verse Eudora "Dora" Creech. 9 children.
- 1177. LOUISA AQUILLA BIGGER, b. 1854, m. Dolph Holt.

118. SARAH ISABEL "Sally" BIGGER, b. 1818 in Mo., d. 1862 in Randolph Co., Ark., m. c.1832 or 1836 in Arkansas City, Ark. to Henry M. Waddle, b. 1800, d. 1849. 10 children.

119. MARGARET ELIZABETH "Polly" BIGGER, b. 1 JAN 1823 in Mo., d. 1900 in Bowie, Montgaue Co., Tex., m. James Wagstaff, b. 1817, d. 1865. Child:
- 1191. MARY ARAMINTA WAGSTAFF, b. 1843, d. 1880, m. George Solomon Hutto.

11(10). ROBERT T. BIGGER, b. 1825 in Mo., age 10 when his family moved to Tex., d. 1900 in Montague Co., Tex., m. Jane (unknown), d. 1882. He served in the C.S.A. 7 children.

11(11). WILLIAM GARRISON BIGGER, b. 1828 in Lawrence Co., Ark., d. 1845 in Cooke Co., Tex., m. Mary E. (unknown), served in the Mexican War.

11(12). GEORGE WASHINGTON BIGGER, b. 1 JAN 1831 in Randolph Co., Ark., d. 30 OCT 1881 in Shelby Co., Tex., m. Julia A. Cartwright, d. 25 MAR 1917, dau. of Hezekiah L. Cartwright. Children:
- 11(12)1. HEZZIE BIGGER, b. 1846.

11(12)2.   NANCY BIGGER, b. 1858, m. Joseph Hern.

11(12)3.   ANNIE BIGGER, b. 1859, m. E.W. Martin.

11(12)4.   THOMAS ARCHER BIGGER, b. c.1860 in Shelby Co., Tex., d. 28 FEB 1924 in Shelby Co., Tex., m. Laura Milta Harris, b. 11 MAR 1872, d. 2 DEC 1961.

12.   THOMAS BIGGER. No further information.

13.   MARY "Polly" RICHARDSON BIGGER, b. 13 OCT 1781 in Goochland Co., Va., bapt. 9 JUL 1782,[1] perhaps in Louisa Co., Va., d. 1843 in Ralls Co., Mo., m. Girard Fagan.

14.   LANDIE BIGGER(S), b. 20 SEP 1785 in Goochland Co., Va., bapt. 23 APR 1786,[2] d. 19 OCT 1864, m. 17 AUG 1824 in Clark Co., Ky. to Nancy Gatson. He served in the Williams' Company of the Kentucky Militia during the War of 1812.[3]

15.   HANNAH BIGGER, b. c.1800, d. 1864 in Danville, Ind., m. 27 JUL 1826 in Clark Co., Ky. to Thomas Gatson, b. 1802, d. 1879.

---

[1] *The Douglas Register*, p. 159.
[2] *The Douglas Register*, p. 159.
[3] See National Archives, War of 1812 Pension Files, WC-11615.

DAVISON FAMILY

The earliest ancestor for whom we have a record is George Davison who was born about 1747 in Armagh Town, County Armagh, Ireland. Armagh is located in the Ulster Province in the northeastern part of the country. No further information has been found about the Davison Family in Ireland. It was not a prominent clan. George Davison was married about 1768 to Eleanor "Nelly" Allen before coming to America, through New York, in July 1770. A large amount of Irish records have been destroyed, so no data about George's ancestry has been learned. Details about how the family arrived in America and how they moved to Westmoreland County, Pennsylvania are unknown. Therefore it is not known if George Allen and his wife Eleanor were alone or if either of them had siblings nearby. The Davison surname is common in early Pennsylvania records, and quite a few Davison men served in the Revolutionary War.

Figure 50 - Diagram of Counties in Ireland

On 2 FEB 1787, George Davison of Westmoreland County, Pennsylvania, assigned his rights to a piece of property to Henry Enman. The document appears to be incomplete, but does describe the property being adjacent to that of John McCibins and Samuel Braddley.[1] Westmoreland was established in 1773 from Bedford County. The earliest land warrants for Bedford County include two Davisons: Elias in 1772 and Hugh Davison in 1773.

Only one Davison Family appears on the 1800 Federal census for Westmoreland County, Pennsylvania, and it is headed by John Davison in North Huntington Township. His household contains 1 male between the age of 10-15, three males between 16-25, 1 male 45 and upwards, with 1 female 16-25 and 1 female upward of 45 years.

The family of George Davison appears on the Federal census for 1810, Clermont County, Ohio, Batavia Township [page 41]. Nothing is known about the death time or place of George and Eleanor Allen.

---

[1] Westmoreland Co., Pa., Deeds, Book 2, p. 95. The initial statement is that Davison assigns his rights to the "above," to Henry Enman, yet it is not clear why he did this. The previous document is a mortgage by David Morrow to Thomas Gallagher of a parcel known as "Hibenia" as appears on a land patent in Patent Book 18 p. 400, on the river Conemaugh, Derry Township, adjoining Robert McConochy and others, containing 207 acres.

Children of George Davison and Eleanor Allen:

+   1. ROBERT DAVISON, b. 17 MAY 1770, presumably in Co. Armagh, Ire., m. 14 APR 1792 by Rev. Valentine Cook in Chestnut Ridge, Westmoreland Co., Pa., to Florence Hamilton, daughter of James Hamilton and Elizabeth Clemmons. Robert d. in Brownsburg, Hendricks Co., Ind., which is located about 14 miles northwest of Indianapolis, Ind.

+   2. JAMES DAVISON (my ancestor), b. c.1773, probably in Westmoreland Co., Pa., m. c.1795 to Catherine (perhaps Long). They removed to Clermont Co., Ohio where we presume they both died.

3. GEORGE DAVISON, b. c.1775, probably in Westmoreland Co., Pa., d. 1836, m. Sarah Brannon, daughter of Alexander Brannon, who d. prior to 29 OCT 1836 in Clermont Co., Ohio. In April 1803, he purchased 111 acres from Col. Thomas Paxton and wife Martha, in Miami Township of Clermont Co.[1] This land was part of 1,000 acres that Paxton purchased in 1795 when he brought his family from Kentucky. George added 42¼ acres in 1813.[2] He was in Hamilton Co. on the 1820 and 1830 Federal census, and sold 137 acres to John Chapman for $800.[3] He perhaps removed to Indiana where he may have died. In 1836, George Davison and wife Sarah, John Anderson and wife Jane, and Ephraim Pierce and wife Martha (whose wives were alias Brannon) sold 124 acres in Clermont Co. to George P. Brannon.[4] Possible issue:

31.   WILLIAM W. DAVISON, SR., b. 1822 in Ohio, m. c.1842, perhaps in Ind., to Catherine T. (unknown), d. February 1899 in Hamilton Co. They settled in Harrison, Hamilton Co., Ohio where he was a cooper in 1850 and a cooper and merchant in 1860. He owned a woolen mill in Hamilton Co.[5] Children:

311.   LEWIS DAVISON, b. 1845 in Ind.
312.   EMILY DAVISON, b. 1847 in Ohio.
313.   ALICE DAVISON, b. 1849 in Ohio.
314.   WILLIAM W. DAVISON, JR., b. 1854 in Ohio.
315.   FRANCIS DAVISON, b. 1858 in Ohio.

32.   EDWARD WILSON DAVISON, cooper, b. December 1828 in Ohio, d. Homer, Ill., m. 2 AUG 1848 in Hamilton Co., Ohio to Cordelia B. Pearce, b. 1829 in Ohio. They were residing in Harrison, Hamilton Co. in 1850 and perhaps returned to Indiana by 1860. Children:

321.   JAMES DAVISON, b. June 1849 in Hamilton Co., Ohio.
322.   THOMAS EDWARD DAVISON, b. 1851 in Hamilton Co., Ohio, d. 15 MAR 1879 in Philo, Ill.
323.   JOHN W. DAVISON, b. 1855 in Harrison, Dearborn Co., Ind.
324.   CHARLES L. DAVISON, b. 1856 in Harrison, Ind.
325.   LUELLA FLORENCE DAVISON, b. 6 SEP 1859 in Harrison, Ind., d. 8

---

[1] Clermont Co., Ohio Deeds, Bk. 2, p. 74.
[2] Clermont Co., Ohio Deeds, B k. 10, p. 159.
[3] Clermont Co., Ohio Deeds, Bk. 35, p. 357.
[4] Clermont Co., Ohio Deeds, Bk. 37, p. 62, recorded 29 OCT 1836.
[5] See 1875 Atlas of Hamilton County, Ohio; also Henry A. Ford, *History of Hamilton County, Ohio* (Cleveland, Ohio: L.A. Williams, 1881), p. 314.

NOV 1950 in Champaign, Ill., m. 9 SEP 1882 to William Albert Christy.

326.　ALBERT M. DAVISON, b. 1862 in Ind.

327.　EMMA JANE DAVISON, b. 10 NOV 1863 [5 on tombstone] in Harrison, Ind., d. 24 NOV 1931 in Sidney, Champaign Co., Ill., m. Albert Lawhead, b. 1867 in Ill., d. 1942, whose father was from Northern Ireland. In 1930 they res. in Sidney, Ill.　Son:

　　3271.　　GUY E. LAWHEAD, b. 1908 in Ill.

328.　JENNIE DAVISON, b. 1864 in Harrison, Ind.

329.　CATHERINE M. "Kate" DAVISON, b. 1865 in Harrison, Ind.

32(10).　WILLIAM F. DAVISON, b. 1867.

32(11).　MARLEY B. DAVISON, b. 13 MAR 1870 in Harrison, Ind., res. in Champaign, Ill., d. 15 JUL 1964 in Paulding Co., Ohio, m. 28 DEC 1900 in Champaign, Ill. to Sadie E. White.

32(12).　MINNIE MAUDE DAVISON, b. 1872 in Philo, Ill., d. April 1929 in Sidney, Ill.

+　4.　JOHN DAVISON, b. 15 MAR 1777, probably in Westmoreland Co., Pa., m. (1) 1 AUG 1797 in Ky. to Mary Satterfield Long. He m. (2) in 1802 to Isabella Hamilton. John d. intestate 12 MAY 1847 in Clermont Co., Ohio.

+　5.　WILLIAM DAVISON, b. c.1780 in Westmoreland Co., Pa., m. (1) 26 JUL 1810 to Susannah Keeth, and m. (2) 15 JUL 1813 in Clermont Co., Ohio to Susan Knaus.

1. Robert Davison
(1770-1848)

The first child we have on record for George Davison and Eleanor Allen is Robert Davison, born in County Armagh, Ireland on 17 MAY 1770. He was married 14 APR 1792 by Rev. Valentine Cook, Methodist Circuit Rider, in Chestnut Ridge, Westmoreland County, Pennsylvania to Florence Hamilton, daughter of James Hamilton from Scotland, and his wife Elizabeth Clemmons.

Florence Hamilton was born 5 March 1777 in Chestnut Ridge, Pennsylvania, and died November 9, 1864 in Charleston, Illinois. The family moved to Clermont County, Ohio about 1796. In April 1804, he voted in the first election held in Miami Township of Clermont County.[1] In 1821, he purchased 32-1/3 acres from Silas Hutchinson and wife Margery.[2] Silas was a grandson of Col. Thomas Paxton. In 1836, Robert and Florence Davison sold 73 acres to Thomas Paxton for $1,200.[3]

Robert Davison died in November 1848 in Brownsburg, Hendricks County, Indiana.

---

[1] See Louis H. Ever, *History of Clermont County* (1882), p. 468.
[2] Clermont Co., Ohio Deeds, Bk. 20, p. 325; survey 720.
[3] Clermont Co., Ohio Deeds, Bk. 37, p. 176; survey 720.

Children of Robert Davison and Florence Hamilton:

11. PHEBE DAVISON, m. 27 MAR 1819 by Jasper Shotwell, J.P. in Clermont Co., to Lewis Fry.[1]

12. JOHN DAVISON, b. between 1790-1800, m. 5 DEC 1821 by A. McGuire, M.G., in Clermont Co. to Fanny Murphy.[2] They left the county. Perhaps five children.

13. JOSEPH DAVISON, b. between 1795-1802, m. (1) 10 DEC 1821 by Peter Yost, M.G., in Clermont Co. to Emily Holley.[3] He was m. (2) 1 MAY 1830 by J.W. Robinson, J.P., in Clermont Co. to Edith Vansuhlo.[4]

14. ROBERT DAVISON, JR., b. between 1800-1810, was m. 15 JUN 1826 by David Kern, J.P., in Clermont Co. to Polly Duncan,[5] who d. prior to 1830. Five children.

15. MARGARET DAVISON, was m. 18 JAN 1827 in Clermont Co. to William Fry, b. Ky., d. bef. 1860. Children:
    151. ALBERT FRY.
    152. HARRIET ELLEN FRY, b. 1834.
    153. CYNTHIA FRY.
    154. ORTHO P. FRY.

+ 16. JAMES HAMILTON DAVISON, b. December 13, 1806 in Williamsburg, Clermont Co., Ohio.[6] He was m. 20 SEP 1827 by J.W. Robinson, J.P.,[7] in Clermont Co., Ohio to his cousin, 44. ELIZABETH DAVISON, q.v., dau. of John Davison and Isabella Hamilton.

17. JANE DAVISON, b. 1819, d. 1902, m. (1) 3 NOV 1828 in Clermont Co. to Jesse Henwood, and m. (2) William South, b. 7 OCT 1815, d. 5 AUG 1875, bur. the I.O.O.F. Boston Lodge No. 189 Cem., Stonelick Twp., Clermont Co., Ohio. Children:
    171. MARCUS SOUTH, b. 10 FEB 1842, d. 28 OCT 1864.
    172. JOHN M. SOUTH, b. August 1845, d. 26 MAY 1907.

18. FLORENCE DAVISON, m. 11 NOV 1828 in Clermont Co., Ohio to Arthur Duncan, b. 1812 in Ky., d. 1880, who m. (2) 16 MAR 1843 in Hendricks Co., Ind. to Jemima Ward. In 1839, Robert Davison conveyed property to Arthur Duncan in Hendricks Co., Ind.[8]

19. GEORGE DAVISON, b. between 1800-1810, was m. 29 MAY 1831 by Rezin Hill,

---

[1] Clermont Co., Ohio Marriages, Record Bk. No. 1, p. 121.
[2] Clermont Co., Ohio Marriages, Record Bk. No. 2, p. 20.
[3] Clermont Co., Ohio Marriages, Record Bk. No. 2, p. 23.
[4] Clermont Co., Ohio Marriages, Record Bk. No. 2, p. 324.
[5] Clermont Co., Ohio Marriages, Record Bk. No. 2, p. 158.
[6] Another source gives December 15.
[7] Clermont Co., Ohio Marriages, Record Bk. No. 2, p. 205.
[8] Hendricks Co., Ind. Deeds, Bk. 7, p. 235, dated 14 JUN 1836.

J.P., in Clermont Co., Ohio to Rachel Knott.[1] Two children.

1(10). ELIZABETH DAVISON, b. November 16, 1822 in Clermont Co., Ohio, was m. 1 FEB 1838 there by James McKimme, J.P., to Isaiah Prickett, Sr., b. 31 OCT 1817, d. 23 FEB 1852. Children:[2]
    1(10)1.   ROBERT D. PRICKETT, b. 11 DEC 1839.
    1(10)2.   FLORENCE VIOLA PRICKETT, b. 24 DEC 1841 in Clermont Co., d. 3 JAN 1892.
    1(10)3.   ANDREW JACKSON PRICKETT, b. 15 MAY 184[3].
    1(10)4.   FRANCIS MARION PRICKETT, b. 3 JAN 1846.
    1(10)5.   WILLIAM PRICETT, b. 27 JAN 1849.
    1(10)6.   ISAIAH PRICKETT, JR., b. 17 MAY 1850, d. 14 FEB 1882 from the effects of a boat excursion, m. 12 JUN 1871 to Lucy Ferrell, b. 16 NOV 1848, d. 23 NOV 1918, dau. of Ezekiel Ferrell and Mornen Roy. Child:
        1(10)61.   ELDON PRICKETT, res. in Newtown, Ohio in 1969 and had the family Bible in 1982.[3]

16. <u>James Hamilton Davison</u>
(1806-1899)

James Hamilton Davison, son of Robert Davison and Florence Hamilton, was born 15 DEC 1806 in Williamsburg, Clermont County, Ohio. He was married 20 SEP 1827 in Clermont County, Ohio to his cousin 44. ELIZABETH [Hamilton] DAVISON, the daughter of John Davison and Isabella Hamilton, *q.v.* James H. Davison was a farmer.

Elizabeth was born 15 NOV 1809 in Milford, Clermont County, Ohio, and died on 13 DEC 1891 about 1½ miles northwest of Hidalgo, Jasper County, Illinois.

They are enumerated on the Federal census of 11 DEC 1850 for Crooked Creek Precinct of Jasper County, Illinois [family #545; page 299, as James Davidson]. James H. Davison died 2 MAR 1899 in Hidalgo, Jasper County, Illinois.

Children of James Hamilton Davison and Elizabeth [Hamilton] Davison:

161.   ISABELLA DAVISON, b. 28 AUG 1828 in Clermont Co., Ohio, d. 29 APR 1910 in Sidel, Vermillion Co., Ill. m. 28 JAN 1846 by J. Kiger in Madison, Jefferson Co., Ind. to James Torbutt, b. 1825, d. 1882. 9 children.
162.   FLORINDA DAVISON, b. 7 DEC 1829 in Clermont Co., Ohio, d. 4 JUL 1849.
163.   NANCY HANNAH DAVISON, b. 20 JUN 1832, d. in February 1878 in Greenup, Ill., m. 1 SEP 1853 near Hidalgo, Ill. to Milan Cramer Carr, b. 1832, d. 1918. 4 children.
164.   ROBERT H. DAVISON, b. 30 NOV 1833 in Clermont Co., Ohio, d. 26 NOV 1916 near Hidalgo, Ill., bur. Hays Cem., served in Co. E, 97th Ill. Inf. during the Civil War, res. in 1880 at Crooked Creek, Jasper Co., Ill.

---

[1] Clermont Co., Ohio Marriages, Record Bk. No. 2, p. 379.
[2] Also see Prickett Family Bible, in Robert D. Craig, *Clermont County Records*, Vol. VI (1969), p. 34.
[3] Letter to Judy Everhart from Jim Wooddell of Okeana, Ohio, dated 8 JUN 1982.

165.   ELLEN ISABEL DAVISON, b. 2 JUL 1835 in Clermont Co., Ohio, d. 4 OCT 1859 in Jasper Co., Ill.

166.   MARTHA DAVISON, b./d. inf. in 1837.

167.   MARGARET ANNE DAVISON, m. 7 JAN 1858 in Jasper Co., Ill. to Michael S. Hays; both bur. Hays Cem. Child:

   1671.   CLINTON HAYS.

168.   MORGAN DAVISON, b. 1838, d. 1884.

169.   JAMES FINLAY DAVISON, b. 12 JUL 1840 in Clermont Co., Ohio, d. 1924 in Jasper Co., Ill., m. 13 OCT 1861 in Chauncey, Jasper Co., Ill. to Helen Tevis, res. in 1910 at Crooked Creek, Jasper Co., Ill. Child:

   1691.   CHARLES ELLIOTT DAVISON, b. 1866 in Ill., d. 1944, bur. Seminary Cem., Vandalia, Fayette Co., Ill., m. 14 MAR 1889 in Jasper Co. to Lou Ella Songer, b. 1868, d. 1942.

16(10).   JOHN DAVISON, b. 3 FEB 1842 in Clermont Co., d. bef. 1884.

16(11).   MARY DAVISON, b. 1844 in Ohio, d. bef. 1884.

16(12).   HESTER DAVISON, b. 1848 in Ohio.

16(13).   CHARLES DAVISON, b. 1852 in Jasper Co., Ill., d. 1878 in Greenup, Cumberland Co., Ill.

2. James Davison
(1773-c.1852)

The ancestor through which we descend is James Davison, son of George Davison and Eleanor Allen, who was born about 1773 in Westmoreland County, Pennsylvania. He was married, perhaps in Pennsylvania, about 1795 to Catherine (perhaps Long), born about 1780 in Hamilton County, Ohio. Hamilton County was divided in 1800 to form Clermont County, Ohio.

James Davison served with General Arthur St. Clair in Ohio in 1791 and was with his Army when it went from Fort Washington (now Cincinnati) to Fort Hamilton (now Hamilton, Ohio), but was defeated on November 4 of that year near Fort Greenville (now Greenville, Ohio). James then served in the army under General Anthony Wayne. Upon his return it is believed he married, and soon thereafter removed to Kentucky, and then in spring 1800 to newly-formed Clermont County, Ohio.

The family for James Davison appears on the local 1802 Census for Clermont County, Ohio, as well as on the 1810 Ohio Tax List for Clermont County. In April 1804, he voted in the first election held in Miami Township of Clermont County.[1] In 1805, James Davison purchased 50 acres of land from Thomas Paxton in Clermont County for $150.[2] In 1810, James and Catherine Davison sold 36-1/16 acres of land in Clermont County to Thomas Cottaral.[3] In 1818, James Davison purchased 199 acres of land from William Lytle.[4] In 1826, James was living in Batavia Township. In 1833, James Taylor and attorney, sold 4

---

[1] See Louis H. Evers, *History of Clermont County* (1882), p. 468.
[2] Clermont Co., Ohio Deeds, Bk. 3, p. 51.
[3] Clermont Co., Ohio Deeds, Bk. 6, p. 80.
[4] Clermont Co., Ohio Deeds, Bk. 17, p. 365; survey 4459.

acres in Clermont County, to James Davison.[1]

We find this family on the Federal census for 1840 and 1850 U.S. in Clermont County, Ohio, Batavia Township. James (age 77) is enumerated with his son John, on page 310 of the census taken July 30, 1850. He had apparently sold his 2-acre residence in 1845 and moved in with his eldest son John Davison.[2] James died prior to 4 JUN 1852, and the whereabouts of the grave for him or his wife is unknown.

On 4 JUN 1852, an administrator's bond in the amount of $500 was granted to Milton Jamison (attested by Elias Fitzwater and James Davidson) to settle the estate of James Davison/Davidson.[3] As administrator, Jamieson purchased 199 acres from the estate proceedings.[4] An inventory of the estate of James Davison, Sr. was filed on June 18, 1853 by Thomas Kain and John Jamison.

Children of James Davison and Catherine (perhaps Long):

21. ELLEN [or Eleanor] DAVISON, b. c.1797, m. 20 APR 1817 in Clermont Co., Ohio by Robert Allen, J.P., to John Bingaman (Bengeman).[5] The couple was enumerated on the 1820 Federal census for Clay Twp. of Brown Co., Ohio [page 394], and 1830 Federal census for Scott Twp., Brown Co., Ohio [page 474]. Ellen may have m. (2) by 1840 to Mr. Fields, and d. after 1850 in Brown Co., Ohio.[6] Perhaps seven children.

+ 22. JOHN DAVISON, b. 15 DEC 1799 in Ky., m. 13 APR 1818 to Areanna Chalmers.

+ 23. ELIZABETH DAVISON, b. 16 NOV 1802 in Clermont Co., Ohio, m. 7 AUG 1823 to Elias Fitzwater.

24. MARY "Polly" DAVISON, b. 1 APR 1807 in Clermont Co., Ohio, m. 3 JUN 1825 by David Morris, J.P., there to Henry Mayham. She d. 29 DEC 1875. Perhaps three children.

+ 25. JAMES C. DAVISON, b. 14 JAN 1812 in Clermont Co., Ohio, d. 29 DEC 1904 there at the age of 92y 11m 17d, m. 31 DEC 1835 there to Lenor Mayham.

+ 26. ROBERT DAVISON, b. 16 NOV 1815 in Clermont Co., Ohio, d. 1880, m. 14 MAR 1839 there to Esther Needham.

+ 27. GEORGE W. DAVISON (my ancestor), b. 7 MAR 1816 in Batavia Township, Clermont Co., Ohio, was m. (1) to Paulina F. Kain and m. (2) to Caroline Smith.

+ 28. WILLIAM DAVISON, b. c.1817 in Clermont Co., Ohio, m. Mary Ann Waits.

---

[1] Clermont Co., Ohio Deeds, Bk. 29, p. 281; survey 4783. This may have been his last residence.
[2] Clermont Co., Ohio Deeds, Bk. 44, p. 45; survey 4783.
[3] Clermont Co. Ohio Accounts, Bk. 3, p. 450.
[4] Clermont Co., Ohio Deeds, Bk. 59, p. 432; survey 4459.
[5] Clermont Co., Ohio Marriages, Record Bk. No. 1, p. 89.
[6] One researcher questioned if she married 2nd to Mr. Fields in Brown Co., Ohio.

29.   CHRISTOPHER DAVISON, laborer b. c.1820 in Ohio, d. after 1880, living with his brother Samuel in Brown Co., Ohio in 1880.

+ 2(10). SAMUEL DAVISON, b. c.1822 in Clermont Co., Ohio, m. 12 APR 1841 in Clermont Co., Ohio to Mary Lukemeier.

22. John Davison
(1799-1886)

John Davison, son of James Davison and Catherine (perhaps Long), was born 15 DEC 1799 in Kentucky. John served in the military during the War of 1812. He was married 13 APR 1818 by William Kelly, J.P. in Miami Township, Clermont County, Ohio to Areanna Chalmers.[1] The couple is enumerated on the 1850 Federal census for Batavia Township of Clermont County, Ohio [page 619], and on the 1860 Federal census for that location [family 969, page 341]. John was a farmer.

John died 21 JUL 1886 in Clermont County, Ohio, and was buried there in the Old Owensville Cemetery of Stonelick Township. Araenor/Areanna, the daughter of Andrew Chalmers and Alice Beasley, was born 10 JUL 1799 in Fulton, Hamilton County, Ohio, and died 24 JUL 1873 of paralysis, age 74y and 14d, and was also buried in the Old Owensville Cemetery. Andrew Chalmers, born 17 MAR 1755, served in the Revolutionary War, and died 25 NOV 1833. He was wounded at Bunker Hill. Alice was born 14 NOV 1768, and died 5 FEB 1855.[2]

Children of John Davison and Areanna Chalmers, order uncertain:

221.   GEORGE DAVISON, b. c.1818 in Ohio.

+ 222.   PHILIP DAVISON, b. 17 MAY 1819 in Clermont Co., Ohio, m. 13 SEP 1838 there to Roxaline Allison, *q.v.*

223.   CHRISTOPHER DAVISON.

224.   ROBERT DAVISON, b. c.1824 in Ohio, d. c.1853, m. Mary (unknown). After Robert's death, Mary m. (2) c.1855 to William Nordike, farmer, b. 1820 in Ohio. William and Mary are found on the Federal census of 28 JUN 1860 for Tate Twp., Clermont Co. [family 469, page 305]. Children:
2241.   FRANCIS DAVISON, b. 1849 in Ohio.
2242.   JOSEPHINE DAVISON, b. 1853 in Ohio, d. 23 OCT 1876, unmarried.

225.   MARGARET DAVISON.

226.   HENRY DAVISON, b. 28 AUG 1829, d. 29 JUL 1848, age 18y, 11m, 2d, bur. in

---

[1] Clermont Co., Ohio Marriages, Record Bk. No. 1, p. 106.
[2] Cemetery records, and death date confirmed by Clermont County Death Records, Volume 1, page 98, entry #2202.

Old Owensville Cem.

227.   ALICE DAVISON, b. c.1836 in Ohio, m. 1 OCT 1852 by James Perrine, J.P., in Clermont Co. to her cousin 422. JOHN REEVES, b. 1833. Res. in Auglaize Co., Ohio in 1860. Children:
2271.   OLIVE REEVES, b. 1853.
2272.   LAURA E. REEVES, b. 1855.
2273.   ELVIRA B. REEVES, b. 1858.
2274.   SUSAN G. REEVES, b. 1859.

228.   JAMES DAVISON, b. 22 OCT 1837 in Clermont Co., d. 23 FEB 1928 in Clermont Co., m. 1 SEP 1859 in Clermont Co., Ohio to Martha J. Simons [or Summers], b. 1837. Children:
2281.   JOSEPH DAVISON, b. c.APR 1860.
2282.   CHARLES DAVISON, rem. to Kan.
2283.   THOMAS DAVISON.
2284.   JOHN DAVISON, m. Harriet Moyer. Child:
22841.   HUGH DAVISON, attorney, m. Ethel M. Howell.
2285.   EMMA DAVISON, m. John Burnside.
2286.   HERMAN DAVISON, m. Julia Chatterton.
2287.   NELLIE DAVISON.
2288.   HARVEY DAVISON, m. Emma Dickerson, res. in Windsor, Colo.
2289.   ALICE DAVISON.

229.   MARY ELEANOR DAVISON, b. c.1840 in Ohio.
22(10).   JOHN DAVISON.
22(11).   ELIZABETH DAVISON.
22(12).   CATHERINE DAVISON.
22(13).   JANE DAVISON.

222. Philip Davison
(1819-1900)

Philip Davison, son of James Davison and Catherine (perhaps Long), was born 17 MAY 1819, probably in Clermont County, Ohio. He was married there on 13 SEP 1838 by John Hill, M.G., to Roxaline Allison. Philip was a farmer.

His family was enumerated on the 1850 Federal census for Jackson Township, Clermont County, Ohio [family 184; page 67A], and also on 22 JUN 1860 in Jackson Township [family 397, page 375]. They are found on the 1870 Federal census for Jackson Township [family 207]. Philip heads family 42 in Jackson Township on the 1880 Federal census [page 98], and his household includes his father John Davison, aged 80 years, born in Kentucky, with parents born in Ireland and Ohio. Philip belonged to Maple Grove Methodist Episcopal Church.[1]

---

[1] Also see Louis H. Evers, *History of Clermont County, Ohio* (188w), p. 553.

Philip Davison died 5 APR 1900 in Clermont County, and was buried in the I.O.O.F. Boston Lodge No. 189 Cemetery, located on Route 50 between Owensville and Stonelick. "Roxana" Davison, born 8 SEP 1817, died 6 AUG 1894, was also buried in the I.O.O.F. Boston Lodge No. 189 Cemetery.

Children of Philip Davison and Roxaline Allison:

2221. MARGARET JANE DAVISON, b. c.1842 in Ohio, m. 25 MAY 1862 by Benjamin Glasscock, M.G. in Clermont Co., Ohio to Leonidas Marsh, b. 1842.

2222. HULDA S. DAVISON, b. 1845 in Ohio, d. 1914, m. 25 DEC 1864 in Clermont Co., Ohio to David Hand Hill, b. 1838, d. 1916, both bur. Greenlawn Cem., Milford, Clermont Co., Ohio. Children:
22221. LAURA B. HILL, b. 1866, d. 1899.
22222. LOUELLA A. HILL, b. 1869, d. 1881.
22223. ALICE MAY HILL, b. 1876, d. 1940, m. Mr. Snider.

+ 2223. HENRY W. DAVISON, b. 18 SEP 1848 in Ohio, d. 14 MAR 1929, m. 29 MAY 1872 in Clermont Co., to Rebecca Hulick, b. 20 MAR 1852, d. 29 MAR 1923.

2224. Infant DAVISON, d. 21 NOV 1851, bur. in Old Owensville Cem., Clermont Co., Ohio.

2225. RUTH E. DAVISON, d. 14 JUL 1855, age 2y 7m 7d, bur. in Old Owensville Cem.

2226. RICHARD M. DAVISON, b. 1855 in Ohio, m. Harriet M. Sweet.

2227. ARIA ANN DAVISON, b. 1858 in Ohio, m. William Ireton.

2228. ALBERT L. DAVISON, b. 14 FEB 1860 in Ohio, d. 11 DEC 1864, age 5y 9m 27d, bur. in Old Owensville Cem.

2229. MARY BELLE DAVISON, b. in Ohio, d. 12 MAR 1898 of pneumonia in Monterey, Clermont Co., Ohio, age 38y 3m 16d.[1]

2223. Henry W. Davison
(1848-1929)

Henry W. Davison, son of Philip Davison and Roxaline Allison, was born 18 SEP 1848 in Ohio. He was married 29 MAY 1872 in Clermont County, Ohio to Rebecca Hulick, born 20 MAR 1852. Henry died 14 MAR 1929, and Rebecca died 29 MAR 1923. Both are buried in Williamsburg Cemetery of Clermont County, Ohio.

---

[1]Death information from Clermont County Death Register of 1896, Page 40, entry #8.

Children of Henry W. Davison and Rebecca Hulick:

22231. ALMA DAVISON, b. 27 DEC 1873, d. 1 FEB 187_.

22232. GEORGIE HULICK DAVISON, b. 24 JUN 1875, m. (1) 3 JUL to Charles Runyan, b. 16 SEP 1869, d. 12 JUN 1910, m. (2) 25 JAN 1917 to John W. Lytle, b. 13 MAR 1867, d. 6 NOV 1943. Son:
222321. JOHN W. LYTLE, b. 19 DEC 1917, m. 1 MAY 1948 to Eloise Quinton.

22233. MINA DAVISON, b. 14 JUL 1877, m. 17 JUN 1909 to Morris Rice, attorney.

22234. OWEN CLARENCE DAVISON, physician, b. 13 SEP 1881 in Jackson Twp., Clermont Co., Ohio, d. 19 SEP 1959 in Bethesda Oak Hospital of Cincinnati, Ohio, m. 31 MAY 1906 to Marie Richards, res. in West St., Bethel, Ohio. Children:
222341. REBECCA ELIZABETH DAVISON, b. 21 DEC 1908, d. MAY 1916.
222342. FRANCES MARIE DAVISON, b. 13 JAN 1912.
222343. ROBERT O. DAVISON, b. 12 JAN 1914.
222344. OWEN RICHARDS DAVISON, b. 6 JAN 1915.

22235. FRANK LORAIN DAVISON, dentist, b. 16 MAY 1883, d. 1 OCT 1964 at Westerville, Franklin Co., Ohio, bur. Greenlawn Cem., Columbus, Franklin Co., Ohio, m. (1) 30 SEP 1906 to Rose Alice Gaskins, daughter of Dr. Gaskins, had nine children and were divorced. Frank m. (2) Mary (unknown), the daughter of the mayor of Delaware, Ohio. Children:
222351. FRANK LORAIN DAVISON, b. 11 NOV 1907, d. 7 OCT 1966 in Cincinnati, Ohio.
222352. HAROLD EUGENE DAVISON, SR., b. 1 DEC 1909 in Ohio, d. 28 FEB 1988 in Columbus, Ohio, bur. Riverside Cem., Columbus, Ohio, m. Helen L. Lytle, b. 27 JUN 1908 in Ohio, d. 26 FEB 1980 in Lancaster, Fairfield Co., Ohio, bur. Riverside Cem., daughter of Lewis Fillmore Lytle (1875-1952) and Lulu Bellle Westonbarger (1878-1963). Chilldren:
2223521. PEGGY ANN DAVISON.
2223522. JUDY I. DAVISON.
2223523. BETTY MAE DAVISON.
2223524. HAROLD EUGENE DAVISON, JR.
2223525. JANE LOUISE DAVISON, b. 28 JUN 1946 in Columbus, Ohio, d. 9 SEP 2010, m. Philip Carl Brokaw, bur. Riverside Cem., Columbus, Ohio.
222353. DONALD LEE DAVISON, b. 7 JUN 1911, d. 8 FEB 1998 in Elwood, Ind.
222354. RUSSELL L. DAVISON, b. 1913, d. 3 JUL 1982.
222355. ROBERT ALLEN DAVISON, b. 7 JAN 1914 in Delaware Co., Ohio, d. 19 FEB 1994 in Memphis, Tenn.
222356. RICHARD PARKS DAVISON, b. 9 MAR 1917 in Columbus, Ohio, res. in Malden, Dunklin Co., Mo., d. 11 JUL 2006 in Missouri Southern Healthcare of Dexter, Mo., bur. Elder Cem. of Campbell, Mo., m. 24 JUN 1948 in Lynchburg, Ohio to Dorothy Carolyn Hart, b. 1925, d. 2010.

222357. DOROTHEA JEAN DAVISON, b. 16 MAY 1920, d. 2 APR 2011 in Denver, Colo.

222358. ELIZABETH ANN DAVISON, b. 1921, d. 2005.

222359. ALICE HULICK DAVISON.

23. Elizabeth Davison Fitzwater
(1802-1885)

Elizabeth Davison, born 16 NOV 1802 in Clermont County, Ohio, was a daughter of James Davison and Catherine (perhaps Long). She was married in the same county on 7 AUG 1823 to Elias Fitzwater. Elias, a son of David Fitzwater and Jane Gilkeson, was born 11 JUL 1801 in Ontario County, New York.

The couple is enumerated on the 1850 Federal census for Batavia Township, Clermont County [family 438, page 624]. On 31 JUL 1860, they were enumerated as family 937 in Batavia Township [page 339]. Elizabeth died 3 AUG 1885 in Clermont County, Ohio, age 82y 8m 19d, and was buried in Batavia Union Cemetery. Elias was a farmer.

On 9 JAN 1864, Elizas Fitzwater wrote his last will and testament. It was proved 31 MAR 1864.[1] He died 11 JAN 1864, age 62y and 6m, and was buried in Batavia Union Cemetery.

Children of Elias Fitzwater and Elizabeth Davison:

231. PHILIP J. FITZWATER, b. 17 JUN 1822 in Clermont Co., d. 23 MAR 1908 in Batavia, Clermont Co., m. Adeline Hendley (1829-1913); both bur. Batavia Union Cem.

232. HESTER FITZWATER, b. 1824, d. 1910, bur. Batavia Union Cem., m. William Glancy, b. 1812, d. 6 DEC 1891 in Clermont Co.

233. DAVID FITZWATER, b. 20 APR 1830, d. 31 JAN 1854, bur. Batavia Union Cem.

234. DORCAS FITZWATER, b. 15 SEP 1833 in Clermont Co., d. 3 SEP 1918 in Oconto, Custer Co., Nebr., bur. Oconto Cem., m. 10 JUL 1850 in Clermont Co. to Elias Tower Stairs (1830-1906).

235. HARRIET FITZWATER, b. 12 JUL 1835 in Ohio, d. 23 JUN 1906 in Vigo Twp., Ind., m. 22 DEC 1850 in Clermont Co. to William Calvin Forbus.

236. SARAH FITZWATER, b. 5 AUG 1837 in Ohio, d. 18 DEC 1862, m. James Skelley (1833-1865); both bur. Batavia Union Cem.

237. KITTURA FITZWATER, b. 10 OCT 1840 in Batavia, Ohio, d. 21 DEC 1921 in Batavia, m. 30 DEC 1858 in Clermont Co. to Francis M. Smith; both bur. Batavia

---

[1] Clermont Co., Ohio Wills, Bk. I, pp. 353, 366.

Union Cem.

238.   GEORGE W. FITZWATER, b. 1844 in Ohio, d. 14 NOV 1929 in Clermont Co., m. 19 FEB 1863 in Clermont Co. to Amanda Smith.

25. James Davison
(1812-1904)

This James Davison, a son of James Davison and Catherine (perhaps Long), was born 14 JAN 1812 in Clermont County, Ohio. He was married 31 DEC 1835 by Alexander Blair, J.P., in Clermont County to Eleanor or Lenor Mayham. Lenor was born in Ohio about 1816 and died after 1880. Her parents were from Wales.

On 31 JUN 1850, the family was listed on the Federal census as family 437 [page 624] in Batavia Township, Clermont County, Ohio. They were listed as family 600 on page 316 of the census for 1860 in the same township, then on the 1870 census for the same location [family 308].

James Davison died 29 DEC 1904 in Clermont County, Ohio,[1] and we have no information about the death of Lenor Mayham.

Children of James Davison and Lenor Mayham:

251.   ELIZABETH S. DAVISON, b. 1838 in Ohio.

252.   SAMUEL DAVISON, b. 1840 in Ohio, m. 1 SEP 1861 in Clermont Co., Ohio to Frances Jane Brooks, b. 25 JAN 1846, d. 17 JUL 1899, bur. Williamsburg Cem.

253.   ASHER DAVISON [Davidson], b. 1842 in Ohio, d. 1911, bur. Oak Hill Cem., Elk City, Montgomery Co., Kan., m. 29 OCT 1861 in Clermont Co., Ohio[2] to Deborah Curlis, b. 28 DEC 1833, d. 24 JAN 1915.

254.   ANGELINE DAVISON, b. 1846 in Ohio.

255.   LYDIA A. DAVISON, b. 1849 in Ohio.

256.   GEORGE DAVIDSON, b. 1852 in Ohio, m. 1 APR 1872 in Clermont Co. to Harriet Curlis. Listed on the 1880 Federal census for Batavia Twp., Clermont Co. [family 404].

257.   AMANDA DAVISON, b. 1855 in Ohio.

---

[1] Clermont Co., Ohio Death Register, p. 43.
[2] Clermont Co., Ohio Marriages, p. 15.

26. Robert Davison
(1815-1880)

Robert Davison, son of James Davison and Catherine (perhaps Long), was born 16 NOV 1815 in Clermont County, Ohio. He was married in the same county on 14 MAR 1839 by David Whitcomb, J.P., to Esther Needham. He was a shoemaker.

The family was enumerated on the 1850 Federal census for Stonelick Township, Clermont County, Ohio [family 533, page 179], and on the 1860 Federal census for Stonelick Township [family 717; page 398]. On the 1870 Federal census he is enumerated as Robert Davidson in Stonelick Township, with wife Hester [family 300; page 290]. Esther is head of household in Boston, Ohio in 1880, and showing that her father was born in England [family 42; page 258A].

Robert died 19 MAR 1880 at the age of 64 years, 4 months and 14 days and was buried in the I.O.O.F. Boston Lodge No. 189 Cemetery between Owensville and Stonelick, Clermont Co., Ohio. His will was dated 21 MAR 1872 and proved 14 APR 1880 in Clermont County.[1] Esther, born 4 OCT 1820, died 3 FEB 1891, was also buried in the I.O.O.F. Boston Lodge No. 189 Cemetery.

Children of Robert Davison and Esther Needham:

261.	JOHN N. DAVISON, school teacher, b. 7 APR 1840 in Ohio, d. 15 JUN 1865, age 25y 2m 8d, in Summit Point, Va. during the Civil War, and bur. I.O.O.F. Boston Lodge No. 189 Cem., perhaps m. Maude Connell. He served in Co. F, 195th Ohio Vol. Inf.

262.	ELIZA ANN DAVISON, b. 1846 in Ohio, m. Mr. Fletcher.

263.	OLIVE DAVISON, b. 20 OCT 1850, d. 23 MAR 1851, age 5m 11d, bur. in I.O.O.F. Boston Lodge No. 189 Cem.

264.	MAUDE CAMILLE[2] DAVISON, b. 1861 in Ohio, alive in 1880.

---

[1] Clermont Co., Ohio Wills, Bk. M, p. 356, witnesses include Alexander Davison, of Equality, Gallatin Co., Ill.
[2] She is listed as Maria C. Davidson on the 1870 census.

27. <u>George W. Davison</u>
(1816-1893)

George W. Davison (my ancestor) was the grandfather of Chester Leland Davison, and died long before Chester was born, and was obviously unknown to him. Naturally it was a surprise to unveil this relation and find him buried in the Union Cemetery in Chester Davison's native town of Kansas City, Missouri. George W. Davison, son of George Davison and Eleanor Allen, was born 7 MAR 1816 in Clermont County, Ohio. He was a farmer and a member of the Tabernacle Church.

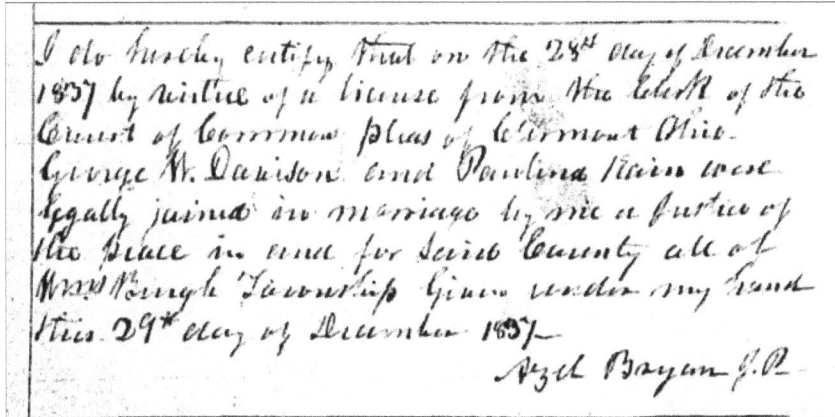

Figure 51 - Davison to Kain marriage, 1837

He was first married 29 DEC 1837 by Azel Bryan, J.P., in Williamsburg, Clermont County, Ohio to Paulina F. Kain[1] who died at the age of 30 years on 18 JAN 1848. Paulina Davison was buried in the Williamsburg Cemetery, and was a daughter of Thomas Kain. Next to Paulina F. Kain in the cemetery is Sarah Kain, wife of Dr. W.G. Gage, who died 4 FEB 1861 at the age of 49 years.

George W. Davison is enumerated on the 1840 Federal census for Stonelick Township, Clermont County, Ohio [page 245]. He is enumerated on 6 AUG 1850 on the Federal census for Williamsburg Township [page 644].[2]

George W. Davison married second on 12 OCT 1848 by Henry Wharton, M.G. in Clermont County, Ohio[3] to Caroline Smith who was born about 1828 in Williamsburg, Ohio. They are enumerated on the Federal census of 6 AUG 1850 for Williamsburg Township of Clermont County [family 592, page 644]. The couple removed from Clermont County, Ohio to Carrollton, Missouri in 1865, and are enumerated in the 1870 Federal census for Grand River Township, Carroll County, Missouri. In 1880, we find the family living in Salt Pond Township, Saline County, Missouri, next to the Kirkpatrick Family [family 327; page 428]; and in 1890, Kansas City, Jackson County, Missouri. On the 1880 census, both parents of Caroline were born in Ohio.

George W. Davison died 8 FEB 1893 at his home in Kansas City, Missouri, and was buried on 11 FEB 1893 in the old Union Cemetery of Kansas City [section 8, grave 2-48].

---

[1] Clermont Co., Ohio Marriages, Volume 3, p. 128, by Azel Bryan, J.P.
[2] Also enumerated on the 1850 census is a child Henry A. Davison, aged 4 months. This adds further puzzle to the actual birth year of Henry, yet seems to disprove all other dates of 1851, 1853 and 1857.
[3] Clermont Co. Ohio Marriages, Bk. 5, p. 38, Henry Wharton, M.G.

Caroline Smith died 24 NOV 1899 at 314 West 13th Street,[1] Kansas City, Missouri and was buried on 26 NOV 1899 in the old Union Cemetery, yet not adjacent to her husband [section 11, grave 5-38].

Children of George W. Davison and his second wife Caroline Smith:

+ 271. HENRY AUGUSTUS DAVISON, b. 9 FEB 1851 in Williamsburg, Clermont Co., Ohio., m. 24 SEP 1871, in possibly Carroll Co., Mo. to Sarah Jane Woods. He d. 2 DEC 1918 in Kansas City, Wyandotte Co., Kan., bur. 5 DEC 1918 in Elmwood Cem. of Kansas City, Mo.

+ 272. CHARLES CONDUS DAVISON (my ancestor), b. 4 JUL 1853 in Clermont Co., Ohio, m. 25 DEC 1884 in Moberly, Randolph Co., Mo., to 41(11). FLORENCE EVELYN RIDGEWAY, *q.v.* He d. 14 NOV 1917 in Kansas City, Mo., bur. 17 NOV 1917 in Elmwood Cem.

273. ANNA BELLE DAVISON, b. 11 DEC 1855 in Fletcher, Miami Co., Ohio, m. lin Jackson Co., Mo. to August Pfeiffer.[2] Anna Pfeiffer d. 20 DEC 1913 of cancer at 2718 Cleveland Ave., Kansas City, Mo., bur. 23 DEC 1913 Elmwood Cem. Children:
    2731. GEORGE PFEIFFER, lived at 85th and Woodland in Kansas City, Mo.
    2732. Infant Pfeiffer, b./d. 23 SEP 1890, bur. 24 SEP 1890 in Union Cem. [sect. 6 lot 5]
    2733. Infant Pfeiffer, bur. 24 DEC 1891 in Union Cem. [sect. 6 lot 5]

274. NANCY CAROLINE DAVISON, b. 10 MAY 1859 in Ohio.

+ 275. IDA ELIZABETH DAVISON, b. 3 APR 1861 in Ohio, m. 3 APR 1881 to Alexander King.

276. LAURA ELLA DAVISON, b. 18 JAN 1864 in Ohio, m. 31 MAR 1881 by John C. Howard, J.P. in Saline Co., Mo. to James J. Jeffries, b. AUG 1850 in Mo. They were on the 1900 Federal census for Kaw Twp., Jackson Co., Mo., on Holmes St. Children:
    2761. ADOLPH JEFFRIES, b. JAN 1881 in Mo.
    2762. NETTIE JEFFRIES, b. FEB 1882 in Mo., m. (1) Otto Therald, m. (2) Arthur Brown. Enumerated on the 1900 Federal census for Kansas City, Mo., Kaw Twp., Holmes St., and with them is living her uncle Franklin L. Davison. They owned a cleaning shop at about 9th St. in Kansas City, but later moved to San Antonio, Tex. Child:
    27621. OTTO HAROLD BROWN.

277. GEORGE WILLIAM DAVISON, b. 6 MAR 1870 in Carroll Co., Mo., perhaps m. Ella (unknown), moved to Bartlesville, Washington Co., Okla. He appeared in

---

[1] Information from Kansas City city death register. The *Kansas City Star* for 25 NOV 1899 says Caroline Davison of 1614 Holmes Street, died of heart disease.
[2] Grandmother always wrote this last name as Pluffer.

the 1930 city directory there as a laborer, while residing at 1612 West 3rd St.

278.   FRANKLIN LeCLAIR DAVISON, b. 3 NOV 1872 in Carroll Co., Mo. He is listed in the 1930 Bartlesville, Oklahoma city directory as "Frank Davidson, switchman A.T. & S.F Railway, residence 218 S. Quapaw Avenue."

Davison Bible Record[1]

George W. Davison was married to Caroline Smith in 1849
Henry Augustus Davison, (born) February 9, 1851
Charlie C. Davison, born July 4, 1853
Annabelle Davison, born December 4, 1855
Ida Elizabeth Davison, born April 3, 1861
Laura Ella Davison, born January 18, 1864
George William Davison, born March 6, 1870
Frank LeClair Davison, born November 3, 1872
Caroline Davison (died) November 4, 1899
George W. Davison Died February 8, 1893

275. Ida Elizabeth Davison King
(1861-1928)

Ida Elizabeth Davison, daughter of George W. Davison and Caroline Smith, was born 3 APR 1861 in Ohio.[2] She was married 8 APR 1881 by John C. Howard, J.P.,[3] in Saline County, Missouri to Alexander King. The family was enumerated on the 1900 and 1910 Federal census for Elmwood Township, Blackburn, Saline County, Missouri.

Alexander King, a son of Steven King of Canada and his wife Columbia Stafford of Virginia, was born 9 JAN 1853 in Sweet Springs, Saline County, Missouri. He was a carpenter. Alexander died 22 DEC 1916 of emphysema in Blackburn, Missouri and was buried 23 DEC 1916 in the city cemetery there. Ida E. King, a hotel proprietor (according to her death certificate), died 27 SEP 1928 of a heart condition in Blackburn, Missouri at 11:20 p.m., and was buried 30 SEP 1928 in the city cemetery there.

Child of Alexander King and Ida Elizabeth Davison:

2751.   LAURA B. KING, b. JAN 1882 in Mo., m. Charles A. Guenther, a barber, son of C.C. Guenther of Germany and Emily Mueller of Newark, N.J. Laura bur. Blackburn Cem., Saline Co., Mo. Charles A., b. 21 FEB 1879 in Higginsville, Mo., d. 20 OCT 1944 in Warrensburg, Mo., bur. 1944 in Blackburn Cem.

---

[1] Notes discovered in the bible in possession of Marguerite Sullivan, Kansas City, Mo., later (1984) in the possession of Henry O. Davison of Chandler, Ariz.
[2] Her death certificate states she was born April 3, 1862 in Pickilog, Ohio - a location which has not been identified.
[3] Saline Co., Mo. Marriages, Bk. D, p. 492.

271. Henry Augustus Davison
(1851-1918)

For some time we knew little of Henry Augustus Davison, son of George W. Davison and Caroline Smith. Mrs. Alberta Towne of Topeka, Kansas has helped a great deal in providing updated information for this family.

Henry Augustus Davison was born 9 FEB 1851[1] in Williamsburg, Clermont County, Ohio. On 24 SEP 1871 he was married to Sarah Jane Wood(s), born 7 MAY 1855/6 in Nodaway or Carroll County, Missouri, the daughter of James Wood(s) and Margaret McCarty. James Wood(s) was a son of William T. Wood and Mary Glaze, and was born in Rutherford County, Tennessee and died 7 JAN 1902 in Carrollton, Missouri. Both he and his wife are buried in Big Creek Cemetery of Bosworth, Carroll County, Missouri, as is his first wife Jennie Wilson. Margaret McCarty, born 27 MAY 1827 in Nodaway County, Missouri, died 22 JUL 1882 in Carroll County, Missouri.

Henry A. Davison died 2 DEC 1918 of endocarditis at 3722 Cambridge, Kansas City, Wyandotte County, Kansas, and was buried 5 DEC 1918 in Elmwood Cemetery of Kansas City, Missouri [block 15 lot 148]. His death certificate is full of errors, but it does show that he was a railroad gateman, working at the Kansas City terminal.

Sarah Jane (Woods) Davison, died 24 AUG 1924 of cancer in Eldorado Springs, Cedar County, Missouri, and was buried 26 AUG 1924 in Elmwood Cemetery [block 15 lot 148].

Children of Henry Augustus Davison and Sarah Jane Woods:[2]

2711. JAMES W. DAVISON, b. 23 AUG 1872/3, perhaps in Carroll Co., Mo., d. 1 NOV 1873.

2712. MARGARET "Maggie" DAVISON, b. 6 MAR 1874/5 in Carrollton, Carroll Co., Mo., d. 8 MAY 1952 of cerebral apoplexy at 2020 Esterly, Kansas City, Kan., bur. 10 MAY 1952 in Elmwood Cem. [block 4 lot 205], m. James Franklin Sullivan, b. 2 JUN 1876 in Spidmore, Mo., d. 9 SEP 1957 in Kansas City, Kan., bur. 12 SEP 1958 in Elmwood Cem. [block 4 lot 205] Children:

27121. MARGUERITE J. SULLIVAN, b. 26 MAY 1916 at 512 Warden St., Kansas City, Kan.
27122. DOROTHY FRANCES SULLIVAN, b. 4 NOV 1908 at 2020 Esterly St., d. 6 APR 1911 at 512 Warden St., Kansas City, Kan.
27123. MAE ALBERTA SULLIVAN, b. 29 NOV 1898 at 617 East 14th St., Kansas City, Mo., m. L.D. Vining.

2713. THOMAS W. DAVISON, b. 9 FEB 1877 in Mo.

---

[1] U.S. Federal census records generally record him with an age which indicates he was born in either 1846 or 1853, but if that were the case he would be a son of George W. Davison's first wife, Paulina F. Kain. The birthdate on his tombstone is 1851, and we are certain the mother was Caroline Smith.
[2] Dates of birth come from a Family Bible that passed from Marguerite Sullivan of Kansas City, Mo., to Henry O. Davison of Chandler, Ariz.

2714. DORA MAY DAVISON, b. 24 MAR 1878.

+ 2715. LEE ALBERT DAVISON, b. 12 APR 1881 in Blackburn, Saline Co., Mo., d. 11 JUN 1966, m. 29 JUN 1905 in Kansas City, Mo. to Martha Maude Coie.

2716. WILLIAM HENRY DAVISON, b. 12 MAR 1892, d. 9 NOV 1963 of cancer at 3815 Blue Ridge, Kansas City, Mo., bur. Elmwood Cem. [block 5 lot 91], m. Rose M. (unknown), d. 13 JUN 1928 of dialition of the heart, age 34, bur. Elmwood Cem. [block 5 lot 91].

2715. <u>Lee Albert Davison</u>[1]
(1881-1966)

Lee Albert Davison, son of Henry Augustus Davison and Sarah J. Woods, was born 12 APR 1881 in Blackburn, Saline County, Missouri. On 29 JUN 1905, he was married in Kansas City, Jackson County, Missouri to Martha Maude Coie. My grandmother thought that in about 1927, "Albert" owned a candy store at 31st and Prospect Street in Kansas City.

Lee died 11 JUN 1966 in Kansas City, and was buried 15 JUN 1866 in Forest Hill Cemetery there. Martha, born 4 APR 1881 in Wayne County, Iowa, died 18 AUG 1968 in Topeka, Kansas and was buried 21 AUG 1968 in Forest Hill Cemetery.

Children of Lee Albert Davision and Martha Maud Coie:

27151. ALBERTA LEE DAVISON, b. 6 APR 1906 in Kansas City, Mo., d. 25 MAY 1995, m. 28 FEB 1942 in Lawrence, Kan. to Harlan Beal Towne, b. 22 APR 1893 in Valencia, Kan., d. 11 MAR 1976 in Topeka, Kan.; both bur. Memorial Park Cem. of Topeka, Shawnee Co., Kan.

+ 27152. THOMAS COIE DAVISON, b. 15 APR 1909 in Kansas City, Mo., m. (1) JUL 1932 to Irene Barlow, div. 1936.

27153. MARY ELIZABETH DAVISON, b. 1 APR 1916 in Kansas City, Mo., d. 9 OCT 1921 of infantile paralysis at 4633 S. Benton in Kansas City, bur. 11 OCT 1921 in Forest Hill Cem.

+ 27154. HENRY ORVILLE "Dave" DAVISON, b. 30 NOV 1918 in Kansas City, Mo., m. 20 OCT 1941 to Kathleen Frances Hart.

---

[1]Information in part provided by Alberta L. Towne of 1204 Frazier, Topeka KS 66604, on 21 MAY 1981.

27152. <u>Thomas Coie Davison</u>
(1909-1984)

Thomas Coie Davison, son Lee Albert Davison and Martha Maude Coie, was born 15 APR 1909 in Kansas City, Jackson County, Missouri, where he was married in July 1932 to Irene Barlow from whom he was divorced about 1936. Irene was born 23 JUN 1911.

Thomas, a painter who resided at 3934 Wabash Avenue, died Wednesday, 4 APR 1984 in Baptist Medical Center of Kansas City, and was buried 9 APR 1984 in Forest Hill Cemetery of Kansas City, Missouri.

Children of Thomas Coie Davison and Irene Barlow:

271521.   JOAN LEE DAVISON, b. 30 JAN 1933 in Kansas City, Mo., resided in Washington State in 1984.
271522.   MARY IRENE DAVISON, b. 1 OCT 1934 in Kansas City, Mo., m. 14 AUG 1957 in San Francisco, Calif. to Bertrand Ross Vielle, b. 14 FEB 1929 in Browning, Mont. The couple resided in Great Falls, Mont. in 1984. Children:
　2715221. THOMAS ROSS VIELLE, b. 24 MAY 1958 in San Francisco, Calif.
　2715222. MICHAEL FRANCIS VIELLE, b. 24 JAN 1960 in San Mateo, Calif.
　2715223. PAUL ANDREW VIELLE, b. 1 JAN 1965 in Portland, Ore.
　2715224. LAUREL ROSE VIELLE, b. 13 SEP 1973 in Browning, Mont.

27154. <u>Henry Orville Davison</u>
(1918-   )

Henry Orville Davison, son of Lee Albert Davison and Martha Maude Coie, was born 30 NOV 1918 in Kansas City, Missouri. He was married 20 OCT 1941 in Lewiston, Nez Perce County, Idaho to Kathleen Frances Hart, born 14 JAN 1923 in Walla Walla, Washington. Henry resided in Chandler, Arizona.

Children of Henry Orville "Dave" Davison and Kathleen Frances Hart:

271541.   DIANA CHERYL DAVISON, b. 3 SEP 1943 in Topeka, Kan., m. 5 MAY 1962 in Moses Lake, Wash. to Verdus Eugene Gosch, b. 14 DEC 1938 in Ute, Iowa. Children:
　2715411. DEBRA MARIE GOSCH, b. 9 OCT 1964 at the R.A.F. Hospital in Wegburg, Ger.
　2715412. BRIAN HENRY GOSCH, b. 6 NOV 1965 at the R.A.F. Hospital in Webgurg, Ger.
　2715413. JEFFREY ALLEN GOSCH, b. 7 SEP 1971 in Duluth, Minn.
271542.   DONNA CHRISTINE DAVISON, b. 28 MAY 1946 in Pendleton, Ore., m. 4 JUL 1965 in Moses Lake, Wash. to Albert Joseph McCabe, Jr., b. 22 JUL 1942 in Boston, Mass. Children:
　2715421. IRENE MARIE McCABE, b. 13 FEB 1966 in Milton, Mass.

2715422. THOMAS ALBERT McCABE, b. 25 SEP 1968 in Quincy, Mass.

2715423. DENNIS MICHAEL McCABE, b. 10 FEB 1969 in Quincy, Mass.

2715424. CHRISTOPHER SEAN McCABE, b. 30 JAN 1970 in Quincy, Mass.

271543. SHELLEY KAYE DAVISON, b. 8 SEP 1949 in Pendleton, Ore., m. 6 APR 1973 in Agana, Guam to Luis Heriberto Marquez, b. 21 JAN 1951 in Fajardo, Puerto Rico. They div. 23 DEC 1976. Shelly m. (2) 12 AUG 1977 in Omaha, Nebr. to Ted Ryon, b. 24 MAY 1940 in Brownsville, Tex. Children:

2715431. JESSICA CONCEPCION MARQUEZ, b. 11 NOV 1973 at the U.S. Air Force Academy in Colorado Springs, Colo.

2715432. JENNIFER RYON, b. 3 JAN 1980 in Omaha, Nebr.

271544. HOLLY LYN DAVISON, b. 10 NOV 1954 in the U.S. Air Force Hospital, Ruislop Air Base, South Ruislop, Middlesex Co., Eng.

272. <u>Charles Condus Davison</u>
(1853-1917)

My ancestor, Charles Condus Davison, was born 4 JUL 1853 in Clermont County, Ohio and was the second child of George W. Davison and his second wife Caroline Smith. Charles was married 25 DEC 1884 in Moberly, Randolph County, Missouri by W.R. Painter, Minister of the Gospel, to 41(11). FLORENCE EVELYN RIDGEWAY, *q.v.* Previous to moving to Corder and later Kansas City, the family of Charles C. Davison lived in Dover Township, Saline County, Missouri.

Florence was born 11 DEC 1864 in Corder, Lafayette County, Missouri, and was a daughter of Samuel Ridgeway and his second wife Jennettie A. Fowler. Her parents were from Kentucky and Tennessee, respectively, but nothing further has been learned about them.

The 1909 City Directory for Kansas City lists Charles C. Davison, carpenter, residing at 2307 Agnes, and later in the 1912 directory he is listed as working at Union Depot while residing at 2415 Cleveland Avenue in Kansas City. The 1935 City Directory lists Florence Davison, widow, residing at 1810 Cleveland Avenue, Kansas City.

Figure 52 - Florence E. Ridgeway and Charles C. Davison, wedding, 1861

Charles Condus Davison died 14 NOV 1917 of nephritis at 2417 Cleveland Avenue in Kansas City, Jackson County, Missouri and was buried 17 NOV 1917 in Elmwood

Cemetery[1] in Kansas City [block 15 lot 112]. While on a visit in Aurora, Colorado, with her son Chester and family, Florence died 21 AUG 1936 of a stroke at 3:15 a.m. at 1731 Dayton. She was buried on 24 AUG 1936 in Elmwood Cemetery back in Kansas City.

Children of Charles Condus Davision and Florence Evelyn Ridgeway:

+ 2721. HALLIE MAY DAVISON, b. 13 MAY 1886 in Blackburn, Saline Co., Mo., Missouri, m. 19 NOV 1906 to Bernard Alvin Parker.

+ 2722. ALVIN EARL DAVISON, b. 5 OCT 1888 in Blackburn, Mo., m. (1) 11 NOV 1911 to Mary V. Payne, and m. (2) 17 JUN 1925 to Ellie May Beasley.

+ 2723. WILLIAM ROY DAVISON, b. 15 FEB 1890 in Blackburn, Mo., m. (1) in 1918 to Oma Lela Pyle, he m. (2) to Rowetta Louise Schrader, who was remarried to Melvin Sharp, and Roy m. (3) to Marjorie Saphronia Ellison.

+ 2724. EFFIE FERN DAVISON, b. 20 FEB 1894 in Blackburn, Mo., m. (1) Gurnest W. Livingston, and m. (2) Byron E. Thornhill.

+ 2725. ROBERT JEWELL DAVISON, b. 28 SEP 1898 in Corder, Lafayette Co., Mo., m. Bertha Elizabeth Ritschel.

+ 2726. CHESTER LELAND DAVISON (my grandfather), b. 16 SEP 1901 in Kansas City, Mo., d. 31 MAR 1991, m. 6221. VELMA PEARL ALLEN, *q.v.*

Figure 54 - Chester, Robert, Wm. Roy and their father Charles C. Davison, 1910

Figure 53 - Robert J., Chester L. and Effie F. Davison, 1904

[1] Elmwood Cemetery is located at 15th and Van Brunt near Truman Road in Kansas City, Mo.

Figure 55 - Davison Siblings: Alvin, Roy, Bob, Effie, Chester, and Hallie.

2721. <u>Hallie May Davison Parker</u>
(1886-1958)

Hallie May Davison, daughter of Charles Condus Davison and Florence Evelyn Ridgeway, was born 13 MAY 1886 in Blackburn, Saline County, Missouri. She was married 19 NOV 1906 by a Baptist minister in Kansas City, Jackson County, Missouri to Bernard Alvin Parker, born 3 DEC 1885. In September 1918, Bernard was drafted for service in World War I; however, he was disqualified because of a short left limb. His draft card showed he resided as 2309 Bellfountaine in Kansas City, and worked as a checker at Armour Packing Company.

In 1952, the couple resided at 3234 Montgall and later at 2800 E. 73rd St. in Kansas City, Missouri. Hallie Parker died 19 JUL 1958 of myocardial infarction in St. Luke's Hospital of Kansas City, Missouri and was buried in Forest Hill Cemetery there two days later [grave 16/95-101]. Bernard A. Parker was a member of the Odd Fellows Lodge, the Swope Park Masonic Lodge, and the Ararat Shrine. He died 17 FEB 1963 at the Odd Fellows Hospital in Liberty, Missouri, and was buried 19 FEB 1963 in Forest Hill Cemetery [grave 15/95-101].

Only child of Bernard Alvin Parker and Hallie May Davison:

27211.   DOROTHY EVELYN PARKER, b. 4 JUL 1907 in Kansas City, Mo., d. 29 JUL 1974 in General Hospital of Kansas City, Mo., bur. 1 AUG 1974 in Forest Hill Cem., m. Jack W. Allen. Dorothy had information on the history of the family, and sent grandmother the birth and death dates of Florence E. (Ridgeway) Davison's parents Samuel Ridgeway and Jennettie A. Fowler. Dorothy retired from the Standard Oil Co. At the time of her death, her residence was 2800 E. 73rd St., Kansas City, and she was bur. 1 AUG 1974 in Forest Hill Cem. there. After Dorothy died, Jack remarried a woman named Opal who lived only a few years afterwards. Jack, a son of John F. Allen and Ella Crosswhite, d. 16 FEB 1981 at Research Hospital of Kansas City and was bur. 19 FEB 1981 by D.W. Newcomer Funeral Home in a lot owned by Bernard A. Parker (13/95-101) at Forest Hill Cem. His last residence was 12942 Wornall Rd., and funeral expenses were billed to John Spurlock. Other relatives were a niece Mrs. Grace Spurlock; a sister Anna Koetting of 3863 Holmes in Kansas City; and Mrs. Drew J. Spurlock of Versailles, Mo. No children.

Figure 56 - (L-R) Fran Davison, Chester Davison, Richard Davison, J.C. Davison, Jan Giese, Dorothy Parker, Peggy Davison, Eileene Pippenger, Pearl Davison, Charlie Pippenger, Alvin Davison, and Jack Parker. November 1965.

2722. Alvin Earl Davison
(1888-1969)

Alvin Earl Davison, son of Charles Condus Davison and Florence Evelyn Ridgeway, was born 5 OCT 1888 in Blackburn, Saline County, Missouri. Alvin was first married on 11 NOV 1911 to Mary V. Payne from whom he was divorced.

Alvin Davison was remarried 17 JUN 1925 by Reverend Henry W. Tolson in Washington, District of Columbia (D.C.) to Mrs. Ellie May Beasley Atkinson, who had been recently divorced from Hiram Atkinson. Ellie was born 3 MAY 1890 in Albemarle County, Virginia and was the daughter of Charles Lewis Beasley and Mary W. Wilkerson.

On 18 JUN 1900, Alvin was enumerated on the Federal census as a resident in the home of William O. Kirkpatrick, near Sedalia in Longwood Township (E.D. 105, sheet 9) of Pettis County, Missouri. The 1905 City Directory for Kansas City, Missouri lists Alvin E. Davison as a soda clerk for W.P. Hucke, with his residence at 2307 Agnes. The 1915 City Directory lists Alvin E. Davison, electrician, residing at 2417 Cleveland Avenue. He had a candy store at 22nd and Agnes Streets in Kansas City, Missouri. The draft registration card for World War I lists him in Dayton, Montgomery County, Ohio, and employed by William Hall Electric Company, age 28, and residing at 222 W. Monument Avenue.

The couple resided in Alleghany County, Virginia in 1930, and in Newport News, Virginia in 1936. By the time draft registration cards were issued for World War II, he resided in Botetourt County, Virginia. By 1952, the couple resided in Buchanan, Virginia.

Ellie Beasley Davison died 11 OCT 1965 in Montvale, near Buchanan, Botetourt County, Virginia, and was buried 14 OCT 1965 in Mountain View Cemetery near Clifton Forge, Alleghany County, Virginia. Alvin died 3 APR 1969 in Florissant, a suburb of St. Louis, Missouri and was buried 7 APR 1969 in Mountain View Cemetery near Clifton Forge.

Child of Alvin Earl Davision and second wife Ellie May Beasley:

27221. RICHARD EARL DAVISON, b. 4 AUG 1926 in Clifton Forge, Alleghany Co., Va., m. (1) in Alliance, Stark Co., Ohio to Erma A. Acierni. He m. (2) to Miss Eckiss, and m. (3) 27 NOV 1954 in St. Louis, Mo. to Frances Ruth "Fran" Buchanan, daughter of James Paul Buchanan and Vera I. Holmes, b. 27 NOV 1933 in Orient, Adair Co., Iowa. Richard E. Davison served in the U.S. Air Force. He d. 11 JAN 1983 of a heart attack in St. Louis, Mo., bur. 14 JAN 1983 in National Cem. near Jefferson Barracks, Mo. Fran resided in Loveland, Colo. in 1988. Children:

272211. RICHARD EARL DAVISON, JR., son of the second marriage, b. 29 DEC 1951 in St. Louis, Mo., resided in Orange, Calif.

272212. PAMELA LEE DAVISON, daughter of the third marriage, b. 10 SEP 1955 in St. Louis, Mo., m. 12 APR 1980 in Florissant, Mo. to Ted C. Tauser.

272213. VIRGINIA LEE DAVISON, daughter of the third marriage, b. 8 SEP 1958 in Florissant, Mo., m. Joe Duncan.

272214. Infant Davison.

27222. (Step-son) Frank L. Atkinson, of Lewisburg, W.Va.

2723. <u>William Roy Davison</u>
(1890-1974)

William "Roy" Davison, son of Charles Condus Davison and Florence Evelyn Ridgeway, was born 15 FEB 1890 in Blackburn, Saline County, Missouri. He was married three times: first 10 APR 1918 in Kansas City to Oma Lela Pyle of Jefferson County, Illinois, by whom he had no children. The 1918 City Directory for Kansas City, Missouri lists Wm. Roy Davison, an electrician, residing at 2417 Cleveland Avenue. Later, Roy worked as an electrician for the Tennessee Valley Authority, and was a member of the First United Methodist Church in Tuscumbia, Alabama.

Roy was married second in Stanley, Johnson County, Kansas to Rowetta Louise Schrader, by whom he had two children. Rowetta, the daughter of John Schrader and Effie Deister, was born 10 SEP 1907 in Stanley, Kansas, and after being divorced from William Roy Davison about 1928, she remarried Melvin Sharp. Rowetta died 22 FEB 1982 in Loma Linda, San Bernardino County, California, and was buried 27 FEB 1982 in San Jacinto Valley Cemetery, of San Jacinto, California.

Roy Davison was married third 24 AUG 1937 to Mrs. Marjorie Saphronia Ellison who had been previously married in 1906 to Archibald W. Tarwater. Marjorie, born c.1886 in Carthage, Missouri, died 30 SEP 1971 in Sheffield, Colbert County, Alabama, and was buried 5 OCT 1971 in Mount Olivet Cemetery of Raytown, Missouri. Marjorie's daughter by previous marriage, Saphronia Tarwater, married Enos Axtell, Sr., who died in October 1987. She resided in Grandview, Missouri. The Axtell house, built in 1900, caught fire in 1992, and Saphronia suffered minor burns.

Roy Davison died 24 FEB 1974 in Sheffield, Colbert County, Alabama and was buried 28 FEB 1974 in Mount Olivet Cemetery of Raytown, Missouri.

Children of William Roy Davison and his second wife Rowetta Louise Schrader:

27231. BETTY JEAN DAVISON, b. 27 JUL 1925 in Stanley, Johnson Co., Kan., m. (1) in Quartzite, Lapaz Co., Ariz. to Michael Francis McCann who d. in 1975. Betty m. (2) in Las Vegas, Nev. to John Weymes. She resided in Hemet, Calif. Child:
  272311. MICHAEL F. McCANN, m. 13 NOV 1965 at St. Stephens Episcopal Church, Banning, Calif. to Colleen Rene Schram, daughter of Leo Schram.
27232. JOHN CONDON "JACK" DAVISON, b. 25 JUN 1927 in San Jacinto, Riverside Co., Calif., m. 3 JUL 1960 to Oma Jane McHan, b. 10 DEC 1937. Children:
  272321. CAROL LOUISE DAVISON, b. 14 DEC 1961, m. 6 JUN 1987 to Ross Williams. Son:
    2723212. SCOT ENGLE WILLIAMS, b. 30 DEC 1988.
  272322. DAVID WILLIAM DAVISON, b. 25 JAN 1964, m. 19 MAY 1984 to Angie (unknown)
  272323. JOHN CONDON DAVISON, JR., b. 19 JUN 1972.

2724. <u>Effie Fern Davison Thornhill</u>
(1894-1978)

E ffie Fern Davison, daughter of Charles Condus Davison and Florence Evelyn Ridgeway, was born 20 FEB 1894 in Blackburn, Saline County, Missouri. She was married twice: first on 19 FEB 1916 in Jackson County, Missouri to Gurnest W. Livingston[1] (of whom she would not mention), who was under age 21. She was married second on 10 JAN 1921 by Rev. Elmer Brown in Kansas City, Wyandotte County, Kansas, to Byron E. Thornhill.

The 1915 City Directory for Kansas City lists Effie, employed as a clerk, residing at 2417 Cleveland Avenue, and in 1918 she is shown as residing at 1824 Washington Street.

Effie died 23 NOV 1978 of cardiac arrest in Lee's Summit, Jackson County, Missouri at the John Knox Retirement Village, and was buried 27 NOV 1978 in Forest Hill Cemetery of Kansas City, Missouri. Byron,

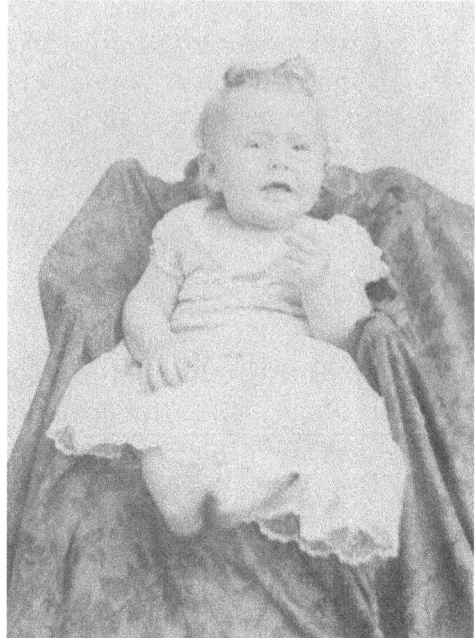
Figure 57 - Effie F. Davison

who was born 16 OCT 1894, died 29 MAY 1970 at St. Luke's Hospital in Kansas City, Missouri, age 75y 7m 13d, and was buried 1 JUN 1970 in Forest Hill Cemetery there.

They had no children, but raised two sons from another part of Mr. Thornhill's family:

27241a.   Robert L. Thornhill, Sr., m. Virginia L. Rittermeyer, daughter of Ludwig F. Rittermeyer of Sedalia, Mo. Virginia, d. 3 AUG 1981 at St. Luke's Hospital in Kansas City, Mo., bur. Forest Hill Cem. Res. Blue Springs, Mo. Children:
27241a1. Robert L. Thornhill, Jr., res. in Blue Springs, Mo.
27241a2. Linda Thornhill, m. Mr. Walker, of Overland Park, Kan.

27242a.   Richard Van Thornhill, Sr., b. in Englewood, Mo., d. 4 NOV 1991 at Liberty Hospital while a resident of Gallatin, Mo., bur. Forest Hill Cem. He worked for General Motors and was a member of the United Auto Workers Union. Children:
27242a1. Richard Van Thornhill, Jr., of Leawood, Calif.
27242a2. Daniel J. Thornhill, of Kansas City, Mo.

---

[1] In an undated letter I received from Grandmother Davison, she says "Aunt Effie wouldn't tell me anything about 'Gurney' Livingston. He had a brother Harold, it's about all I know. She was married to him long before Grandpa and I was married - I didn't know him. They stood up with Uncle Bob and Aunt Bertha when they were married, so they must have been married between 1915 and 1920 sometime."

2725. Robert Jewell Davison
(1898-1952)

Robert Jewell "Bob" Davison, son of Charles Condus Davison and Florence Evelyn Ridgeway, was born 28 SEP 1898 in Corder Village, Lafayette County, Missouri. He was married 30 JUN 1920 in Kansas City, Missouri to Bertha Elizabeth Ritschel, born 28 JUN 1901 in Kansas City, Missouri. According to her death certificate, Bertha's parents were John F. Ritschel and Mary Elizabeth Swantz. Bob was a mail carrier. In 1936 they resided at 3336 Spruce Ave. in Kansas City, and later at 5704 James Reed Road.

"Bob" Davison died 2 APR 1952 of acute coronary thrombosis in Kansas City, Missouri and was buried 7 APR 1952 in Woodlawn Cemetery of Independence, Jackson County, Missouri. Bertha E. Davison died 13 JUN 1954 of stomach cancer or a gastric ulcer in Kansas City, Missouri and was buried 16 JUN 1954 in Woodlawn Cemetery.

Children of Robert Jewell Davison and Bertha Elizabeth Ritschel:

27251.   JOHN CHARLES "J.C." DAVISON, SR., b. 14 JUL 1923, d. 9 SEP 2000, bur. Mount Moriah Cem., m. (1) 16 JUN 1955 in Joplin, Jasper Co., Mo., to Madge Cohen, from whom he was divorced 8 MAY 1958 in Clinton, Henry Co., Mo., having no children. J.C. m. (2) on 19 APR 1963 to Peggy L. Shields. They resided in Raytown, Mo. Children:
272511a. PAMELA L. SHIELDS DAVISON, daughter of Peggy L. Shields, b. 16 JUN 1953 in Waco, McLennan Co., Tex., adopted 21 JAN 1964 in Kansas City, Mo., by J.C. Davison. Pam m. 26 MAR 1976 in Kansas City, Mo. to Wesley Paul Waguespack. Children:
272511a1.   NICOLE WAGUESPACK, b. 22 JUL 1982.
272511a2.   BRETT WAGUESPACK, b. 29 MAR 1985.
272511a3.   BRANDON WAGUESPACK, b. 27 NOV 1986 in Kansas City, d. 7 APR 1988 at Children's Mercy Hospital of Kansas City, Mo. after open heart surgery. Funeral services were Sat., 9 APR 1988 in Kansas City, Mo., bur. Floral Hills Cem.
272512.   LEONE E. DAVISON, b. 9 NOV 1964 at St. Luke's Hospital of Kansas City, Mo., resided in Springfield, Mo., m. 20 AUG 1988.
272513.   JOHN C. DAVISON, JR., b. 2 JUL 1966 in St. Luke's Hospital.
272514.   LINDA K. DAVISON, b. 2 OCT 1969 in St. Luke's Hospital.

2726. Chester Leland Davison
(1901-1991)

Chester was a son of Charles Condus Davison and Florence Evelyn Ridgeway, and was born 16 SEP 1901 at 2307 Agnes Street, Kansas City, Missouri. In 1907 he moved with his family to 2417 Cleveland Avenue, and attended the Greenwood Elementary School at 27th and Cleveland Avenue. Soon after the age of 16 years, Chester quit school and was first employed as a wagon boy to deliver packaged goods for Emery Bird Thayer Dry Goods Store in Kansas City. He did not really have any hobbies, but loved fishing with his dad who died 14 NOV 1917 while still employed at old Union Station located at 8th and Mulberry Streets. The 1918 City Directory for Kansas City, Missouri lists Chester L. Davison, an employee of the Bell Telephone Company, and residing at 2417 Cleveland Avenue. He also worked for Herb Battery. See additional information following at "Twenty Questions."

On October 11, 1922, Chester Leland Davison and Velma Pearl Allen, my grandparents, eloped to the courthouse in Olathe, Johnson County, Kansas and were married by Ernest J. Vigour, a probate judge. I wrote a letter to the courthouse in Olathe, but they indicated no record of this marriage could be found. After this alarming response, I sent an inquiry to Topeka, Kansas from where I was sent a brief State record of marriage.

This couple bought their first home in December 1922. Grandmother wrote in a letter to me, dated 15 JUL 1985, that "I had a hundred dollars my folks gave us for a wedding present, and Grandpa had fifty dollars—that was our down payment on a $5,000 new house. I was making $20 per week and Grandpa $24, of course we had a second mortgage to pay interest on, but we made it." Grandmother describes that she and her husband held many other occupations or positions. "Grandpa was Associate Guardian of Jobs Daughters Bethel #9 at East Gate Lodge for 6 years in the late 1950's, and was Patron of Eastern Star #367 at East Gate in 1960." At one time as Associate Guardian of Jobs Daughters he had 90 girls from the ages of 12 to 20 years old, and he participated with them on hay rack rides, wiener roasts and roller skating outings. Grandmother was president of PTA: two years at Yeager School (about 1946 and 1947), one year at the grade school in Raytown, Missouri, two years at Raytown High School; and served as District

Figure 58 - Chester and Pearl, wedding, 1922

President on Missouri Congress of Parents and Teachers. Pearl attended installation proceedings for the Congress which had jurisdiction over the five area Missouri counties of Jackson, Clay, Platte, Ray and Cass, and served as matron of the Order of Eastern Star.

Chester was past worthy patron of the East Gate chapter of the Order of Eastern Star, and a past associate guardian of Job's Daughters. Pearl worked part time for A.T.&.T. The 1930 City Directory lists Chester L. Davison as a mechanic, residing at 1810 Cleveland Avenue, and the 1935 City Directory adds that he was employed by United Motor Service.

Grandpa has always been known throughout the family for his potato salad, "black with pepper and swimming in mayo," and was frequently asked to bring it for special occasions. See discussion next entitled "Twenty Questions" for more details on the lives of my grandparents. Grandmother was always a good letter writer and kept me current on family affairs. I have kept letters since about 1977, and every now and then when I review these, I get a chuckle. In one letter grandmother wrote to me: "Grandpa is fine - is working today - Me, I'm a general Mess - allergy, arthritis, and aches and pains - What have you? The garden is fine."

In the 1970s, the couple spent time at their cottage at Sunrise Beach, Missouri. They eventually sold the lake cottage and returned to Kansas City, living at several locations (see list of residences). They regularly attended Colonial Presbyterian Church.

Velma Pearl (Allen) Davison died 14 JUL 1990 of cancer and was buried three days later in Memorial Park Cemetery. While a resident of Oakwood Manor, Chester died 30 MAR 1991 at St. Joseph's Health Center in Kansas City, and was buried in Memorial Park Cemetery there.

Children of Chester Leland Davison and Velma Pearl Allen:

+ 211. JANICE LOUISE DAVISON, b. 23 DEC 1925 at home at 1810 Cleveland Avenue, Kansas City, Mo., m. 7 JUL 1946 by the Reverend Lee Soxman at the Cleveland Avenue Methodist Church of Kansas City, to Walter Raymond Giese. See mention elsewhere.

+ 212. ZORA EILEENE DAVISON, b. 5 MAR 1932 at 8:30 in the morning, at home at 1810 Cleveland Avenue, m. 7 JUN 1953 at four o'clock in the afternoon at the Cleveland Avenue Methodist Church, to Charles Wesley Pippenger [Jr.]. See mention elsewhere.[1]

Figure 59 - Eileene Davison

Figure 60 - Eileene and her new husband Charlie Pippenger, 1953

[1] See also Wesley E. Pippenger, *Pippenger and Pittenger Families: A Genealogical History of the Descendants of William Pippenger of New Jersey, and Allied Families* (Baltimore, Md.: Gateway Press, Inc., 1988); and Wesley E. Pippenger, *Alexander Family: Migrations From Maryland* (Tappahannock, Va.: Barbour Printing Services, 2012).

Figure 61 - C.W. and Marguerite Pippenger, Charlie Pippenger and new bride Eileene Davison, Pearl and Chester Davison, 1953

"Twenty Questions"
Denver, Colorado - March 1985

One Sunday afternoon while my Davison grandparents were visiting my parents at their home at 7447 South Lamar Street, Littleton, Colorado, I called to my grandfather who, for the record is Chester Leland Davison (husband of Velma Pearl Allen), and said we were going to play a game. I was going to ask "twenty questions" and we would see how good he did. With humor and curiosity we began.

When I asked him to remember, way back when, what was his first job, he replied that he worked as a wagon boy for a company called Emery Bird Thayer (EBT) Dry Goods Store, in Kansas City, Missouri. He delivered packages of goods to customers' doors. Soon after he started working there he quit school at the age of 16 years.

As a kid, grandfather lived with his parents at 2307 Agnes Street, then moved in about 1907 to 2417 Cleveland Avenue, all in Kansas City, Missouri.

He only attended one school, the Greenwood Elementary School, at 27th and Cleveland Avenue in Kansas City. He remembered his teacher was Mabel Caughman [or Kauffman] who taught general subjects through the 6th grade. He used to walk home every day to eat lunch, then return to school.

When asked about hobbies, he said he didn't have any as a kid—didn't collect anything. Of course he loved going fishing with his Dad and brother Bob Davison. "I had a dog named Brownie, at 2417 Cleveland. One time he started frothing at the mouth, so Dad took it out and beat its head off and killed it." Dad had a dog named Smut, when they were kids. "Couldn't get rid of it, and we put it in a box car and it still came back."

My grandpa's father Charles Condus Davison worked at the old Union Station in Kansas City, located at 8th and Mulberry Streets. When he wasn't there he was a carpenter by trade. Chester's brother Alvin Davison wired the big clock in the present Union Station. He said it was so big that Alvin could stand up inside.

Grandpa's first car that he had was a 1927 Chevrolet; a grey, 2-door coupe. It was a good car, but then he got a 1928 coupe, followed by a 1930 Chevy. You wonder if the first one was such a good car, why others so soon?

His best buddies were Frank and Alfonse Pelletier who lived next door at 2415 Cleveland Avenue. Max and Louis Sheber lived down the street at 2410 Cleveland, and they all used to play around together. He remembers that Gretchen Meyers was the little girl across the street, who, last time he knew, still lived around Center High School in Kansas City. Other friends he could remember were members of a gang who all seemed to hang out together: Jesse Gladman, Violet Cox, Chester Ruffner, Miss Jessie Steadman, and Byron Smith. It seemed as though he was having fun remembering back in time, for he kept thinking of his old friends. He then said Freda Ebert and Sally Rand. Sally lived on the 2300 block of Mercington Street and he carried her books. He said that her original name was Helen Beck, then she changed her name and became the world renowned "fan" dancer. She was a cousin of Catherine Baker.

Now by this time my questioning had caused quite a stir in the house, and I had most of the family gathered around. Then I started to zero in on his love life, and asked who was his first girl friend. It was funny to see grandmother's face blush, but he was quick to look at her and say that "Grandma was my first love—met her when she was 14 years old." I don't remember where he said they met. He had a couple of dates with Irene Goodman, and used to go to the nickel picture show on 24th and Elmwood Streets with Pauline Hoppis. Grandpa said at that place they only played the piano, for there were silent pictures.

Figure 62 - Telephone Building

Grandpa said he wanted to go sign up for the Navy, but when he brought the papers home for his mother (Florence Evelyn Ridgeway Davison) to sign, she said she would not. He was too young, only 17 years old. I imagine that since Chester's father died early, that having boys around the house was important to the mother. Chester's mother Florence Davison died in Denver, Colorado and the funeral was handled by Olinger Mortuary.

Chester L. Davison retired from the Pinkerton Security Company on October 8, 1966. Other notes that I wrote down while were talking was that Grandpa indicated that the Davison ancestors had an argument in Ireland, and some knocked the "d" out of the name. Of course, he said, "those who kept the "d" kept the money."

After talking with Grandfather, I thought that I would also quiz

Grandmother on lifetime events. For the record, I am talking with Velma Pearl (Allen) Davison.

Figure 63 - Pearl Allen and her brother Wayne Allen

Pearl Allen was born in a little log cabin near Springtown, Benton County, Arkansas. You have to hunt to find evidence of the town now, but even back then it was barely enough to have a post office. It was just over the county line from Washington County. While still young the family moved to Texas for a while where her brother Samuel Wayne Allen was born.

The first house in Kansas City, Missouri in which she remembers living, was a big green house located at 19th and Monroe Streets. There she lived until about age twelve. Things of note about this house were that it had a furnace and a bathroom inside. About 1913 the house at 1927 Mercington Street was built. The next house was located at 1810 Cleveland Avenue, where she lived as wife to Chester L. Davison.

About the age of 13 years, Pearl played basketball, wore long underwear when it snowed, and played the piano—taking lessons in grade school. She said that at her last piano recital she played a 9-page piece. When I was a child she sat down and played our piano, and said at that time she could remember only one song.

I then asked her about her first job, since Grandfather started as a wagon boy for Emery Bird Thayer (EBT) Dry Goods Store, surely she did something of note. Yes, her first job was to sort towels for the Wayne Towel Company, 15th and Prospect Street in Kansas City. This she did after attending high school each day. Somehow connected to this she told me that her mother and dad moved to Filley, Missouri in about 1916, and it was nearly 19 miles out of Eldorado Springs. Her second job was to work for 6 months for Southwestern Bell Telephone Company, located at 9th and Baltimore Streets in Kansas City. This honorable position was known as a "Plug Molly."

After working this short term with the telephone company, she went to the farm in Filley, Missouri and stayed with her folks for a while, and said that she "made breakfast every morning while the folks milked cows." Pearl had a riding horse for a pet, but she couldn't do much with it but ride because he wouldn't tote a buggy or anything else.

Figure 64 - Filley, Missouri, 1920

Years later, Pearl Allen returned to Kansas City to answer a blind newspaper advertisement for a telephone job, in May 1921. The location was at 6th and Wyandotte Streets in Kansas City, and her supervisor was Helen Billow who remained in her friendship for many years to come.

Now that all the small talk was over and done with, I asked Grandmother who her first boyfriend was, surely it wasn't "Grandpa?" "No, Ray Miles" came to mind as her first boyfriend, who she met at Linn Creek, Missouri at her Aunt Hattie's house. "He was older than me, and never married." Grandfather piped up and said "Then a guy named George!, He knew better than to try and get fresh with her!" Chuckle. Another one of whom we had pictures of somewhere was Elmer Bybee. His mother was a switchboard operator at Filley, Missouri.

Pearl Davison remembers that they had the funeral for "Granny" Lewis [Sarah Elizabeth Adair, wife of William Martin [or F.] at her parents house on 1927 Mercington Street, Kansas City, where her dad brought the casket in the house and put it in the front room. "Chester and I brought our rug from the 1810 Cleveland house to put on Mother's floor."

"During the 1930's, Dad owned a farm at Kenneth, Kansas near Stanley, Kansas; it was 38 acres. Mr. and Mrs. York lived nearby. We had to heat water on the coal stove for bath water."

Pearl's best friend in school was Louise Cutler, with whom she would walk to Central School all the time. She was also a neighbor when they lived on Cleveland Avenue, and lived for many more years in Kansas City.

"Bernice Biddle, Violet Cox—they all went to Oakhurst Methodist Church." Oakhurst was located at 18th and Spruce Streets "where Grandpa and I met." It was at this church where Pearl was first baptized. "Grandpa was baptized in Cleveland Avenue Methodist Church."

Grandmother said she had a boy friend who worked at Emery Bird's with his Mother who said that "I was pure as the pearl buttons she sewed." Chester apparently got wind of this and he and Jesse Gladman were going to beat the kid up and make sure he got on a bus and left town.

Still stuck on the many "loves" that she apparently had, Grandmother continued to say that "one was named Ferman Mullins. We played games together, and he had a crush on me." Then, at cousin Eula Downey's graduation from high school in Rogers, Arkansas, "I took her boy friend Pete Hanson away from her. She was so mad she about died."

Figure 65 - Pearl Davison and daughter Eileene

To find out more information about the life in Rhea's Mill, Washington County, Arkansas, we got started talking about Grandmother's grandparents Samuel Gillion Allen and his wife Mary Ann Hicks. Pearl started off by saying that "she (her grandmother Mary Ann Allen) was wonderful, and made the best plum butter;

she was quite a character." She was generally slow in nature, deliberate, and slow talking. She was nice looking. Mary Allen wove rugs, making them for all over the house. She washed her clothes in a black kettle, and scrubbed it out and made apple butter.

Figure 66 - Chester Davison and Eula Downey

"She [Mary Allen] passed away when Janice [Davison] was about 4 or 5 years old, and we went to the funeral. The undertaker laid her on boards in front of the living room picture window. She had a printed dress on, and had not been embalmed. It was summer."

The old house down there [Rhea's Mill, Arkansas] got to be in quite sad repair. Chester helped Homer Allen re-roof the old house with oak shingles. My grandparents had a buggy. Aunt Clara Allen bought a Model T Ford just before Grandpa Allen died. She kept it in the shed by the smoke house on the farm. She covered the car with sheets and kept rugs under the clutch. If that wasn't enough she kept chick feed in the car, and the lawn mower under her bed so no one would take them. Clara spent a dollar a week on gas, and bought it in Prairie Grove, Arkansas.

My mother Zora Eileene Davison went to Yeager School in Kansas City, as did Grandmother. Mother started the third grade at Spring Valley School in Kansas City, Missouri.

Figure 67 - Sisters, Janice and Eileene Davison

Figure 68 - Cowgirl Eileene

Figure 69 - Janice Davison

Residence Addresses
of Chester Leland Davison and wife
Velma Pearl Allen

1. 1810 Cleveland Avenue, Kansas City, Missouri (first home as a married couple (1922 to 1940)

2. 1731 Dayton, Aurora, Colorado (1936)

3. 8524 East Colfax Avenue, Aurora, Colorado (1936)

4. 8421 Blue Ridge Extension, Kansas City, Missouri (30 MAY 1940 to 1968)

5. Lake of the Ozarks, Rural Route E, Box 9, Sunrise Beach, Missouri (1968 to 1974)

6. 623A Willow Drive, Lee's Summit, Missouri (John Knox Village) (1974 to 1976)

7. 1911-D Cherry, Lee's Summit, Missouri 64063 (1976 to 15 JUN 1981)

8. 119 West 99th Terrace, #309, Kansas City, Missouri 64114 (14 JUN 1981 to 20 MAR 1983)

9. 10244 Locust, Kansas City, Missouri 64131 (28 MAR 1983 to Pearl's death)

10. 7300 W. 107th, Apt. 320, Shawnee Mission, Kansas 66212 (1991 to until Chester's death)

Figure 70 - While at the Dayton house

Figure 71 - Initial construction at the lake

28. William Davison
(ca. 1817-aft. 1860)

William Davison, born about 1817 in Clermont County, Ohio, and was a son of James Davison and Catherine (perhaps Long). He was married 11 DEC 1834 by Samuel Hill, J.P. in Clermont County, Ohio to Mary Ann Waits.

On the Federal census for 23 JUL 1850, William Davison heads household #188 in Jackson Township of Clermont County. He was a laborer, and neither he nor his wife could read or write. William was enumerated on the 1860 Federal census as being a patient in the Clermont County Infirmary, and died in the county soon afterwards. Mary Ann was listed on the 1860 Federal census as an inmate of the county infirmary [dwelling 813, page 330, with children Mary, Lucy and Charles], and died after 1860.

Children of William Davison and Mary Ann Waits:

281.   JOSEPH J. DAVISON, b. c.1835 in Ohio, m. c.1855 to Kate (unknown), b. Ire. Children:
  2811.   HARRIET DAVISON, b. 1857.
  2812.   GEORGE DAVISON, b. 1859.
282.   WILLIAM M. DAVISON, b. c.1837 in Ohio.
283.   Daughter Davison, d. before 1850.
284.   JOSHUA F. DAVISON, b. c.1841 in Ohio.
285.   CYNTHIA ANN DAVISON, b. c.1843 in Ohio.
286.   JACKSON DAVISON, b. c.1845 in Ohio.
287.   LUCINDA DAVISON, b. c.1848 in Ohio.
288.   MARY ANN DAVISON, b. c.1852 in Ohio.
289.   LUCY N. DAVISON, b. c.1854 in Ohio.
28(10).   CATHERINE DAVISON, b. c.1855, not enumerated in 1860.
28(11). CHARLES H. DAVISON, b. c.1856 in Ohio.

2(11). Samuel Davison
(c.1822-after 1860)

Samuel Davison, son of James Davison and Catherine (perhaps Long), was born c.1822 in Clermont County, Ohio. He was married 21 APR 1841 in Clermont County, to Mary Lukemeier.[1] They were enumerated on the 1850 Federal census for Pike Township, Brown County [family 1419]. They were enumerated on the 1860 Federal census for Batavia Township, Clermont County, Ohio [family 762, page 326]. Samuel was a farmer. The Federal census for June 1880 lists the family in Pike Township of Brown County, Ohio [family #106; page 191, place of birth for his parents appear incorrectly as Kentucky and Pennsylvania].

---

[1] Records submitted to the LDS Church, Salt Lake City, Utah for the I.G.I. indicate he was married on July 20, 1841.

Children of Samuel Davison and Mary Lukemeier:

2(11)1. DELOS DAVISON, b. 1846 in Ohio.
2(11)2. LORENZO D.S. DAVISON, b. c.1849 in Ohio.
2(11)3. TABITHA DAVISON, b. 1853 in Ohio.
2(11)4. EBENEZER DAVISON, b. c.1855 in Ohio.
2(11)5. MARY E. DAVISON, b. c.1858 in Ohio.
  2(11)6. Male child, b. 1860.

4. John Davison
(1777-1847)

John Davison, son of George Davison and Eleanor Allen, was born 15 MAR 1777 at Chestnut Ridge, Westmoreland County, Pennsylvania. He was first married 1 AUG 1797 in Mason County, Kentucky to Mrs. Mary (Satterfield) Long. John Davison was remarried second in 1802 in Clermont County, Ohio to Isabella Hamilton.

John Davison is mentioned in the *History of Clermont County, Ohio*, where it indicates in 1802 he settled in Miami Township, Clermont County, Ohio, and "in 1807 [original says 1870, but is in error as he was long dead] bought the farm now owned by the heirs of James Roudebush."[1] In April 1804, he voted in the first election held in Miami Township of Clermont County.[2] In 1845, John and Isabella Davison, of Stonelick Township, sold 1 acre to William Needham.[3]

James Davison made his will 12 MAY 1847,[4] and died the same day in Boston, Clermont County, Ohio.

Isabella was alive when her husband John made his will. She was born 22 FEB 1782 in Westmoreland County, Pennsylvania, and was the daughter of James Hamilton and Elizabeth Clemmons. James Hamilton was born in Scotland about 1745 and was drafted into the English Army and sent to America. He was married in Scotland in 1767 to Elizabeth Clemmons of Scotland, and during the Revolutionary War he sent for his wife to came to America about 1774.[5]

Isabella (Hamilton) Davison died 11 MAR 1848 in Boston, Clermont County, Ohio.

Children of John Davison and his first wife Mary (Satterfield) Long:

41. GEORGE DAVISON, b. c.1798 in Mason Co., Ky., m. (1) 6 MAR 1818 by Samuel Hill, J.P., in Stonelick Twp., Clermont Co., to Catherine Reeves,[6] and m.

---

[1] *History of Clermont County, Ohio* (1880), p. 248.
[2] See Louis H. Evers, *History of Clermont County* (1882), p. 468.
[3] Clermont Co., Ohio Deeds, Bk. 44, p. 6; survey 4449.
[4] Clermont Co., Ohio Wills, Bk. F, p. 167, proved 27 JUL 1847 by administrator William South, Sr. Division to be made among daughters who are not named. Proved by the oaths of James McKimmie and John Hamilton.
[5] Material from Marie (Mrs. E.E. Davidson) of P.O. Box 314, Burley, ID 83318.
[6] Clermont Co., Ohio Marriages, Record Bk. No. 1, p. 107.

(2) 4 AUG 1826 by William Davis, J.P., to Rebecca Sly.[1] They are found on the 1860 Federal census for Jackson Twp., Clermont Co. [family 574, page 388].

42. MARGARET "Peggy" DAVISON, b. c.1800, prob. in Mason Co., Ky., d. 14 NOV 1874, m. 12 FEB 1818 by William Kelly, J.P., at the house of her father John Davison in Clermont Co. to Elijah S. Reeves,[2] b. 1798 in Ohio, d. 1865 in Ohio, son of Nathaniel Reeves (1756-1848) and Mary Skinner. The family is enumerated on the 1850 Federal census for Stonelick Twp., Clermont Co. [family 573, page 189]. Children:

421. RHEUHAMA REEVES, b. 1819, d. 1911, m. 3 APR 1838 in Clermont Co., Ohio to Wesley Worman, b. 1817. Two children.

422. JOHN D. REEVES, cooper, b. 21 OCT 1823 in Clermont Co., Ohio, d. 20 FEB 1907 in Lima, Allen Co., Ohio, m. his cousin 226. ALICE DAVISON, b. 1836, d. 1869, daughter of John Davison and Areanna Chalmers, *q.v.* They are found on the 1860 Federal census for Noble Twp., Brown Co., Ohio [family 956, page 368]. Children:

4221. OLIVE REEVES, b. 1853 in Ohio, m. 9 JUN 1876 in Auglaize Co., Ohio to John Franklin Sprague, b. 1856, d. 1931. Six children.

4222. LAURA E. REEVES, b. 1855 in Ohio, m. 1882 to Amos E. Grant, b. 1857, d. 1900. Three children.

4223. CLARA B. REEVES, b. 28 NOV 1857 in Ohio, d. September 1948 in Lima, Ohio, m. 12 SEP 1875 in Auglaize Co. to Jacob Curtis Young. Six children.

4224. SUSAN CATHARINE REEVES, b. 20 SEP 1860 in Noble, Auglaize Co., Ohio, d. 22 JUL 1945 in St. Mary's, Auglaize Co., m. her cousin 456. CHARLES C. DAVISON, *q.v.*, b. 1 SEP 1851, d. 19 JAN 1918 in Dayton, Ohio. Children:[3]

42241. ESTELIA DAVISON, b. 27 OCT 1878.

42242. PERLIE DAVISON, b. 18 APR 1880.

42243. RUSSELL DAVISON, b. 21 JUN 1882.

4225. HANNAH REEVES, b. 26 FEB 1866, d. 16 JUL 1923 in Allen Co., Ohio, bur. Woodlawn Cem., m. 1891 to George G. Grant, b. 1868, d. 1927. Child:

42251. EARL GRANT, b. 1896.

423. WARREN REEVES, farmer, b. December 1828 in Clermont Co., d. 28 MAR 1910 of apoplexy in Auglaize Co., Ohio, bur. Elm Grove Cem.

424. NATHANIEL REEVES, b. 25 APR 1830 in Stonelick Twp., Clermont Co., d. 26 OCT 1915, m. 3 JUL 1859 in Auglaize Co., Ohio to Susan Langsden.

425. THOMAS REEVES, b. 28 FEB 1834 in Stonelick Twp., d. 10 MAR 1907.

426. SUSANNAH CATHERINE REEVES, b. 16 AUG 1837 in Stonelick Twp., d. 14 APR 1929, m. 15 APR 1863 in Wabash, Ind. to Robert Yates Votaw, b. 1838, d. 1919. Three children.

427. MARGARET REEVES, b. 1840.

---

[1] Clermont Co., Ohio Marriages, Record Bk. No. 2, p. 159.
[2] Clermont Co., Ohio Marriages, Record Bk. No. 1, p. 104.
[3] From a Bible page sent to me in 2003 by Pam Wells.

43. WILLIAM DAVISON, b. c.1801 in Clermont Co., Ohio, d. before 1851, m. 15 APR 1830 by Ichabod Temple, Baptist Preacher, in Clermont Co., to Sarah Armstrong,[1] b. c.1805 in Ind. She m. (2) 16 FEB 1851 by David Kirgan, J.P., in Clermont Co. to Jesse Price, b. 1806. Jesse and Sarah are found on the 1860 Federal census for Batavia Twp., Clermont Co. [family 633, page 318]. Children:
   431. SARAH S. DAVISON, b. 1832.
   432. WILLIAM DAVISON, b. 1835.
   433. FRANCIS DAVISON, b. 1838, perhaps d. 1865 in Clermont Co.
   434. Son Davison, b. 1835/1840.

Children of John Davison and his second wife Isabella Hamilton:

+ 44. ELIZABETH [Hamilton] DAVISON, b. 15 NOV 1802[2] in Milford, Clermont Co., Ohio, m. 20 SEP 1827 by J.W. Robinson, J.P.,[3] in Clermont Co. to 16. JAMES HAMILTON DAVISON, *q.v.*, son of Robert Davison and Florence Hamilton. She d. 13 DEC 1891 about 1½ miles northwest of Hidalgo, Jasper Co., Ill.

45. CHRISTOPHER "Christian" DAVISON, shoemaker and farmer, b. 1804, m. Eliza Clark, b. 1806 in Pa. In 1838, Christopher Davison purchased 6-7/8 acres of land in Clermont Co., from Ezekiel Dimmitt.[4] On 20 FEB 1847, Christopher and Eliza Davidson of Clermont Co., conveyed 6 acres to Frederick Shard of Clermont Co.[5] They were residing in Brown Co., Ohio when in 1847 they sold Lot 41 of the town of Cynthian, Ohio to Andrew Black.[6] Christopher Davison, a shoemaker, and Eliza his wife are enumerated 12 SEP 1850 on the Federal census for Pike Township, Brown Co., Ohio. They are found on the 1860 Federal census for Noble Twp., Auglaize Co., Ohio [family 954, page 368]. Children:
   451. Daughter Davison, b. c.1829.
   452. MARY A. DAVISON, b. 1831 in Ohio.
   453. EDITH DAVISON, b. 1840 in Ohio.
   454. THOMAS DAVISON, b. 1842 in Ohio, may have owned land in Auglaize Co.
   455. SAMANTHA DAVISON, b. 1842 in Ohio.
   456. CHARLES C. DAVISON, b. 1 SEP 1851, d. 19 JAN 1918 in Dayton, Ohio, m. his cousin 4224. SUSAN CATHARINE REEVES, *q.v.*, b. 20 SEP 1860 in Noble, Auglaize Co., Ohio.

46. JANE DAVISON, b. c.1805,[7] m. (1) 21 SEP 1828 to Jesse Henwood,[8] and m. (2) 21 SEP 1837 by James McKimme, J.P., in Clermont Co., to William South, a cooper and carpenter, b. 17 OCT 1815 in Ohio, d. 6 AUG 1875 in Clermont Co.

---

[1] Clermont Co., Ohio Marriages, Record Bk. No. 2, p. 328.
[2] Another source provides the birthyear as 1809. This is entirely possible since the next child recorded was not born until 1812.
[3] Clermont Co., Ohio Marriages, Record Bk. No. 2, p. 205.
[4] Clermont Co., Ohio Deeds, Bk. 39, p. 269; surveys 13536 and 4459.
[5] Clermont Co, Ohio Deeds, Bk. 46, p. 81, dated 20 FEB 1847; surveys 13536, 4459.
[6] Clermont Co., Ohio Deeds, Bk. 46, p. 264, dated 9 JUN 1847.
[7] Another source gives birthyear as 1819.
[8] Marriage information provided by a genealogist hired by Judy Everhart; however records of the LDS church indicate Jane Davison was m. 3 NOV 1828 to Jesse Henwood, and yet another source says this is untrue and Jane Davison was m. 21 SEP 1837 in Clermont Co., Ohio to William South. The later is indeed true as it was a second marriage for Jane Davison.

In 1850, they were enumerated in Stonelick Twp. of Clermont Co. [family 549, page 181], and on the 1860 Federal census [family 686, page 396]. William and his two sons are bur. in the I.O.O.F. Boston Lodge No. 189 Cem. between Owensville and Stonelick. Children:

461. VIOLA SOUTH, b. 1840 in Ohio.
462. MARCUS B. SOUTH, b. 10 FEB 1842 in Ohio, d. 28 OCT 1864 while serving in the Civil War.
463. JOHN M. SOUTH, b. 1846 in Ohio, served in Co. I, 153rd Ohio Inf. during the Civil War.
464. AMINA R. SOUTH, b. 1858 in Ohio.

47. ELEANOR DAVISON, b. c.1812, m. 13 APR 1834 in Clermont Co., to Lewis Sly. They were enumerated on the 1850 Federal census for Batavia Twp., Clermont Co. [family 415, page 621], and on 22 JUN 1860 in the Federal census [family 416] in Jackson Twp., Clermont Co. On the 1880 Federal census they were enumerated as family 78 in Jackson Twp. Children:

471. I.J. SLY, b. 1835.
472. WILLIAM EZRA SLY, b. 1837.
473. JOHN SLY, b. 1839.
474. THOMAS H. SLY, b. 1845.
475. JAMES H. SLY, b. 1846 in Ohio.
476. MARTHA A. SLY, b. 1851 in Ohio.

+ 48. JOHN HENRY DAVISON (twin), b. c.1813 in Clermont Co., d. 1865, m. 1 JAN 1835 in Clermont Co., to Tabitha Lukemyers.

49. (Rev.[1]) JAMES H. DAVISON (twin), farmer, b. c.1813 in Clermont Co., m. 19 MAR 1835 by J.C. Hunter, J.P., in Clermont Co., to Sarah Ann Duckwall, b. 1818 in Ohio. The family was enumerated on the 1850 Federal census for Jackson Twp., Clermont Co. [family 185; page 67A]. Children:

491. PHEBE F. DAVISON, b. 1837 in Ohio.
492. MARSELIUS DAVISON, b. 1839 in Ohio.
493. THOMAS A. DAVISON, b. 1842 in Ohio.
494. EVELINE DAVISON, b. 1845 in Ohio.
495. REBECCA J. DAVISON, b. 1846 in Ohio.
496. JACOB H. DAVISON, b. 1849 in Ohio.

4(10). FLORENCE DAVISON, b. c.1820 in Clermont Co., d. 6 FEB 1903 in Clermont Co., m. 15 MAR 1840 by David C. Bryan, J.P., in Clermont Co. to Ausborn Cooper,[2] b. 1816 in Ohio. They are found on the 1850 Federal census for Stonelick Twp., Clermont Co. [family 572, page 189]. Children:

4(10)1. MELISSA COOPER, b. 1843.
4(10)2. VIOLA COOPER, b. 1846.

---

[1] Believed to be the pastor of Maple Grove Methodist Episcopal Church in Jackson Township when it was organized in 1849.
[2] Material submitted by Mrs. E.E. Davidson suggests Florence was married to a Mr. Hollis.

+ 4(11). ROBERT ERASTUS DAVISON, b. c.1824 in Clermont Co., d. 1861, m. (1) Mary Lukemire, m. (2) Margaret Culver.

4(12). CATHERINE DAVISON, b. c.1826[1] in Clermont Co., m. 8 JUN 1848 by her brother, Rev. James H. Davidson (Methodist), in Clermont Co., to William Hunter, farmer, b. 1821 or 2 in Ohio, d. 16 NOV 1907 in Clermont Co. They are listed on the 1860 Federal census for Jackson Twp., Clermont Co. [family 494, page 382]. Children:
4(12)1. JAMES H. HUNTER, b. 1849 in Ohio.
4(12)2. ROBERT HUNTER, b. 1851 in Ohio.
4(12)3. AMANDA HUNTER, b. 1853 in Ohio.

4(13). ALEXANDER DAVISON, shoemaker, inherited 23 acres of land by his father's 1847 will, b. 1 MAR 1825 in Clermont Co., d. 14 NOV 1906, m. (1) 15 OCT 1846 there by J. McLaughlin to Eliza Needham, b. 21 JUL 1829 in Ohio, d. 23 MAR 1886. The family was listed on the Federal census for 1 AUG 1850 in Batavia Twp., Clermont Co. [family 458, page 626]. May have removed to Equality, Gallatin Co., Ill., and witnessed the 1880 will of Robert Davison.[2] Alexander m. (2) Martha Catherine Wiggins Willis Carter, d. 12 APR 1913. Children:
4(13)1. AMANDA JANE DAVISON, b. 19 JUL 1848 in Ohio, m. John Miller, b. 19 JUL 1848.
4(13)2. SARAH A. "Sallie" DAVISON, b. 1849 in Ohio, m. George Leming, b. 26 DEC 1860, d. 2 DEC 1886.
4(13)3. LOWELL MORRIS DAVISON, b. 15 MAR 1853 in Ohio, d. 19 MAY 1927, m. to Louise Rodgers, b. 20 DEC 1860, d. 15 OCT 1925. Three children.
4(13)4. JOHN HOWARD DAVISON, b. 2 NOV 1857 in Stonelick Twp., Clermont Co.,[3] d. 1 JAN 1933.
4(13)5. RUSSELL DAVISON, b. 1860 in Ohio, d. before 1897, m. Sarah E. French.
4(13)6. JESSIE LENORA DAVISON, b. 24 OCT 1865 in Ohio, d. 19 FEB 1925, m. Buck Massey.

48. John Henry Davison
(c.1813-1865)

This John Henry Davison (not to be confused with John Hamilton Davison who was a son of Robert Davison and Florence Hamilton), was a child of John Davison and Isabella Hamilton. He was born about 1813 in Ohio, and was married 1 JAN 1835 by J.C. Hunter, in Clermont County, Ohio to Tabitha Lukemire or Lukemyers. Tabitha, a daughter of John Lukemire and Lydia Baldwin, was born about 1813 in New Jersey. John H. Davison was a farmer.

---

[1] Another source gives 1798 as her birth year.
[2] Clermont Co., Ohio Wills, Bk. M, pp. 356, 365.
[3] Clermont Co., Ohio Register of Births, 1857.

In 1837, John and Tabitha sold Lots 19, 20 and 66 in the town of Boston, Clermont County, Ohio to Robert Davison.[1] They were enumerated on Federal census for 1 AUG 1850 for Batavia Township, Clermont County [family 452, page 626]. Tabitha died about 1861 in Clermont County, and John H. Davison died there about 1865.

Children of John H. Davison and Tabitha Lukemyers (all born in Batavia Township, Clermont County, Ohio):[2]

481. DEBORAH A. DAVISON, b. 1838 in Ohio.
482. PERMILIA DAVISON, b. 1841 in Ohio.
483. OLIVE DAVISON, b. February 1843 in Ohio, m. c.1860 to Richard Hague, and d. in the 1920's in Vincennes, Knox Co., Ind.
484. LIZZIE FRANCES DAVISON, b. 1846 in Ohio, m. (1) Mr. Ringwater, then m. (2) Mr. Johnston.
485. DOCK FRANKLIN DAVISON, b. 22 FEB 1848 in Clermont Co., m. 4 APR 1869 in Macon Co., Mo. to Cassinda Emmaline "Cassie" Sneed. Cassie, daughter of Hezekiah Sneed and Mary A. Wilson, b. 8 DEC 1845 in Macon Co. Dock d. 17 DEC 1935 in Randolph Co., Mo., bur. in Mount Salem Cem. near Excello, Macon Co., Mo. Cassie d. 23 DEC 1941 in Adair Co., Mo., bur. in Mount Salem Cem. Children, all b. in Chariton Township, Macon Co., Mo.:[3]
    4851. GEORGIA ETTA DAVISON, b. 2 SEP 1870, d. 17 APR 1937, bur. in Mount Salem Cem., m. 11 DEC 1887 to Benjamin Mullinix.
    4852. JAMES H. DAVISON, b. 5 MAY 1874, m. (1) 4 DEC 1895 to Elizabeth Teter, and m. (2) in 1906 to Viola Teter. James d. 21 NOV 1944, bur. in Teter Cem. of Macon Co., Mo.
    4853. JOHN E. DAVISON, b. 26 AUG 1876, m. 30 JAN 1902 to Mary E. Green, d. 28 JAN 1962, bur. in Moberly, Randolph Co., Mo.
    4854. WILLARD DOCK DAVISON (twin), b. in December 1880, m. c.1903 to Ida Bissoux. Willard d. in 1958 and bur. in Moberly, Mo.
    4855. WILBERT DOCK DAVISON (twin), b. in December 1880, d. as an infant in 1881 and bur. in Sneed Cem. of Macon Co., Mo.
    4856. Stillborn male child, 9 SEP 1884, bur. in Sneed Cem.
    4857. MARTHA FRANCES DAVISON, b. 5 OCT 1885 in Macon Co., Mo., m. 1 JAN 1902 to Daniel Iven Cooley, b. 22 JUL 1881 in Macon Co., Mo., d. 8 JUL 1964 in Adair Co., Mo., son of John I. Cooley and Martha I. Youngblood. Martha d. 3 MAR 1954, bur. in Kirksville, Adair Co., Mo. Daughter:
        48571. DELTA MAUREEN COOLEY, m. 21 DEC 1922 in Adair Co., Mo., \m. 20 AUG 1945 to Ottie L. Walker, res. Ojai, Calif.
    4858. BENJAMIN F. DAVISON, b. 30 MAR 1888, m. 2 JUN 1907 to Eva Summers. He d. 11 OCT 1977, bur. at Moberly, Mo.
    4859. EVAN T. DAVISON, b. 27 MAR 1890, m. 3 OCT 1915 to Mable Reed, d. 7 JUN 1931, bur. at Mount Salem Cem., Macon Co., Mo.
486. JOHN BERKLEY DAVISON, b. 27 MAR 1853, m. (1) 14 NOV 1874 to Mary Etta

---

[1] Clermont Co., Ohio Deeds, Bk. 47, p. 121.
[2] Information in part by Dale Patrick Walker of St. Louis, Mo. Similar information published in the *History of Clermont County, Ohio*, by Clermont County Genealogical Society (1980), Vol. 1, pp. 185-6.
[3] Information in part provided by D.L. "Pat" Walker, 4256 Botanical Avenue, St. Louis, Mo. 63110.

164

Kindles, b. 17 FEB 1854, d. December 1895, and m. (2) 20 DEC 1896 to Susie Frances Tiller, b. 9 MAR 1876, d. 3 APR 1956. He d. 21 MAY 1932, bur. near Bevier, Macon Co., Mo. Ten children.

4(11). <u>Robert Erastus Davison</u>
(c.1824-1861)

Robert Erastus Davison, a son of John Davison and Isabella Hamilton, was born about 1824 in Clermont County, Ohio. He was married first in 1848 to Mary Lukemire. Robert was married second on 28 SEP 1854 in Crawford County, Indiana to Margaret Culver. Margaret Culver, daughter of Daniel Culver and Susan Coy, was born 16 SEP 1832 in Hardin County, Kentucky, and died 18 JUL 1920 in Ravenna, Nebraska. Robert died in November 1861 in Crawford County, Indiana.

Robert and Margaret were enumerated on the 1850 Federal census for Clermont County, Ohio [page 310]. After the death of her husband Robert Davison, Margaret was remarried in 1865 to John Wiseman.

Children of Robert Davison and Margaret Culver:[1]

4(11)1.   FRANCIS DAVISON, b. c.1848.

4(11)2.   GEORGE WASHINGTON DAVISON, b. 28 JUL 1855 in Crawford Co., Ind., d. 27 MAY 1939, m. 11 MAR 1880 to Clarinda Gardner.

4(11)3.   CHARLES NATHANIEL DAVISON, b. 10 MAR 1857 in Alton, Crawford Co., Ind., d. 31 MAR 1948 in Baldwin Park, Los Angeles Co., Calif., m. 2 NOV 1883 in Ravenna, Nebr. to Laura Smith, b. 18 JUL 1867 in Des Moines, Iowa, d. 30 JUN 1905 in Ravenna, Nebr., daughter of Erastus Smith and Mary Jane Person.

4(11)4.   DANIEL JAMES DAVISON, b. 22 JUN 1858 in Crawford Co., Ind., d. 31 AUG 1945 in Canyon Co., Idaho, m. 3 DEC 1883 in Ravenna, Nebr. to Mary Elizabeth Herbaugh, b. 26 OCT 1866 in Ind., d. 22 JUN 1918 in Scotts Bluff, Nebr., daughter of John William Herbaugh (1843-1916) and Rachel Owen Crawford (1842-1908). Children:

4(11)41.   WILLIAM HARMON DAVISON, b. 4 FEB 1885 in Ravenna, Nebr., d. 11 JUL 1957, m. Emma Boeh.

4(11)42.   EDITH MARGARET DAVISON, b. 26 OCT 1887 in Ravenna, Nebr., d. 4 APR 1960 in Canyon Co., Idaho.

Figure 72 - Daniel J. Davison and Mary E. Herbaugh wedding

---

[1] Information provided in part by Carolyn Carey, 7105 East Powers Ave., Greenwood Village, Colo. 80111, in March 1988.

4(11)43. ELLA CECIL DAVISON, b. 27 JUN 1891 in Ravenna, Nebr., d. 5 DEC 1972 in Portland, Ore., poss. m. Luther Owen.

4(11)44. IVA L. DAVISON, b. 5 AUG 1893 in Ravenna, Nebr., d. 20 JAN 1913 in Logan, Nebr.

4(11)45. ROBERT ELLSWORTH DAVISON, b. 12 MAR 1898 in Ravenna, Nebr., d. 25 JAN 1968 in Yuma Co., Ariz.

4(11)46. MYRTLE ALICE DAVISON, b. 1 MAY 1904 in Ravenna, Nebr., d. 16 FEB 1989.

5. William Davison
(c.1775-bef. 1840)

William Davison, son of George Davison and Eleanor Allen, was born between 1775 and 1780, probably in Westmoreland County, Pennsylvania. He was married first on 26 JUL 1810 by R.W. Waring, J.P., to Susannah Keeth,[1] and married second on 24 JUN or 15 JUL 1813 by Henry Chapman, J.P., in Clermont County, Ohio to Susan Knaus.[2]

In 1811, William Davison purchased from William Vaughan, lots number 7 and 8 in the village of Williamsburg, Clermont County, Ohio.[3] In 1816 purchased from Col. Robert Higgins, Lot 7 in the town of Higginsport, Ohio when it was laid out.[4] William Davison probably died before 1840 in Higginsport, Brown Co., Ohio. William Davison owned and operated a mill in Higginsport.

Children of William Davison and his second wife Susan Knaus:

51. HENRY DAVISON, b. 1814, m. c.1840 to Elizabeth (unknown). Children:
   511. MARTHA DAVISON, b. 1840.
   512. LUCY M. DAVISON, b. 1843.
   513. MARY DAVISON, b. 1844.
   514. EMILY DAVISON, b. 1847.
   515. ELLA DAVISON, b. MAY 1850.

52. Son Davison, b. 1815/1820.

53. Son Davison, b. 1815/1820.

54. Daughter Davison, b. 1815/1820.

55. ELIZABETH DAVISON, b. 1824.

56. LEWIS DAVIDSON, b. 1820/1825, perhaps the same on the 1850 Federal census

---

[1] Clermont Co., Ohio Marriages, Record Bk. No. 1, p. 15.
[2] Clermont Co., Ohio Marriages, 1810-1811, p. 42 and Record Bk. No. 1, p. 38, with different dates.
[3] Clermont Co., Ohio Deeds, Bk. 7, p. 73.
[4] Clermont Co., Ohio Deeds, Bk. 13, p. 217.

for Brown Co., Ohio, m. Frances M. (unknown), and had son Jacob R. Davidson.

57.   CATHERINE DAVISON, b. 1826.

58.   ANNE C. DAVISON, b. 1828.

59.   SARAH DAVISON, b. 1830.

5(10).   PENNBROOK DAVISON, b. 1835.

RIDGEWAY FAMILY

From the records kept through many years by my grandmother Velma Pearl (Allen) Davison, we know that the parents of Florence Evelyn Ridgeway, wife of Charles Condus Davison, were Samuel and Jennettie Ridgeway. Florence had no birth certificate, and on her death certificate the informant, Chester Davison, only provided parental information for her father as Mr. Ridgeway.

Samuel Ridgeway was born 7 SEP 1804 in Lincoln County, Kentucky, and had two marriages. We descend from his second marriage. This fact of more than one marriage is quickly learned upon examination of census records that give the age of children and their place of birth. We find Samuel Ridgeway living in Sugar Creek Township of Randolph County, Missouri on the 1850 Federal census [26 SEP 1850, page 233], with a wife Fanny who was born about 1801 in Virginia.

Lineage of many branches of the Ridgway/Ridgeway Family has been published in a book entitled, *Ridgways U.S.A.* by Thurman Ridgway and Gertrude N. Brick. After close examination, the lineage of our Samuel Ridgeway is correct, and has been enhanced by other records, as below:

Ridgeway Family Lineage

A. **JOHN RIDGWAY, SR.,** [1] a planter of Prince Georges Co., Md., b. prior to 1690, perhaps in Charles Co., Md., d. after September 1733, m. c.1712 to Elizabeth Simmons, d. before September 1733, daughter of Jonathan Simmons and Elizabeth Isaac. In 1715, John Ridgway, planter, purchased from Robert Clarke, lawyer, a 192-acre tract called *Clarkson's Purchase* in Prince Georges Co., Md.,[2] formerly part of Charles Co., Md. In 1718, John Ridgway, sold the tract to William Tyler, carpenter.[3] In 1733, he deeded to his son Robert[4] much of his personal property.[5] Five children, of whom:

B. **JOHN RIDGEWAY, JR.,** b. 1 SEP 1716 in St. John's Parish of Prince Georges Co., Md., d. intestate 1793 in Berkeley Co., Va.[6] (now part of Jefferson Co., West Va.), m. Mary Tenley, daughter of Philip Tenley and Grace Thomas, d. testate 1809 in Berkeley Co., Va. Philip Tenley m. Grace Thomas on 2 JUL 1720 in St. John's Parish, and he died testate, will dated 13 NOV 1772 in Prince Georges Co., Md.[7] In 1769, John Ridgeway acquired a plantation called "Dan," in Frederick Co., Md., that was located on the north side of Potomac River.[8] In 1775, John acquired 413

---

[1] According to an article published in *History of Mt. Pulaski, Illinois, 1836-1986* at the Sangamon Co., Ill. Genealogical Society, John Ridgeway, Sr. was a son of Richard Ridgeway who was born in Wallingsford, Buckinghamshire, England in 1654 and died in 1723 after which he was buried in Burlington Co., N.J. However, Gertrude N. Brick in her *Ridgways U.S.A.* states that there is often confusion of two John Ridgways for this time period, and that our John who married Mary Tenley is not the same as the son of Richard, progenitor of the family in America.

[2] Prince Georges Co., Md. Deeds, Liber F, fol. 473, dated 23 APR 1715.

[3] Prince Georges Co., Md. Deeds, Liber 22, fol. 690, dated 12 JUL 1718, and wit. by his wife Elizabeth and two others.

[4] The register of St. John's Church, Broad Creek, shows the birth of Robert, son of John, as 25 MAR 1713.

[5] Prince Georges Co., Md. Deeds, Bk. Q, p. 690, dated 10 SEP 1733; as there is no mention of his wife Elizabeth, she is presumed dead.

[6] Berkeley Co., W.Va. Wills, Bk. 2, p. 223, for estate appraisal of John Ridgeway, Sr. Also see Administrator Bonds Bk. 2, p. 62.

[7] Prince Georges Co., Md. Wills, Liber T No. 1, fol. 38.

[8] Frederick Co., Md. Deeds, Bk. M, p. 67.

acres from John Briscoe in Berkeley Co., Va.,[1] which was just a few miles west of his "Dan" tract, and about 1½ miles southeast of Charles Town, W.Va. Thirteen children, of whom:

+ C. PHILIP RIDGEWAY, b. c.1750/2, d. May 1794 in Salisbury District of Rowan Co., N.C., m. Mary (perhaps Payne[2]), d. c.1815. He served in the Revolutionary War.[3] Twelve children, of whom:

+ D. AUSBURN RIDGEWAY [RIDGWAY], of Berkeley Co., Va., m. 29 SEP 1803 in Rowan Co., N.C. to Jane Phelps, daughter John Phelps and Mary Williams. He removed to Lincoln Co., Ky.; Washington Co., Ky.; then Sangamon Co., Ill. where he d. 8 AUG 1841. Ausburn voted 2 AUG 1830 in an election in Springfield, Ill. The 1835 Tax List for Sangamon Co., Ill.[4] shows Ausburn Ridgeway as owner of over 480 acres of land which he bought in parcels (himself 80 acres on 17 MAY 1830: 2½ SW 24, 16 twp. 2 range) from Forga Milligan (patented 26 NOV 1830: 3½ SE 23, 16 twp. 2 range), Joseph Bondurant (patented 27 NOV 1829: 2½ NE 26, 16 twp. 2 range), and William Bridges (2½ NW 21, twp. 17, range 3). His signature in 1825 and 1840 is written "Ridgway." Fifteen children, of whom:

+ E. SAMUEL RIDGEWAY (my ancestor), b. 7 SEP 1804 in Lincoln Co., Ky., d. 1879, was m. there (1) 28 FEB 1825 to Fanny R. Page, and m. (2) Jennettie A. Fowler.

C. **Philip Ridgeway**
(c.1752-1794)

Philip Ridgeway was born c.1752, and a son of John Ridgeway and Mary Tenley. He died intestate in May 1794 in Salisbury District of Rowan County, North Carolina. He was married, perhaps in Prince Georges County, Maryland to Mary (perhaps Payne[5]), who died 16 OCT 1815.

The heirs and devisees of Philip Ridgeway, deceased, formerly of Rowan County, North Carolina, on 12 OCT 1812, appointed Osbern [Ausburn] Ridgeway (also one of the devisees) as their attorney to "go to the state of North Carolina, Rowan County, and make a deed of conveyance ... to John Miller" for 397 acres of land in Rowan County on the waters of the Yadkin adjoining on the upper side the lands of Joseph Boner and binding on the Yadkin River ... being the same tract of land of their deceased father, Philip Ridgeway, which was to be divided in accordance with his will among the above named children and which said tract was sold by Osbern Ridgeway to John Miller for $1,500.[6]

[1] Berkeley Co., Va. Deeds, Bk. 3, p. 425, dated 9 OCT 1775.
[2] One researcher believes Mary's maiden name is Williams.
[3] See NSDAR Number 4740879 A535.
[4] Marilyn W. Thomas and Hazelmae T. Temple, *1835 Tax List of Sangamon County, Illinois*, p. 4 of the original tax book.
[5] One researcher believes Mary's maiden name is Williams, and data on *Findagrave.com* gives maiden name as Heirs.
[6] The heirs were Elizabeth Ridgeway, Elijah Ridgeway, Samuel Ridgeway, Isaac Ridgeway, William Ridgeway, Thomas Ridgeway, David McBride and wife Nelly, late Nelly Ridgeway, and Patsy Ridgeway, of Lincoln County, Kentucky.

The heirs of Philip Ridgeway are listed in an indenture of 12 AUG 1813 in Jefferson County, West Virginia, along with a plat. It is between Betsey Ridgeway, Elijah Ridgeway, Rebecca Ridgeway, Osburn Ridgeway, Jane Ridgeway, Samuel Ridgeway, Betsey Ridgeway, Isaac Ridgeway, David McBride, Nelly McBride, and Patsey Ridgeway, heirs-at-law of Philip Ridgeway, deceased, who was one of the sons of John Ridgeway, deceased, all of Lincoln County, Kentucky, of the one part, and to Henry Haines, of Jefferson County, Virginia [now West Virginia], of the other part.

Children of Philip Ridgeway and Mary (perhaps Payne):

1. JOHN RIDGEWAY, b. c.1772, d. MAR 1827, m. in 1790[1] by Rev. John Jenkins in Pittsylvania Co., Va. to Ann Compton. Moved via Rowan Co., N.C. to Jefferson Co., Ky., and was there in 1803 when he was an administrator to his father's estate. Son:
    11. ENOCH RIDGEWAY, b. 28 FEB 1796 in Rowan Co., N.C., d. 15 DEC 1870, bur. Fairview Cem., Randolph Co., Mo., m. 27 DEC 1828 to Alcy J. Barnes, b. November 1805, d. 26 JUL 1877. Ten children.

2. ELIJAH RIDGEWAY, b. 12 JUL 1773 in Berkeley Co., Va., d. testate 12 JUN 1852 in Howard Co., Mo.,[2] bur. Richland Christ Church Cem., Howard Co., m. 1793 in Rowan Co., N.C. to Rebecca Caton, b. 1772, d. after 1851, daughter of Charles Caton, Sr.; both bur. Drake-Campbell Cem. Children:[3]
    21. THOMAS RIDGEWAY, b. 16 SEP 1800 in Lincoln Co., Ky., d. 9 SEP 1872 testate in Rocheport, Howard Co., Mo.,[4] m. 28 DEC 1820 in Howard Co., Mo. to Sarah "Sally" Staniford, b. 23 FEB 1801, d. 2 MAR 1876; both bur. Drake-Campbell Cem. Thirteen children.
    22. CHARLES RIDGEWAY, m. 5 JAN 1826 in Howard Co. to Ibby Head.
    23. JESSE SAMUEL RIDGEWAY, b. 12 FEB 1807 in Lincoln Co., Ky., d. 1 FEB 1893 in St. Clair Co., Mo., m. (1) 29 DEC 1836 in Howard Co. to Ann Wiley Booth, b. 17 MAY 1816 in Lincoln Co., Ky., m. (2) Mary Moore Boots, b. 1821, d. 1900. Twelve children.
    24. WILLIAM RIDGEWAY, b. 1810, d. 11 SEP 1857, bur. Drake-Campbell Cem., m. 17 NOV 1835 in Howard Co. to Hannah Price. Child:
        241. HANNAH C. RIDGEWAY, b. 3 AUG 1843, d. 7 JUL 1852, bur. Drake-Campbell Cem.
    25. POLLY RIDGEWAY, b. 1813, m. 11 DEC 1834 in Howard Co. to Joshua Wiley.
    26. SARAH RIDGEWAY, m. 13 JUN 1831 in Howard Co. to Frederick Fulkerson.
    27. JAMES RIDGEWAY, b. 1816, m. (1) Sarah (unknown), m. (2) 14 SEP 1837 in Howard Co. to Mary Prince.
    28. ANN RIDGEWAY, b. 1817, m. 21 SEP 1852 in Howard Co. to Francis D. Searcy. Children:

---

[1] Pittsylvania Co., Va. Marriage Bonds, p. 13, Only the year is in the record. Rev. Jenkins also married James Ridgeway to Ann Henderson in 1804, but he appears to be a son of James Ridgeway and Elizabeth Chizenhall.
[2] Howard Co., Mo. Wills, Bk. 4, p. 241., dated 6 OCT 1851, prov. 21 JUL 1852.
[3] Brick & Ridgway, p. 607.
[4] Howard Co., Mo. Wills, Bk. 7, pp. 123, 145.

281. ELIJAH SEARCY.
282. NANCY SEARCY, b. 1853, d. October 1928, m. Raybourn Burke.

3. SAMUEL RIDGEWAY, b. 10 MAY 1777 in Berkeley Co., Va., d. 22 JUN 1847 in Sangamon Co., Ill., bur. Stout Cem., Ball Twp., Chatham, Sangamon Co., m. by bond[1] of 22 APR 1799 in Surry Co., N.C. to Elizabeth Caton, b. 25 AUG 1775 in Berkeley Co., Va., d. 28 FEB 1847 in Sangamon Co., Ill., bur. Stout Cem. Couple removed to Lincoln Co., Ky., and in November 1829 to what is now Clear Lake Twp. of Sangamon Co., Ill.,[2] about 5 miles northeast of Springfield, Ill. Elizabeth was a dau. of Charles Caton and Jemima Summers. Children:

31. CHARLES M. RIDGEWAY, farmer, b. 22 APR 1801 in Ky., d. 15 AUG 1875 at Danville, Ky., m. 19 FEB 1824 in Garrard Co., Ky. to Sarah "Sally" Wilson, b. 9 APR 1805, d. 30 DEC 1880 in Danville, Ky.; both bur. Bellevue Cem., Danville, Boyle Co., Ky.

32. AUSBURN RIDGEWAY, b. 8 JUN 1803, d. 12 AUG 1826 in Ky. within about 2 weeks of his scheduled marriage.

33. PHILIP RIDGEWAY, b. 1 JAN 1806 in Ky., d. 8 SEP 1838, m. 8 MAR 1832 in Sangamon Co., Ill. to Margaret Henderson; rem. to Hancock Co., Ill. Three children.

34. JOHN RIDGEWAY, b. 30 MAR 1808 in Ky., d. 1872, m. (1) 1 JAN 1835 to Nancy Kelly [or Kelsey] who died within 6 mos., m. (2) 21 APR 1836 in Sangamon Co., Ill. to Tabitha Wilson, moved to Mo.; by 1845 took up a Donation Land Claim in Polk Co., Ore. Ten children by second wife.

35. MARY RIDGEWAY, b. 14 DEC 1811 in Lincoln Co., Ky., m. 21 FEB 1833 in Sangamon Co., Ill. to James Watson, b. 1808, d. 1861; both bur. Kings Valley Cem., Benton Co., Ore. The Watson home that was built in 1852 and barn still stand on Hoskins Rd., Benton Co., Ore. Children:
    351. BENJAMIN F. WATSON, b. 1845 in Sangamon Co., Ill., d. 17 SEP 1850 in Benton Co., Ore., age 5y 7m 28d, bur. Kings Valley Cem.
    352. MARY E. WATSON, b. 20 DEC 1846 in Sangamon Co., Ill., d. 31 JAN 1865 in Benton Co., Ore., bur. Kings Valley Cem.

36. SAMUEL LESLIE RIDGEWAY, b. 25 APR 1813 in Lincoln Co., Ky., m. 10 AUG 1837 in Sangamon Co., Ill. to Charlotte A. Stout, daughter of Philemon Stout and Penelope Anderson, b. 13 OCT 1817; rem. in July 1872 to Maryville, Nodaway Co., Mo. Philemon Stout, b. 15 MAY 1785 in Hunterdon Co., N.J., d. 31 JAN 1836 in Sangamon Co., Ill., m. 8 FEB 1810 in Woodford Co., Ky. to Penelope Anderson, d. 23 NOV 1860; both bur. Stout Cem. Eight children.

37. BENJAMIN R. RIDGEWAY, farmer, b. 15 FEB 1815 in Lincoln Co., Ky., m. 13 JUL 1839 in Sangamon Co., Ill. to Catherine Rape, daughter of John Rape of S.C., b. 21 DEC 1821 in Tenn. Six children.

38. LINDSAY RIDGEWAY, farmer, b. 20 JAN 1818 near Stanton, Lincoln Co., Ky., d. 13 MAR 1895, bur. Oak Ridge Cem., Springfield, Ill., m. (1) 7 DEC 1841 in Sangamon Co., Ill. to Lucy Melvina Dawson, b. 7 MAR 1825, d.

---

[1] With his brother Ausburn Ridgeway as bondsman.
[2] Also see *History of Early Settlers of Sangamon County, Illinois*, by John Carroll Power (1876), p. 617.

August 1889, bur. Oak Ridge Cem., daughter of John Dawson and Cary Jones, m. (2) Nancy Logan. Five children.

+ 4. AUSBURN RIDGEWAY (my ancestor), b. c.1770 in Berkeley Co., Va., d. 8 AUG 1841 in Sangamon Co., Ill., m. 29 SEP 1803 in Rowan Co., N.C. to Jane Phelps.

5. ISAAC RIDGEWAY, b. c.1783. No further information.

6. ELEANOR RIDGEWAY, b. 11 APR 1784, d. 3 AUG 1847 in Boone Co., Mo., m. 14 SEP 1802 to David McBride, b. 19 JAN 1784 in Md., d. 12 JAN 1852, son of John and Henrietta McBride. Twelve children.

7. JANE RIDGEWAY. No further information.

8. WILLIAM RIDGEWAY, b. c.1787 in Rowan Co., N.C., d. 29 JUN 1870 in Columbia, Boone Co., Mo., m. May 1812 to Sarah Barnes, b. 1787 in Madison Co., Ky., dau. of Shadrack Barnes who was a soldier in the Revolutionary War, d. 20 AUG 1873 in Boone Co., Mo., and Hannah Turner. He served in the military at the Battle of New Orleans during the War of 1812. He owned 320 acres of land that adjoined the town of Columbia, Mo. Both bur. Ridgeway Farm that is now a part of Columbia Country Club. Five children.

9. PATSY RIDGEWAY, b. c.1790 in Rowan Co., N.C., d. before 1829, m. 7 APR 1823 in Lincoln Co., Ky., to Peyton R. Skidmore, b. 1795, d. about February 1833, son of John Skidmore and Sarah McClure. Three children.

10. THOMAS RIDGEWAY, d. 9 JAN 1861, unmarried, Boone Co., Mo.

4. Ausburn Ridgeway
(c.1770-1841)

Ausburn Ridgeway (my ancestor) was a son of Philip Ridgeway and his wife Mary (perhaps Payne), and was born c.1770 in Berkeley County, Virginia. Ausburn was bondsman for the marriage of his brother Samuel Ridgeway in 1799 in Surry County, North Carolina. Ausburn was married by bond[1] of 29 SEP 1803 in Rowan County, North Carolina to Jane Phelps, daughter of John Phelps and Mary Williams.

About 1805, he moved to Lincoln County, Kentucky where he is listed on the 1810 Federal census [page 131]. He remained for time in Lincoln County, where he was enumerated on 7 AUG 1820 at Crab Orchard, with 13 white persons in his household. Then he moved to Washington County, Kentucky, and finally in 1828 to Sangamon County, Illinois. He is listed as Austin Ridgeway on the 1830 Federal census in Sangamon County where his household contains 12 free white persons [page 186].

---

[1] Bondsman was brother-in-law David McBride, and wit. by J. Hunt.

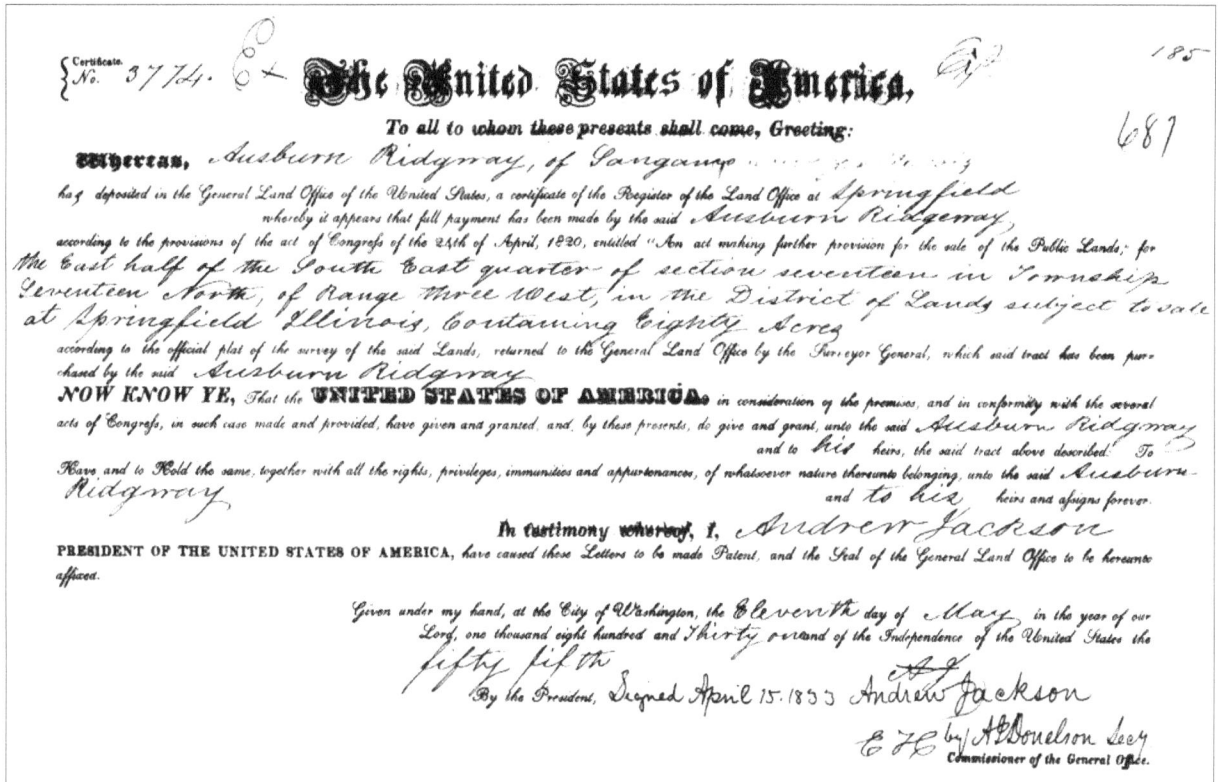

Figure 73 - Land grant for 80 acres in Sangamon County, Illinois to Ausburn Ridgway, filed in 1833

On 11 MAY 1831, he obtained a land grant of 80 acres in Sangamon County, Illinois,[1] and about that time he lived in Buffalo Township, Sangamon County.[2] His brother Philip Ridgway was an overseer of the roads on Muddy Creek in Stokes County, North Carolina. There is a power of attorney from the Philip Ridgeway heirs to Ausburn Ridgeway in Stokes County, for settlement of land in Stokes County that was once in Rowan County.

Osburn Ridgeway is enumerated on the 1840 Federal census for Sangamon County, Illinois [page 78], with 13 free white persons in his household.

The will of Osburn Ridgeway is dated 27 JUN 1840 in Sangamon County, Illinois. He died 8 AUG 1841 in Sangamon County.

Children of Ausburn Ridgeway and Jane Phelps:[3]

+   41.   SAMUEL RIDGEWAY (my ancestor), b. 7 SEP 1804 in Lincoln Co., Ky., d. 4 SEP 1879 in Randolph Co., Mo., m. (1) 28 FEB 1825 by Walter Anderson in Lincoln Co., Ky. to Fanny R. Page,[4] m. (2) Jennettie A. Fowler, *q.v.*

---

[1] U.S. General Land Office Records, dated 11 MAY 1831, for 80 acres in T 17N, R 3W, Sect. 17 of Sangamon Co., Ill., filed 15 APR 1833 in the Land Office.
[2] *History of Sangamon County, Illinois* (Chicago, Ill.: Interstate Publishing Co., 1881), p. 804.
[3] Also see *History of the Early Settlers of Sangamon County, Illiinois*, by John Carroll Power (Springfield, Ill.: Edwin A. Wilson & Co., 1876), pp. 617-19.
[4] When Samuel Ridgeway married Fanny R. Page, the surety was Dillard Page, 28 FEB 1825. Osborn Ridgeway gave consent for his son to marry, 21 FEB 1825.

42.   JOHN RIDGEWAY, b. 23 FEB 1806 in Lincoln Co., Ky., d. 28 OCT 1858 in Sangamon Co., Ill., m. 12 FEB 1829 in Sangamon Co., to Sarah Bridges, b. 14 NOV 1812 in Xenia, Ohio, d. 5 DEC 1879, daughter of William Bridges and Martha Patsy Martin. Sarah m. (2) 20 DEC 1860 in Sangamon Co. to Jonathan Constant, b. 30 SEP 1809 in Fleming Co., Ky., son of Jacob Constant. John served as a private in the Blackhawk War of 1832.[1] Enumerated on the 1850 Federal census for Sangamon Co., Ill. [#2325]. Children:

421.   MARTHA JANE RIDGEWAY, b. 3 JAN 1830, m. 5 MAR 1846 by C.W. Luis in Sangamon Co., Ill. to Charles T. Eckel.; rem. to Ottawa, Kan. Five children.

422.   ALFRED A. RIDGEWAY, b. 13 MAR 1834 in Ill., d. 1857.

423.   ADELINE MELINDA RIDGEWAY (twin), b. 17 JAN 1837 in South Wheatland Twp., Macon Co., Ill., d. 10 JAN 1915, bur. Salem Cem., m. 1 OCT 1857 in Sangamon Co., Ill. to Benjamin Franklin Hill, b. 20 FEB 1836, d. 1874, son of Francis Green Hill and Rachel Wilson; res. Decatur, Ill. Seven children.

424.   CAROLINE RIDGEWAY (twin), b. 17 JAN 1837 in Ill., d. 2 NOV 1864 in Illiopolis, Sangamon Co., Ill., m. in Illiopolis to Henry Lee.

425.   LEVI S. RIDGEWAY, b. 29 SEP 1839 in Ill., d. 2 AUG 1868 in Sangamon Co., Ill., m. (1) Essie Eckel, and m. (2) Rhoda E. Fletcher, b. 1841, d. 1919. Levi and Rhoda bur. Mechanicsburg Cem., Sangamon Co., Ill. Five children.

43.   EDWARD RIDGEWAY, b. c.1808 in Lincoln Co., Ky., d. 1834, m. 1 OCT 1829 in Sangamon Co., Ill. to Ann Cantrell, b. 1817, d. 1852. Widow Ann m. (2) Frederick Meeker, bur. Turley Cem., Elkhart, Logan Co., Ill. Children:

431.   NANCY JANE RIDGEWAY, b. 16 OCT 1829 in Athens, Ill., d. 9 SEP 1915 in Laurens, Iowa, bur. Turley Cem., m. 15 FEB 1848 to James H. Mileham, b. 27 JUL 1825, d. 25 MAR 1892 in Ill. Nine children.

432.   ELIZA RIDGEWAY, b. 9 APR 1833 in Sangamon Co., Ill., d. 9 DEC 1874, m. 28 APR 1850 to Andrew Wells, b. 28 MAR 1824 in Louisiana, Pike Co., Mo., d. 19 JUL 1890 at Mount Carroll, Carroll Co., Ill., bur. Woodland Brethren Cem. Seven children.

44.   WILLIAM RIDGEWAY, b. 18 JAN 1810 in Hangingford, Lincoln Co., Ky., d. 10 FEB 1895 in Lebanon, Ore., bur. Lebanon Pioneer Cem., m. (1) 14 FEB 1833 in Sangamon Co., Ill. to Elizabeth Ann Lucas, b. 1812, d. 1844, dau. of Thomas Lucas and Sarah Hoblit, m. (2) Sarah Ann Dannals, b. 11 JUL 1822, d. 7 JAN 1890. This family moved from Logan Co., Ill. to Jasper Co., Iowa, and then on to Linn Co., Ore. William and Sarah are bur. in Lebanon Pioneer Cem. of Lebanon, Ore. Eighteen children (five by first marriage), some descendants in Idaho and Oregon.

45.   JAMES RIDGEWAY, b. 12 JAN 1812 in Lincoln Co., Ky., d. 30 NOV 1888 in Lebanon, Ore., bur. Lebanon Pioneer Cem., m. (1) 13 FEB 1835 in Sangamon Co., Ill. to Dulceme Fletcher, m. (2) Dulcina Paine, b. 28 JUN 1820, d. 2 MAY 1896. Ten children, some descendants in Oregon.

---

[1] <u>Brick & Ridgway</u>, p. 621.

46.   PATTERSON RIDGEWAY, b. 19 NOV 1813 in Lincoln Co., Ky., d. c.1893 in Laomi, m. (1) 9 DEC 1844 by Ira Mosher in Sangamon Co., Ill. to Nancy Huddleston, b. 1817, d. before 1852, m. (2) 6 JUL 1852 in Sangamon Co., Ill. to Rhoda J. Withrow Walker, widow of Theophilus Walker. Children:[1]

   461.   NORMAN RIDGEWAY, b. 18 DEC 1846 in Sangamon Co., Ill., m. 18 AUG 1898 to Alice Dillon, daughter of Ebenezer and Lucretia Dillon, b. 22 MAR 1873 in Sangamon Co., Ill.

   462.   MARGARET RIDGEWAY, b. 1848 in Va.

   463.   ROBERT RIDGEWAY, b. c.1854, d. 2 MAR 1906 in Springfield, Ill., bur. Oak Ridge Cem., m. 6 MAY 1877 to Emaline A. Rude. Five children.

47.   LOUISA ANN RIDGEWAY, b. 22 JUN 1822 in Lincoln Co., Ky., d. 6 OCT 1865 in Sangamon Co., Ill., age 43y 3m 15d, bur. Cass Cem., of Buffalo Hart Twp., Sangamon Co., m. (1) 3 MAR 1836 by John Dawson in Sangamon Co., Ill. to Benjamin Franklin Burns, b. 6 AUG 1816, d. 16 MAR 1870, bur. Cass Cem., Buffalo Hart, Sangamon Co., Ill., son of Thomas Burns and Elizabeth Ridgeway, m. (2) in 1852 to Charles Hempstead. Child:

   71.   LOUVENIA E. BURNS, d. 22 SEP 1870, age 19y 6m 14d, bur. Cass Cem.

48.   MARY RIDGEWAY, b. c.1817 in Lincoln Co., Ky., d. before 1874, m. 19 DEC 1833 in Sangamon Co., Ill. to Stephen L. Cantrell, b. April 1815. Three children.

49.   GEORGE RIDGEWAY, b. 1819 in Ky., m. 24 OCT 1841 in Sangamon Co., Ill. to Sarah J. Cast. Six children, res. in Sangamon Co., Ill.

4(10). ALEXANDER RIDGEWAY, b. c.1821 in Lincoln Co., Ky., d. 26 MAY 1873 in Decatur, Iowa, m. 30 AUG 1844 by James T. Robinson in Sangamon Co., Ill. to Cynthia Ann Johnson. Eight children.

4(11). ENOCH OSBORN RIDGEWAY, b. 1823 in Buffalo Hart Twp., Lincoln Co., Ky., bur. Constant Cem., m. 28 NOV 1841 to Mary Jane [or Ellen[2]] Likens, b. 25 JAN 1820 in Ind., d. 6 FEB 1909 at Buffalo Hart, Sangamon Co., Ill. Five children.

4(12). MARINDA JANE RIDGEWAY, b. 1827 in Lincoln Co., Ky., d. c.1858 at Buffalo Gap, Sangamon Co., Ill., m. 26 NOV 1844 by James T. Robinson in Sangamon Co., Ill. to Ballard Huddleston, b. 1822, d. 1903.

4(13). SARAH L. RIDGEWAY, b. c.1829 in Lincoln Co., Ky., m. 2 AUG 1843 by Henry McDaniel in Sangamon Co., Ill. to Dennis T. Provine.

4(14). MALINDA E. RIDGEWAY, b. 26 JAN 1831 in Sangamon Co., Ill., m. 12 APR 1847 by John England in Sangamon Co., Ill. to Charles Alexander Dickerson, b. 11 APR 1827, son of Samuel Dickerson and Susan Kane. Eight children.

---

[1] Also see *Historical Encyclopedia of Illinois and History of Sangamon County, Illinois*, ed. by Newton Bateman (Chicago, Ill.: Munsell Publishing Co., 1912), Vol. II, p. 1565.
[2] See *The Circuit Rider*, Vol. XVI No. 3 (July 1984), p. 91.

4(15).   LUCINDA RIDGEWAY, b. 1833 in Buffalo Gap, Ill., d. 17 SEP 1881 in Grand River Twp., Decatur Co., Iowa, m. 27 MAY 1852 by W.T. Bennett in Sangamon Co., Ill. to James Hall, b. 1821, d. 1898. Child:

4(15)1.   BELLE HALL, b. 1862, d. 1908.

41. <u>Samuel Ridgeway</u>
(1804-1879)

Samuel Ridgeway (my ancestor) was a son of Ausburn Ridgeway and Jane Phelps and he was born 7 SEP 1804 in Lincoln County, Kentucky. He was married first on 28 FEB 1825 to Fanny R. Page. She died 24 DEC 1854 at the age of 54y, 1m and 23d and is buried in the Coulter-McCanne Burying Ground of Randolph County, Missouri.

In the 1835 Tax Book of Sangamon Co., Illinois[1] we find he purchased two 80-acre parcels (23 NOV 1829: E½ NE 20, twp. 16, range 4; and 7 NOV 1829: E½ NW 28, twp. 16, range 4), and was owner of a tract (80 acres: 2½ NE 20, twp. 16, range 4) originally purchased 3 APR 1825 by Levi Abrams. On 2 AUG 1830 Samuel voted in an election held in Springfield, Illinois.

On 9 APR 1850, Samuel Ridgeway purchased 40 acres in Randolph County from William Hunt and wife Nancy for $400.[2] On 20 MAR 1852, Samuel Ridgeway and his wife Fanny R. sold the same 40 acres to Thomas B. Reed for $181.[3]

Samuel Ridgeway was married second on 5 NOV 1855 to Jennettie A. Fowler, born 11 JAN [or 24 FEB] 1820 in Tennessee. The place of this marriage has not yet been determined, and a county record of the event has not been located.

The family is found on the Federal census of 26 SEP 1850 for Sugar Creek Township, Randolph County, Missouri. Samuel was a farmer; with wife Fanny he has listed four children. During the early 1850's it is known that Samuel Ridgeway bought two 40-acre parcels of land southwest of Jacksonville, Missouri in Section 9, which he later mortgaged. He owned Lots 4, 5, 10, 11 and 12 in Block L of the City of Jacksonville, and "opened the first hotel (in Jacksonville) and continued to occupy it until his death which occurred in (1879)."[4]

On 2 SEP 1860, the family of Samuel and Jennettie Ridgeway was enumerated on the Federal census in Jacksonville, Randolph County, Missouri [family 1137], and was listed in Jackson Township of that county in 1870. On 18 JUL 1879, Samuel Ridgeway conveyed to his wife Jennettie, lots 4, 5, 6, 10, 11 and 12 in Block L in the town of Jacksonville, Missouri.

---

[1] Ibid., page 36 of the original tax book.
[2] Randolph Co., Mo. Deeds, Bk. H, p. 701.
[3] Randolph Co., Mo. Deeds, Bk. H, p. 702, mortgage at p. 763.
[4] History of Randolph County, Missouri by Alexander H. Waller (1920), page 157.

Samuel Ridgeway died September 4, 1879, presumably in Randolph County. He was buried in the McCanne Burying Ground (now known as Coulter Cemetery), which is located on Randolph County Road B20 on the Randolph and Macon County line, about 1½ miles east of Highway #63.

On the 1880 Federal census for Jackson Township, Randolph County, Missouri, Jennettie Ridgeway is shown as the head of household, age 60 [page 6]. She died 4 OCT 1883.[1] In the Randolph County public death records we find that she died at 5:30 a.m. on that date at the age of 63 years, 7 months and 10 days, making her birth date 24 FEB 1820. The death record shows Jennettie died in Moberly, Missouri of stomach and bowel cancer and was buried in Jacksonville, Missouri by Williams and Brothers Funeral Home of Moberly. Jennettie was buried Friday, 5 OCT 1883 in McCanne Burying Ground (now known as Coulter Cemetery). A newspaper notice states cause of death was stomach cancer.

Figure 74 - Highlighted lots in Jacksonville owned by heirs of Samuel and Jenetta Ridgeway

On 23 MAY 1884, Susan Ridgeway and Florence Ridgeway, *heirs to the estate of Jenetta Ridgeway, dec.*, conveyed title to Lots 4, 5, 6, 10, 11 and 12 in Block L of the City of Jacksonville, Missouri to D.L. Freeman for the consideration of $275.[2]

Children of Samuel Ridgeway and his first wife Fanny R. Page:

+ 411. JOHN PAGE RIDGEWAY, b. c.1826 in Ky., prob. m. 3 OCT 1850 in Macon Co., Mo. to Sarah J. Brock. He d. 18 JUL 1904, bur. Mount Salem Cem. near Excello in Macon Co., Mo.

  412. LUCY[3] ANN RIDGEWAY, b. c.1828 in Ky., m. 22 FEB 1855 by L.C. Davis in Randolph Co., Mo.[4] as the second wife of Nimrod S. Esry, b. 3 DEC 1819 in Mercer, Ky., d. 22 FEB 1885 in Randolph Co., Mo. The family was enumerated on the Federal census of 20 JUL 1860 in Narrows Twp., Macon Co., Mo. [page 319, post office McLandesville], with Nimrod, age 40, b. Ky., and Nancy A., age 32, born Ky. It appears that Mr. Esry had a previous marriage by which he had at least four children. Children:

    4121. WILLIAM ESRY, b. 28 JAN 1857 (age 3 in 1860) in Mo., m. 7 FEB 1878 in Mason Co. to Martha E. Brook.

    4122. ELDORA BELLE ESRY, b. April 1859 in Mo., d. 2 MAY 1938 in Lajunta, Colo., m. Albert E. Wisdom, b. 1856, d. 1925. Four Children.

    4123. ROBERT McCLELLAN ESRY, b. 26 JAN 1861 in Macon Co., Mo., d. 11

---

[1] Death date initially provided by Dorothy (Parker) Allen.
[2] Randolph Co., Mo. Deeds, Bk. 25, p. 337.
[3] Her name is sometimes seen as Nancy Ridgeway.
[4] Randolph Co., Mo. Marriages, Bk. A, p. 176.

MAR 1936 in Dallas, Tex., bur. Laurel Land Memorial Park, m. (1) 7 DEC 1898 in Randolph Co., Mo. to Iva Patrick, m. (2) Flora Belle Wilson, b. 31 MAY 1866, d. 7 DEC 1965.

4124. LUCY A. ESRY, b. 1863 in Macon Co., Mo.

4125. FANNIE E. ESRY, b. 3 AUG 1864 in Macon Co., Mo., d. 22 SEP 1955 in Randolph Co., Mo., m. 16 FEB 1883 in Randolph Co. to Curtis Drury Hudson, b. 1862, d. 1935. Ten Children.

4126. GEORGE ESRY, b. 1867 in Macon Co., Mo.

4127. SAMUEL ESRY, b. 1869 in Macon Co., Mo.

+ 413. ELIZABETH RIDGEWAY, b. 5 DEC 1833 in Ky., c. 12 FEB 1888, m. 6 MAY 1852 by Benjamin Polson in Randolph Co., Mo.[1] to Richard Coffey Bennett, b. 20 DEC 1824 in Casey Co., Ky.

414. JOSEPH RIDGEWAY, b. c.1835 in Ky., m. (1) 8 FEB 1857 by John W. Jones, J.P., in Randolph Co., Mo. to Georgia Ann Halliburton.[2] On the Federal census of 2 SEP 1860, his family was enumerated in Jacksonville, Randolph Co., Mo., and Georgia A. was listed as age 22, and born in Tenn. Child:

4141. F. RIDGEWAY (female), b. c.1858 (age 2 in 1860) in Mo.

+ 415. JENNETTIE A. RIDGEWAY, b. 27 AUG 1837 in poss. Lincoln Co., Ky., m. 22 AUG 1864 at the home of Rufus O. Kirkpatrick in Sweet Springs, Saline Co., Mo.[3] to John Samuel Tiller. Jennettie d. 24 OCT 1892.

416. GEORGE WILLIAM RIDGEWAY, bur. in McCanne Burying Ground, "son of S. and F.", died 24 JUL 1845, aged 4y, 4m and 9d.

417. MARY JANE RIDGEWAY, b. 15 MAR 1841, bur. in McCanne Burying Ground, "dau. of S. and F.", d. 28 OCT 1846, aged 5y, 7m and 4d.

Children of Samuel Ridgeway and his second wife Jennettie A. Fowler:

418. WILLIAM HUGH RIDGEWAY, b. 9 SEP 1856, d. 8 JUL 1860 in Randolph Co., unmarried, bur. in McCanne Burying Ground, d. "3y, 9m and 29d".

419. SUSAN HARRIETT RIDGEWAY, b. 31 JUL 1858 in Jacksonville, Randolph Co., m. 8 JUL 1896 in Kansas City to Charles L. Knight, b. 1849, d. 1918, bur. Mount Washington Cem. of

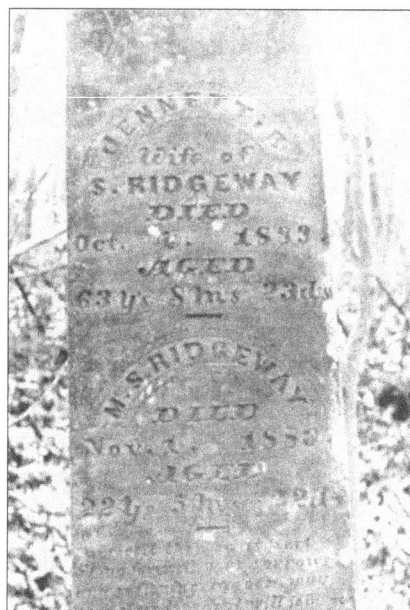

Figure 75 - One face of the grave marker for Ridgeway Family showing Samuel's second wife Jennettie. McCanne Cemetery.

[1] Randolph Co., Mo. Marriages, Bk. A, p. 150.
[2] Randolph Co., Mo. Marriages, Bk. A, p. 199.
[3] Saline Co., Mo. Marriages, Bk. A, p. 289.

Kansas City, Mo. She d. 28 SEP 1934 at 2926 Victor St., Kansas City, Mo. and was bur. 1 OCT 1934 Mount Washington Cem. (Section E, Block 10, grave 93). Her newspaper death notice says she was found dead in bed. Charles L. Knight was b. 3 JUN 1849 and before his marriage, was employed as a ticket agent for Wabash, St. Louis and Pacific Railway in Moberly, Mo. He was a popular guy, not married, and well liked by the ladies.[1] Child:

    4191. ELEANOR RIDGEWAY "Ella" KNIGHT, m. 7 AUG 1901 in Jackson Co. to Earl L. Swope, b. 23 JUN 1867 in Philadelphia, Pa., d. 19 MAR 1936 of cerebral hemorrhage, cremated, son of John W. Swope and Thresa Hines.

    41(10). MARTIN S. RIDGEWAY, b. 9 MAY 1861 in Randolph Co., d. 1 NOV 1883 in Clifton, Randolph Co., age 22y 5m 23d [sic], unmarried, bur. by Williams and Brothers Funeral Home of Moberly, Mo. in McCanne (Coulter) Burying Ground, located at Excello, Macon Co., Mo. He worked as a brakeman for the railroad, and died east of Clinton, Randolph Co., Mo. after suffering a fractured skull in a fall from a railroad car.

+ 41(11). FLORENCE EVELYN RIDGEWAY (my ancesstor), b. 11 DEC 1863 near Corder, Lafayette Co., Mo., d. 21 AUG 1936 in Aurora, Colo., m. 25 DEC 1884 in Moberly, Mo. to 272. CHARLES CONDUS DAVISON, *q.v.* See Davison Family.

Figure 76 - Florence Evelyn Ridgeway

---

[1] *History of Randolph and Macon Counties, Missouri* (St. Louis, Mo.: National Historical Co., 1884).

411. <u>John Page Ridgeway</u>
(1826-1904)

John Page Ridgeway, son of Samuel Ridgeway and Fanny R. Page, was born 4 JAN 1826 in Lincoln County, Kentucky. He was probably married 3 OCT 1850 in Macon County, Missouri to Sarah James Brock, daughter of Davis Brock (1792-1840) and Sarah King (1790-1845). Sarah was born 21 DEC 1833 in Lincoln County, Kentucky, and died 28 FEB 1886 in Macon County, Illinois. Both John and Sarah were buried in Mount Salem Cemetery near Excello, Macon County, Missouri.

The family was enumerated 2 SEP 1860 on the Federal census for Jacksonville, Randolph County, Missouri. On the 1880 Federal census for Narrows Township, Macon County, Missouri this family was enumerated on page 22. John died 18 JUL 1904 and was buried in Mount Salem Cemetery near Excello, Macon, Missouri.

Possible children of John Page Ridgeway ande Sarah James Brock:

4111. LUCINDA ANN RIDGEWAY, b. 29 AUG 1853 in Mo., d. 3 FEB 1934, m. 11 DEC 1877 in Macon Co., Mo. to Matthew Theodore Esry, b. 1842, d. 1917, bur. Coulter-Wright Cem., Jacksonville, Randolph Co., Mo. Children:
   41111. Infant Esry, b. 1878, bur. Coulter-Wright Cem.
   41112. LENA MAE ESRY, b. 11 MAY 1881, d. 24 OCT 1960 in Moberly, Mo., m. 25 DEC 1910 in Randolph Co. to John Oliver Broaddus, b. 22 MAR 1888 in Mo., d. 5 APR 1921 in Moberly, Mo., son of John McKenzie Broaddus (1862-1917) and Agness C. Edwards (1864-1918).
   41113. LESLIE ESRY, b. 1896, d. 1969.
4112. J.L. RIDGEWAY, male, b. c.1856 (age 4 in 1860) in Mo.
4113. M.F. RIDGEWAY, female, b. March 1860 in prob. Randolph Co., Mo.
4114. MARIA JANE RIDGEWAY, b. 23 FEB 1860 in Excello, Mo., d. 26 AUG 1933 in Narrows Twp., Macon Co., Mo., m. 16 OCT 1881 in Macon Co. to Perry Thomas Coulter, b. 7 APR 1847, d. 23 FEB 1925 in Narrows, Macon Co., Mo.; both bur. Mount Salem Cem. Children:
   41141. PEARL G. COULTER, b. 1882, d. 1957, m. 14 MAY 1905 in Excello, Mo. to Benjamin V. Cross.
   41142. MABEL C. COULTER, b. 3 DEC 1885, d. 26 NOV 1918, m. 29 DEC 1909 in Mexico, Audrain Co., Mo. to John Butler Lawrence.
   41143. FLOSSIE COULTER, b. 31 DEC 1891, d. 19 MAY 1953, m. 27 JAN 1915 in Macon Co., Mo. to Wesley T. Butler.
4115. SALLIE D. RIDGEWAY, b. c.1866 (age 14 in 1880) in Mo.
4116a. George R. Brock, b. c.1872 (age 8 in 1880) in Mo.

413. <u>Elizabeth Ridgeway Bennett</u>
(1833-1888)

E lizabeth Ridgeway, daughter of Samuel Ridgeway and Fanny R. Page, was born 4 DEC 1833[1] in Kentucky. She was married 6 MAY 1852 in Randolph County, Missouri to Richard Coffee Bennett of Hustonville, Lincoln County, Kentucky.

On 5 SEP 1860 this family was enumerated on the Federal census for Salt River Township, Randolph County, Missouri [family 291, post office Milton], with Richard C. age 35, born in Kentucky. At the time of the 1860 Federal census, Nancy Bennett, age 79, born in Pennsylvania, was residing in the same household, as well as Richard's sister Charlotte Bennett, age 40, who was born in Virginia. We find Charlotte's grave in Liberty Cemetery of Cairo, Missouri, with dates 12 FEB 1810 to 3 NOV 1890. Elizabeth Bennett died 12 FEB 1882 in Randolph County, Missouri and was buried in Liberty Cemetery.

Richard, the son of Moses Bennett, Jr. and Nancy Cooper (daughter of William Cooper of Scotland), was born 20 DEC 1824 in Casey County, Kentucky, and died 20 JAN 1903 in Randolph County, Missouri. He too was buried in Liberty Cemetery. Moses Bennett, Jr. died in Grundy County, Missouri and was a son of Moses Bennett, Sr. who was from Botetourt County, Virginia. Both Elizabeth and her husband Richard were buried in Liberty Cemetery which was across the road from their farm, 2 miles east of Cairo, Missouri, in Salt River Township.

Children of Richard Coffee Bennett and Elizabeth Ridgeway:[2]

4131. JAMES HAMILTON BENNETT, stillborn 14 JAN 1853 in Randolph Co., Mo.
4132. MARY JANE BENNETT, b. 6 FEB 1854 in Mo., m. 4 NOV 1880 in Randolph Co. to George Brown (1852-1926). She d. in 1936 and bur. in Liberty Cem. Children:
   41321. CARL BROWN, b. 4 JUN 1885, d. unmarried 11 APR 1921.
   41322. VERNIE BROWN, b. 1889, d. 1935, m. 26 NOV 1913 in Randolph Co. to Melvin Edwards (1888-1930). Buried at Liberty Cem. No children.
4133. ALEXANDER BENNETT, b. 10 DEC 1855 in Ralls, Mo., d. 12 DEC 1927 in Cairo, Mo., m. 14 OCT 1878 to Miria Wright, bur. Oakland Cem. near Moberly, Mo. Children:
   41331. MATTIE KATE BENNETT, m. 17 DEC 1913 in Jackson Co. to Frank M. Sanders.
   41332. MAE BENNETT, m. 15 SEP 1909 in Randolph Co. to Lacy N. Gooding, bur. Oakland Cem. of Moberly, Mo. Child:
      413321. JAMES BENNETT GOODING, may have had a farm near Cairo, Mo. and moved to Calif.
4134. CHARLES BEAL BENNETT, b. 4 MAR 1858 in Randolph Co., Mo., m. Mary "Jannie" Roberts (1880-21 DEC 1964). He d. 19 MAY 1933 in Moberly, Mo., and bur. in Liberty Cem., 2 miles east of Cairo, Mo. Child:
   41341. MARY EVELYN BENNETT, m. 18 NOV 1942 in Randolph Co. to Clay T.

---

[1] The birthdate on her tombstone in Liberty Cemetery is 18 NOV 1834.
[2] Information in part provided by Mr. Ellis N. Bennett, 130 Berwick, San Antonio TX 78201 as provided in an undated letter to him by Claudette Whitefield, 621 Lilac Drive, Liberal KS 67901.

Mayfield, resided in Centerview, Mo.

4135. JOHN BENNETT, b. 4 MAR 1860 in Randolph Co., d. 1 MAR 1915 in Cairo, Mo., bur. in Liberty Cem.,[1] m. 11 MAR 1887 in Randolph Co. to Lelah Darby, b. 11 NOV 1866. Children:

    41351.   CURT BENNETT, res. in Kansas City, Mo.

    41352.   ROY BENNETT, lived at 4472 Fort Drive, S.E., Washington, D.C.

    41353.   EARL BENNETT, res. at 401 S. Williams in Moberly, Mo.

    41354.   FLETA M. BENNETT, m. 1 SEP 1913 in Randolph Co. to Everett Edwards and moved to Tucson, Ariz. where she died. Child:

        413541.   RUTH EDWARDS.

4136. CHARLOTTE FRANCES "Fannie" BENNETT, b. 22 JAN 1862 in Randolph Co., Mo., d. 26 MAY 1922 in Randolph Co., bur. Liberty Cem., m. 22 JAN 1888 to Smith Asa Ridgway, b. 6 NOV 1851, d. 23 FEB 1935, bur. Liberty Cem., son of Strother Ridgway (1814-1894) and Ann Maria Roush (1819-1913). No children.

4137. NANCY ANN BENNETT, b. 5 MAY 1864 in Randolph Co., Mo., d. 28 AUG 1864 in Randolph Co.

4138. SARAH SUSAN BENNETT (twin), b. 3 JUL 1866, d. 14 OCT 1866.

4139. LIZZIE LUELLEN RIDGEWAY (twin), b. July 3, 1866, d. 8 SEP 1866.

413(10). IZORA BELLE BENNETT, b. 11 SEP 1867 in Randolph Co., Mo., d. 18 MAR 1904 in Cairo, Mo., unmarried, bur. Liberty Cem.

413(11). MILLIE ALICE BENNETT, b. 18 OCT 1869, d. 5 JUL 1916, bur. Liberty Cem., m. 19 APR 1893 in Randolph Co. as the second wife of a distant cousin, Marion B. Ridgway (1856-1937), bur. Liberty Cem., son of Strother Ridgway[2] and Ann Maria Roush. Marion was m. (1) to Sarah E. Halliburton, and (3) to Carrie Austin Bobbitt, 1876-1930 who was bur. in Liberty Cem. Children:

    413(11)1.   ETNA RIDGWAY, b. 2 JUN 1894, d.inf.

    413(11)2.   MABEL RIDGWAY, b. 19 JUN 1897, d. inf.

    413(11)3.   GLEN RIDGWAY, b. 2 MAR 1901, d. 7 JUL 1974, res. in Independence, Mo.

413(12). EVERETT BENNETT, b. 5 FEB 1872 in Randolph Co., Mo., d. 16 NOV 1952 in Guyman, Okla., m. 19 OCT 1892 to Annie Lee Rogers, b. 1877, d. 1954. Nine children.

413(13). EMMETT BENNETT, b. 15 JUL 1874, m. Nettie Miller. Child:

    413(13)1.   MARY GLADYS BENNETT, b. 2 JUL 1907, d. 14 NOV 1916, bur. Liberty Cem.

---

[1] His grave stone in Liberty Cem. indicates his wife Lela; however the place for her date of death is blank.

[2] According to *Ridgway Families* by Thurman Ridgway and Gertrude N. Brick (Baltimore: Gateway Press, 1980), p. 266.

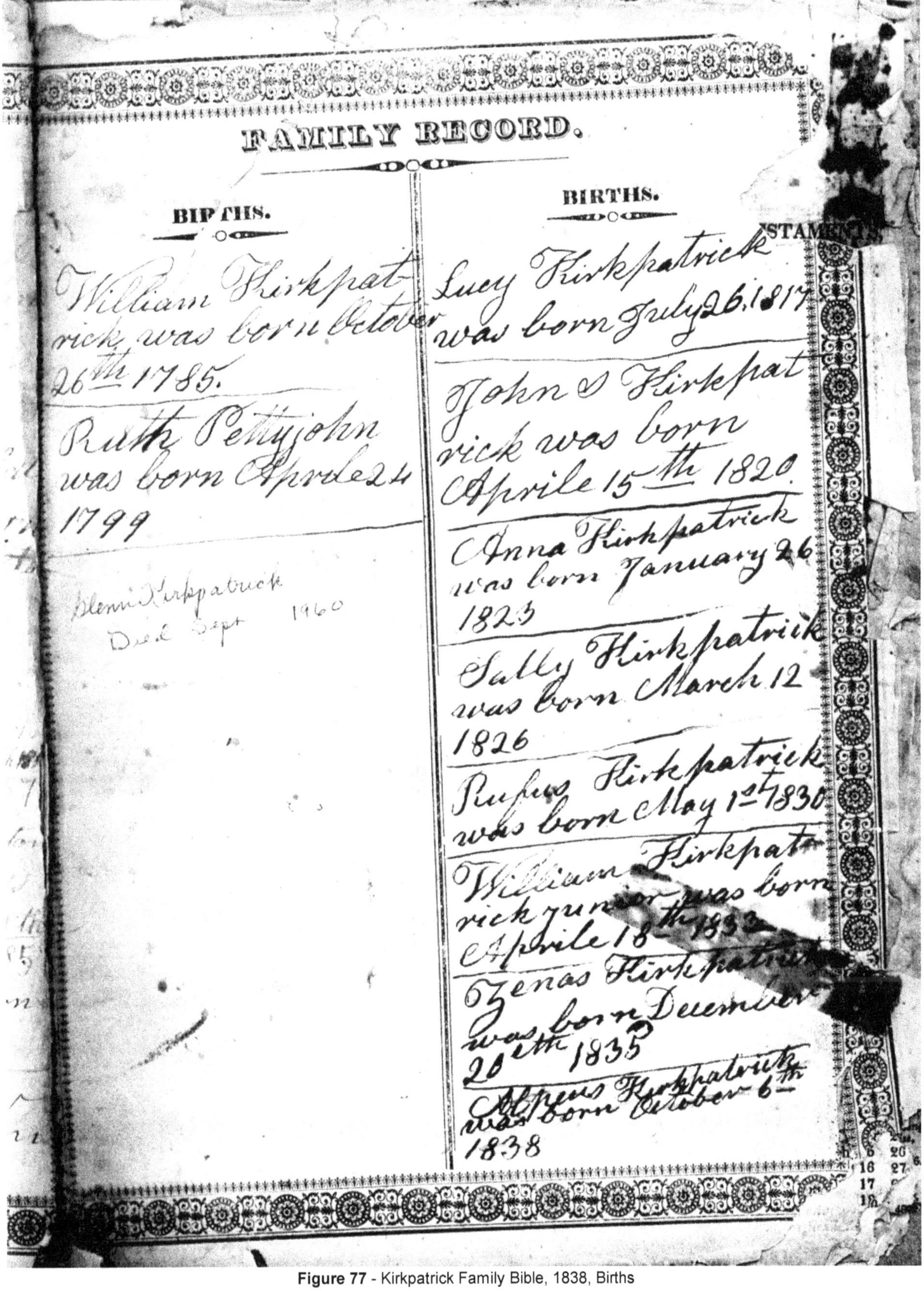

FAMILY RECORD.

BIRTHS.

William Kirkpatrick was born October 26th 1785.

Ruth Pettyjohn was born Aprile 24 1799

Glenn Kirkpatrick Died Sept 1960

BIRTHS.

Lucy Kirkpatrick was born July 26, 1817

John S Kirkpatrick was born Aprile 15th 1820.

Anna Kirkpatrick was born January 26 1823

Sally Kirkpatrick was born March 12 1826

Rufus Kirkpatrick was born May 1st 1830

William Kirkpatrick junior was born Aprile 18th 1832

Zenas Kirkpatrick was born December 20th 1835

Alpheus Kirkpatrick was born October 6th 1838

Figure 77 - Kirkpatrick Family Bible, 1838, Births

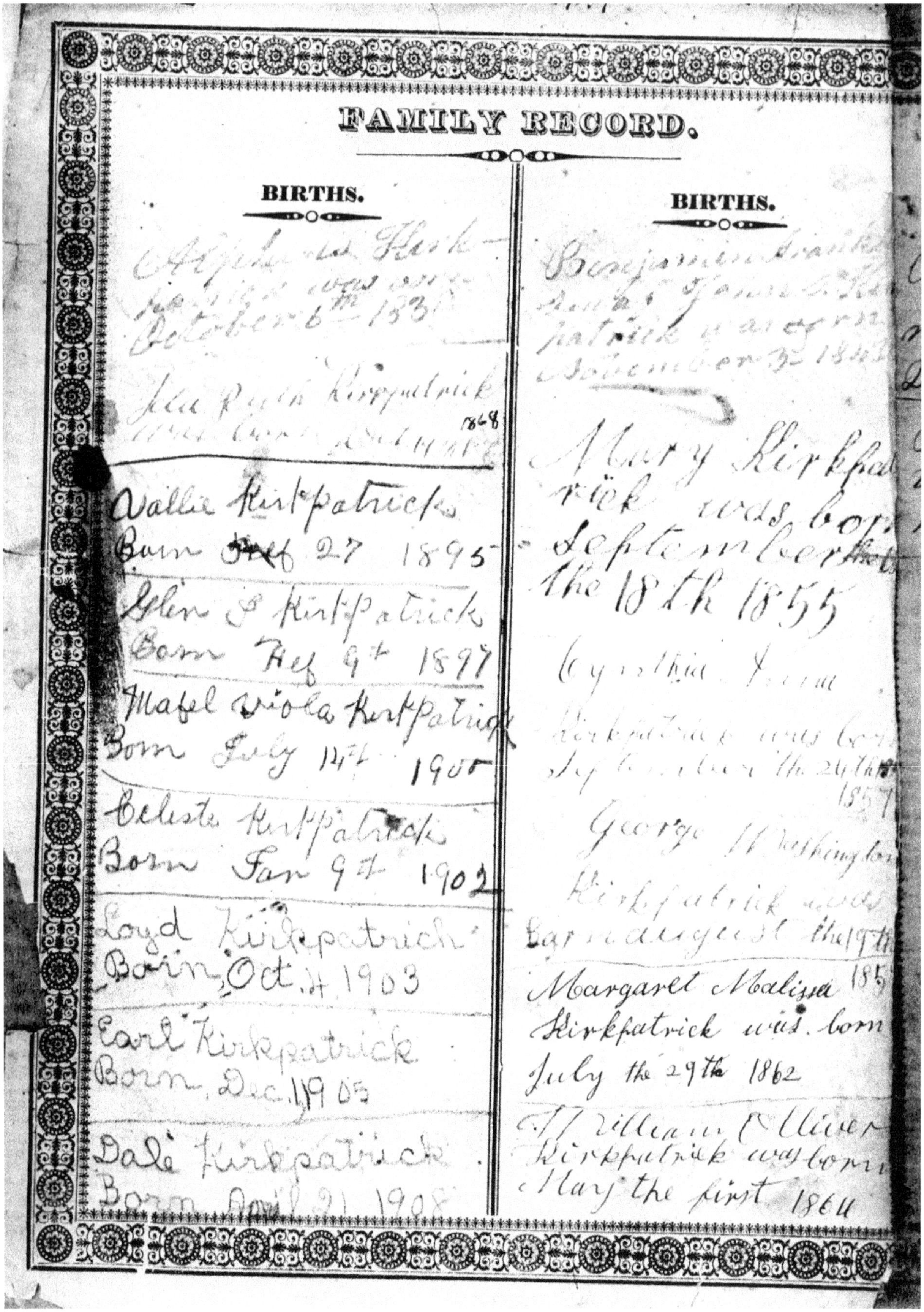

FAMILY RECORD.

BIRTHS.

Ageh ... Flesh
... was ...
October 6th 183[?]

Ilea Ryan Kirkpatrick
was born Oct 11 1868

Vallie Kirkpatrick
Born Oct 27 1895

Glen J Kirkpatrick
Born Feb 9th 1897

Mabel Viola Kirkpatrick
Born July 14th 1900

Celeste Kirkpatrick
Born Jan 9th 1902

Loyd Kirkpatrick
Born Oct 4 1903

Carl Kirkpatrick
Born Dec 1 1905

Dale Kirkpatrick
Born April 21 1908

BIRTHS.

Benjamin Frank...
... James ...
patrick was born
November 3 184[?]

Mary Kirkpat-
rick was born
September
the 18th 1855

Cynthia Ann
Kirkpatrick was born
September the 24th
185[?]

George Washington
Kirkpatrick was
born august the 19th

Margaret Malissa 185[?]
Kirkpatrick was born
July the 29th 1862

William Oliver
Kirkpatrick was born
May the first 1864

Figure 78 - Kirkpatrick Family Bible, 1838, Births (continued)

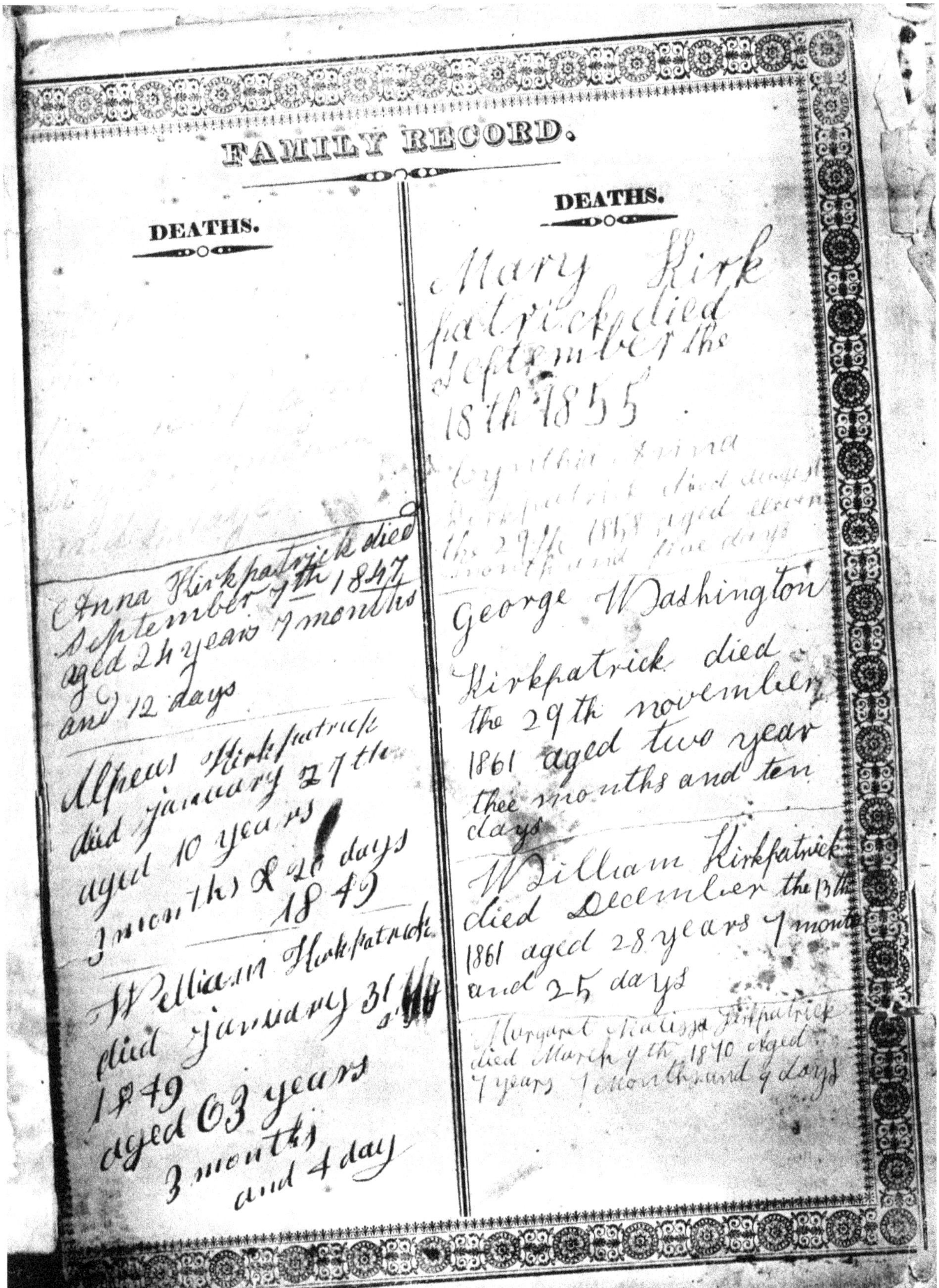

FAMILY RECORD.

DEATHS.

Anna Kirkpatrick died September 7th 1847 aged 24 years 7 months and 12 days

Alpeus Kirkpatrick died january 27th aged 10 years 7 months & 20 days 1849

William Kirkpatrick died January 31st 1849 aged 63 years 3 months and 4 day

DEATHS.

Mary Kirkpatrick died September the 18th 1855

Cynthia Anna Kirkpatrick died august the 29th 1858 aged eleven months and five days

George Washington Kirkpatrick died the 29th november 1861 aged two year thee months and ten days

William Kirkpatrick died December the 13th 1861 aged 28 years 7 months and 25 days

Margaret Malissa Kirkpatrick died March 9th 1840 aged 7 years 1 months and 9 Days

Figure 79 - Kirkpatrick Family Bible, 1838, Deaths

FAMILY RECORD

Rufus Kirkpatrick was born
May 1. A.D. 1830.

Margaret Elizabeth McCullough
was born May 26. 1830.

Mary Kirkpatrick was born
September 18. 1855.

Cynthia Anna Kirkpatrick
was born September 24. 1857.

Geo. Washington Kirkpatrick
was born August 19. 1859.
Margaret Malissa Kirkpatrick
was born July 29. 1862.
William Oliver Kirkpatrick
was born May 1. 1864.
Ida Ruth Kirkpatrick
was born October 19. 1868

Figure 80 - Kirkpatrick Family Bible, 1838, Family Record

Figure 81 - Kirkpatrick Family Bible, 1838, Marriages

415. <u>Jennettie A. Ridgeway Tiller</u>
(1837-1892)

Jennettie A. Ridgeway, daughter of Samuel Ridgeway and Fanny R. Page, was born 27 AUG 1837 in Kentucky, possibly Lincoln County. According to county marriage records, Jennettie was married 22 AUG 1864 in Sweet Springs, Randolph County, Missouri[1] to John Samuel Tiller, a wagon maker from Limestone County, Alabama where he was born on 8 DEC 1826. We believe that the parents of John Samuel Tiller were from Tennessee, and that he may have had brothers Robert Tiller and David Tiller. J.S. Tiller was previously married to Lucy Duvall and had three children: Susan Elizabeth Tiller (b. 8 OCT 1853 in Jacksonville, Mo., d. 13 OCT 1926 in Moberly, Mo., m. 25 APR 1872 to Nathaniel Francisco Haworth (1850-1927)), Robert F. Tiller (1857-1869), and Charles V. Tiller (1860-1869).

The family was enumerated on the 1870 Federal census for Jackson Township of Randolph County, Missouri [family 97, page 170], Cairo Post Office. According to Mrs. Chester (Dorothy) Kirkpatrick of Sedalia, Missouri, Jennettie Tiller died on 24 OCT 1892. On the 1900 Federal census we find John Tiller living with William Kirkpatrick in Pettis County, Missouri [E.D. 105, Sheet 9]. John S. Tiller died about 1906 in Pettis County, Missouri.

Children of John Samuel Tiller and his second wife Jennettie A. Ridgeway:

4151. GEORGE S. TILLER, b. 20 APR 1866 in Mo., d. 21 AUG 1907, perhaps bur. in Linwood Cem. of Paragould, Green Co., Ark., m. 12 MAY 1889 at Rufus Kirkpatrick's in Sweet Springs, Saline Co., Mo. to Ida Ruth Kirkpatrick, b. 19 OCT 1868 in Sweet Springs, Saline Co., Mo., d. 13 JUN 1959 in Sedalia, Mo., daughter of Margaret Elizabeth Spotts (b. 1830) and Rufus Kirkpatrick, b. 1 MAY 1830 in Eagle Creek, Ohio, d. 17 JAN 1899, a son of Rev. William Kirkpatrick (1785-1849)[2] and Ruth Pettyjohn (1799-1887). Rufus m. 16 OCT 1854 in Saline Co., Mo. to Margaret Elizabeth McCullough, b. 26 MAY 1830. Children:
- 41511.   HENRY KIRKPATRICK TILLER, b. 28 AUG 1894 in Mo.
- 41512.   MARGARET RUTH TILLER, b. JUL 1898 in Mo., m. 1 JUN 1939 in Jackson Co., Mo. to Albert Samuel Arenson, b. c.1888.
- 41513.   MABEL TILLER, b. 1901 in Mo.

4152. CELIA ANN TILLER, b. 8 MAR 1869 in Jacksonville, Randolph Co., Mo., d. 15 JUN 1942 of progressive muscular atrophy in Bothwell Memorial Hospital of Sedalia, Mo., bur. Memorial Park Cem., m. 14 NOV 1893 to William Oliver Kirkpatrick, b. 29 JUL 1862, son of Rufus Kirkpatrick and Margaret Elizabeth McCullough of Tenn. The family was enumerated on the 1900 Federal census for Longwood Twp., Pettis Co., Mo. [E.D. 105, Sheet 9], shows that William Kirkpatrick's mother and father were from Ohio and Tennessee respectively. William O. Kirkpatrick d. in Saline Co., Mo. on 17 JAN 1899. Margaret, bur. in Paragould, Ark., possibly Linwood Cem. On the

---

[1] Randolph Co., Mo. Mariages, Bk. A, p. 289.
[2] William Kirkpatrick, the progenitor of this line, was from Charles Co., Md. He owned a tract called *Patrick's Close* iin sight of the Wicomico River. He died there, testate, about 1803. He was both a farmer and a millwright.

1910 Federal census, the family was shown living at 670 East 15th Street in Sedalia, Mo. [E.D. 133, Sheet 2]. William O. Kirkpatrick d. 19 DEC 1932 at 4:20 a.m. at 1104 South Mass in Sedalia, Pettis Co., Mo., bur. Memorial Park Cem., Sedalia, Mo. (Rose Hill B, Lot 212, grave 3). Children:

41521. VALLIE KIRKPATRICK, b. 27 FEB 1895 in Saline Co., Mo., d. 16 NOV 1976 in Sedalia, Mo., m. 16 JUN 1919 in Sedalia, Pettis Co. to Marion Oscar Hart, b. 25 NOV 1892 in Camden, Mo., d. 3 AUG 1962, son of Elza Marshall Hart and Mary Elizabeth Noland, bur. Memorial Park Cem. of Sedalia. Children:

415211. MARION LLOYD HART, b. 27 JUL 1921, d. 19 SEP 1936.

415212. WILLIAM LEE HART, b. 1 JUL 1924, d. 14 JUN 1941.

415213. DONNA JEAN HART, b. 1925, d. 1961, m. 17 AUG 1946 in Sedalia, Mo. to Jack R. Venable.

415214. KENNETH ELZIE HART, b. 15 AUG 1927, d. 1 DEC 2010 in Kankakee, Ill., m. 12 MAR 1950 to Norma Jean Bland.

415215. MARY RUTH HART, b. 29 JUN 1929, d. 19 SEP 1989 in Sedalia, Mo.

415216. RICHARD J. HART, b. 13 AUG 1939, d. 3 OCT 1997.

41522. GLENN J. KIRKPATRICK, b. 9 FEB 1897 in Sweet Springs, Saline Co., Mo., m. 2 JUN 1925 in Pettis Co., Mo. to Lydia Pearl Dillow. Glenn, a postman and former secretary of the Missouri Rural Letter Carriers association, died in Bothwell Memorial Hospital of Sedalia, Mo. on 6 SEP 1960 of a heart attack, and was bur. 8 SEP 1960 in Memorial Park Cem. there. Glenn was a past master of Masonic lodge, past commander of the Knights Templar, patron of the Order of Eastern Star chapter 279, and a member of the Knights of York Cross of Honor and the High Priesthood of the Silver Trowel. The survivors listed in his newspaper obituary included three sisters Mrs. M.O. Hart, Mrs. George F. Chambers and Mrs. Paul B. Baum. From another newspaper obituary, we learned that Lydia was born November 6, 1900 in Anna, Ill., and was a member of the First Baptist Church as well as the Eastern Star and the Social Order of Beauceant. Lydia died at the age of 67 years on 5 MAR 1968 in Sedalia, and bur. in Memorial Park Cem. Her obituary also indicated the survivors included sisters, Mrs. Lloyd Kirkpatrick and Daisy Parker, both of Sedalia. Children:

415221. DR. CHESTER A. KIRKPATRICK, a retired optometrist of Sedalia, Mo., b. 1 OCT 1925 in Sedalia, m. 18 JAN 1952 in Sedalia to Dorothy Elaine Towner.

415222. HAZEL ANN KIRKPATRICK, b. 17 MAR 1927 in Sedalia, m. there 29 MAY 1949 to James William Middleton, a retired employee of Sears and Roebuck of Kansas City, Mo. who was b. 5 SEP 1927 in Sedalia. Hazel resided in Leawood, Kan. and sold real estate. Children:

4152221. JAMIE LOU MIDDLETON.

4152222. JAMES CLINTON MIDDLETON.

4152223. DANIEL JAY MIDDLETON.

415223. ROSALIE KIRKPATRICK, b. 4 SEP 1928 in Sedalia, m. (1) 17 OCT 1953 in Sedalia to Leonard Eugene Pressley, and m. (2) to Donald Heerman, and m. (3) on 10 SEP 1982 to Frank Zahringer. She resided in Sedalia. Child:

4152231. RONALD EUGENE PRESSLEY.

41523. MABEL VIOLA KIRKPATRICK, b. 14 JUL 1900 in Newland (now Sedalia), Pettis Co., Mo., d. 1997, m. 25 SEP 1921 in Pettis Co. to George F. Chambers, b. 1899, d. 1964; both bur. Memorial Park Cem. of Sedalia, Mo. Children:
    415231. ROBERT WILLIAM CHAMBERS, b. 1922, d. 1991, res. 2801 Wing in Sedalia, bur. Memorial Park Cem.
    415232. JACK LeROY CHAMBERS, b. 30 MAR 1928, d. 29 MAR 2009 in Sedalia, res. 2801 Wing in Sedalia, bur. Memorial Park Cem.
41524. CELESTE KIRKPATRICK, b. 9 JAN 1902 in Newland, Mo., d. 3 MAR 1978, m. 6 JUL 1952 in Pettis Co. to Paul Baum; bur. Memorial Park Cem.
41525. LLOYD KIRKPATRICK, b. 4 OCT 1903 in Sedalia, d. 4 MAR 1993, m. 26 JAN 1929 to Camilla Elizabeth Dillow, b. 7 JUL 1906 in Ill., d. 17 JUL 2002 in Sedalia, daughter of James Monroe Dillow and Fannie Caroline Montgomery; both bur. Memorial Park Cem.
41526. EARL KIRKPATRICK, b. 1 DEC 1905 in Sedalia, d. 30 JAN 1979 in Sun City, Ariz., m. 3 AUG 1935 in Pettis Co. to Helen Louise Scott, b. 10 MAY 1909 in Sweet Springs, Saline Co., Mo., d. 16 OCT 1997 in Sun City, Ariz.; both bur. Memorial Park Cem. of Sedalia, Mo.
41527. DALE KIRKPATRICK, b. 21 APR 1908 in Mo., d. July 26, 1910 of acute colitis in Sedalia, Mo., bur. in Memorial Park Cem. of Sedalia, Mo.

4153. HUGH JAMES TILLER, engineer, b. 22 SEP 1867 in Jacksonville, Randolph Co., Mo., d. 17 FEB 1933 of cerebral thrombosis in Lafayette Co., Mo., m. c.1890 to Laura Frances Wicker, b. 17 JAN 1869, d. 10 JUL 1936, both bur. Higginsville Cem., Higginsville, Mo. Child:
41531. CHARLES J. TILLER, b. 1895, d. 1959, bur. Higginsville Cem.

4154. LUTHER ORA TILLER, b. 1871.

4155. MINNIE LEE TILLER, b. 1875.

Davison Family *(continued)*

211. <u>Janice Louise Davison Giese</u>
(1925-1998)

Janice Louise Davison, daughter of Chester Leland Davison and Velma Pearl Allen, was born 23 DEC 1925 at 1810 Cleveland Avenue in Kansas City, Missouri. She was married 7 JUL 1946 at Cleveland Avenue Methodist Church to Walter Raymond Giese, born 16 NOV 1926 in Kansas City, Jackson County, Missouri, son of Herbert Frederick Giese and Dorothy Adelia Skelsey.

Janice was an active member of Colonial Presbyterian Church for 44 years: serving as a library volunteer, assisting with Vacation Bible School and as a Sunday School teacher. She was a Girl Scout leader and volunteered at her local hospital. After suffering with CREST Syndrome[1] for 15 years, Janice died 9 SEP 1998 at St. Mary's Hospital in Rochester, Minnesota. She was buried in Mount Moriah Cemetery of Kansas City, Missouri.

Figure 82 - Janice L. Davison and Walter R. Giese

Walt Giese was married second on 4 SEP 1999 at Colonial Presbyterian Church to Mrs. Vera Reames. They reside in Kansas City.

Children of Walter Raymond Giese and Janice Louise Davison:

1. ROBERT DALE GIESE, b. 10 JAN 1947 in Kansas City, Mo., m. (1) 20 MAR 1965 in Kansas City to Sandee Ann Eads, b. 28 AUG 1946 at a Marine base in Ill., div. 1987. He m. (2) 4 MAY 1971 in Miami, Okla. to Karla Rae Spencer, b. 23 MAY 1950 in Kansas City, m. (3) his first wife, and m. (4) 5 FEB 1994 to Anita Gail Stump, b. 10 OCT 1949. Child:
    11.   LONNY DALE GIESE, b. 8 SEP 1965 in Kansas City.

2. DIANE LOUISE GIESE, b. 23 MAY 1949 in Kansas City, m. 7 APR 1973 at Colonial Presbyterian Church in Kansas City to Robert Dean Darby, son of Scott Ellison Darby and Hester Lillian Kirk, b. 30 SEP 1945 in Independence, Mo., d. 29 MAY 2013 in Liberty, Mo., an avid outdoorsman. Children:
    21.   DAVID RYAN DARBY, m. 7 JUN 1997 to Amanda Elizabeth Weeks. Children:
        211.   MAKAYLA ELISE DARBY, b. 17 FEB 2006 in Houston Methodist Hospital, Sugar Land, Tex.

---

[1] CREST refers to the disease's five main features: Calcinosis, Raynaud's phenomenon, Esophageal dysmotility, Sclerodactyly and Telangiectasia.

212. DEREK ETHAN DARBY, b. 15 FEB 2008 in Houston Methodist Hospital.
22. STEPHEN KIRK DARBY, b. 30 JUN 1980 at St. Luke's Hospital in Kansas City.

3. LORIANN GIESE, b. 3 MAY 1956 in Kansas City, m. 29 JUL 1978 at Colonial Presbyterian Church in Kansas City to Gerald L. Richardson, son of George B. Richardson, div. Children:
   31. ELAINE RICHARDSON, b. 6 SEP 1984 in Kansas City, Mo., m. JUN 2005 to Rob Ross, d. 2006. Child:
     311. ROMAN ROSS, b. 10 SEP 2005 in Bolivar, Mo.
   32. KELLEY RICHARDSON, b. 29 DEC 1987 at 12:45 a.m. in Kansas City, Mo.
   33. SCOTT MITCHELL RICHARDSON, b. 3 MAR 1990 in Kansas City, Mo.

4. PAMELA GIESE, b. 3 APR 1958 in Kansas City, d. 10 DEC 2002 of breast cancer at her home in Baldwin, Kan., bur. Stony Point Cem., m. 30 DEC 1978 at Colonial Presbyterian Church in Kansas City to David Wagner, son of Duane E. and Sylvia Wagner of Great Bend, Kan., res. Vinland Valley Ranch. Children:
   41. PAIGE WAGNER, b. 16 SEP 1988 at 5:14 a.m. in Lawrence, Kan.
   42. CASEY EVAN WAGNER, b. 3 OCT 1990 in Lawrence, Kan.

5. DAVID LEE GIESE, b. 5 OCT 1962 in Kansas City, Mo., m. (1) Jeanette Goodman, div. in 1984, m. (2) c.1990 to Tammy Davidson, d. 1992, m. (3) 1 JUL 2000 to Jennifer Anne Light, b. 1 JAN 1971. Child:
   51. CHERLYN ANN GIESE, b. 14 JUN 1982 in St. Luke's Hospital of Kansas City.

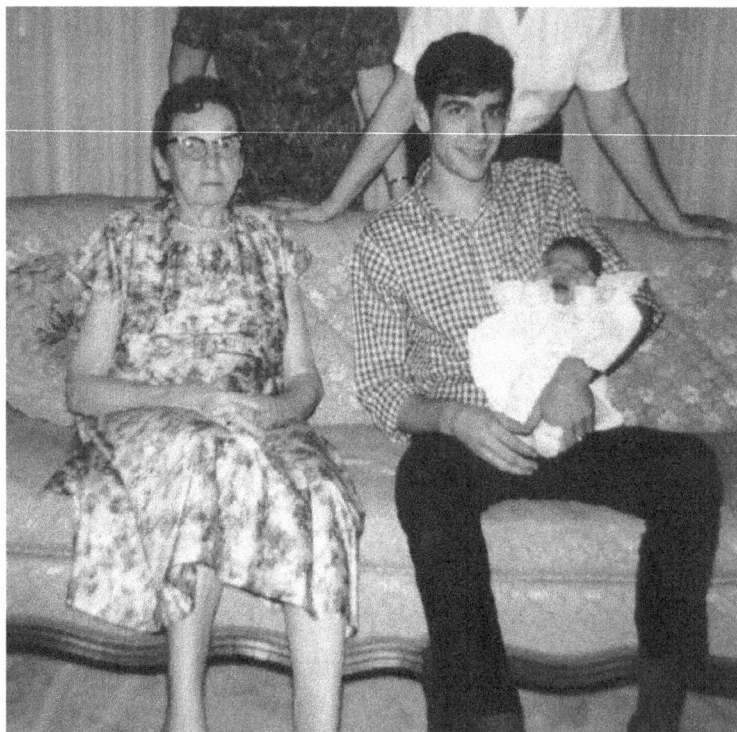

Figure 83 - Aunt Betty Henning, Bob Giese and newborn son Lonny, 1965. Pearl Advison and Janice Giese stand behind.

Figure 84 - Wedding photograph of Janice Davison and Walter Giese, with Chester and Pearl Davison, and Dorothy and Herbert Giese, at Clevelland Avenue Methodist Church, 1946

GIESE FAMILY

Much information about the Giese Family is gleaned from grandfather Giese's German Bible.[1] In it he wrote: "I left my old home and fatherland in April 1872 and emigrated to America, where on the 30th of April of the same year I was happy to arrive in New York. From there I went further into the interior of the country and in due time arrived at Batavia, Illinois."

Frederick Giese was born 28 NOV 1818 in Germany, and died 7 APR 1887 in Batavia, Kane County, Illinois where he was buried in East Batavia Cemetery. He was married in Germany to Henrietta Klatt, born 16 AUG 1822, who died 7 MAR 1876, and was buried in Germany. He raised a family in Batavia, Illinois. Children:

---

[1] Carl Ludwig Giese.

1. CARL LUDWIG GIESE, b. 17 FEB 1847 in Gerdshagen, Province Bommem, Prussia, Ger., d. 7 SEP 1929 of chronic myocarditis at 164 Cleveland Ave., Batavia, Ill., bur. 9 SEP 1929 in East Batavia Cem., m. 27 APR 1873 in Batavia, Ill., to Emilie Karoline Johanna Groener, b. 13 MAR 1853 at Rackow, Regenwalde, near Stettin, Prussia, d. 15 JAN 1944 of uremia at 164 Cleveland Ave., Batavia, Ill., bur. 18 JAN 1944 in East Batavia Cem., daughter of William Groner [sic] (1818-1882) and Augusta Schneider (1817-1878) from Ger., bur. East Batavia Cem. Carl served in the Franco-Prussian War in 1870, as a sharpshooter. He came to America with Christ and William Miller. He was a farmer for 12 years and a blacksmith at Newton's. As a staunch church member he enjoyed reading. Emilie came to America in 1870 with her parents. The family resided at Batavia, Ill. Children:

   11. ALVINA ANNA MARIA GIESE, dress-maker, b. 30 DEC 1874 in Kane Co., Ill., d. 26 OCT 1948 at church of cardia failure, worked at Elgin Watch Factory, bur. 29 OCT 1848 in East Batavia Cem., m. Edgar W. Bull, b. 6 JAN 1873, d. 7 FEB 1938 in Elgin, Ill., bur. East Batavia Cem., worked at the Elgin Watch Factory, res. Elgin, Ill.

   12. AUGUSTA LOUISE GIESE, secretary, b. 16 APR 1878 in Batavia, Ill., d. 29 NOV 1947 in Elmhurst, DuPage Co., Ill., m. 30 SEP 1919 in Chicago, Ill. to John Christopher Klein, b. 30 SEP 1886, d. 4 AUG 1968 in Daytona Beach, Fla., freight manager for Southern Pacific Railroad; both bur. East Batavia Cem.

   13. AMANDA MARTHA GIESE, b. 1 JUN 1880 in Batavia, Ill., d. 8 MAR 1956 or uremic acidosis and broncho-pneumonia in Naperville, Ill., m. Alfred Frederick Marckhoff, b. 18 OCT 1875, d. 29 APR 1953 of sudden heart failure at 444 Cleveland Co., Batavia, Ill., bur. East Batavia Cem., bricklayer and head mason at Mooseheart, served in the Spanish-American War, son of Carl Marckhoff and Sophia Sonneborn, bur. East Batavia Cem., res. Batavia, Ill. Children:

      131. VERDELLE SOPHIA MARCKHOFF, b. 26 AUG 1903, m. Elmer Alvin Koerner, music teacher, b. 7 SEP 1900, d. 24 NOV 1965. Children:

         1311. HAROLD LEE KOERNER, b. 22 JUN 1930, m. Nancy Jean Springborn, b. 2 OCT 1933, res. Naperville, Ill.

         1312. ROLLAND RAY KOERNER, b. 20 MAY 1934, m. Yvonne Jeannette Layton, b. 18 SEP 1934, res. Naperville, Ill.

      132. ALBERTA AMELIA MARCKHOFF, b. 18 SEP 1910, m. Ralph Lawrence Esterly, b. 26 SEP 1906, d. 22 MAR 1958, res. in Minn., and Naperville, Ill. Children:

         1321. MERLYN RUTH ESTERLY, b. 8 FEB 1934, m. Samuel Holzman, b. 9 JUL 1906, res. Chicago, Ill.

         1322. CAROL JOYCE ESTERLY, b. 23 JUN 1936, m. Thomas Henry Eck, b. 9 JUL 1938, res. Ill. and Whitehall, Mich. Four children.

         1323. LORRAINE JANET ESTERLY, b. 27 NOV 1940, m. Howard Taylor Pierce III, b. 12 JUL 1938, res. Chicago, Ill. and Lansing, Mich.

      133. CARLENE AMANDA MARCKHOFF, b. 11 FEB 1918, m. Donald Eugene Brown, b. 15 AUG 1918, res. Bacyrus, Ohio.

   14. ELSIE HELENA GIESE, b. 21 MAY 1885, d. 26 MAR 1959, bur. East Batavia Cem., was graduated from North Central College, a teacher of Latin and German, m. Henry A. Lipp, b. 30 NOV 1881, d. 5 SEP 1926, science teacher and athletics coach, res. Ottawa, Ill. and Fond du Lac, Wisc.

2. WILHELMIENE GIESE, b. 15 SEP 1851/2, d. 25 JUL 1909, m. Carl Joecks, b. 8 JAN 1850, d. 8 AUG 1900, res. Stettin, Ger. Children:
   21.   MARTHA JOECKS, b. 4 OCT 1882, starved during the war in 1945, m. Ernst Grahl.
   22.   HERMANN JOECKS, b. 17 JUL 1884, d. 1944, m. Marie Ronnebeck, res. Ost, Ger. Children:
      221.   ERNST JOECKS, b. 16 JUL 1912.
      222.   GERTRUD JOECKS, b. 21 AUG 1913.
      223.   HERMAN JOECKS, b. 6 AUG 1920.
   23.   HELENE JOECKS, b. 10 JUL 1889, d. 23 JAN 1961, m. Karl Voss, b. 21 NOV 1884, died missing during World War I. Children:
      231.   HANS GEORG FREDERICK VOSS, b. 22 JAN 1914, m. Herta Mina Hedwig Aumann, b. 11 APR 1915, res. Cologne, Ger.
   24.   FRIEDA JOECKS, b. 23 DEC 1890, m. Wilhelm Boeck, b. 23 JAN 1880, res. Hanover, Ger. Child:
      241.   ELFRIEDE BOECK, b. 11 JUL 1920, m. Will. Kalkbrenner, res. Hanover, Ger.
   25.   ERNST JOECKS, b. 14 FEB 1893, m. Frieda Eschen, res. Ost, Ger. Children:
      251.   ANNELIESE JOECKS.
      252.   INGEBORG JOECKS.

3. EDWARD GIESE, b. 30 MAR 1856, d. 30 NOV 1874.

4. HERMAN W. GIESE, blacksmith, b. 21 APR 1862 in Gerdshagen, Province Pommem, Prussia, Ger., d. 22 NOV 1952 of ruptured aortix at Community Hospital, res. 112 N. Prairie, Batavia, Ill., bur. East Batavia Cem., m. (1) Caroline "Lena" Runge, b. 15 SEP 1860 in Elgin, Ill., d. 24 MAR 1917 in Aurora, Ill., he m. (2) Mary Schwahn, b. 1873, d. 1930, dressmaker. Children:
   41.   HERBERT FREDERICK GIESE, estimator for construction firms, b. 20 DEC 1893 in Batavia, Kane Co., Ill., d. 13 APR 1968 in Kansas City, Mo., bur. Floral Hills Cem., m. 25 OCT 1922 in Geneva, Ill.[1] to Dorothy Adelia Skelsey, b. 20 APR 1899 in Aurora, Ill., d. 30 MAY 1987 at St. Joseph Health Center, res. Kansas City, Mo., daughter of John W. Skelsey (1857-1915) and Catherine Calista Bronson. After Herb's death, Dorothy m. (2) to Ira Victor Pinnick, b. 29 MAY 1897 in Fowler, Kan., d. 14 MAR 1989 in Kansas City. She was a founding member of Trinity Evangelical Church (now Meyer Boulevard United Methodist Church), and was a member of the local D.A.R. Children:
      411.   JOHN RICHARD "Jack" GIESE, petroleum engineer and project manager, b. 4 JUL 1924, d. 23 NOV 2005 in Templeton, San Louis Obispo Co., Calif., m. 28 MAY 1950 by Rev. Glenn C. Weinert in Kansas City, Mo. to Shirley Coleen Standish, medical lab technician, b. 28 AUG 1924, res. Templeton, Calif. Children:
         4111. GAIL GIESE, environmental engineer, b. 23 DEC 1950 in Kansas City, Mo., m. 28 APR 1973 at Holy Shepherd Lutheran Church in Orinda, Calif. to Peter Lawrence Mattson, div. 14 FEB 2000, res. Calif.

---

[1] Kane Co., Ill. Marriages, Bk. 10, p. 54, license no. 35008.

4112.   NANN GIESE, dental hygienist, b. 17 NOV 1953 in Kansas City, Mo., m. 14 FEB 199_ in Discovery Bay, Calif. to Paul Stark. Children:

    41121.   EMILY ANN STARK, b. 25 JUN 1999.

    41122.   JONATHAN PAUL STARK, b. 15 AUG 2005.

4113.   JILLIAN GIESE, massage therapist, b. 25 JUL 1956 in Kansas City, Mo., m. Mr. Standish.

4114.   GLENN RICHARD GIESE, b. 14 MAY 1958, m. 18 JUN 1993 at St. Patrick's Catholic Church in Arroyo Grande, Calif. to Florencia "Angie" Rico.

4115.   JOHN MILES GIESE, industrial engineer, b. 5 MAY 1960 in Kansas City, Mo., m. 24 MAY 1986 at St. Francis Catholic Church in Concord, Calif. to Dianne Elizabeth Gross. Children:

    41151.   HOWARD GRAHAM GIESE, b. 18 FEB 1994.

    41152.   JULES THOMAS GIESE, b. 26 MAY 1995.

    41153.   ALDEN MILES GIESE, b. 17 DEC 1997.

412.   WALTER RAYMOND GIESE, architect, b. 16 NOV 1925, m. 7 JUL 1946 in Cleveland Avenue Methodist Church of Kansas City, Mo. to 211. JANICE LOUISE DAVISON, *q.v.*

413.   HERBERT DAVIS "Herbie" GIESE, b. 28 JAN 1932, d. 21 JUL 2008.

42.   MILDRED CAROLINE GIESE, b. 27 JAN 1896.

43.   MIRIAM IRENE GIESE, b. 2 MAR 1899.

44.   CARL RUNGE GIESE, b. 28 MAR 1903 at 44 Prairie St., East Batavia, Ill.

5. AUGUSTA GIESE, b. 26 JAN 1864, d. 31 JAN 1950 at Community Hospital in Geneva, Ill., bur. East Batavia Cem.

Figure 85 - Davison Daughters and Families: (L-R) Lori and Jan Giese, Pearl and Chester Davison, Diane Giese, Eileene Pippenger holding daughter Rachel, with son Wes below, Charlie Pippenger, Walt Giese holding daughter Pam, with son Bob below

Figure 86 - Wedding photo of Diane Giese to Robert Darby, at Colonial Presbyterian Church, 1973

Figure 87 - Janice and Walt Giese

Davison Family (continued)

212. <u>Zora Eileene Davison Pippenger</u>
(1932-   )

Zora Eileene Davison, daughter of Chester Leland Davison and Velma Pearl Allen, was born 5 MAR 1932 at 1810 Cleveland Avenue in Kansas City, Missouri. Her birth was announced in the newspaper. Mother is a direct descendant of the Davison Family of County Armagh, Ireland, as well as of Philip Ridgeway who fought in the Revolutionary War. Data about the history of the Pippenger Family was previously published by this compiler in 1988.[1]

She was baptized April 17, 1938 at Cleveland Avenue Methodist Church where her family attended for a number of years. In 1944, she was promoted within the church from the junior to intermediate department by superintendent Mrs. Emil B. Sartori.

Figure 88 - Chester, Janice and Eileene Davison, c.1933

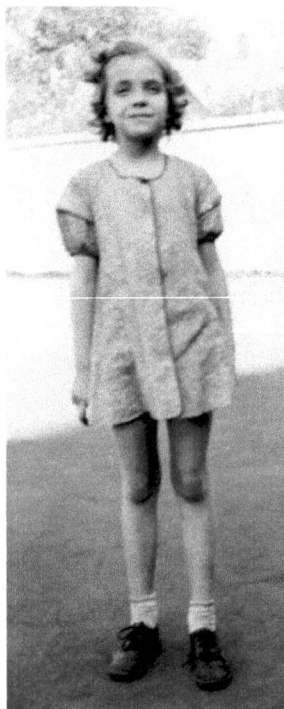

Figure 89 - Eileene, 1939

In the late 1980s, I interviewed my mother and her parents and asked a number of questions about their early lives. Mother remembered little about the family's house on Cleveland Avenue where she was born, other than that she and her sister Janice slept in the front room which had been converted into a bedroom. While in the third grade, the family moved to a larger home on Blue Ridge. While growing up she enjoyed pets, but they were difficult to keep, as her dad ran over her first puppy with the car; a cat named "Beans" wasn't quite right and always acted a bit odd; then a Scotty dog was stolen. Her sister Janice kept a black Chow dog for a while when a boyfriend entered into the military.

Eileene's schooling began at Yeager School in Kansas City, and her teachers in the Kindergarten, first and second grades were Misses Hunton, Scherer and Stubbs. Two interesting remarks from teachers during this time were that: (a) very seldom did she keep her hands and materials away from her mouth, but (b) practically always did she obey rules promptly and cheerfully, and pay attention when others were talking and did not interrupt. For a writing exercise in 1939, Eileene wrote that she had a doll named Patricia to liked soap and water. "She is a good doll [and] she is coming to school." Eva Lee Caldwell was teacher from 1939 to 1940. Throughout the next several school years Eileene was recognized in the pupils reading circle or for her achievements in prose. In April 1945, she tested

---

[1] *Pippenger and Pittenger Families: A Genealogical History of the Descendants of William Pippenger of New Jersey, and Allied Families* (Baltimore, Md.: Gateway Press, Inc., 1988).

negative for tuberculosis while living at 4441 Bales Street.

From the third through the eighth grade she was a student at Spring Valley School from which she was graduated in May 1946.[1] Spring Valley was located at 79th and James A. Reed Road, and was about 3/4 of a mile walking distance from their home. The grading scale was E (Escellent), S (Superior), M (Medium), I (Inferior) and F (Failing). Eileene's best marks in the fifth grade were in music, reading, spelling and geography. The principal there, Mrs. Leah Smith, was pretty strict for grades six through eight, but there were only five in the graduating class: Shirley Dimoush, Bev Morse (who later married Dick Drake), Marilyn Winter, Maurice "Scotty" Scott, and Eileene.

Raytown High School

Figure 90 - Raytown High School, from the Baccalaureate Exercises program, May 1950

When she was just four years old in 1936, the Davison Family took a visit to Denver, Colorado where her grandmother Florence Evelyn (Ridgeway) Davison, widow of Charles Condus Davison, died of a stoke in the house where they were staying on Dayton Street in Aurora, Colorado. Mother remembered that she and her mother returned to Kansas City via train with her grandmother's body. While staying on Dayton Street, she dared a neighbor in a rock toss, but lost after being hit in the head with a large chunk of quartz. Her other grandparents, Robert Edward and Mary Ellen (Lewis) Allen often wintered in Tucson, Arizona where her uncle Samuel Wayne Allen lived, and Eileene would go there to visit. Her great grandmother Sarah Elizabeth (Adair) Lewis, "Granny" Lewis, lived at Filley, Missouri, and Eileene enjoyed visits there during summer. It was at her grandpa Allen's farm in Stanley, Kansas that she accidentally stepped on a log and cut her foot so bad that her grandmother packed it in mud.

One of mother's best friends was Sally Vokoun, a good friend at school who was also a neighbor with whom she would ride bikes from home to Swope Park and back. The return trip was always the workout as it was completely up hill. Eileene used to love to swim, and would even jump off the diving board once in a while, but later in life her desire of water or even being in a swimming pool became overshadowed by a phobia of not liking to get her head wet. Mother's hobbies always included music, and she pursued this interest while at Raytown High School where she sang her first solo in a spring program and was heard by a Mr. Huckstep who encouraged her to take voice lessons. After doing so, Eileene entered various contests for vocal achievement, and after being defeated in a contest the very first year, later received awards for district and State competitions. After moving to Colorado, she took up voice lessons again with Mary Ward, and continued to be a lead soprano in the church choir at St. James Presbyterian Church for many years.

Mother recounted several boyfriends before my father Charles Wesley Pippenger entered the scene. Tommy Horrell, who lived in Oldham Farms where the kids used to trick or treat during Halloween, was a year ahead of Eileene in grade school, had wavy hair and later

---

[1] Her graduation certificate on the graduation exercise program list her as Lora Eileene Davison.

married Eva Purdum. There was a guy named Don, who years later died while trying to save his step-child who drowned in the ocean. Don was remembered for being the first to kiss Eileene, and besides that, the event took place in her mother's front room while Mrs. Davison was away at work. Pete Newby was a friend she met at Playmore Roller Rink, but things got real serious with J.R. Herman (who ported red hair), but she averted any marriage plans because of differences in social and religious habits. Eileene also remembered that a guy she dated while a junior in high school was Jim Oldham who died of polio very soon following graduation, after he had contracted the disease while in Minnesota.

Mr. Pippenger came into the picture when Eileene met him in the music department at Raytown High School. In about 1948, she and Charlie went on a date to a banquet in which he was featured as Kawani of the Week. Even though he was one grade ahead of her, she claims they never kissed until 5 years later. Apparently Eileene's mother saw Charlie singing in a music competition and remarked that he was "the most pathetic thing" she had seen, but they became good buddies during a time when Charlie did various construction jobs at the Davison home. Eileene went on to complete

Figure 91 - Four generations: Great-grandfather Robert E. Allen, Eileene Pippenger holding son Wes, and her father Chester Davison

one year of college at Central Methodist College in Fayette, Missouri where she majored in music, and carried a minor concentration in English.

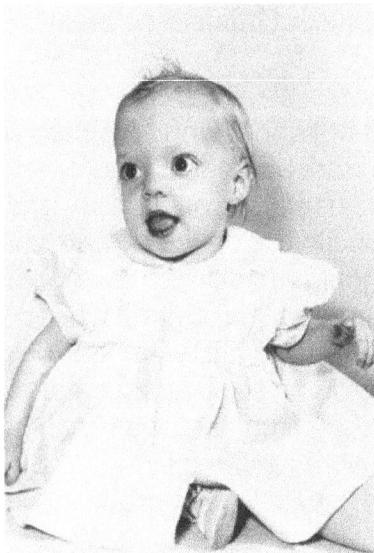

Figure 92 - Patrice Pippenger

Eileene and Charlie were married 7 JUN 1953 at four o'clock in the afternoon at the Cleveland Avenue Methodist Church. Their first child Wesley was born in 1956. Next, daughter Patrice was born in 1957; however, due to a heart defect she soon died about 18 months later in 1959. Rachel was born in 1959. In October 1960, father got a job with *Martin Marietta*, and the family from from their home at 9700 Beacon in Kansas City, to 7980 South Elmhurst Drive outside of Littleton, Colorado. Later, some wizard decided that the street was miss-classified, and the house address was changed to 5766 West Elmhurst Drive. The phone number there was Pyramid [79]8-4393.

Many years were filled with every weekend of taking trips to the mountains; often with camping supplies (a Coleman stove, and always Aunt Betty's pan), a trailer, a dirt bike, or a pop-up tent; and quite often with the Carpenter Family. Dad routinely chose the most rugged, narrow, and virtually un-driveable roads to explore. Rachel and I sat in the back seat and jumped up and down with fear and excitement. Mother and Dad's parents would visit frequently from Kansas City, after the long 444-mile drive across Kansas—the Davisons in a Dodge, the Pippengers in a Pontiac car. In 1975, the family sold the Elmhurst house and moved about a mile north to 7447 South Lamar Street, where Mother and Dad still reside. Wes and Rachel grew up as kids and eventually left the nest—both coming back for a short time while zeroing in on what direction life was going to take.

During my lifetime, both Mother and Dad have been continually active in choir and other activities at St. James Presbyterian Church in Littleton, Colorado, where in early times they joined the Mariners, and Mother was the children's choir director and later wedding coordinator for many years. Mother attended classes and became quite proficient at decorative painting, specializing in tole painting, and after teaching classes for quite a few years, obtained her highest honor of a Master Painter from the National

Figure 93 - Pearl Davison, Eileene Pippenger, Diane Giese, and Rachel and Wes Pippenger, on a visit to Central City in the nearby Colorado mountains

Society for the same.

Most recently, my folks have enjoyed traveling away from their home base in Littleton, Colorado, and are fondly known as the "roamin' Pipps". The two have visited every continent on the globe—from the Antarctica to Africa—and have taken rides on just about any kind of transportation about, including a hot air balloon. After each trip, Mom meticulously documents every detail of the travel experience, and she and Dad merge and select photos to create a lasting journal and photo extravaganza. What an archive!

Children of Charles Wesley Pippenger and Zora Eileene Davison:

2121.   WESLEY EUGENE PIPPENGER, management analyst, historian, pianist, b. 22 JUN 1956 at St. Mary's Hospital in Kansas City, was graduated from Columbine High School of Littleton, Colo. in 1975, moved to the east coast in September 1982, retired from NASA Headquarters, Washington, D.C. in 2011, res. at *Little Egypt* in Tappahannock, Essex Co., Va., with his partner David Henderson, born 1 NOV 1951 in Glendale Sanitorium and Hospital of Glendale, Calif., son of John Henderson and Virginia Pierce Gammons of Mass. Wes and David were m. 21 AUG

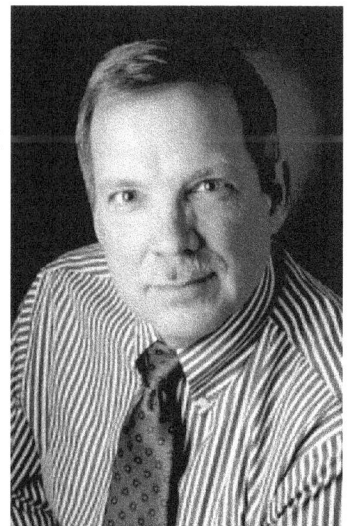

Figure 94 - Wesley E. Pippenger

2014 by Rev. Jeffrey L. Maszal at 1712 Swann Street, N.W. in Washington, D.C. after a 19-year courtship. Compiler of this genealogy.

2122. PATRICE PIPPENGER, b. 15 DEC 1957 in Kansas City, d. 16 JUL 1959 of heart insufficiency in Kansas City, bur. 18 JUL 1959 in Memorial Park Cem.

2123. RACHEL PIPPENGER, b. 31 JAN 1959 at St. Mary's Hospital in Kansas City, *q.v.*, m. (1) 21 MAY 1982 at St. James Presbyterian Church of Littleton, Colo. to Alan Garfield Swanson, b. 28 NOV 1950, div. 1983, m. (2) 1 MAR 1985 at St. James Presbyterian Church to Logan James Lucas. They res. in Littleton, Colo. Child:

21231. CHRISTOPHER WESLEY LUCAS, b. 12 OCT 1982, on 2 MAY 1988 was adopted by his step-father Lucas and had his name legally changed from Christopher William Swanson.

EXCURSUS–LUCAS

Rachel Pippenger Lucas. Christ follower, life-long student, book reader, gardener, seamstress, singer, painter, writer, sticky bun baker, husband helper. I was born in 1959 in Kansas City, Missouri, the third child in a wonderful family; brother Wes is 3 years older, sister Patrice was only 14 or so months older and passed almost 6 months after my birth. Neither Patty nor I were given a middle name. Our family moved to the Littleton, Colorado area in 1960 and my father, Charlie Pippenger worked for *Martin Marietta*. My parents carried my brother and me into St. James Presbyterian Church in 1961, I was two. Because my parents were very involved in Mariners and small groups and choir, I had many sets of secondary parents as I was growing up. I often came to choir and sat with mom. I loved hearing her sing, it always made me feel special. I enjoyed listening to Tom Miyake as the choir director. And I was allowed into the kid's choir before I was old enough because Mom, Eileene Pippenger, was the kid's choir director and our good friend Cynthia Carpenter was the pianist. Wes was also in the kid's choir for a while. I think my first solo was probably in one of the kid's choir musicals. I remember "It's Cool in the Furnace" best. That was fun. At that time the sanctuary was

Figure 95 - Wes and Rachel visiting Grandma Davison on Blue Ridge

what is now the gym. And there was a raised choir/organ/pulpit area where the upper rooms are now in the far end. I still have dreams occasionally about being up there in the choir area or at some event in that room.

Most of my friends as I was growing up came from St. James. There were many youth group trips and events. I loved bible studies with Sally Stuart and the girls. Jim Stuart was wonderful as the youth group director. I remember a trip through some of the lakes of Minnesota with backpacks and canoes. It was not a lot of fun to carry the canoes between the lakes, but we had a great time. There was a bus that we occasionally had to push and jump start. Although high school was a time of incredible confusion and insecurity, I remember it with warmth because of the St. James youth group.

My mother taught me the creative things along with life skills. Her mother taught me how to make bread. My father encouraged me to help him with projects around the house, from painting walls to loading shot gun shells for his next hunting trip. He also threw the baseball with me. His mother taught me the love of plants. I remember camping in a tent, and eating Spam and "ground round." For some reason I didn't want to eat hamburgers when I was really young, so Dad cooked the meat on the ground, called it ground round and handed it to me. It was good. I remember put-put golf and road trips with a pop-up trailer. We visited many of the state parks and sights to see all

Figure 96 - Rachel Pippenger, 1973

over the U.S. I remember being on the back of a motorcycle with either Dad or Wes; that was in my teens. I remember the big slate board on the basement wall of the Elmhurst house. I don't know how Dad ever got that home and hung on the wall, it was incredibly heavy. Friend Cynthia Carpenter's watch died while their family was visiting our house; Dad whacked it with a hammer to make sure it was really dead and then buried it in the back garden; they said a little prayer for it. I remember Mom's holiday decorations. One of my favorites was the valentines she cut out of red construction paper, strung with thread, and hung from the kitchen lamp over the table every year. One year she made five or six little elves with felt, pipe cleaners and shiny ornament balls for faces. She put them in the Christmas greenery above the cabinets between the kitchen and family room. It would always be fun to find them. I have them at my house now. I remember playing "I Spy" by the Christmas tree while we waited for Dad to get home for dinner. I remember going to some of Mom's painting classes with her. Most of the time I had my nose in some book. I did eventually take some painting lessons from her when she taught a class held at St. James. Mom was a Den Mother part of the time Wes was in Cub Scouts; I got to sit in on some of that. I was in the Brownies and then the Girl Scouts for a time. Sometimes on Sunday mornings while Mom and Dad sang in the choir I sat with Bob Hendrix and his wife Frances. On one of these mornings Bob took me back behind the coat rack and turned me upside down because I had swallowed a piece of candy and was choking. Back then the choir had these blue shiny robes with white stoles; they were really pretty. When I was in second or third grade and Mom was the children's choir director, Mom and Cynthia made red robes for the children's choir. Mom took voice lessons from Mary Ward and I went along; somewhere along the way I began voice lessons also. Wes and I were both encouraged to take piano lessons. Wes did much better with that than I did. In high school I tried my hand at guitar, that didn't last very long for me either, but I still have it. Although there were a few spankings along the way, Mom and Dad have always been very supportive of whatever I was interested in doing. They are always there to help whenever I need them; always giving hugs. My parents are faithful to their God and have always been a great example to me of good people in all they do. I have been truly blessed to be their daughter.

My first jobs were for Temporary Office Personnel Service, Charm Cove Nursing Home, Littleton Travel, Columbine Hills Elementary School as a teacher aide, American Diamond Company as a telephone appointment setter, and Microfilm Associates. I lasted only a month setting telephone appointments; the phone is not my favorite thing. My favorite job of the bunch was the last where we photographed hospital-typed information and x-rays for microfilm. I did this for two summers and Christmas break while at college. In the fall of 1977, I moved into a dorm at Colorado State University in Ft. Collins, Colorado and began a 5-year journey studying accounting, music therapy and music education. Grandpa Pippenger's passing in the fall of 1981 affected me deeply; that was the first major family death I experienced. In the spring of 1982 I was to perform a senior recital and then student teach in the fall; I found both of those events overwhelmingly scary. I also thought I was in love; a man I met when I worked at The Kipling Inn over the summer. Mix all of that together and the result wasn't good. I compromised my values and became pregnant. When I finished school for the semester, Al and I were married at St. James, but it wasn't long before I knew that the marriage was a huge mistake. What I didn't know at the time was that you don't marry everyone you fall in love with; that some people are not supposed to stay in your life for the long haul. Christopher was born October 12, 1982 on Christopher Columbus Day that year. He was baptized in April 1983 by Rev. Les Avery. Al and I divorced in the fall.

Figure 97 - Christopher Lucas

Soon after Christmas of 1982 I began a job with the National Independent Study Center of the Office of Personnel Management (O.P.M.). I had interviewed with them in August or so. They saw something in this very pregnant woman and wanted me. This was where I first began learning about computers. I stayed with O.P.M. until August 1984 when I went to work for Coors Transportation Company as an administrative assistant until 1985. Then it was onward in computer-related functions for Don McCullough Law Office for a year and a half, University of Colorado Foundation for a year and a half, Utah Gas Service Company from August 1988 to October 1994, then Carl Walker Engineers to 1999, Modern Plastics to 2002, and Arapahoe Community College in 2003. Utah Gas was my favorite job because I ran billing programs for them; I was always trying to make the whole process more efficient. It was with Carl Walker where I really began to use the Microsoft's Access database skills I had begun to learn about when I went back to college at Regis University. I graduated Magna Cum Laude in May 1991 with a Business Administration Major and Computer Information Systems Minor. I have always loved learning things, especially when I can see a particular use for them in my life.

My first husband wanted less and less to do with church, so I didn't go as often as I wanted to. I met my second husband, Logan James Lucas, at St. James; a man who worked with wood and owned a pop-up trailer. I returned to St. James full time later in 1983 when I was going through the divorce. I received counseling there and I have always been surrounded by people who love me there. In the fall of 1983 I attended a relationship seminar (divorce recovery workshop) and found this really neat guy to talk to. He had been through a divorce a few years earlier and he had a lot of really good things to tell me, he helped me a lot. Then I found him in the choir; he was my father's choir folder partner and they got along well. For our first outing, Logan asked me one night after the divorce recovery workshop session if I wanted to go get something to eat. He had come straight from work and hadn't had dinner yet. I told him yes, and also said I would have to go get my son from the nursery first. He said okay and we went down the street to Pizza Hut.

For our first official date, Logan picked me up at my parents' house. I had moved back in with them until I could get my life back together after the divorce. Our lives together progressed from there. Logan also had a son, Ryan, and one of their habits was to go get donuts at Donut Hut just down the street after church every other weekend. So that became our Sunday pattern—singing in the choir and donuts after church. We were married in 1985 and have attended many of the church's couples and family retreats. Logan has been an incredible blessing and encourager to me over the years. We are well-matched and do many projects together, from gardening to household repairs to building a 5-sided garden house in the back yard to building a small cabin from scratch on 4.2 acres in Indian Mountain just this side of Fairplay, Colorado. At the time of this writing, we have completed almost all the finish work on the first level; the upstairs is smaller and will be easier. No built-in bookshelves or murals on that level. In the cabin I took my stamps and put aspen leaves on some panels in between the ceiling joists in one room. At home over the years I had done some murals on the walls in three rooms.

Son Ryan is currently the Principle of Elk Creek Elementary School located near Bailey, Colorado. We are very proud of the godly man he has become. Logan and I were honored to be involved in Ryan's baptism last October. Logan baptized Ryan and then Ryan baptized Logan and me—in the Blue River beside Kingdom Park in Breckenridge, Colorado, with patches of snow still on the ground—brrrrrr. What a neat experience! As kids Wes and I often swam at Harlow Park; I was there yesterday for the baptism of my friend Amy Lodwig and a bunch of others from Horizon Christian Fellowship professing their faith in Jesus Christ. It brought back memories. They have a couple of really fun-looking water slides now.

Somewhere over the years I figured out that I am a behind the scenes women's ministry person. It is with women that I feel most helpful (second to my husband). I have enjoyed the many women's retreats. I think I began attending them in the later 1980's and then began doing the little devotional booklets for them in 1994. In 1995 I also made my first women's retreat banner titled "Becoming Women of Excellence." There were five banners

Figure 98 - Lucas and Pippenger Family, 2001: Ryan, Logan and Rachel Lucas, Eileene and Charlie Pippenger, Christopher Lucas

that I made and then the Stitch-N-Chatter ladies took that challenge on when I gave it up.

I have enjoyed doing the devotional booklets over the years. They are a collection of things I have come across, new and old, picture and word, things friends have written, things I have written, put in booklet form and given out mainly around women's retreat time. The booklet became really important for me to do in March 2010. I almost didn't do it, but then I thought about how I would feel if retreat time came and went and I didn't do it. It became a way for me to express some of my grief.

In December 2009, our 27-year-old son, Christopher, passed away. It is such a heartbreak for someone so young to die, such a loss of all the things this young man could have been. St. James is an incredible place of healing for hurt and broken people. We have been surrounded with love and care. Christopher grew up in the middle of St. James also. He rebelled for a while and then we made him go to youth group starting in 6th grade when we "made" him go on a Noah's Ark trip with Terry Buchanan. Christopher was so mad that we would make him do these things. He found out that it was here in the youth group friends and activities that he found meaning and significance and joy. Christopher was one of the speakers on Youth Sunday of 1998 where he gave his testimony. In his freshman year at Columbine High School, he was in the cafeteria when the shooting began and we found out later that he covered a friend who was a girl with his body to protect her. One of the teachers got them out of the school shortly after that. Because of his death, I went back through the Sunday service archives and found that recording. It's neat to hear his voice again.

Figure 99 - Logan J. Lucas and Rachel Pippenger, 2004

We knew over the years that even though Christopher struggled to find his place in the world, he had a heart for people. In the stories we heard from his friends while we were in the hospital and the stories told at the memorial service in December, we saw how he was drawn to the outcasts and the marginalized people—they were his mission field, we understand that now. As he was growing up we wanted to protect him from those we felt would hurt him. Christopher learned to use his whole being to help others. So, in the 2010 Women's Retreat booklets I put together a main one with devotional materials and some of my writings around Christopher's death, and then I made a second one just about Christopher. It is always my hope and prayer that these booklets will speak to the hearts of those who read them, and that is especially true with this set—that even in Christopher's death, he would still be able to help people whose hearts hurt.

Abercrombie, Janice Luck, *Louisa Co., Virginia, Judgments, 1766-1790* (Athens, Ga.: Iberian Publishing Co., 1998)

Biographical and Historical Memoirs of Northeast Arkansas, Illustrated (Chicago, Ill.: The Goodspeed Publishing Company, 1889)

Bradshaw, Herbert Clarence, *History of Prince Edward County, Virginia* (Richmond: Dietz Press, 1955)

Brick, Gertrude N. and Thurman Ridgway, *Ridgways, U.S.A.* (Baltimore, Md.: Gateway Press, Inc., 1980)

Brown, Margie G., *Genealogical Abstracts Revolutionary War Veterans, Scrip Act 1852* (Decorah, Ia.: The Anundsen Publishing Co., 1990)

Chisholm, Claudia Anderson and Ellen Gray Lillie, *Old Home Places of Louisa County* (Louisa, Va.: Louisa County Historical Society, 1979)

Cook, Michael L., *Pioneer Lewis Families* (Evansville, Ind.: Cook Publications, 1978)

Craig, Robert D., *Clermont County Records*, Vol. VI (1969)

Crosby County Historical Commission, *A History of Crosby County, [Texas] 1876-1977* (Taylor Publishing Co., 1978)

Dorman, John Frederick, ed., *Adventurers of Purse and Person*, 4th Ed. (Baltimore, Md.: Genealogical Publishing Co., Inc., 2007), Volume 3

Evers, Louis H., *History of Clermont County* (1882)

Ford, Henry A., *History of Hamilton County, Ohio* (Cleveland, Ohio: L.A. Williams, 1881)

History of Edwards, Lawrence and Wabash Counties, Illinois (Philadelphia, Pa.: J.L. McDonough & Co., 1883)

History of Mt. Pulaski, Illinois, 1836-1986

History of Randolph and Macon Counties, Missouri (St. Louis, Mo.: National Historical Co., 1884)

History of Randolph County, Arkansas (Little Rock, Ark.: Democrat Printing and Lithographers Company, 1946)

Illinois Historical and Lawrence County Biographical (Chicago: Munsell Publishing Co., 1910)

Jones, W. Mac, Ed., *The Douglas Register: Being a detailed record of Births, Marriages and Deaths together with other interesting notes, as kept by the Rev. William Douglas, from 1750 to 1797* (Richmond, Va.: J.W. Fergusson & Sons, Printers and Publishers, 1928)

Lawrence County Historical Society, *Lawrence County, Illinois Commemorative Edition* (Paducah, Ky.: Turner Publishing Co., 1995)

Lewis, Q., *A Short History of the Lewis Family in Lawrence County* (Lawrenceville, Ill.: 1940)

Odel, Cecil, *Pioneers of Old Frederick County, Virginia* (Marceline, Mo.: Walsworth Publishing Co., 1995)

Pippenger, Wesley E., *Pippenger and Pittenger Families: A Genealogical History of the Descendants of William Pippenger of New Jersey, and Allied Families* (Baltimore, Md.: Gateway Press, Inc., 1988)

Power, John Carroll, *History of Early Settlers of Sangamon County, Illinois* (1876)

Pritchett, John W., *Southside Virginia Genealogies* (2007)

Randolph County, Arkansas: A Pictorial History (Morley, Mo.: Acclaim Press)

Stephen, Homer, *History of Erath County, Texas* (Stephensville, Tex.: By the Author, 1950)

Thomas, Marilyn W. and Hazelmae T. Temple, *1835 Tax List of Sangamon County, Illinois*

Torrence, Clayton, *Winston of Virginia and Allied Families* (Richmond, Va.: Whittet & Shepperson, 1927)

Tyler, Lyon Gardiner, ed., *Encyclopedia of Virginia Biography* (New York: Lewis Historical Publishing Co., 1915), Volume 5

INDEX

211

C

220

226

236

241

Heritage Books by Wesley E. Pippenger:

Alexander Family: Migrations from Maryland

Alexandria (Arlington) County, Virginia Death Records, 1853–1896

Alexandria City and Arlington County, Virginia Records Index: Vol. 1

Alexandria City and Arlington County, Virginia Records Index: Vol. 2

Alexandria County, Virginia Marriage Records, 1853–1895

Alexandria, Virginia Marriage Index, January 10, 1893 to August 31, 1905

Alexandria, Virginia Marriages, 1870–1892

Alexandria, Virginia Town Lots, 1749–1801
Together with the Proceedings of the Board of Trustees, 1749–1780

Alexandria, Virginia Wills, Administrations and Guardianships, 1786–1800

Alexandria, Virginia 1808 Census (Wards 1, 2, 3, and 4)

Alexandria, Virginia Death Records, 1863–1896

Alexandria, Virginia Hustings Court Orders, Volume 1, 1780–1787

Connections and Separations: Divorce, Name Change and Other
Genealogical Tidbits from the Acts of the Virginia General Assembly

Daily National Intelligencer *Index to Deaths, 1855–1870*

Daily National Intelligencer, *Washington, District of Columbia*
Marriages and Deaths Notices (January 1, 1851 to December 30, 1854)

Dead People on the Move: Reconstruction of the Georgetown Presbyterian
Burying Ground, Holmead's (Western) Burying Ground, and
Other Removals in the District of Columbia

Death Notices from Richmond, Virginia Newspapers, 1841–1853

District of Columbia Ancestors,
A Guide to Records of the District of Columbia

District of Columbia Death Records: August 1, 1874–July 31, 1879

District of Columbia Foreign Deaths, 1888–1923

District of Columbia Guardianship Index, 1802–1928

District of Columbia Interments (Index to Deaths)
January 1, 1855 to July 31, 1874

District of Columbia Marriage Licenses, Register 1: 1811–1858

District of Columbia Marriage Licenses, Register 2: 1858–1870

District of Columbia Marriage Records Index
June 28, 1877 to October 19, 1885: Marriage Record Books 11 to 20
Wesley E. Pippenger and Dorothy S. Provine

District of Columbia Marriage Records Index
October 20, 1885 to January 20, 1892: Marriage Record Books 21 to 30

District of Columbia Marriage Records Index
January 20, 1892 to August 30, 1896: Marriage Record Books 31 to 40

District of Columbia Marriage Records Index
August 31, 1896 to December 17, 1900: Marriage Record Books 41 to 65

District of Columbia Probate Records, 1801–1852

District of Columbia: Original Land Owners, 1791–1800

Early Church Records of Alexandria City and Fairfax County, Virginia

Essex County, Virginia Deed Abstracts, 1786–1805, Deed Books 33 to 36

Essex County, Virginia Deed Abstracts, 1805–1819, Deed Books 37 to 39

Essex County, Virginia Guardianship and Orphans Records, 1707–1888: A Descriptive Index

Essex County, Virginia Marriage Bonds, 1804–1850, Annotated

Essex County, Virginia Newspaper Notices, 1738–1938

Essex County, Virginia Newspaper Notices, Vol. 2, 1735–1952

Essex County, Virginia Will Abstracts, 1751-1842 and Estate Records Index, 1751–1799

*Georgetown, District of Columbia 1850 Federal Population Census (Schedule I)
and 1853 Directory of Residents of Georgetown*

Georgetown, District of Columbia Marriage and Death Notices, 1801–1838

*Husbands and Wives Associated with Early Alexandria, Virginia
(and the Surrounding Area), 3rd Edition, Revised*

Index to District of Columbia Estates, 1801–1929

Index to District of Columbia Land Records, 1792–1817

*Index to Virginia Estates, 1800–1865
Volumes 4, 5 and 6*

John Alexander, a Northern Neck Proprietor, His Family, Friends and Kin

Legislative Petitions of Alexandria, 1778–1861

Pippenger and Pittenger Families

Proceedings of the Orphan's Court, Washington County, District of Columbia, 1801–1808

Richmond County, Virginia Marriage Records, 1854–1890, Annotated

The Georgetown Courier *Marriage and Death Notices:
Georgetown, District of Columbia, November 18, 1865 to May 6, 1876*

*The Georgetown Directory for the Year 1830: to which is appended, a Short Description
of the Churches, Public Institutions, and the Original Charter of Georgetown, and
Extracts of the Laws Pertaining to the Chesapeake and Ohio Canal Company*

The Virginia Gazette and Alexandria Advertiser:
Volume 1, September 3, 1789 to November 11, 1790

The Virginia Journal and Alexandria Advertiser:
Volume I (February 5, 1784 to January 27, 1785)

Volume II (February 3, 1785 to January 26, 1786)

Volume III (March 2, 1786 to January 25, 1787)

Volume IV (February 8, 1787 to May 21, 1789)

The Washington and Georgetown Directory of 1853

Tombstone Inscriptions of Alexandria, Volumes 1–4

Virginia's Lost Wills: An Index

Westmoreland County, Virginia Marriage Records, 1850–1880, Annotated

www.ingramcontent.com/pod-product-compliance
Lightning Source LLC
Chambersburg PA
CBHW080234270326
41926CB00020B/4230